QuickBooks® 2014
The Guide

About the Author

Leslie Capachietti, MBA, is an Advanced Certified QuickBooks ProAdvisor, Authorized Intuit Reseller, and a member of Intuit's Accountant Training Network. As a national speaker and trainer, she has taught thousands of accounting professionals on best practices to employ when supporting their QuickBooks clients. Her firm, Automated Financial Solutions, has been recognized by Intuit as a Top Performer for outstanding achievement in supporting QuickBooks users. Leslie has written several books about QuickBooks, including *QuickBooks 2013 The Guide*.

About the Technical Reviewer

Thomas E. Barich is a QuickBooks Certified ProAdvisor, consultant, and author of numerous QuickBooks titles, including *QuickBooks 2013 QuickSteps*.

QuickBooks® 2014
The Guide

LESLIE CAPACHIETTI

New York   Chicago   San Francisco
Athens   London   Madrid   Mexico City
Milan   New Delhi   Singapore   Sydney   Toronto

Cataloging-in-Publication Data is on file with the Library of Congress

QuickBooks® 2014 The Guide

1 2 3 4 5 6 7 8 9 0   DOC DOC   1 0 9 8 7 6 5 4 3

ISBN   978-0-07-182339-5
MHID   0-07-182339-5

Sponsoring Editor
Roger Stewart

Technical Editor
Thomas E. Barich

Production Supervisor
George Anderson

Editorial Supervisor
Patty Mon

Copy Editors
Lisa Theobald, Lisa McCoy

Composition
Cenveo® Publisher Services

Project Editor
LeeAnn Pickrell

Proofreader
Susie Elkind

Illustration
Cenveo® Publisher Services

Acquisitions Coordinator
Amanda Russell

Indexer
Rebecca Plunkett

Art Director, Cover
Jeff Weeks

For the countless small business owners
with whom I've the privilege to work.

Contents at a Glance

Part One

Getting Started Using QuickBooks

Part Two

Daily Operations Using QuickBooks

Part Three

Other Tasks You May Need to Complete in QuickBooks

Part Four

Tracking Time and Paying Your Employees

Part Five

Sharing, Securing, and Customizing Your Data

Part Six

Using QuickBooks Reports, Budgets, and Planning Tools

Part Seven

Appendixes

Contents

Part Two

Daily Operations Using QuickBooks

Part Three
Other Tasks You May Need to Complete in QuickBooks

Part Five
Sharing, Securing, and Customizing Your Data

Part Six
Using QuickBooks Reports, Budgets, and Planning Tools

Part Seven
Appendixes

Acknowledgments

It took a team of dedicated and talented professionals to deliver this book to you.

A special thanks to Roger Stewart at McGraw Hill for the opportunity to author this book for another year. Thanks to Thomas E. Barich, whose adept technical-editing skills helped ensure the clarity and accuracy of the content contained in the pages of this guide.

It's been a pleasure to again work with Project Editor LeeAnn Pickrell. I appreciate her professionalism and organizational skills as I do the insightful suggestions offered by Copy Editors Lisa Theobald and Lisa McCoy. Kudos to Editorial Coordinator Amanda Russell who helped keep us all on track.

I would not have been able to meet the many deadlines associated with this project without the help of my able assistant, Katherine Murphy.

Finally, I especially want to thank my family whose support and patience during my "writing season" have made it possible for me to do this book for the last five years.

Introduction

Use This Book to Get the Most from QuickBooks

Whether you're a novice or an experienced QuickBooks user, the information in this book is organized and presented in a way that can benefit you. If you're brand new to QuickBooks, the chapters that make up Parts One and Two are required reading. Following the advice and detailed steps outlined in these chapters will help ensure that your QuickBooks file is set up correctly—from the start. You'll also learn about all the day-to-day bookkeeping chores you'll be performing in QuickBooks. If you're already a more experienced QuickBooks user or you've mastered the basics, you'll find the information in Parts Three through Six relevant. You can refer to these chapters to confirm that you're on the right track or to learn how to use some of the more advanced features QuickBooks offers.

When you have an immediate need to know how to do something, both the Contents and the Index are designed to make it easy for you to identify quickly where in the book a specific task or feature is covered.

"Extras" Provided in This Book to Help You

This book contains some extra elements that are my way of sharing with you, from my perspective as a QuickBooks ProAdvisor, an occasional best practice and, in some cases, "lessons learned" from years of supporting QuickBooks users. Specifically,

- **ProAdvisor Tips**   Gives you some additional insight about a subject or a task. Sometimes they're shortcuts, and sometimes they're workarounds.
- **Cautions**   Helps you avoid making some common mistakes.
- **ProAdvisor Recommends boxes**   Contains more detailed insights that may be useful. Sometimes they provide information about what happens behind the scenes when you perform a task; others are designed to point out how other QuickBooks users perform a task in the program to run their business.

You and Your Accountant

There are a number of places throughout this book where you'll be reminded to call your accountant before making a decision about the best way to enter a beginning balance or handle a particular transaction in QuickBooks. I encourage you to heed this advice. While QuickBooks gives you the tools you need to manage your business's financial operations, your accountant can play a vital role in helping you maintain a healthy and viable business by providing you with valuable tax and strategic business-planning advice. In addition, to help *your accountant* better assist *you*, throughout the book I identify information that I think you should share with your accountant because it tells him or her how QuickBooks handles certain accounting functions—like payroll and inventory, for example.

If you don't have an accountant and want to connect with one, there are also accountants in your area who are certified by Intuit as QuickBooks experts. They often provide onsite assistance with setup and troubleshooting and are a great resource if you get "stuck" while setting up your QuickBooks file—or just want to have an expert review the information you've entered in your system. To locate a Certified QuickBooks ProAdvisor in your area, select Find A Local QuickBooks Expert from the QuickBooks Help menu.

Part One

Getting Started Using QuickBooks

So you've decided to use QuickBooks to help you manage your business. If this is a brand-new business, congratulations! If you've been newly charged with keeping the books for a business, your decision to use QuickBooks is a smart one.

You'll soon see that QuickBooks can be used as more than just a bookkeeping program. When set up and maintained properly, it will likely become one of your company's most valuable assets. Not only will you use it to track your bank balances and what your customers owe you, but you'll also refer to it as you make important decisions such as hiring more employees, making a price change, or even selling your business.

In Part One of this book, you'll learn how to gather the information you need to get started so you can create and start using your company file. You'll also gain an understanding of what steps are most important, what you can do on your own, and when you may need help to ensure that your file is set up right from the start. Part One also includes chapters containing instructions and hints about putting all the important elements into your QuickBooks system, such as customers, vendors, general ledger information, and the other lists that contain data to help you track your finances more accurately.

Using QuickBooks for the First Time

Chapter 1

The first time you open QuickBooks, the QuickBooks Setup window launches. From here, you can begin the process of either creating a brand-new company file or working with an existing file. The focus of this chapter is on ensuring that you have what you need to set up your new QuickBooks company file and to help you get familiar with basic navigation so that you can begin to work in the program right away.

What to Do Ahead of Time

New clients will often ask me what they can do to prepare for their QuickBooks installation. I give them a "To Do" list telling them what information they need to pull together and the decisions they have to make *before* their QuickBooks system is installed and launched for the first time.

That list—and the details behind why they're important—are outlined for you in the next several sections. Later in this chapter, you'll learn about the options you have when entering key information about your business into your new QuickBooks file.

So now would be a good time to get out that shoebox, binder, or the spreadsheet you've been using to keep track of your business so far, because you'll need to have the following handy:

- Your last tax return for the business
- Your bank register and statements for the year
- Loan statements and terms
- A list of the customers that owe you money and how much they owe as of the date you want to start using QuickBooks
- A list of the suppliers that you owe money to and how much you owe them as of the date you want to start using QuickBooks
- A list of any special equipment, machinery, or computers you own, including their current value and amounts previously depreciated
- A written tally of the money you've put into your business

Why should you take the time to gather all this information before you start working in QuickBooks? Because you want the most accurate and complete information you have about your business to make its way into your new QuickBooks file. It's not that you can't change things in QuickBooks later on; it's just that if you start with incorrect or even incomplete data, you sometimes can't figure out what was wrong to begin with. And if you can't find the source of a problem, you run the risk of the problem becoming permanent.

Decide on the Start Date

Your *start date* is the date that you begin tracking your business in QuickBooks. Even though activities may have occurred before this date, it is from this date on that your transactions will be entered into your new file.

Choosing a start date is an important decision, since the date you choose can affect how much work it's going to be to set up your QuickBooks file. For example, a September 1 start date means that the nine months of activity that happened in your business, from January 1 through September 1, has to be reflected in your QuickBooks system before you start entering September transactions. If it's March, this task is a lot easier because you'll be entering transactions only from January to March.

Here's what to think about as you make your choice.

If your goal is to have your new QuickBooks file reflect every detail of your company as of your start date, then you'll want to have every individual transaction in the system. This includes every invoice you sent to customers and all the payments you've received on them, every check you wrote to vendors, every payroll check you gave an employee, and so on.

If you're not so ambitious, the second best way to create your new QuickBooks file is to enter summary totals for each of your company's transaction types up until the day before your QuickBooks start date. Entering monthly summary totals will allow you to run valuable reports (such as the Profit & Loss statement and Balance Sheet) with month-to-month comparisons.

If it's the first half of the year when you read this, make your start date the first day of the year and then enter everything you've done so far this year. It sounds like a lot of work, but it really isn't. When you start entering transactions in QuickBooks, such as customer invoices, you just pick the customer, enter a little information, and move on to the next invoice. Of course, you have to enter all your customers, but you'd have to do that even if you weren't entering every transaction for the current year.

If it's the middle of the year, you can choose either option. If you have a lot of transactions every month, you might want to enter summary totals to get you up to date and then enter real transactions as they occur, beginning with the start date.

If it's late in the year as you read this, perhaps October or November or later, and you usually send a lot of invoices to customers, write a lot of checks, and do your own payroll, think about waiting until the new year to start using QuickBooks.

More About the Information You'll Need

It's a good idea to have all the information you'll need to complete the setup of your QuickBooks together and in one place rather than trying to locate each piece of information during the setup. So in addition to your last tax return, bank registers, and the lists mentioned in the previous section, check out this section for more details about the numbers and information QuickBooks needs to get started. Step-by-step instructions on how to actually enter your starting balances and transactions into your new company file can be found in Chapter 7.

Cash Balances

You have to tell QuickBooks what the balance is for each bank account you use in your business. The balance being referred to here is the *reconciled* balance and not simply the balance from your check register. And it should be a reconciled balance as of your QuickBooks starting date.

If you haven't balanced your checkbooks against the bank statements for a while, now would be a good time to do it. In addition to the reconciled balance and the statement itself, you need to have a list of the dates and the amounts (both deposits in transit and checks) of the transactions that haven't yet cleared.

Customer Balances

If any customer owes you money as of your start date, you have to tell QuickBooks about it. Enter each unpaid customer invoice, using the real, original dates for each invoice. Those dates must be earlier than your QuickBooks start date. This means you have to assemble all the information about unpaid customer invoices, including such details as how much of each invoice was for services, for items sold, for shipping, and for sales tax. To learn how to set up a customer, refer to Chapter 3. As you enter your open customer balances, QuickBooks will automatically create the accounts receivable balance for you. Refer to Chapter 7 for additional guidance on how to enter these important balances in QuickBooks.

Vendor Balances

The money you owe as of your start date will make up your Accounts Payable. Similar to the way you entered your Accounts Receivable, each unpaid bill should be entered into QuickBooks using its original date. Chapter 4 covers what you need to know about setting up and using vendors.

Asset Balances

Besides your bank accounts, you have to know the balance of the rest of your businesses assets. For example, you'll need to know the current value of your fixed assets (such as equipment and furniture) and any accumulated depreciation on those assets (you can likely ask your tax preparer for this information). Refer to the section in Chapter 2 titled "The Accounts that QuickBooks Uses" to learn more about how QuickBooks handles the other assets your business may own.

Liability Balances

Get all the information about your company's liabilities (outside obligations) together. Although the open vendor bills you enter determine your accounts payable balance automatically, you'll need to know the current balance of any loans or mortgages, for example. If there are unpaid withholding amounts from payroll, they also must be entered. Refer to the section in Chapter 2 titled "The Accounts that QuickBooks Uses" to learn more about how to identify the other liabilities your business may be responsible for.

Payroll Information

If you do the payroll yourself instead of using a payroll service, you'll need to know everything about each employee: social security number, all the information that goes into determining tax status (federal, state, and local), and which deductions are taken for health or pension. You have all this information, of course; you just have to get it together. If your employees are on salary, you've probably been repeating the check information every payday, with no need to look up these items. Dig up the W-4 forms and all your notes about who's on what deduction plan.

You also need to know which payroll items you have to track: salary, wages, federal deductions, state deductions (tax, SUI, SDI), local income tax deductions, benefits, pension, and any other deductions (garnishments, for example). And that's not all—you also have to know the name of the vendor to whom these withholding amounts are remitted (government tax agencies, insurance companies, and so on). Running payroll in QuickBooks is covered in Chapter 20.

Inventory Information

You need to decide on the names you want to assign to every inventory item you carry, and, most importantly, how much you paid for each item and how many of each you have in stock as of the start date. QuickBooks needs these last two key pieces of information in order to keep an accurate inventory valuation for you. It is also a good time to be thinking about any other information you want to track for each of the items you carry in inventory. For example, what description do you want your customers to see on their invoices? Do you have a preferred vendor that you purchase an item from? Learn more about setting up your inventory in Chapter 15.

You're now ready to set up and configure your QuickBooks company file! Let's get started.

Install and Launch the Software

Whether you're installing QuickBooks from a CD or using a download link from Intuit, the installation process is quite straightforward. Simply follow the installation wizard to where you'll read and accept the Software License Agreement, select where on your computer you want to install the program, and tell the wizard whether you'll be installing the program for multiple users (who will need access to the company file across a network). Refer to Appendix A to learn more about installing QuickBooks on your computer and in a networked environment as well.

Once the installation of the program is complete, QuickBooks places a shortcut to the software on your desktop, and that's the easiest way to open the program. If you have other windows covering the desktop, you can use the Start menu, where you'll find QuickBooks in the Programs menu. Place your pointer on the QuickBooks listing in the Programs menu and choose QuickBooks from the submenu (choose Programs | QuickBooks).

P r o A d v i s o r   T i p : For even faster access to QuickBooks, copy or move the desktop shortcut to your Quick Launch toolbar (Windows XP and Vista), which requires only a single click to open software. Right-drag the shortcut icon onto the Quick Launch toolbar, and then choose Move Here (or Copy Here, if you want a shortcut in both places). If you're a Windows 7 or 8 user, you can pin QuickBooks to the Start menu (right-click the icon and select Pin To Start Menu).

When QuickBooks launches for the first time, the QuickBooks Setup window opens and provides links to help you get started with creating a new company file, updating an existing file, and other useful information. On subsequent launches, the Login page for the last file that you were working in opens. If you choose not to work in this particular file (maybe you want to work in another file or want to check out the sample company files), click the Cancel button on the QuickBooks Login screen. The No Company Open window opens, giving you the following options:

- **Create A New Company**   Select this option to begin the process of creating a company file. All of the steps involved in this task are covered in the next section.
- **Open Or Restore An Existing Company**   Select this option if you're upgrading from a previous version of QuickBooks. Go through the windows in the Open Or Restore Company wizard to select your company file. QuickBooks offers to upgrade the file to your new version. Place a check mark in the I Understand That My Company File Will Be Updated To This New Version Of QuickBooks box to accept the offer. QuickBooks then requires that you make a backup of your file in its current version. When the backup is complete, you'll see a message reminding you that the file is being converted to a newer version—in this case, QuickBooks Pro 2014. Click OK and you can now begin working in your updated file.

C a u t i o n : If you're working in a network environment and you installed QuickBooks Pro 2014 as an upgrade to a previous version, upgrade QuickBooks on the computer that holds the company data file first. Then upgrade QuickBooks on the other computers.

- **Open A Sample File**   Click this option to display a list of sample companies you can explore and play with to get familiar with QuickBooks. One company is designed for product-based businesses, the other for service-based businesses.

ProAdvisor Tip: Many QuickBooks users (especially accountants) maintain more than one QuickBooks company file. As you open and work in different files, they will automatically be listed and available for selection in the No Company File Open window. If you find that you no longer want or need a file to be listed here, use the Edit List link to hide a particular file. This action does not remove the file from your computer or network, it only hides it from the list of company files visible from this particular window. If you work in that file again on a future date, it will reappear on the list again for easy access.

Create Your Company File

For now, choose Create A New Company, because that's what this chapter is all about. The QuickBooks Setup window opens, giving you various options to help you begin the process of creating your company file (see Figure 1-1):

- **Express Start**, where you need only enter some very basic information about your business.
- **Advanced Setup**, a wizard that moves you through several screens, answering questions and providing information to fine-tune your setup.
- **Other Options**, which allows you to create a new file from an existing Quicken file or from Microsoft Office Accounting and Small Business Accounting, or Peachtree Accounting. Select the Convert Other Accounting Software Data option and follow the onscreen directions to launch the QuickBooks Conversion Tool.

ProAdvisor Tip: The Accountant and Professional Bookkeeper versions of QuickBooks offer the option of creating a new QuickBooks file based on an existing one. When this option is selected, QuickBooks creates a new company file using the existing company's Chart of Accounts, Items, Preferences, and Sales Tax Items.

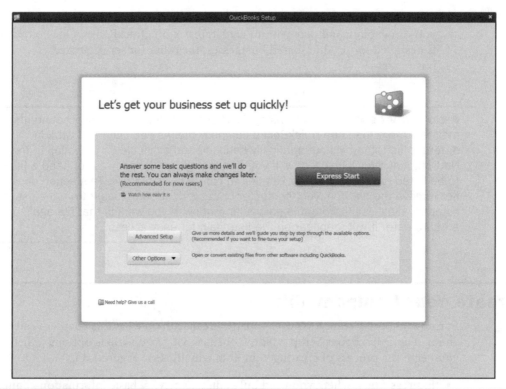

FIGURE 1-1 The QuickBooks Setup window gives you more than one option for creating a company file.

Using Express Start

Express Start is a two-screen wizard designed to get your company file created—albeit with only basic information—in just two steps. In the first window, you'll be required to enter your company name, the industry you're in, and the company type. Your choice here also indicates the type of tax return you'll likely be filing. In the second window, you'll be required to enter your ZIP code and phone number—with the option to enter the rest of your company's contact information. From there, you go straight to having QuickBooks create your company file. The Preview Your Company Settings window lets you preview the features that will be enabled and the accounts that QuickBooks recommends for you, based on the industry and company type you selected.

It's a good idea to take a look at these settings. You can add or remove the accounts listed on the Chart Of Accounts tab and confirm the location where your new company file will be saved:

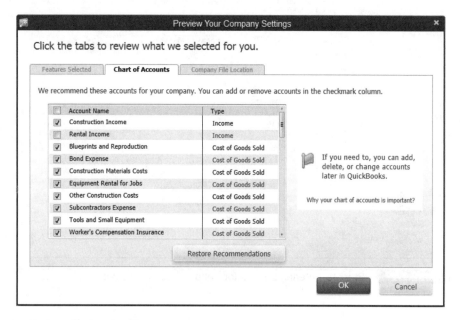

Using Advanced Setup

To select this setup path, click Advanced Setup on the QuickBooks Setup window. The Easy Step Interview wizard is launched, providing you with a step-by-step approach to creating your company file. You'll click Next to move through the windows.

Entering Company Information

To begin, QuickBooks needs basic information about your company (see Figure 1-2). Notice that the information about your company name has two entry fields. The first field is for the real company name, the one you do business as. The second field, for your company's legal name, is optional and is used only if the legal name of your company differs from the company name you use for doing business. For instance, your company may do business as Win Contracting, but your legal or corporate name might be Winchester Contracting, Inc.

Enter the company tax ID number. If you have a federal employer ID number (EIN), it's a nine-digit number in the format *XX-YYYYYYY*. You'll need a tax ID number if you have employees. If you don't have an EIN, enter your social security number.

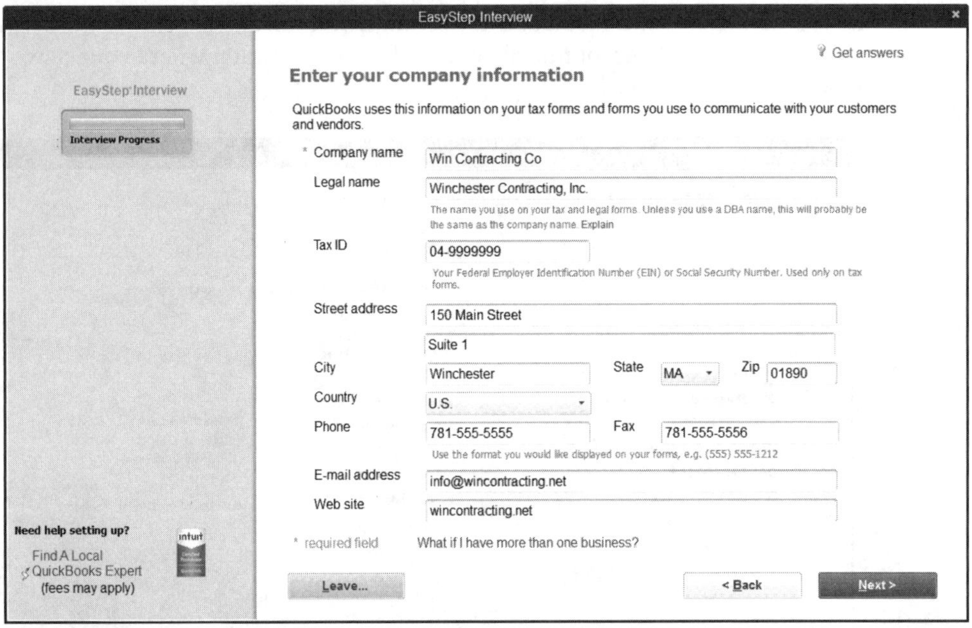

FIGURE 1-2 Start by entering basic information about your business.

If you are a sole proprietor using your social security number for business purposes, consider applying for a federal ID number. This can help you separate your business and personal finances by using the EIN for business transactions and maintaining a separate bank account in your business name. As your business grows and you hire subcontractors, consultants, or employees, you'll eventually need an EIN to pay these folks.

Enter the contact information (address, telephone, and so on). This data is used on the transactions you print (such as invoices), so enter this data as you want it to appear on printed documents. Click Next when you've filled in your company data.

Selecting the Type of Business

In the next window, select the industry that matches the type of business you have (see Figure 1-3). If you don't see an exact match for your business type, choose one that comes close. Alternatively, you can simply select either of the General Product/Service-based Business options that are located at the very bottom of the industry list.

Selecting Your Legal Entity Type

The next window displays the various types of legal entities for businesses, such as proprietorship, partnership, corporation, and so on. Select the one that matches the way your business is organized.

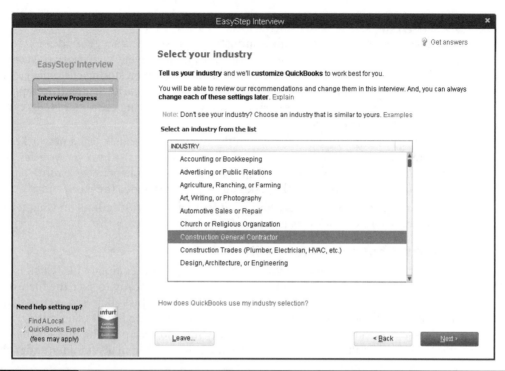

FIGURE 1-3 Find the type of business that matches yours.

If you're not sure, ask your accountant, or find a copy of the business income tax you filed last year (unless this is your first year in business) and match the form number to the list in the window. If you can't find the information, select Other/None. You can change it later via the My Company window, which can be accessed from the Company menu. QuickBooks uses this information to attach tax-line information to all your accounts that affect your taxes. If you use an Intuit tax preparation program, this information can then be used to prepare a tax return for your business.

Configuring Your Fiscal Year

In the next window, enter the first month of your fiscal year. QuickBooks enters January as the default entry, but if you're not using a calendar year, select the appropriate month from the drop-down list. The month you choose here will automatically set the default year-to-date ranges for many QuickBooks reports, including the Profit and Loss report.

Setting Up the Administrator

The next window asks you for an administrator password. It's a good idea to create a password to limit access to your company file and to prevent unauthorized access to your business's financial information, especially if you plan on storing customer credit card information. PCI DSS (Payment Card Industry Data Security Standard) compliance standards also require a complex password if you are storing customer credit card information in QuickBooks.

If multiple users will need to work in the file simultaneously (on a network), user names are required (and each should have a password). However, you can wait until after you've finished the EasyStep Interview and implement the feature later, when you can concentrate on the task and make notes about the passwords.

Creating user logins and passwords that let you place restrictions on what users can do and see in QuickBooks is covered in Chapter 8.

Creating Your Company File

The next window explains that you're about to save your company file. Click Next to see the Filename For New Company dialog, which is ready to save the file using a filename based on the company name you've entered. Just click Save to use that filename. Or, if you prefer, you can change the name of the file. It takes a few seconds for QuickBooks to save the company file and set up all the files for the company. By default, QuickBooks saves your company file in a subfolder under the Documents subfolder.

Consider creating a folder on your hard drive for your QuickBooks data (for instance, C:\QBDataFiles). This makes it easier to find and back up your data.

P r o A d v i s o r   T i p : If you run QuickBooks on a network, or another user works in QuickBooks on your computer, make sure the folder you create for your data has permissions set properly. Specifically, the Everyone group must be given Full Control. To learn more about setting up QuickBooks in a multi-user environment, refer to Appendix A.

Customizing QuickBooks for Your Business

The remaining EasyStep Interview windows provide a series of choices and options about the way you do business. For example, you're asked what you sell (services, products, or both), whether you charge sales tax, whether you use estimates, and so on. The questions are clearly stated and easy to answer and you won't necessarily have to perform any setup tasks right away if you answer Yes; for example, if you answer Yes when you're asked if you have employees, you don't have to create employee information immediately—you can do all of that later.

Essentially, the wizard is setting configuration options for you, but you can set any of those options for yourself at any time in the future. Information about the options you need to perform certain tasks is found throughout this book, in the appropriate chapters.

Selecting a Start Date and Creating the Chart of Accounts

Before you begin the process of creating your chart of accounts, you'll be asked to choose a QuickBooks start date. And before filling in your answer, be sure to read the section "Decide on a Start Date" earlier in this chapter. Click Next after you've completed this page to review the Income and Expense accounts that QuickBooks suggests you use.

The wizard displays the income and expense accounts it has established for your company, based on the responses you made to the interview question regarding your type of business (see Figure 1-4).

You can select or deselect specific accounts if you know you need or don't need any of the accounts listed. However, it may be easier to go through that process later. You'll likely need additional accounts in your chart of accounts, but it's easier

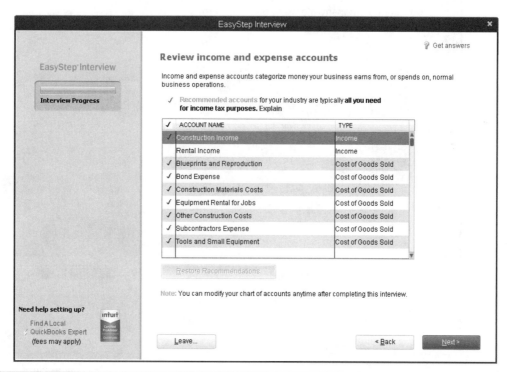

FIGURE 1-4 You can select or deselect accounts now, or wait until you begin using QuickBooks.

to add them after you've finished this company setup task. Learn more about setting up your chart of accounts in Chapter 2.

Click Next and you're finished with the basics of creating your QuickBooks company file. You can now continue the work of building out your file by clicking the Go To Setup button and launching the QuickBooks Setup window.

The QuickBooks Setup Wizard

The QuickBooks Setup wizard (which launches after either an Advanced or Express Setup) gives you three import options designed to help simplify the task of getting information into your new company file, as shown in the following illustration:

Click the Add or Add More button next to the list type that you want to enter. QuickBooks will tell you about where you can import your data from and any fixes that need to be made to the information prior to importing it.

If you prefer to start exploring your file now and work on your lists at a later time, click the Start Working button at the bottom of the window. This will bring you to the Quick Start Center. If you're ready to start working in your new file, close this window to go to the standard QuickBooks Home page. If you're still not ready to dive into the program on your own, you can instead work in the Quick Start Center, which offers a simplified view of the regular QuickBooks Home page. It is also where you can access training videos and other resources that will help prepare you for the important tasks you'll be completing in your QuickBooks file.

Navigate in QuickBooks

With your new file created, let's take a look at how to get around in the software.

The Home page window shows the following elements:

- **Title Bar**, located at the very top of the QuickBooks window, displays the name of your QuickBooks company file.
- **Menu Bar**, which gives you access to all areas in QuickBooks.
- **Icon Bar**, which contains buttons for quick access to frequently used functions. Learn how to change the location and functions on the Icon Bar in the section "Customize the Icon Bar," later in this chapter.

Home Page

The heart of the Home page has links and icons you can use to access the features and functions you need to run your business in QuickBooks. In addition, it's divided into sections to make it easy to find icons and see the workflow those icons represent. Take a moment to review the Home page and identify the Vendor, Customer, Employees, Company, and Banking areas on it.

The Home page is dynamic; that is, the icons and workflow arrows it contains change as you enable the various features available in QuickBooks. For example, if you enable inventory tracking, QuickBooks adds icons in the Vendors section for inventory-related tasks, as shown next:

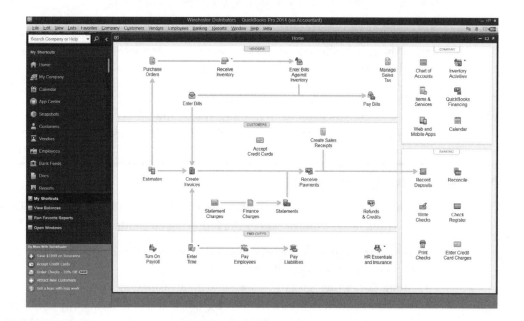

QuickBooks Centers

QuickBooks centers are windows in which information is displayed about specific areas of your company. Most centers have a dedicated button on the Icon Bar or directly in the middle of the Home page, while others are accessible from the menu bar. You can see current data, analyze that data, and perform tasks. QuickBooks centers include the following:

- Customer Center
- Vendor Center
- Employee Center
- Report Center
- Bank Feeds Center
- Doc Center
- App Center
- Lead Center

Customer Center

To open the Customer Center, select Customer Center from the Customers menu at the top of the QuickBooks window. This Center holds everything you'd ever need to know about your customers. It's where QuickBooks stores your list of customers and all the information about each customer. You can also perform routine customer-related tasks using the buttons at the top of the Customer Center window. Information about using and customizing the Customer Center is in Chapter 3.

Vendor Center

Like the Customer Center, the Vendor Center makes it easy to view detailed information about your vendors and to enter transactions into QuickBooks related to them. Select Vendor Center from the Vendors menu on the menu bar to open this center. Learn how to use and customize the Vendor Center in Chapter 4.

Employee Center

Whether you process your own payroll or use a QuickBooks payroll service, the Employee Center is where you can find detailed information about each employee, your payroll liabilities, and the payroll transactions for each employee. It is accessed from the Employees menu. Refer to Chapter 20 to learn more about the ways you can process payroll in QuickBooks.

Report Center

The Report Center, seen in Figure 1-5, can be opened directly from the Icon Bar. There are three views in the Report Center: the Carousel view, the List view, and the Grid view. For each view, the major category of reports is displayed in the left pane. The first time you open the Report Center, you'll open to the Grid view, which allows you to scroll through a visual display of the reports available for each category. The Grid view shows a sample of the actual reports available in each category in a single window and makes it easy to add a report to your Favorites reports list—just click the red heart under the sample report you want to use.

To change the way you view a category, use the view icons located in the top-right corner of the Report Center window. You can also use the Report Center to access memorized reports as well as a collection of popular reports that other QuickBooks users find useful.

Bank Feeds Center

From the Icon Bar, you can also launch the Bank Feeds Center, where you can go to download and enter transactions directly from your credit card and bank accounts into QuickBooks. This QuickBooks feature is designed to save you from having to enter this information manually into your QuickBooks file. Not every QuickBooks user takes advantage of online banking—but they should.

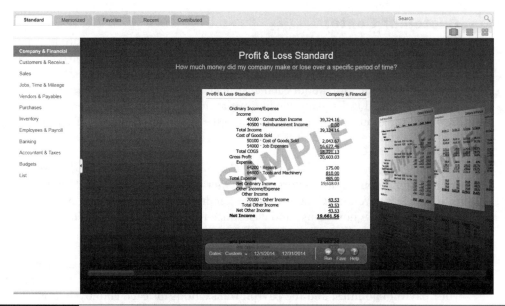

FIGURE 1-5 The Report Center makes it easy to choose the right report.

Doc Center

The Doc Center holds documents and files on your computer that you can then "attach" to or associate with a specific transaction or record in QuickBooks. For example, a purchase order a customer sends to you via e-mail or snail mail can be saved or scanned into the Doc Center. Later, with the customer's invoice open, click the attach (paper clip) icon at the top of the Create Invoices window and browse to the document that you've saved on your computer through the Doc Center. A copy of the PO will then be easily retrievable right from their invoice. To open the Doc Center, click the Docs button on the Icon Bar.

Lead Center

Unlike the other centers, the Lead Center doesn't have a button of its own on the Icon Bar (although you can add it if you wish by customizing the Icon Bar, as explained in the next section). You access the Lead Center from the Customers menu. You can choose to enter your leads manually, one by one, or by copying and pasting multiple leads from Excel into a preformatted grid and import them all at once. Regardless of the method you choose, you'll be able to keep track of key contact and sales lead information as well as maintain detailed notes on your progress with each prospect. Tracking your prospects in QuickBooks gives you the advantage of working in one program and makes it easy to turn a lead into a customer once the sale is closed.

Calendar

While not a "center" per se, the QuickBooks Calendar can give you a unique view of all the important transactions and reminders you need to keep track of to keep your business running smoothly. Click the Calendar button on the Icon Bar to open your calendar for the first time. If you haven't yet entered any transactions into your QuickBooks file, your calendar will be empty. Check back in, however, once you've entered some bills or invoices: your calendar will show you the dates that these bills or invoices were created and are due along with any To Do items that you've added, as shown here:

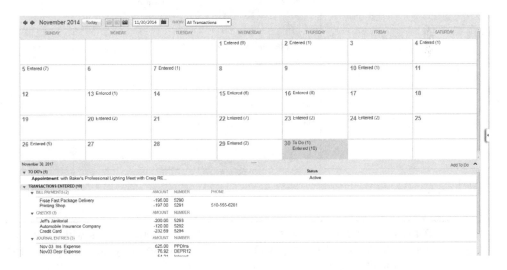

Customize the Icon Bar

To customize the Icon Bar, choose View from the menu. You'll see options that let you move the default location of the Icon Bar from the left-hand side of the window to the top of the window, or you can hide it altogether.

QuickBooks put icons on the Icon Bar, but the icons QuickBooks chose may not match the features you use most frequently. Choose View | Customize Icon Bar to display a list of the icons currently occupying your Icon Bar, as shown next. From here, you can add, remove, or reorder the icons to suit you.

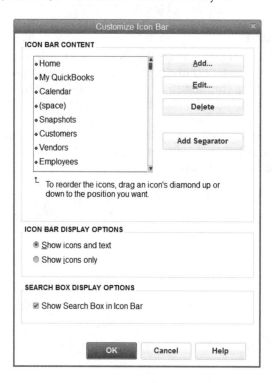

ProAdvisor Tip: When you log into QuickBooks with your own login name, the Icon Bar settings you establish are linked to your login name only. You are not changing the Icon Bar for other users.

Changing the Order of Icons

You can change the order in which icons appear on the Icon Bar. To move an icon, click the small diamond to the left of the icon's listing, hold down the left mouse button, and drag the listing to a new position.

Changing the Icon Bar Display

You can change the way the icons display in many ways. These are covered in this section.

Display Icons Without Title Text

By default, icons and text display on the Icon Bar when it's positioned at the top of the window. You can select Show Icons Only to remove the title text under the icons. As a result, the icons are much smaller (and you can fit more icons on the Icon Bar). Positioning your mouse pointer over a small icon displays the icon's description as a Tool Tip.

Change the Icon's Graphic, Text, or Description

To change an individual icon's appearance, select the icon's listing and click Edit. Then choose a different graphic (the currently selected graphic is enclosed in a box), change the Label (the title), or change the Description (the Tool Tip text).

Separate Icons

You can insert a separator between two icons, which is an effective way to create groups of icons (after you move icons into logical groups). The separator is a black vertical line. In the Customize Icon Bar dialog, select the icon that should appear to the left of the separator bar and click Add Separator. QuickBooks inserts the separator on the Icon Bar and "(space)" in the listing to indicate the location of the separator.

Removing an Icon

You can remove any icons you never use or use infrequently so that you can use the space they take up for icons representing features you use a lot. Select the unwanted icon in the Customize Icon Bar dialog and click Delete. QuickBooks does not ask you to confirm the deletion; the icon is just removed from the Icon Bar. The icon is not gone for good, though. You can add it back at any time by using the Customize Icon Bar feature.

Adding an Icon

You can add an icon to the Icon Bar in either of two ways:

- Choose Add in the Customize Icon Bar dialog.
- Automatically add an icon for a window (transaction or report) you're currently using.

Using the Customize Icon Bar Dialog to Add an Icon

To add an icon from the Customize Icon Bar dialog, click Add to display the Add Icon Bar Item dialog:

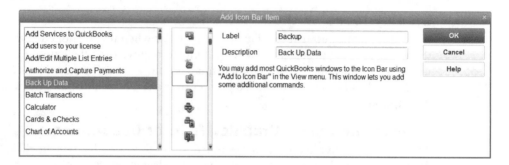

Scroll through the list to select the task you want to add to the Icon Bar. Then choose a graphic to represent the new icon. If you wish, you can change the label and/or the description (the text that appears in the Tool Tip when you hold your mouse pointer over the icon). Click OK to close this dialog when you're done.

Adding an Icon for the Current Window

If you're currently working in a QuickBooks window and it strikes you that it would be handy to have an icon for fast access to this window, while the window is active, choose View | Add *Name Of Window* To Icon Bar. A dialog appears so you can choose a graphic, name, and description for the new icon:

The Favorites Menu

The Favorites menu (located on the menu bar) gives you the flexibility to list up to 30 of the QuickBooks tasks and lists that you use most often, saving you from having to navigate to other areas of the program to complete your most common QuickBooks tasks. To add menu items to your Favorites menu, select Favorites |

Customize Favorites from the menu bar. The Customize Your Menus window opens, as shown next. Select a menu item, and then click the Add button to add it to your Favorites menu. Click OK when finished.

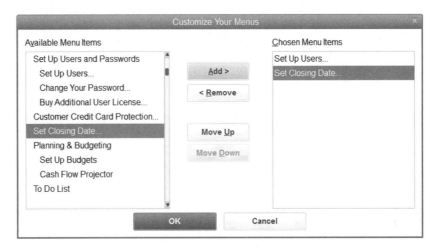

Closing QuickBooks

To exit QuickBooks, click the X in the top-right corner of the QuickBooks window or choose File | Exit from the menu bar. QuickBooks will ask you if you're sure you want to exit. If you choose Yes, the company file open at the time you exit the software is the file that opens the next time you launch QuickBooks.

Using Accounts in QuickBooks

In this chapter:

- Review the accounts that QuickBooks uses

- Decide whether to use numbers for accounts

- Create accounts

- Create subaccounts

- Edit, delete, and merge accounts

Chapter 2

The Accounts that QuickBooks Uses

QuickBooks uses accounts to categorize the many different transactions that occur as you operate your business, and the list where all these accounts live is called the chart of accounts. In addition, these accounts are further categorized by type. Assets, liabilities, income, and expenses, for example, are the account types most frequently used. The good news is that as you enter transactions in QuickBooks, you don't have to worry about the "behind the scenes" entries that need to be made to the accounts that are affected, because QuickBooks takes care of this for you.

For example, when you sell goods or services to a customer and send them an invoice, the Invoice Transaction screen asks you to fill in the name of the customer, the product or service you sold, and the amount you're charging. QuickBooks posts the amounts related to the transaction to the accounts you specify and also posts a record of that transaction in the customer's account. Later, when the customer pays the invoice, QuickBooks will show that the invoice has been paid, and it will also increase your bank account for the amount of the payment.

QuickBooks might have created some accounts for you during the initial setup of your company, but you'll likely need to create additional accounts to ensure that your chart of accounts reflects the activities that are unique to your business. You create the chart of accounts first because some of the other QuickBooks lists you create require you to link the items in those lists to your accounts.

Assets

An asset is something you own, such as

- Money in your bank accounts (sometimes called *cash on hand)*
- Money owed to you by your customers (called *accounts receivable*)
- Equipment, furniture, and so on (called *fixed assets*)
- The inventory you stock for resale if you are a distributor or manufacturer (called *inventory assets*)

Liabilities

A liability is something that you may be holding but does not belong to you. It is something you owe to someone else, such as

- Money you owe your vendors and suppliers (QuickBooks account type: *Accounts Payable*)
- Sales tax you have collected and must turn over to the state (QuickBooks account type: *Current Liability*)
- Money withheld from employees' pay that you must turn over to government agencies (QuickBooks account type: *Current Liability*)
- Outstanding loan balances (QuickBooks account type: *Long Term Liability*)

Equity

Your equity is your business's net worth and is made up of the following:

- The capital invested in your business (called *capital*)
- The capital you've withdrawn from the business (if your business isn't a corporation)
- The profit (or loss) including accumulated earnings in prior years (called *retained earnings*)

Income

Income, also referred to as revenue, is made up of the following:

- Money you collect when you sell products
- Fees you collect for services
- Income derived from interest

Expenses

Expenses are the monies you spend to operate your business. You use the chart of accounts to track or categorize your expenses so you can analyze your business's performance and, of course, also file tax returns. Generally, expenses are divided into two main categories: *cost of goods sold (COGS)* and *general and administrative expenses*.

Cost of goods sold usually comprises the following:

- Cost of raw materials for manufacturing
- Cost of goods you resell in a wholesale or retail business
- Cost of materials consumed/sold in a service business

General and administrative expenses include these:

- Overhead (utilities, rent, insurance, and so on)
- Office supplies
- Payroll
- Services you purchase
- Taxes

Use Account Numbers

By default, QuickBooks uses account names only in the chart of accounts. However, you can change this setting so that your accounts have numbers in addition to the names.

The advantage of using numbers is that you can arrange each section of the chart of accounts by category and subcategory, because within each type of account, QuickBooks displays your chart of accounts in alphanumeric order. Without numbers, QuickBooks displays each section of your chart of accounts in alphabetical order.

You can also use numbered subaccounts (see the section "Use Subaccounts" later in this chapter) to provide subtotals for accounts on many QuickBooks reports and to make it easier to enter transactions. For example, using account numbers gives you the ability to arrange your bank accounts in a logical order, making sure your primary bank account is always at the top of the drop-down list users see when making bank deposits or writing checks. It can also be handy if you open another bank account or if you change banks, because it helps you better control the order in which the accounts appear when selecting them in transactions. So, for instance, if the account number you used for your old checking account was 1000, and you now want to use that number for your new bank account, it's a simple task to edit the original account number to, say, 1150 (which moves it to the bottom of the list) and give the new checking account the 1000 number so that it will appear at the top of the list.

Enabling Account Numbers

To switch to a number format for your accounts, you have to enable the account number feature. Choose Edit | Preferences from the menu bar to open the Preferences dialog, and select the Accounting icon in the left pane. Click the Company Preferences tab, and select the Use Account Numbers check box (see Figure 2-1).

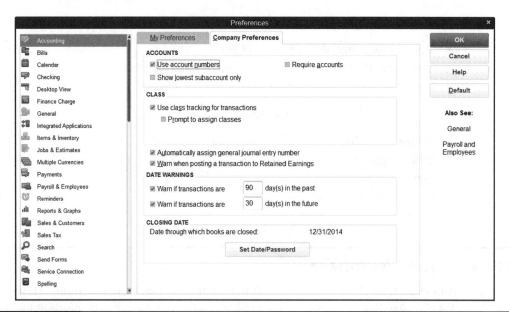

FIGURE 2-1   Enable numbers for your chart of accounts.

▶▶ ProAdvisor Recommends

When You Need to Run Reports Without Account Numbers

As convenient as it is for you (and your accountant) to have numbered accounts so you can track your finances by category and subcategory, you may have to produce reports for an outside stakeholder (such as your bank). They may have certain financial categories that they'll want to look at first, and it's easier for them if your accounts, especially your expenses, are in alphabetical order.

To produce reports without account numbers, putting each account type list back into alphabetical order, turn off the account number feature by deselecting the option in Accounting Preferences (Edit | Preferences | Accounting). Print the reports, and then turn the feature on again. QuickBooks stores account numbers as part of the account name, so when you re-enable account numbers, all your numbers appear exactly as you created them.

If you chose a prebuilt chart of accounts when you set up your company file, those accounts are switched to numbered accounts automatically. However, the QuickBooks numbering scheme is designed to keep accounts in alphabetical order, especially in the Expenses section. This costs you some of the advantages and efficiencies that well-planned numbers bring, but all you have to do is create your own plan and then edit the accounts to change the numbers (see "Edit Accounts" later in this chapter).

Accounts you added yourself (over and above the prebuilt accounts that were automatically brought into your company file) have to be edited to add numbers; QuickBooks doesn't automatically number them.

When you select the option to use account numbers, the option Show Lowest Subaccount Only (refer to Figure 2-1) becomes accessible. This option tells QuickBooks to display only the subaccount on transaction windows instead of both the parent account and the subaccount, making it easier to see precisely which account is receiving the posting.

If all your accounts aren't numbered and you select Show Lowest Subaccount Only, when you click OK, QuickBooks displays an error message that you cannot enable this option until all your accounts have numbers assigned. After you've edited existing accounts that need numbers (any accounts that QuickBooks didn't automatically number for you), you can return to the Preferences dialog and enable this subaccount option.

Creating a Numbering System

After you've set up numbered accounts, you have a more efficient chart of accounts, so you, your bookkeeper, and your accountant will have an easier time managing your chart of accounts. Numbers give you a quick clue about the type and category of the account you're working with. As you create accounts, be sure to maintain the logic of your numbering system, assigning ranges of numbers to account types. A common approach to account numbering is shown here:

- 1xxxx Assets
- 2xxxx Liabilities
- 3xxxx Equity
- 4xxxx Income
- 5xxxx Expenses
- 6xxxx Expenses
- 7xxxx Expenses
- 8xxxx Expenses
- 9xxxx Other Income and Expenses

This example uses five-digit numbers because QuickBooks uses five-digit account numbers. QuickBooks permits account numbers of up to seven digits, so you're not going to run out of numbers no matter how many accounts you need for your business.

Creating Ranges of Numbers

Account types have subtypes, and you need to assign ranges of account numbers to match those subtypes. The starting number of each range has to be the same as the starting number for the account type. That means that if you use numbers starting with a 1 for assets, all of the number ranges for different subtypes of assets must start with a 1.

Let's take assets, for example. You can use 10000 through 10999 for bank accounts, 11000 through 11999 for receivables and other current assets, and then use 12000 through 12999 for tracking fixed assets such as equipment, furniture, and so on. Follow the same pattern for liabilities, starting with current liabilities and moving to long term. It's also a good idea to keep all payroll withholding liability accounts together.

If you have inventory and you track cost of goods, you can reserve a section of the chart of accounts for those account types. Some businesses use 43000 through 49999 for cost of goods, and some companies dedicate the numbers in the 5xxxx range to that purpose.

▶▶ ProAdvisor Recommends

Re-sorting Your Chart of Accounts

When you first set up your chart of accounts, your accounts are sorted by type and then by number. Because the order of these accounts can be changed manually, you may, over time, find it more difficult to find and work with some accounts in your list. You can fix this by re-sorting the list. Open your chart of accounts, click the Account button, and select the Re-Sort List command to return the list to its original order.

You can, if you wish, have a variety of expense types and reserve the starting number for specific types. Some businesses, for example, use 5*xxxx* for sales expenses, then use 60000 through 79999 for general operating expenses and 8*xxxx* and 9*xxxx* for other specific expenses that should appear together in reports such as taxes, penalty fees, and so on. You can also use one range of expense accounts, such as 70000 through 79999 for expenses that fall into the "overhead" category.

Usually, you should create new accounts by increasing the previous account number by 10 or 20 (or even 100 if you don't have a lot of accounts), so you have room to insert more accounts that belong in the same general area of your chart of accounts when they need to be added later.

Name Accounts

Whether or not you choose to enable account numbers, you have to give each account a name. What's more, you should take steps to ensure that your account naming convention is consistent. Why is this important? Because when I visit clients who haven't established and enforced naming conventions, it's not uncommon to find accounts with names such as these:

- Telephone Exp
- Exps-Telephone
- Tele Expense
- Telephone
- Tele

The problem here is that every one of those accounts had amounts posted to them. That's because users "guess" at account names when they see a drop-down list, and they point and click whatever they see that seems remotely related. If they don't find the account the way they would have entered the name, they create a new account (using a name that is logical to them). You can avoid all of those errors by establishing rules about creating account names, limiting which users have authority to create new accounts, and then making sure your users search the account list before applying an account to a transaction.

Here are a few suggestions. You can adjust them to meet your own needs or create different rules that you're more comfortable with. But the important thing is consistency!

- Avoid apostrophes and quotes.
- Set the number of characters for abbreviations. For example, if you permit four characters, telephone is abbreviated "tele"; a three-character rule produces "tel".
- Make a rule about whether spaces are allowed. For example, would you rather have "Repairs & Maintenance" or "Repairs&Maintenance"?

Create Accounts

After you've done your homework and decided on a naming and numbering scheme, creating accounts is a piece of cake:

1. Press CTRL-A to open the Chart Of Accounts window.
2. Press CTRL-N to enter a new account.
3. In the Add New Account: Choose Account Type dialog (see Figure 2-2), select the type of account you're creating. If the account type you need doesn't appear

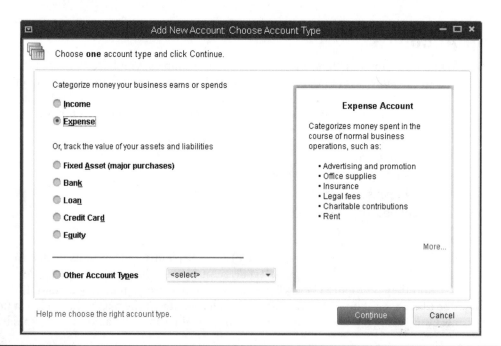

FIGURE 2-2   Start by selecting the type of account you want to add.

in the major category list on the dialog, select Other Account Types and choose an account type from the drop-down list.

4. Click Continue to create the account.

The dialog you see when you fill out account information varies depending on the account type you chose, because different types of accounts require different information. In addition, if you've opted to use numbers for your accounts, there's a field for the account number. Figure 2-3 shows a blank Add New Account dialog for an Expense account.

Select From Examples

If you created your company file in QuickBooks 2014 and you selected an industry type during the setup, a button labeled Select From Examples in the Add New Account dialog will display for certain account types. Clicking the button produces a list of accounts that QuickBooks thinks you might want to consider adding to

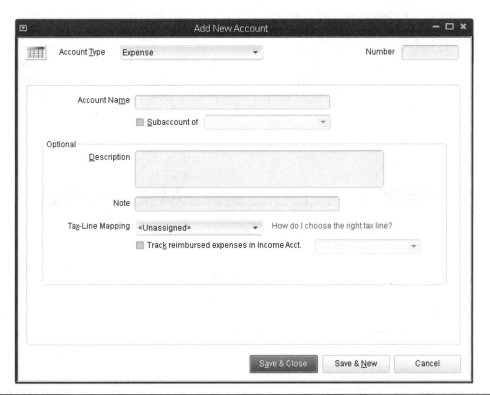

FIGURE 2-3   The only required entry for an account is a name.

your chart of accounts. As you can see in Figure 2-4, the list of accounts matches the account type you selected when you started the process of adding an account.

The accounts suggested are those that were available for the industry you selected when you created your company file but were not selected for inclusion in your chart of accounts.

The following account types do not have the Select From Examples feature:

- Bank
- Credit Card
- Equity
- Accounts Receivable
- Accounts Payable
- Long Term Liability

Optional Fields for Accounts

The Description field in the Add New Account dialog is optional, as is the Note field (which appears only on some account types). You can assign a Tax-Line Mapping to your accounts (see Figure 2-3), which can be a huge timesaver if you do your own taxes or if your tax preparer is using one of Intuit's tax preparation software programs. QuickBooks exports data for each account to the appropriate tax line if you use TurboTax to do your taxes, for example. In order to do this, QuickBooks has to know which tax form you use, and you probably provided that information when you set up your company file. In fact, if you selected a tax form when you set up the company file, QuickBooks automatically inserts a tax line assignment for Income, Cost of Goods Sold, and Expense Accounts.

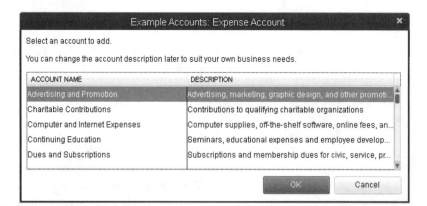

FIGURE 2-4 QuickBooks suggests accounts to add to your chart of accounts.

If you didn't select a tax form, the Tax-Line Mapping field doesn't appear. But you can add the tax-line information in the Company Information window. You get to this window by opening the Company menu, selecting My Company, and then clicking the edit icon on the top-right side of the My Company window. You'll find the Income Tax Form Used drop-down list located on the Report Information tab.

ProAdvisor Tip: You can use QuickBooks without assigning a tax line. Knowing which tax line to assign to an account is not always apparent, so if you're unsure about assigning a tax-line mapping, consult with your accountant or a tax professional first.

Some account types (bank, credit card, assets, liabilities, loan, and equity) have a button labeled Enter Opening Balance. Clicking it opens a dialog in which you can enter an opening balance. While convenient, I recommend that you do not enter opening balances here when you're creating accounts. See "ProAdvisor Recommends: What You Should Know About Entering Opening Balances for Accounts" as well as Chapter 7 to learn about better ways to enter beginning balances.

As you finish creating each account, click Save & New to move to another blank Add New Account dialog. By default, the new dialog is configured for the same account type as the account you just created, but you can change the account type by selecting another type from the drop-down list at the top of the dialog.

When you're finished creating accounts, click Save & Close, and then close the Chart Of Accounts window by clicking the X in the upper-right corner.

Use Subaccounts

Subaccounts provide a way to post transactions more precisely by using subcategories for main account categories, while also giving you the ability to view key reports at both the subaccount and parent account levels. To create a subaccount, you must first create the parent account.

For example, suppose you have the following parent account:

- 6130 Car/Truck Expense

You can create the following subaccounts:

- :6131 Car Lease
- :6132 Gas
- :6135 Mileage
- :6138 Insurance-Auto

▶▶ ProAdvisor Recommends

What You Should Know About Entering Opening Balances for Accounts

Unless you start your business the day you start using QuickBooks, you haven't yet opened a bank account, and you haven't purchased any equipment for your business, many of your accounts already have an existing balance. For example, you probably have money in your business bank account, either because your business has been operating for a long time and you're just getting around to using QuickBooks, or because you provided startup money for your new business.

It is best not to enter any figures in the Opening Balance field of any account that has this option, because QuickBooks (which is a true double-entry accounting application) needs to make an offsetting entry of the same amount you entered into an offsetting account. Of course, QuickBooks has no way of knowing the source of that money, so the offsetting account it uses is called Opening Bal Equity, which is an account QuickBooks invented for just this purpose. In actuality, the money in your bank account may be the result of a loan you made to your business, capital you invested in your business, or sales you made before you started keeping records in QuickBooks.

Your accountant will want to zero-out the balance in Opening Bal Equity, and sometimes that's a difficult job because it's hard to tell how the balance was arrived at—was this opening balance the result of transactions in past years? If so, it needs to be moved to the Retained Earnings account. Is it from the current year? If so, what's the real source of the amount (because it has to be moved to the proper account)? Is it a combination of both? If so, you'll have to remember every entry and explain it to your accountant so the appropriate amounts can be moved to the appropriate accounts.

So it's best to ignore the Opening Balance field when you create an account, and after you've created the account, create a transaction that accurately describes the source of this amount. Chapter 7 details an easy-to-follow process you can use to enter opening balances and historical data correctly and efficiently. Be sure to ask your accountant to help you create the transactions that provide the details behind the opening balances for your accounts.

The colon in the account names listed here is added automatically by QuickBooks on some reports to indicate a parent account: sub account relationship.

> **ProAdvisor Tip:** To get the most out of using subaccounts when viewing reports, you should be sure that, once you create them, you post transactions to the correct subaccount—and not the parent account. Why? Because when you post directly to a parent account that has subaccounts attached to it, reports that include transactions to this account will appear as if they were posted to a subaccount called "Other."

Viewing Subaccounts

When you have subaccounts, the Chart Of Accounts window displays them indented under their parent accounts (see Figure 2-5), as long as you've configured the window to display accounts in Hierarchical view.

If you know you created subaccounts, but you don't see any indented listings, your Chart Of Accounts window has been configured to display accounts in Flat view, which is a simple listing of accounts. To remedy this, click the Account button at the bottom of the window and select Hierarchical View.

Creating Subaccounts

To create a subaccount, you must have already created the parent account. Then take these steps:

1. Open the Chart Of Accounts list.
2. Press CTRL-N to create a new account.
3. Select the appropriate account type.
4. Click Continue.
5. Enter a number (if you're using numbered accounts).
6. Name the account.
7. Click the Subaccount Of check box to place a check mark in it.
8. In the drop-down box next to the check box, select the parent account.
9. Click Save & New to create another account or Save & Close if you're finished creating accounts.

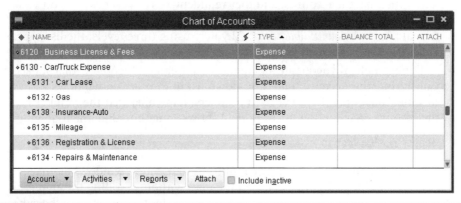

FIGURE 2-5   It's easy to see that the Car/Truck expense account has subaccounts to track expenses more accurately.

Multiple Levels of Subaccounts

You can have multiple levels of subaccounts. For example, you may want to track income in the following manner:

Income

    Income:Consulting

    Income:Consulting:Software Training

Creating the sub-subaccounts is as easy as creating the first-level subaccounts; just make sure you've already created the first-level subaccounts. When you fill in the Add New Account dialog, after you check the Subaccount Of check box, select the appropriate subaccount to act as the parent account.

C a u t i o n : If you plan on using a third-party integrated application that shares data with your QuickBooks data file, it is best to avoid using multiple levels of subaccounts, because the integrated application may not be able to post to an "imbedded" account. Check with the developer of your integrated application just to be sure.

Showing Lowest Subaccounts Only

When you view accounts in the Chart Of Accounts window, subaccounts appear under their parent accounts, and they're indented. However, when you view a subaccount in the drop-down list of a transaction window, it appears in the format: *ParentAccount:Subaccount*. (If you're using three levels, the list appears as *ParentAccount:Subaccount:Sub-subaccount*.)

For example, if you create a parent account named Income with a subaccount Consulting, the Account field drop-down list in transaction windows shows Income:Consulting. If you've used numbers, remember that the number is part of the account name, so the Account field shows something like the following:

```
40000-Income:40010-Consulting
```

Because many of the fields or columns in transaction windows are narrow, you may not be able to see the subaccount names without scrolling through each account. This can be annoying, and it's much easier to work if only the subaccount name is displayed. That's the point of enabling the preference Show Lowest Subaccount Only, discussed earlier in this chapter. When you enable that option, you see only the subaccounts in the drop-down list when you're working in a transaction window, which makes it much easier to select the account you need.

Edit Accounts

If you need to make changes to any account information (including adding a number after you enable numbered accounts), select the account's listing in the Chart Of Accounts window and press CTRL-E. The Edit Account dialog appears, which looks like the account card you just filled out. Make your changes and click Save & Close to save them.

Delete Accounts

It's not uncommon to clean up your chart of accounts to get rid of accounts you'll never use or to remove duplicate accounts. (You can't have two accounts with the same name or number because QuickBooks doesn't permit that, but it's certainly possible to end up with multiple accounts that are similar, such as Tel, Tele, Telephone.)

To delete an account, select its listing in the Chart Of Accounts window and press CTRL-D. QuickBooks asks you to confirm the fact that you want to delete the account. Click OK to remove the account.

You can delete any account that isn't in use, which means the account has never been used in a transaction or linked to a sales or payroll item. You don't have to search all your transactions to find out whether an account has been used in your system; you can just try to delete it, and if it's been assigned to a transaction or item, QuickBooks issues an error message explaining why you can't delete it.

Also, you cannot delete an account that has subaccounts unless you first delete the subaccounts, which can be accomplished only if the subaccounts have never been used in a transaction. However, a workaround for saving the subaccounts and getting rid of the parent account is first to turn the subaccounts into parent accounts. To accomplish this, either drag the subaccount listing to the left in the Chart Of Accounts window (be sure the window is displaying accounts in Hierarchical View and the list is in its original sort order), or edit the subaccount to remove the check mark in the Subaccount Of check box.

If you can't delete an account but you don't want anyone to use it, you can hide it—QuickBooks calls this making it *inactive*. If you have a duplicate account, you can merge it with the other account. Those topics are covered next.

Make Accounts Inactive (Hiding Accounts)

When you make an account inactive, you're hiding the account from users. When an account is inactive, it doesn't appear in drop-down lists in transaction windows, so it can't be selected. The account continues to exist "behind the scenes" and its history remains in the system; it just doesn't appear in drop-down lists during transaction entry.

To make an account inactive, right-click its listing in the Chart Of Accounts window and select Make Account Inactive. QuickBooks doesn't ask you to confirm your action. You can also make an account inactive by selecting it and pressing CTRL-E to open the account record in Edit mode; then select the check box labeled Account Is Inactive to enter a check mark.

By default, inactive accounts aren't displayed in the Chart Of Accounts window, but if you've made any accounts inactive, the Include Inactive check box at the bottom of the window becomes accessible (if it's grayed out that means no inactive accounts exist). Select the check box to insert a check mark, and you can see your inactive accounts, which are displayed with an "X" to the left of the listing.

To return an inactive account to active status, be sure that the Chart Of Accounts window is displaying inactive accounts, and then click the "X" to toggle the account's status to Active.

Merge Accounts

Sometimes you see two accounts that should be one. For instance, you may have accidentally created two accounts for the same purpose. As I discussed earlier in this chapter, I've worked with clients that had accounts named Telephone and Tele, with transactions posted to both accounts. Those accounts are definitely candidates for merging. You can merge accounts only when the following conditions exist:

- Both accounts are of the same account type (for example, you cannot merge an Expense account with an Other Expense account).
- Both accounts are at the same level (you cannot merge a subaccount with a parent account).

Take the following steps to merge two accounts:

1. Open the Chart Of Accounts window.
2. Select (highlight) the account that has the name you do not want to use.
3. Press CTRL-E to open the Edit Account dialog.
4. Change the account name to match the account you want to keep.
5. Click Save & Close.
6. QuickBooks displays a dialog telling you that the account number or name you've entered already exists for another account and asks if you want to merge the accounts. Click Yes to confirm that you want to merge the two accounts.

Remember, the way to do this is to start with the "bad" account and rename it to match the "good" account—the one you want to keep.

Your Customers

Chapter 3

When you create a customer in QuickBooks, you not only have the ability to store basic information such as address, phone number, and e-mail, but you can also track and manage nearly everything and anything you need to know about that customer—and all your other customers—in the Customer Center, shown here:

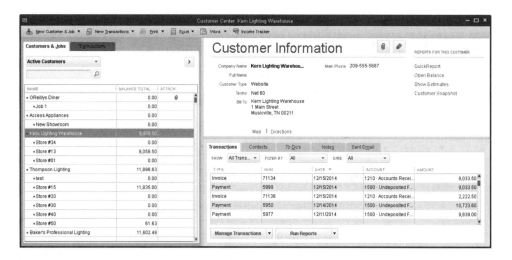

You'll learn more about how to navigate and work in the Customer Center later in this chapter, but first things first. You have to get your customer information into your QuickBooks company file—and there's more than one way to do that. You can create new customers "on the fly" the first time you invoice them, import all your existing customers from a spreadsheet, or enter them manually, one by one. Regardless of the method, your goal should be to enter the most complete and consistent information you can, since this valuable data can then be used for marketing, customer service, and other activities critical to maintaining a great relationship with your customers.

Build Your Customers List

Here are the ways you can add your customers to QuickBooks: You can choose to add them one-by-one (the details for using that method are covered in this section); you can use the Add/Edit Multiple List Entries window (covered in this chapter in the section "Adding Multiple Customer Records"); or, if you've been storing this information in an Excel sheet or a comma-separated (.csv) file, you may want to consider using a special QuickBooks utility designed to import this information. This import utility contains a step-by-step wizard that can be accessed by choosing File | Utilities | Import | Excel Files. You can also use this utility to import your vendors, inventory items, and your chart of accounts.

To create a new customer manually, first open the Customer Center by clicking the Customers button located either on the Icon Bar or on the Home page. Next, click the New Customer & Job drop-down arrow at the top of the Customer Center window (navigating the Customer Center is covered in detail later in this chapter) and select New Customer from the submenu. This action opens the New Customer window (see Figure 3-1). Fill in the appropriate information using the guidelines in the following sections.

Address Info

The New Customer window opens with the Address Info tab in the foreground. The first field in which you'll enter information is the Customer Name field. Consider this field an internal code rather than a customer name. The text you enter here doesn't appear on printed invoices or other sales transactions; instead, what you enter in the Company Name field will appear.

Customer Name

You should create a system for how you complete the Customer Name field so that you'll enter every customer in the same way and avoid the risk of entering the same customer multiple times. For example, if your customer is a business, you can simply enter the name of the business, as shown in Figure 3-1. If your customer is an individual, it's a good practice to enter their last name first in the Customer Name field.

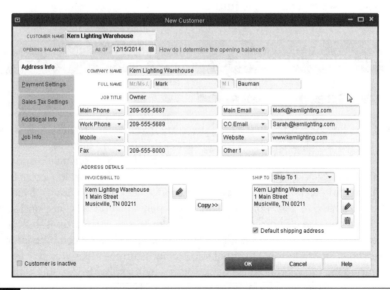

FIGURE 3-1 The customer record holds quite a lot of information.

Each customer must have a unique entry in this field, so if you have a lot of customers named Johnson, for example, you may want to enter them in a way that makes it easy to determine which Johnson this listing represents. For instance, you could have customer names such as JohnsonJack, JohnsonMary, JohnsonRestaurant, and so on. If you have several Jack Johnson customers, you can use JohnsonJackMainSt for the Jack Johnson on Main Street. This field can contain up to 41 characters, so you should be able to create a naming system that works well for you.

Currency

If you've enabled the Multiple Currencies feature, the Currency field appears so you can select the currency for this customer. (Refer to Appendix B if you plan on using the Multiple Currencies feature.)

Opening Balance

QuickBooks makes an Opening Balance field available, along with the date for which this balance applies (by default, the current date is inserted). The field is designed to hold the amount this customer currently owes if an open balance exists for the customer. See "ProAdvisor Recommends: Customer Opening Balance."

Customer Address Info

In the Company and Address Details sections of the window, enter the company name, a contact name (optional), and the billing address. Add any other contact information you want to track for this customer (telephone, e-mail, and so on). Be sure to enter an e-mail address if you want to be able to e-mail this customer invoices or statements in the future.

➠ ProAdvisor Recommends

Customer Opening Balance

It's best not to use the Opening Balance field, because if you enter an amount that includes the balance from more than one outstanding invoice, you'll have no detailed records on how this balance was arrived at, which will then make it difficult to match payments against specific invoices. What's more, QuickBooks posts the amount you enter in this field to Accounts Receivable and makes an offsetting entry into an account named Opening Balance Equity. Eventually, you or your accountant will need to zero-out the balance in Opening Balance Equity, and sometimes that's a difficult job because it's hard to tell how the balance was arrived at: Is this an opening balance you entered from past years? Is it from the current year? Is it a combination of both? Entering transactions that represent the way the customer's current status was reached is far more accurate than using the Opening Balance field. That's why it's better to skip this field and then enter an invoice or multiple invoices to post this customer's balance to your books.

Ship To Addresses

You can maintain multiple shipping addresses for your customers. Give a name of your own choosing to each Ship To address so you can select it from a drop-down list when you're entering sales transactions. If the shipping address isn't different from the billing address (or if you have a service business and never ship products), you can ignore the shipping address field, or click the Copy button to copy the data from the Bill To field.

To create a shipping address, click the plus sign button next to the Ship To address block to open the Add Shipping Address Information dialog:

QuickBooks automatically enters the address name Ship To 1. Feel free to replace that text with a name that reminds you of the address location (such as Boston or Main Street) to make it easier to select this address from a drop-down list when you have to ship goods to this customer.

Enter the address information and specify whether this address should be the default Ship To address, and then click OK. If needed, enter another Ship To address for this customer; it will have a default name of Ship To 2.

Payment Settings

The Payment Settings tab (see Figure 3-2) puts all the important information about customer finances in one place.

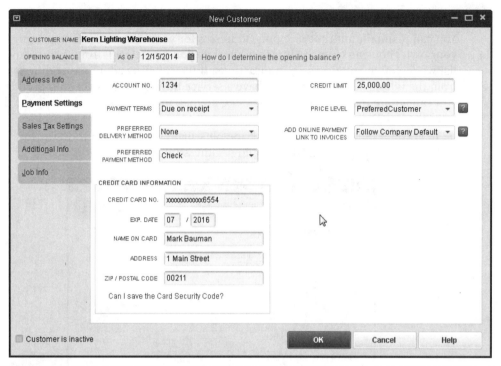

FIGURE 3-2 Use the Payment Settings tab to track details needed for this customer's transactions.

Account No.

This is an optional field you can use if you assign account numbers to your customers.

Credit Limit

A credit limit is a way to set a threshold for the amount of money you'll extend to a customer to make "on account" purchases. If a customer places an order and the new order combined with any unpaid invoices exceeds this threshold, QuickBooks displays a warning. QuickBooks won't prevent you from continuing to sell to and invoice the customer, but you should consider rejecting the order (or shipping it COD).

C a u t i o n : Leaving the Credit Limit field blank is not the same as entering a zero. If you want a data entry/sales person not to sell to this customer, enter a zero in this field.

Payment Terms

Click the arrow to the right of the Payment Terms field to see the list of terms that QuickBooks has already defined, or choose <Add New> to define a new one.

The terms in the Payment Terms List are for both customers and vendors, and you may need additional terms to meet your customers' and vendors' needs. See Chapter 6 to learn how to create different types of terms.

Price Level

Price levels are a way for you to customize your prices on a customer level—usually to offer special discounts when that customer makes a purchase. Select an existing price level or create a new one. See Chapter 6 to learn about creating and assigning price levels.

Add Online Payment Link To Invoices

Use this option to learn more about or to sign up for the Intuit Payment Network. With this service, you can allow your customers to pay their invoices online, via a link, when they receive their invoice via e-mail. You can choose to accept credit card, bank payments, or both (additional fees may apply).

Preferred Delivery Method

This field stores the default value for the way you want to send invoices, statements, or estimates to this customer (it does not refer to the method you use to send products to the customer). The choices are the following:

- **E-mail** You e-mail the documents. This feature lets you attach the documents as PDF files to an e-mail message. You can e-mail using Outlook or your web-based e-mail (such as Yahoo! or Gmail, for example). Chapter 14 has the details.
- **Mail** You use a QuickBooks service to mail the invoices. The data is reproduced on a form that has a tear-off portion your customers enclose with their payment.
- **None** No special features are used to send the documents. You print them and you mail them.

Regardless of the method you choose as your default, you can use any send method when you're creating a transaction. Chapter 14 has more information on setting and using these methods.

Preferred Payment Method

This indicates the customer's preferred method for payments—a list of payment methods is offered in the drop-down list. You can select the appropriate item from the list or add a new one by selecting <Add New> from the drop-down list. See Chapter 6 for more information on this list.

ProAdvisor Tip: The payment method you select automatically appears on the Receive Payments window when you are using this customer in the transaction. You can change the payment method at that time, if necessary.

Credit Card Information

These fields are intended to capture this customer's credit card information, if that's the customer's preferred payment method. If you decide to store this information, be sure to enable QuickBooks Customer Credit Card Protection. For more information on how to turn on this feature, as well as to learn more about important credit card security issues and best practices, see the section "Secure Customer Credit Card Information" later in this chapter.

Sales Tax Settings

If you've configured QuickBooks to collect sales tax, there are a few fields on this tab you should complete. If the customer is liable for sales tax, select the appropriate sales tax code and item for this customer. You can also create a new sales tax item or code here if you need to. If the customer does not pay sales tax, select Non (from the Tax Code drop-down list), and in the Resale No. field, enter the resale number provided by the customer. See Chapter 5 for a complete discussion of sales tax codes and sales tax items.

Additional Info

The information you enter in the Additional Info tab (see Figure 3-3) gives you the opportunity to capture more detailed information about your customers. On this tab, you can use the available fields or create custom fields of your own. You'll then be able to use this extra info to analyze things like buying patterns or how well your sales staff is doing. You'll also be able to design reports based on the data captured in these fields.

Customer Type

Use the Customer Type field to sort your customers by a type you find important. For example, you may want to use customer types to distinguish between wholesale and retail customers, or to track the source of referrals. QuickBooks maintains this information in the Customer Type list (covered in more detail in Chapter 6).

To use the field, click the arrow to select a type that you already entered, or create a new type.

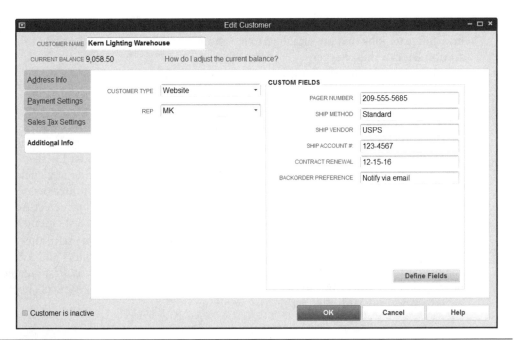

FIGURE 3-3   Entering additional information makes your work in QuickBooks go faster.

Rep

This field is the place to track a sales representative, and it's useful whether you pay commissions or you just want to know who is in charge of a particular customer. Sales reps can be employees, vendors, or "other names" (which means the name is entered in the Other Names list). Select a rep from the list of reps or add a new rep by choosing <Add New> from the drop-down list. Chapter 6 has more information on how this information is used in QuickBooks.

Custom Fields

Custom fields provide an opportunity for you to create fields for tracking special information about your customers (such as contract renewal date, for example). Later, you can sort and arrange your QuickBooks lists and reports using the data from these fields. See the section "Use Custom Fields" later in this chapter.

Job Info Tab

Use the fields on this tab to help you keep track of the status of your work with a customer and to assign a job description and job type. In addition, assigning start and projected end dates will allow you to produce reports that give you feedback on your performance. More information about how this information is used, as well as how to create jobs that are attached to a customer, can be found in the "Use Jobs" section later in this chapter.

When you have finished filling out the fields, click OK.

Adding Multiple Customer Records

If you want to add multiple customers at once (or make changes to the information for existing customer records), you can use the Add/Edit Multiple List Entries window. To access this time-saving feature, open the Customer Center (by clicking the Customers button located on the Icon Bar), select the New Customer & Job drop-down arrow at the top of the Customer Center window, and then select Add Multiple Customer:Jobs (you can also access this window from the Lists menu).

The Add/Edit Multiple List Entries window opens (see Figure 3-4) with the Customers list already selected. From here, you can add new customers and jobs, change customer information, or fill in data you didn't have when you first created the customer record. You can even copy and paste customers from an Excel sheet into the Add/Edit Multiple List Entries window.

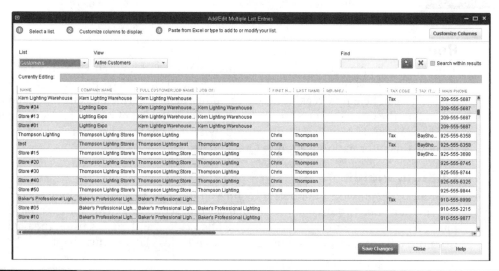

FIGURE 3-4 Adding and editing multiple customer records

Here's a list of some of the important features and functionalities that you should be familiar with to get the most benefit from using the Add/Edit Multiple List Entries window:

- **List and View filters**   Select the List or View drop-down arrow to display only those records in your list that you want to work with.
- **Find field**   Use this field to quickly locate and work with a specific customer record.
- **Customize Columns button**   Click this button to open the Customize Columns window, where you can add columns for the fields within the customer record that you want to modify. For example, if you want to add a job to your Customers list (see the section "Use Jobs" later in this chapter), add the two columns Job Of and Full Customer:Job Name. When you add the Job Of column, it displays a drop-down arrow you can use to associate your new job to its parent customer. The ability to customize the columns also makes it easier to copy and paste from a spreadsheet because you can match the spreadsheet columns to the Add/Edit Multiple List Entry window.

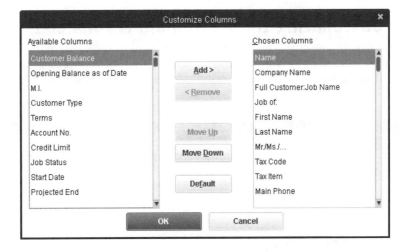

- **Copy Down**   Right-clicking within a field in the table allows you to select the Copy Down command, which copies the contents of a selected field to all the remaining records in the list (note, however, that you can't use the Copy Down command with the Name field).
- **Duplicate Row**   Right-clicking with your cursor placed on any row in the table lets you duplicate the selected record in the row below. The new duplicate record name will start with "DUP".

The Customer Center

The QuickBooks Customer Center is where all your customers and jobs, and detailed information about those customers and jobs, are kept. It's also where you can go to create, edit, and get reports about customers and jobs.

To open the Customer Center (shown in Figure 3-5), click the Customers button located on the Icon Bar or on the Home Page Navigator.

The left pane of the Customer Center has two tabs: Customers & Jobs and Transactions. A customer is always selected in the Customers & Jobs List (by default, the first customer in the list when you first open the Customer Center), and the right pane of the Customer Center displays information about the selected customer or job.

The Transactions tab lists all your customer transactions (invoices, sales receipts, and so on) by transaction type. Selecting a transaction type displays the current transactions of that type in the right pane. The display can be manipulated and filtered by choosing categories and sorting by column.

Customizing the Customers & Jobs List

You can customize the information displayed in the Customers & Jobs List to your own liking. By default, the list has three columns: Name, Balance Total, and Attach (learn about the Attached Documents feature in Chapter 14). The Currency column

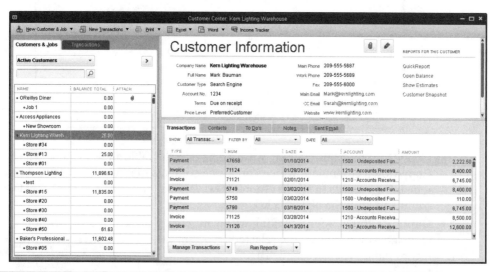

FIGURE 3-5   The Customer Center is your one-stop location to work with and get information about your customers.

will also be visible (unless you've removed it) if you've enabled the multiple currencies feature. You don't even have to select a customer's listing to see the current balance, because the balances for all your customers are displayed next to their names.

You can add more columns to the Customers & Jobs List. To do so, right-click anywhere in the list and choose Customize Columns to open the Customize Columns dialog shown in Figure 3-6. To add a column, select its label in the left pane and click Add. Alternatively, if you want to eliminate a column from your list, highlight its label in the right pane and click Remove.

Some users find it useful to add the Overdue column, so they know which customers have an overdue or almost due invoice. More about this feature and the Customer Collections Center in Chapter 10.

You can rearrange the left-to-right order of the columns. Select a column you want to move, and then choose Move Up to move a column to the left or Move Down to move it to the right. The order of columns displayed in the Chosen Columns pane of the dialog translates as top to bottom = left to right.

If you add columns to the Customers & Jobs List, you won't be able to see all the information unless you widen the list's pane and also widen each column. To maximize this pane, click the Show Full List Only button—the right-pointing arrow located on the top right-hand side of the Customers & Jobs List (see Figure 3-5).

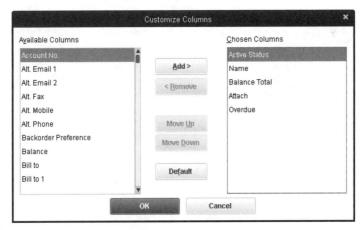

FIGURE 3-6   Choose what you want to see in the Customer Center's Customers & Jobs List.

Working in the Customer Information Pane

The Customer Information pane is where QuickBooks keeps all of the information you've entered for your customers, as well as each and every sales-related transaction (see Figure 3-7). From here you can quickly see the details behind a customer's past due balance, add or update important notes or To Do's that relate to a specific job, and even run key customer reports.

The top half of the Customer Information pane displays basic contact information, along with links to maps, directions, and key reports. The bottom half of the pane is made up of five tabs that contain transaction details, contact information, To Do's, notes, and sent e-mail information. When working in any of these tables, you can click the Manage <*tab name*> button at the bottom of the window to add, edit, or delete the information contained therein.

Transactions Tab

If you want to view only invoices for a particular customer, you can filter for that information on the Transactions tab. In fact, there are several different categories to choose from on the drop-down lists in the Show field. And just as with the Customers list (see previous section), you can add and remove columns of information by right-clicking anywhere on or below the column headings and choosing Customize Columns.

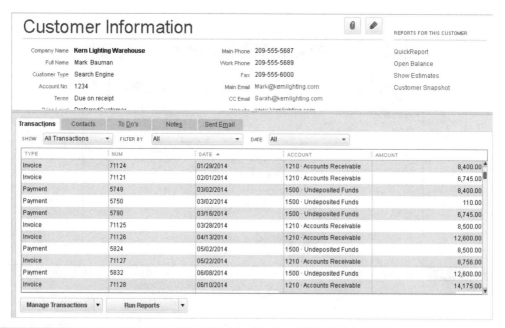

FIGURE 3-7 View, access, and update customer information and transactions directly in the Customer Information pane.

Contacts Tab

On the Contacts tab, you can store pretty much all the ways that you can keep in touch with your customers. Click the drop-down arrows in the available fields and you'll see that there's not only a place for phone and e-mail information but also for LinkedIn and Facebook sites:

To Do's Tab

From the To Do's tab, click the Manage To Do's button and select Create New to compose a reminder specifically for this customer (see Figure 3-8). This is a very useful feature. You get to specify the date on which you want to be reminded (the Due field) and categorize your new To Do as a call or meeting in the Type field, for example. You can then view your To Do note in the Calendar (discussed in Chapter 1) or directly in the Customer Center. When the task is complete, open the reminder and change its status to Done. Click the Run Reports button on the To Do's tab to see a detailed listing of all your To Do's—including those for vendors and employees.

ProAdvisor Tip: If you want to view a list of *all* of your QuickBooks To Do's, select To Do List from the Company menu. From this "global" list, you can add, edit, or delete a To Do or even print a report that shows the details of each task.

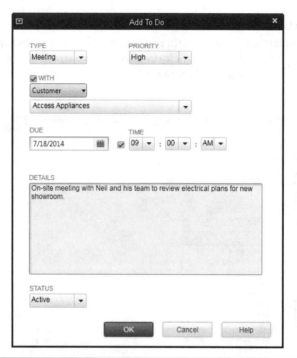

FIGURE 3-8 To Do's are a useful way to keep track of important customer-related tasks.

Notes Tab

From the Notes tab, click the Manage Notes button to add, edit, or delete a note. Use the Date/Time Stamp button to insert the current date and time automatically when you're adding text to the notepad.

Sent Email Tab

This is the best way to keep track of all the sales transactions you've e-mailed a customer. In a single list, you can see who the e-mail was addressed to, the date it was sent, and the form that was sent (invoice, sales receipt, payment receipts, for example), including the reference number and amount.

Editing an Individual Customer Record

There may be times when you want to edit a customer record individually. You can do this from the Customer Center. Simply locate and double-click the customer's listing in the Customers & Jobs List to open the customer record in Edit mode.

When you open the customer record, you can change any information or fill in data you didn't have when you first created the customer entry.

> **ProAdvisor Tip:** Take care when making changes to the Customer Name field, as it may result in some unintended consequences, such as changing the order in which that name appears in the Customers list and customer reports and causing a retroactive change to the customer's name on all past transactions. Also, changes in the Customer Name field do not automatically change the name as it appears in the Bill To or Ship To address field—you'll have to remember to update that manually.

Use Jobs

QuickBooks handles customers and jobs together. That gives you the option of creating a single customer and posting all the invoices to that customer, or creating multiple jobs for that customer and job-level invoices.

Some businesses don't worry about jobs; only the customer is tracked. But if you're a building contractor or subcontractor, an interior decorator, a consultant, or some other kind of service provider who usually sends invoices based on a project, you should track jobs. Jobs don't stand alone; they are always attached to customers, and you can attach as many jobs to a single customer as you need to.

If you plan to track jobs, you can either enter the jobs you know about during your QuickBooks setup phase or enter them as you need to. Jobs are attached to customers—they can't stand alone—so the customer to which the job is attached has to exist in your QuickBooks Customers & Jobs List before you can create the job.

Once the job is created, you can track its progress and keep an eye on the promised end date. If you think this will be the only job you perform for this customer, you can do the same thing for a customer without creating a job, because the customer record also has a Job Info tab. If you're lucky enough to get another project from the customer, you can always add a new job at a later time.

Creating Jobs

To create a job, open the Customer Center and right-click the listing of the customer for whom you're creating a job. Choose Add Job to open the New Job window, shown in Figure 3-9. Create a name for the job (you can use up to 41 characters) and make it descriptive enough for both you and your customer to understand.

If this job requires you to bill the customer at an address that's different from the address you entered for this customer, or to ship goods to a different shipping address, make the appropriate changes in the job's Address Info tab. QuickBooks maintains this information only for this job and won't change the original shipping address in the customer record. Update the Payment Settings and Additional Info tabs as required. The sales tax settings are related to the customer rather than the job, so you won't see the Sales Tax Setting tab.

FIGURE 3-9 To create a new job, enter the job name—all the basic information about the customer is already filled in.

Next, move to the Job Info tab (see Figure 3-10) to fill in the details of this job. All of the information on the Job Info tab is optional.

The Job Status drop-down list offers choices that you can change as the progress of the job moves along. You can change the default text to reflect the way you refer to each progress level, but the changes you make for the text are system-wide and affect every job. Here's how to change the text you use to track job status:

1. Choose Edit | Preferences to open the Preferences dialog.
2. Click the Jobs & Estimates icon in the left pane, and then click the Company Preferences tab in the right pane to see the current descriptive text for each status level (see Figure 3-11).
3. Change the text of any status levels if you have a descriptive phrase you like better. For example, you may prefer using the term "Working" instead of "In Progress."
4. Click OK to save your changes.

The new text is used on every existing and new job in your system.

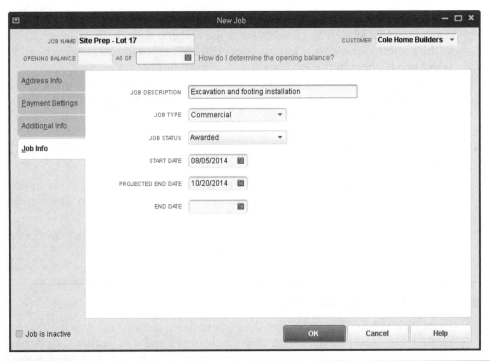

Track job details on the Job Info tab.

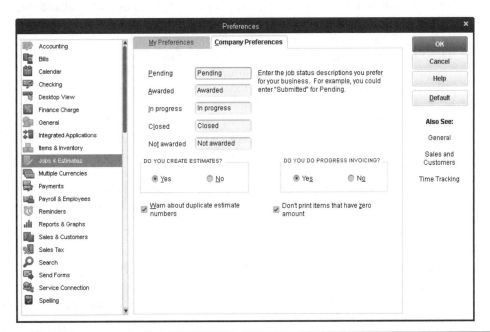

Customize the text to reflect the way you track a project's progress.

The Job Info tab also provides fields to track the start date and the projected end date of the job, as well as a field to enter the real end date (frequently not the same as the projected end date). You can also create job types to categorize jobs and select one of them in the Job Type field (covered in Chapter 6).

When you finish entering all the data about this job, click OK to close the New Job window and return to the Customers & Jobs List. The jobs you create for a customer become part of the customer listing.

Editing Jobs

It's common to open a job record to make changes, because most people track the current status (and occasionally change the projected end date). In addition, you may want to change some of the basic data you entered for a job.

To edit a job, double-click its listing in the Customers & Jobs List. You can make changes to the appropriate fields in any tab.

Delete Customers & Jobs

From time to time, you may have the need to delete a customer or a job that you've created. For example, you might create a customer and then realize it's a duplicate record for a customer that already exists in your Customers list. Deleting a job is a bit more common than deleting customers, because sometimes QuickBooks users add a job when they prepare an estimate for a client for a new project and then delete the job if the project doesn't materialize.

You can delete a customer or a job only if it has never been used in a transaction. I hear from many users who complain that they can't remove a customer that is essentially "dead wood" on their Customers & Jobs List. The customer has a zero balance, and there hasn't been a sale to this customer for a long time, possibly even years. Unfortunately, a zero balance doesn't matter; the rule is that you can delete a customer or a job only if it has never been used in a transaction.

In addition, you cannot delete a customer who has at least one job attached to it. Instead, you must first delete the jobs (if they can be deleted), and then delete the customer.

To delete a customer or job, select it on the Customers & Jobs List and press CTRL-D. QuickBooks asks you to confirm the fact that you want to delete this customer or job. Click OK to remove the customer or job.

Making Customers & Jobs Inactive (Hiding)

If you have a customer that can't be deleted but is no longer active, you can prevent users from selecting this customer in transaction windows by making the customer inactive (hiding the customer so it doesn't appear in drop-down lists). You can do the same thing for any job.

To make a customer or job inactive, right-click its listing in the Customers & Jobs List and choose Make Customer:Job Inactive.

Caution: If you make a customer with jobs inactive, all of the jobs are automatically made inactive. You cannot hide a customer without hiding all the jobs associated with that customer.

If your Customers & Jobs List is configured to show Active Customers (the default view), inactive customers and jobs don't appear on the list. To see which customers and jobs are inactive, select All Customers from the drop-down list at the top of the Customers & Jobs List. Inactive customers and jobs have an "X" to the left of their listings (see Figure 3-12).

To make a customer or job active again, select All Customers as the view, and click the "X" next to the hidden customer or job to toggle the setting back to active. If you're reactivating a customer with jobs, QuickBooks asks if you also want to make all the jobs active. If you click Yes, the customer and all jobs are activated.

If you click No, the customer is activated and all the jobs remain inactive; you can activate any of the jobs individually.

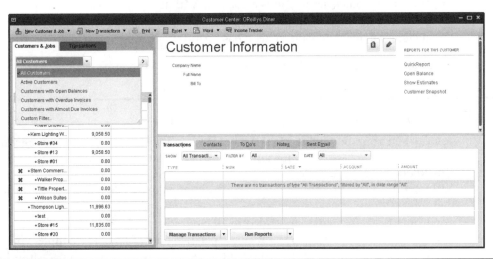

FIGURE 3-12 It's easy to spot inactive customers and jobs.

ProAdvisor Tip: Historical transactions related to inactive customers and jobs are included in reports, so you can continue to get accurate information about a customer's past activities even if you decide to make them inactive.

Merging Customers or Jobs

Sometimes you create a customer or job and enter at least one transaction before you realize it's a duplicate of an existing customer or an existing job for the same customer. The best thing to do in this case is to merge two customers or two jobs and move all the transaction history into one customer record. Follow these steps to do this:

1. Double-click the listing of the customer or job you do not want to keep to put it in Edit mode.
2. Change the customer or job name to match the name of the customer or job you want to keep.
3. Click OK.
4. QuickBooks displays a message telling you that the name is in use and asks if you want to merge the names.
5. Click Yes.

Merging customers works only when one of the following circumstances exists:

- Neither customer has any jobs associated with it.
- The customer name you want to get rid of has no jobs attached (it's OK if the customer name you want to keep has jobs).

Merging jobs works only when both jobs are linked to the same customer.

Use Custom Fields

You can add your own fields to the Customer, Vendor, Employee, and Item records. Custom fields are useful if you want to track particular information but QuickBooks doesn't provide a field for it. For example, if you want to track customer birthdays or annual renewals for a contract, you can add fields to track that information.

Custom fields for names are added to all names lists, but you can configure each field you create to limit its appearance to specific names lists. For example, you might create a custom field that you want to use in only the Customers & Jobs List or in both the Customers & Jobs and Vendors lists.

Adding a Custom Field

To add one or more custom fields to names, follow these steps:

1. Open a Center (Customers & Jobs, Vendors, or Employees).
2. Double-click any name on the list to put the record in Edit mode.
3. Move to the Additional Info tab.
4. Click the Define Fields button to open the Set Up Custom Fields For Names dialog, where you can name the field and indicate the list(s) in which you want to use the new field (see Figure 3-13).

That's all there is to it, except you must click OK to save the information. When you do, QuickBooks displays a message reminding you that if you customize your templates (forms for transactions, such as invoices or sales receipts), you can add these fields. Instructions for adding fields to transaction templates are found in Chapter 24.

The Additional Info tab for every name in the list(s) you selected now shows those fields.

Adding Data to Custom Fields

To add data to the custom fields for a customer, select their name from the Customer Center and double-click the name to put the record into Edit mode. Move to the Additional Info tab where the custom field you created appears (see Figure 3-14).

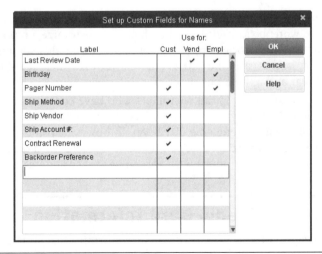

FIGURE 3-13 Custom fields appear on all the records of the list(s) you select.

FIGURE 3-14 Add data to the custom field for each customer to which this custom field is relevant.

Be sure you enter data in a consistent manner for each customer, or the information you retrieve won't be as useful to you when you customize a report to include this custom information. For example, one of the custom fields shown in Figure 3-14 holds a date. In this case, the date is entered in the format: Year-Month, using a four-digit year and a three-character month.

If you use that format for all customers who have contract renewal dates (such as 2012-Jun or 2013-Jan), you can filter a customer list report to show all customers with contracts that are renewing 2012-Sep. If, however, you use Sept for some data entry, and Sep for other data entry, or if you forget to enter a dash and used a space, you won't see all the customers with September renewal dates.

Secure Customer Credit Card Information

QuickBooks provides security features for companies that store customer credit card data in their company files. These features are designed to help you meet the requirements set by the payment card industry that are known as the *Payment Card Industry Data Security Standard* (PCI DSS).

If you log in to your company file as Admin, you may see a reminder about enabling credit card protection when you open the file. The first chore you face is changing your own Admin password so it matches the standards for complex passwords required by the credit card protection feature (see Figure 3-15).

You should enable the credit card protection feature as soon as possible, but if you don't respond to the reminder by selecting Enable Protection, you can perform the task by choosing Company | Customer Credit Card Protection and selecting Enable Protection.

C a u t i o n : You must be logged in as the user named Admin to configure credit card protection.

The Challenge Question section is mandatory. If you forget your password, you can click the Reset Password button on the Login dialog. When you answer the challenge question correctly, QuickBooks lets you change your password to a new complex password. When you complete the dialog and click OK, QuickBooks confirms the fact that you've changed your password and informs you that you'll have to repeat this task every 90 days.

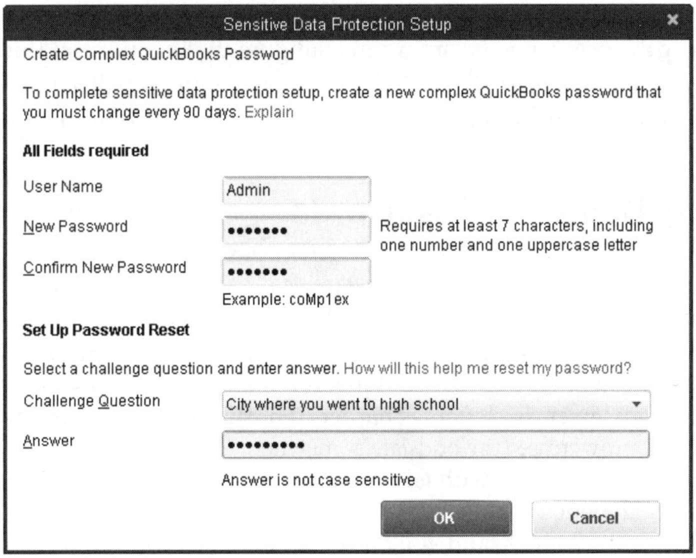

FIGURE 3-15   Start by setting a complex password for the QuickBooks Admin user account.

> **ProAdvisor Tip:** Although not recommended, you can disable the customer credit card protection feature: reopen the Customer Credit Card Protection window, and a dialog appears asking if you want to disable it.

More About QuickBooks Customer Credit Card Protection

Here are some important points to keep in mind when you enable Credit Card Protection:

- All users who have permission to view full credit card detail in the customer record must set up a *complex password* (see the next section, "About Complex Passwords").
- The password must be changed every 90 days. Users who don't change their passwords cannot open the file. If the Admin fails to change their password, the credit card protection feature is disabled (and you see messages about your failure to comply with the rules set for businesses that accept credit cards).
- You cannot reuse any of the last four passwords.
- If a user enters an incorrect password three times (users sometimes guess different passwords when they can't remember their passwords), the company file closes for that user.
- Only the user named Admin can configure the functions in this feature.
- The QuickBooks credit card security audit log tracks all actions that involve credit cards (including viewing customer credit card information).

About Complex Passwords

Complex passwords (sometimes called *strong passwords*) are passwords that can't easily be discovered by hacker software that uses permutations and combinations of letters and numbers to break into password-protected files.

The more complex a password is, the higher the odds are against breaking it. For example, a password that contains seven characters and includes one uppercase letter and six lowercase letters is harder to break than a password that is entirely uppercase or lowercase (the odds are somewhere in the range of one in many millions). When you mix numbers with letters, and at least one letter is in a different case than the others, the odds are even greater. If you add characters and at least two of those characters are numbers, and at least two of the letters are in a different case than the other letters, the odds of breaking it grow to pretty astronomical levels.

User Permissions for Viewing Credit Card Information

With credit card protection enabled, when you set up users and give them Full Access to the Sales and Accounts Receivable area, those users are not given permission to view customer credit card information unless you specifically select that option.

Users who do not have permission to view credit card information see only the last four numbers of the credit card when they open the Payment Info tab of a customer's record (see Figure 3-16).

Users who have permission to view customer information are forced to create a complex password during their next login.

When you set up new users and give them permission to access customer information, it's not necessary to set up a complex password for them. Provide a regular, easy to enter password, and QuickBooks will force a password change during the first login. (See Chapter 8 to learn more about setting up users and permissions.)

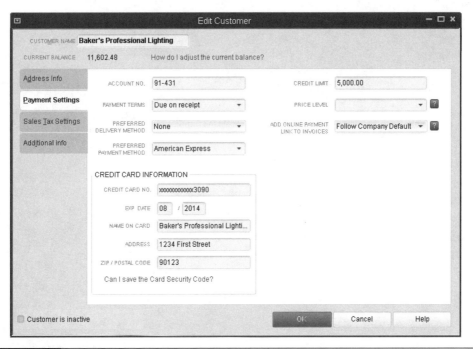

FIGURE 3-16   Users without the proper permissions can't see credit card numbers.

Viewing the Security Log

When credit card protection is enabled, QuickBooks maintains a security log called the Customer Credit Card Audit Trail. This is a special report that can be viewed only by the QuickBooks Admin user. To open the report, choose Reports | Accountant & Taxes Customer Credit Card Audit Trail.

This report is updated each time a customer's credit card information is entered, displayed, edited, or deleted—or if any changes are made to the account information. The most recent activity is always listed at the top of the report.

Your Vendors

In this chapter:

- Build your vendor list
- The Vendor Center
- Edit vendors
- Delete vendors
- Merge vendors
- Create custom fields to track vendor information
- Designate a vendor as eligible to receive a Form 1099

Chapter 4

QuickBooks refers to the businesses or individuals from which you purchase goods and services as *vendors*, and the names of these vendors have to be entered into your QuickBooks system before you can enter bills or otherwise pay them. In most cases, it's easier to enter their information before you start entering transactions. And, just like your list of customers, you not only have the ability to store basic information such as address, phone number, and e-mail, but you can also track and manage nearly everything and anything you need to know about that vendor—and all your other vendors—in the Vendor Center.

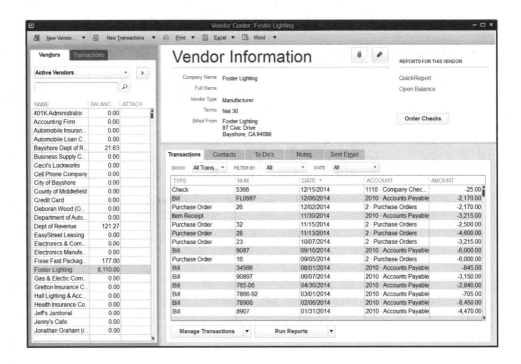

Create Your Vendors List

As with your Customers list, you have a few options when building your list of vendors in QuickBooks. You can choose to add them one-by-one (the details for using that method are covered in this section), you can use the Add/Edit Multiple List Entries window (covered later in this chapter), or, if you've been storing this information in an Excel sheet or a comma-separated file (.csv file), you may want to consider using a special QuickBooks utility designed to import this information. This import utility contains a step-by-step wizard that can be accessed by selecting File | Utilities | Import | Excel Files. The utility can also be used to import your customers, inventory items, and your chart of accounts.

To create a vendor, you'll first need to open the Vendor Center. From the Vendors menu, select Vendor Center. Now click the New Vendor icon above the Vendors list and select New Vendor. The New Vendor dialog opens to the Address Info tab, as seen in Figure 4-1.

Address Info

Start by filling in the Vendor Name field at the top of the window, and then move on to fill in as much information as you think you'll need about this vendor, including contacts, telephone numbers, and so on. The Billed From address block is important if you're planning to print checks and the vendor doesn't enclose a return envelope, because this is where you'll likely send your payment to. You can purchase window envelopes, and when you insert the check in the envelope, the vendor name and address block is located in the right place to show through the window. The Shipped From address is used if your vendor ships from a different place than they bill from.

It's best *not* to enter anything in the Opening Balance field. Instead, separately enter the existing open vendor bills that represent the current open (unpaid) balances. See Chapter 7 to learn how get vendor history into your company file.

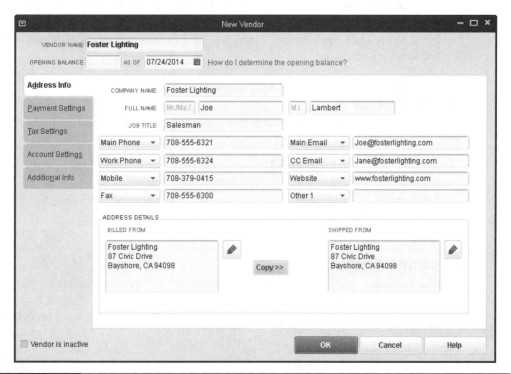

FIGURE 4-1 Enter contact and billing information about your vendor on the Address Info tab.

Currency

If you've enabled multiple currencies, select the appropriate currency for this vendor if the vendor is in another country. (Refer to Appendix B for more information on the QuickBooks multiple currencies feature.)

Payment Settings

The Payment Settings tab allows you to store some useful information:

- **Account No.**   If an account number is associated with this vendor, you can enter it here and the number will appear in the memo field of printed checks.
- **Payment Terms**   The terms you enter here will automatically be applied to all bills entered for this vendor.
- **Credit Limit**   QuickBooks will give you a warning if you enter a bill or write a check that exceeds your credit limit with this vendor.
- **Billing Rate Level**   (This field is available only in the Premier and Enterprise levels of QuickBooks.) If you plan on rebilling your customers for the work performed by this vendor, you can enter either a standard hourly or custom rate here. Then each time you create an invoice with billable time, QuickBooks will automatically fill in the correct rate for each service item based on the vendor that did the work.
- **Print Name On Check As**   Fill in this field if the Payee name is different from the Vendor name used.

Tax Settings

If you plan on issuing a Form 1099 to a vendor at the end of the year, you'll want to be sure to complete the following information:

- **Vendor Tax ID**   Use this field to enter the social security number or employer ID number (EIN) if this vendor receives a Form 1099.
- **1099 status**   If appropriate, select the check box for Vendor Eligible For 1099. Learn more about the 1099 tracking feature later in this chapter.

Account Settings

Prefilling expense accounts is a great way to save time and ensure accuracy when entering bills or writing checks. When you select accounts in this window for this vendor (see Figure 4-2), they'll appear automatically when you enter a bill or a check for the vendor. You can always change the prefilled account before saving the bill or check, if necessary.

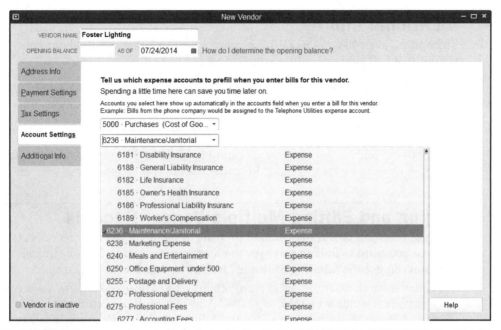

FIGURE 4-2 Prefill the usual posting account for a vendor to save time and avoid errors.

You can prefill up to three accounts for a vendor. This feature can be very useful for your Internet service provider, for example, for which you may want to split out Internet service and telephone service. Another good use is for making loan payments, which require postings to principal and interest.

ProAdvisor Tip: If a vendor needs only one account, but you often split the amount due in order to assign parts of the bill to customers, enter the same account in all three fields of the Account Settings tab. QuickBooks will list all the accounts in the transaction window. For example, parts of your telephone bill (usually long distance charges) may be charged to multiple clients as reimbursable expenses.

Additional Info

The options available on this tab allow you to capture other details about your vendor that will give you enhanced tracking and reporting:

- **Vendor Type** Select a vendor type or create one. The Vendor Type field is handy if you want to sort vendors by type, which makes reports more efficient. For example, you can create vendor types for inventory suppliers, tax authorities, and so on.
- **Custom Fields** You can create custom fields for vendors (see the section "Use Custom Fields in Vendor Records" later in this chapter).

Adding and Editing Multiple Vendor Records

Suppose you want to add information to many or all of your vendor records at once, or you want to find an easy way to enter new vendors in a more streamlined way. You can use the Add/Edit Multiple List Entries window to do just that.

From the Vendor Center, select New Vendor | Add Multiple Vendors. (You can also access this window by selecting Lists | Add/Edit Multiple List Entries and selecting Vendors as the list type.) The Add/Edit Multiple List Entries window opens, as shown in Figure 4-3.

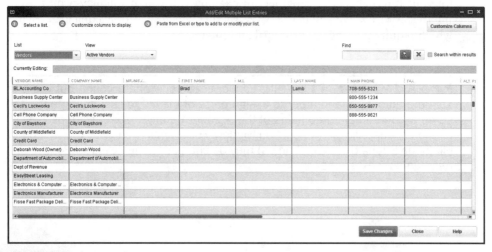

FIGURE 4-3 Add and edit multiple vendor records in the Add/Edit Multiple List Entries window.

From here, you can add new vendors, change or update key information, or fill in data you perhaps didn't have when you first created the vendor. You can even copy and paste vendor information from an Excel worksheet into the Add/Edit Multiple List Entries window to create a new vendor record quickly.

Here's a list of some of the important features and functionality that you should be familiar with to get the most benefit from using the Add/Edit Multiple List Entries window:

- **List and View filters**   Select the List or View drop-down arrow to display only those records in your list that you want to work with.
- **Customize Columns button**   Use this button to open the Customize Columns window. Here you can add the columns to the vendor record that you want to modify or add columns to match those in a spreadsheet that you want to copy and paste from into QuickBooks.
- **Copy Down**   Right-click a field in the table and select the Copy Down command to copy the contents of a selected field to all the remaining records in the list (you can't, however, use the Copy Down command with the Name field).
- **Duplicate Row**   Right-click any row in the table and choose Duplicate Row to duplicate the selected record in the row below. The new duplicate record name will start with *DUP*.

The Vendor Center

The Vendor Center is where your list of vendors is stored, along with all the information about each vendor's transactions. To open the vendor center, choose Vendors | Vendor Center from the menu bar (or click the Vendors icon on the Icon Bar). The Vendor Center displays your Vendors list, gives you quick access to key reports, and makes it easy to enter vendor transactions (see Figure 4-4).

The left pane of the Vendor Center has two tabs: Vendors (which is your Vendors list) and Transactions. A vendor is always selected in the list (by default, the first vendor in the list when you first open the Vendor Center), and the right pane of the Vendor Center displays the details that you'll want to track for the selected vendor as well as any transactions related to that vendor.

Customizing the Vendor Center

You can customize the information displayed in the Vendors list (the Vendors tab in the left pane of the window), as well as the Vendor Information pane on the right side of the window.

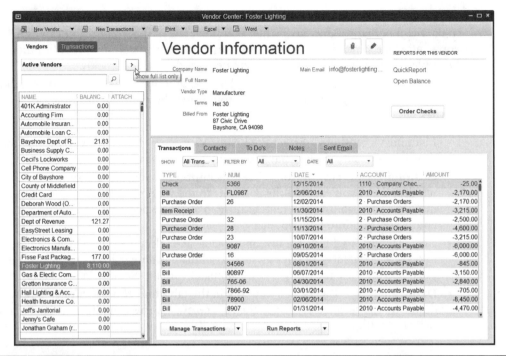

FIGURE 4-4 The Vendor Center is where the key information about your vendors lives.

Customizing the Vendors List

By default, the Vendors list has three columns: Name, Balance Total, and Attach. The Attach column displays a paper clip icon next to the vendor name if you've attached a scanned or other document to that record using the Doc Center (see Chapter 1 for more about the Doc Center). Use the scroll bar to get to the part of the list that has the vendor you want to see.

You can use the drop-down list at the top of the Vendors tab to display your vendors in any of following ways:

- All Vendors
- Active Vendors
- Vendors With Open Balances
- Custom Filter

Use the Custom Filter to display only vendors that match the criteria you set in the Custom Filter dialog. The options in the dialog are easy to understand and use.

You can add more columns to the list by right-clicking anywhere in the list and choosing Customize Columns to open the Customize Columns dialog seen in Figure 4-5.

To add a column, select its label in the left pane and click Add. The information the column describes is displayed for each vendor in the list. As long as the vendor you're interested in is displayed on the portion of the list that's visible, the information is available—you don't have to select the listing or open the record.

You can rearrange the left-to-right order of the columns by opening the Customize Columns dialog and selecting a column you want to move. Choose Move Up to move a column to the left or Move Down to move it to the right. The order of columns displayed in the Chosen Columns pane of the dialog translates as top to bottom = left to right.

If you add columns to the Vendors list, you won't be able to see all the information unless you widen the list's pane and also adjust the width of each column. To maximize this pane, click the Show Full List Only button (shown previously in Figure 4-4).

Working in the Vendor Information Pane

In the Vendor Information pane, you can view all the information you've entered for your vendors as well as each and every purchasing-related transaction (see Figure 4-6). The bottom half of the pane has five tabs that contain transaction details, contact information, To Do's, notes, and a list of e-mails sent to this vendor. Use the Manage <tab name> button at the bottom of the window to create a new entry, edit, or delete the information on any one of these tabs.

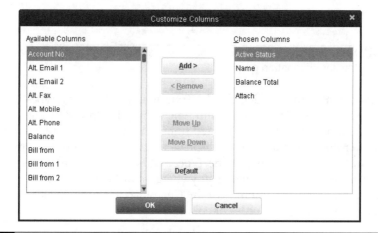

FIGURE 4-5   Customize the Vendors list to see only the information important to you.

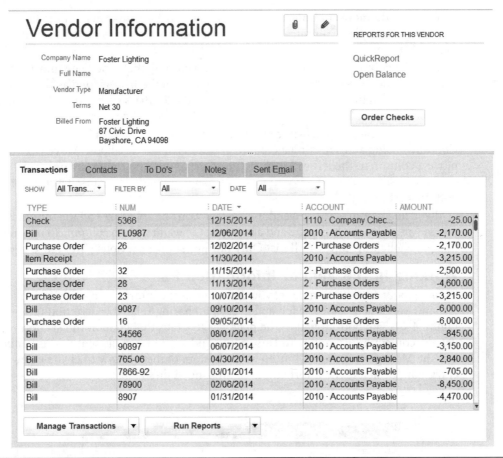

Vendor Information

REPORTS FOR THIS VENDOR

Company Name	Foster Lighting
Full Name	
Vendor Type	Manufacturer
Terms	Net 30
Billed From	Foster Lighting 87 Civic Drive Bayshore, CA 94098

QuickReport
Open Balance

Order Checks

Transactions | Contacts | To Do's | Notes | Sent Email

SHOW All Trans... ▾   FILTER BY All ▾   DATE All ▾

TYPE	NUM	DATE ▾	ACCOUNT	AMOUNT
Check	5366	12/15/2014	1110 · Company Chec...	-25.00
Bill	FL0987	12/06/2014	2010 · Accounts Payable	-2,170.00
Purchase Order	26	12/02/2014	2 · Purchase Orders	-2,170.00
Item Receipt		11/30/2014	2010 · Accounts Payable	-3,215.00
Purchase Order	32	11/15/2014	2 · Purchase Orders	-2,500.00
Purchase Order	28	11/13/2014	2 · Purchase Orders	-4,600.00
Purchase Order	23	10/07/2014	2 · Purchase Orders	-3,215.00
Bill	9087	09/10/2014	2010 · Accounts Payable	-6,000.00
Purchase Order	16	09/05/2014	2 · Purchase Orders	-6,000.00
Bill	34566	08/01/2014	2010 · Accounts Payable	-845.00
Bill	90897	06/07/2014	2010 · Accounts Payable	-3,150.00
Bill	765-06	04/30/2014	2010 · Accounts Payable	-2,840.00
Bill	7866-92	03/01/2014	2010 · Accounts Payable	-705.00
Bill	78900	02/06/2014	2010 · Accounts Payable	-8,450.00
Bill	8907	01/31/2014	2010 · Accounts Payable	-4,470.00

Manage Transactions ▾   **Run Reports** ▾

FIGURE 4-6 View, access, and update vendor information and transactions directly in the Vendor Information pane.

Transactions Tab By default, the Transactions tab lists all types of vendor transactions. Selecting a transaction type (using the drop-down arrow next to the Type field) will filter for the selected transactions for a particular vendor. You can also filter the information that's displayed on the Transactions tab by changing one or all of the three available filters: Type, Status, and Date. In addition, you can add and remove columns by clicking anywhere on or below the column headings and choosing Customize Columns. In the Customize Columns dialog, you can add, remove, and change the order of columns.

Contacts Tab You can add more detail about who to talk to if you have a question about a bill via the Contacts tab. There's even a field for a vendor's Facebook or Twitter information.

To Do's Tab From the To Do's tab, click the Manage To Do's button and select Create New to compose a reminder for a specific vendor in the Add To Do dialog, shown here:

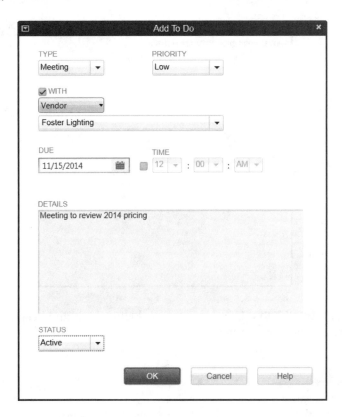

This is a very useful feature that lets you specify the date on which you want to be reminded (the Due date) and categorize your new To Do as a call or meeting, for example. You can then view your To Do note in the Calendar (discussed in Chapter 1) or directly in the Vendor Center. When the task is complete, open the reminder and change its status to Done. Use the Run Reports button to see a detailed listing of all your To Do's—including those for customers and employees as well.

ProAdvisor Tip: If you want to view a list of *all* of your QuickBooks To Do's, select To Do List from the Company menu. From this "global" list you can add, edit, or delete a To Do or even print a report that shows the details of each task.

Notes Tab From the Notes tab, click the Manage Notes button to add, edit, or delete a note in the Notepad dialog, shown next. Click the Date/Time Stamp button to insert the current date automatically when you're adding text to the notepad.

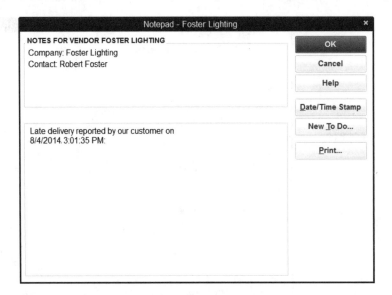

Sent Email Tab Use the Sent Email tab to view and keep track of the purchase orders that you've e-mailed a vendor:

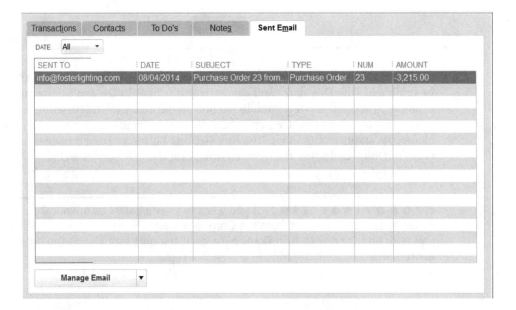

Edit Vendor Information

You can edit a vendor's information by double-clicking the vendor's listing in the Vendors list. The vendor's record opens in Edit mode. From here, you can fill in data details you didn't enter when you first created the vendor. Many QuickBooks users prefer to enter just the vendor name and company name when they set up vendors, so they can start entering historical transactions immediately. Later, when they have some time, they edit the record to fill in the missing data.

You can change any data you've previously entered, but change the data in the Vendor Name field with caution, since doing so will change the way it appears in your Vendors list and key vendor reports. Changing the Vendor Name field can also change the name associated with past transactions that you have cleared in QuickBooks. For example, if your phone company changes from AT&T to Verizon, and you change the vendor name, all past checks and bill payments written to AT&T will show as written to Verizon.

Delete a Vendor

You can remove a vendor from the list only if that vendor has never been involved in a transaction. It doesn't matter if there's no open balance, or the last transaction was a long time ago; the fact that a vendor is in your transaction history means you cannot delete the vendor.

To delete a vendor, select its listing in the Vendors tab of the Vendor Center and press CTRL-D. QuickBooks asks you to confirm the fact that you want to delete the vendor; just click OK to finish the task. If the vendor has ever been involved in a transaction, QuickBooks issues an error message saying you can't delete this vendor.

If you can't delete a vendor but you don't want this vendor used in transactions, you can hide the vendor's listing by making it inactive.

Make a Vendor Inactive

If you can't delete a vendor, but you don't want to use the vendor anymore, you can prevent users from selecting this vendor in transaction windows by making the vendor inactive (hiding the vendor name so it doesn't appear in drop-down lists).

To make a vendor inactive, right-click its listing in the Vendors list and choose Make Vendor Inactive.

If your Vendors list is configured to show Active Vendors (the default view), inactive vendors don't appear on the list. To see which vendors are inactive, click the small down arrow to the right of the View field at the top of the list and select All Vendors from the drop-down list. Inactive vendors have an "X" to the left of their listings. To make a vendor active again, select All Vendors as the view and click the "X" next to the hidden vendor or job to toggle the setting back to active. Inactive vendors are included in reports, so you can continue to get accurate reports on purchases and other vendor activity.

Merge Vendors

Sometimes you create a vendor and enter transactions for them before you realize you've created a duplicate of an existing vendor. In this case, you can merge the two vendors and move all the transaction history into one vendor record. Here are the steps:

1. Double-click the listing of the vendor you do *not* want to keep, which opens its record in Edit mode.
2. Change the data in the Vendor Name field to match exactly the name of the vendor you want to keep.
3. Click OK.
4. QuickBooks displays a message telling you that the name is in use and asks if you want to merge the names.
5. Click Yes.

Remember, the trick to merging is to start with the vendor name you *don't* want and merge into the vendor name you *do* want.

Use Custom Fields in Vendor Records

You can add your own fields to the Vendor, Customer, and Employee records. QuickBooks provides the ability to create custom fields for Names lists (and also offers custom fields for Items).

Custom fields for Names lists are added to all Names lists, but you can configure each custom field you create to limit its appearance to specific Names lists. For example, you might create a custom field that you want to use in only the Vendors list, or in both the Customers & Jobs and Vendors lists.

Custom fields are useful if there's information you want to track but QuickBooks doesn't provide a field for it. For example, if you have vendors with whom you've signed contracts, you might want to add a field that will let you track contract renewal dates.

Adding a Custom Field for Vendors

To add one or more custom fields to the vendor list, follow these steps:

1. Open the Vendor Center.
2. Select any name on the Vendors list and press CTRL-E to put the record in Edit mode.
3. Move to the Additional Info tab.
4. Click the Define Fields button to open the Set Up Custom Fields For Names dialog, where you can name the field and indicate the list(s) in which you want to use the new field (see Figure 4-7).

That's all there is to it, except you must click OK to save the information. When you do, QuickBooks flashes a message reminding you that if you customize your templates (forms for transactions, such as bills or checks), you can add these fields. The Additional Info tab for every name in the list(s) you selected now shows those fields, and you can add data to any name for which these fields have relevance.

Adding Data to Custom Fields

To add data to the custom fields for each name on the list that needs the data, select the name and press CTRL-E to put the record into Edit mode. Move to the Additional Info tab where the custom field you created appears (see Figure 4-8).

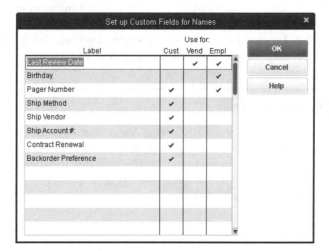

FIGURE 4-7   Design custom fields that you can use for one list or multiple lists.

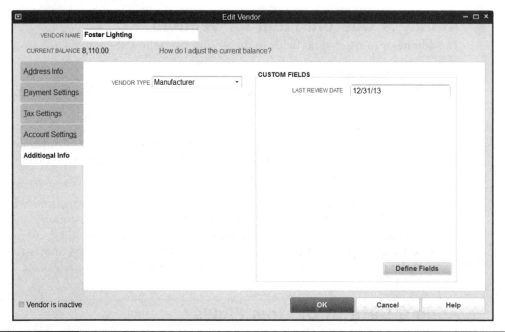

FIGURE 4-8   Add data to the custom field for each vendor to which this custom field is relevant.

Be sure that you enter data in a consistent manner for each vendor, or you won't be able to get accurate information when you customize a report to include this information. For example, consider the data entered in the custom field Last Review Date shown in Figure 4-8. If you enter **Dec 31, 2013** for some vendors and **12/31/2013** for others, and then customize a report looking for 12/31/2013, all the Dec 31, 2013 vendors will be missing from the report.

Create 1099 Vendors

QuickBooks supports only the 1099-MISC form. If any vendors are eligible for 1099 reporting, you need to enter additional information about them when setting them up. The focus of this section is on accomplishing this task before you begin making payments to a 1099 vendor. The process of verifying and filing 1099 forms in QuickBooks is covered in detail in Chapter 18.

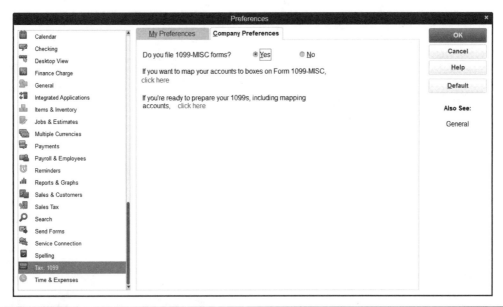

FIGURE 4-9   Be sure to turn on the 1099 tracking feature.

Configuring 1099 Options

First, make sure your file is set up to track and process 1099 forms: choose Edit | Preferences, click the Tax: 1099 icon, and move to the Company Preferences tab to see your settings (see Figure 4-9). Be sure you've clicked Yes next to the question Do You File 1099-MISC Forms?

Marking Vendors as 1099 Recipients

Generally speaking, you are required to issue Form 1099-MISC at the end of the calendar year to a vendor to whom you've paid $600 or more and who operates their business as an individual or partnership.

To issue Form 1099, you must have the vendor's federal Tax Identification Number (TIN), which can be a social security number or an employer identification number (EIN). Open each appropriate vendor listing and open the Sales Tax Settings tab. Select the option labeled Vendor Eligible For 1099, and fill in the Vendor Tax ID number as shown in Figure 4-10.

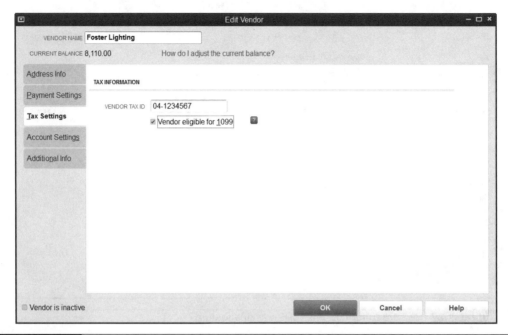

FIGURE 4-10 Mark each eligible vendor for 1099 reporting and fill in their Tax ID number.

ProAdvisor Tip: 1099 reporting rules are becoming more complex each year. It's a very good idea to check in with your accountant about the latest IRS rules regarding which vendors should receive a 1099 from you. Also be sure to ask your accountant if you should be aware of any other guidelines or rules.

Creating Items
for What You Sell

In *this chapter:*

- Understand how QuickBooks uses items

- Understand the different types of items that QuickBooks uses

- Create an item

- Set up sales tax items

In QuickBooks, you use *items* to list the things you sell on an invoice and other sales-related transactions. You can also use items on a bill to tell QuickBooks about the things you're buying from a vendor. An item can be a product (that you may or may not be tracking as inventory), a service, or another necessary entry on a sales or purchase transaction.

What other items could be used in a transaction besides products and services? Well, think about the many different elements you see on an invoice. Are you required to charge sales tax? If you do, that's an item. Do you accept prepayments or give discounts? Those are items. Do you subtotal sections of your invoices to apply discounts or taxes? That subtotal is also an item. Do you charge for shipping or restocking fees? Those are items.

In this chapter, the different types of items you can use in QuickBooks are covered in detail, with the exception of inventory items (which are covered in detail Chapter 15) and payroll items (covered in Chapter 20).

Understand How Items Are Used

Items are most often used in sales-related transactions where each line in an invoice, for example, includes an item that represents a product or service that you sell. What's more, every item you create is linked to an income account in your chart of accounts, so that when you're creating a transaction you don't have to worry about the account to which any individual line item on an invoice or sales receipt is posted—your item takes care of all that behind-the-scenes accounting for you.

Most items are linked to an income account, because most of the items that appear on a sales transaction are things you're selling to the customer. You can link all of your items to one income account in your chart of accounts (called "Income" or "Sales"), or you can track different types of items by linking them to different income accounts. For example, you might want to link all product sales to an income account named "Product Sales" and link the services you sell to an income account named "Service Sales." The advantage of linking certain types of items to certain income accounts is that when you look at a standard Profit & Loss report, you can tell at a glance what your sales totals are for each group of item types. You can also create reports on your items themselves so you can see your sales total, by item, for a particular month, for example. QuickBooks also offers several item reports that give you insight into details such as your best sellers and your most profitable and least profitable items, to name a few. You'll read more about reports in Part Six.

Some items, however, are not linked to income accounts, because they're not considered income. For example, sales tax isn't income to you, it's money you collect on behalf of your state or local government, and eventually you have to account for and turn that money over to them. Because you're holding someone else's money, sales tax items are linked to a liability account.

Discounts you give your customers are items, too, and you should link them to accounts specifically designed for that purpose. That way, you can easily see in your reports the savings and incentives that you've passed on to your customers.

As you can see, items are a bit more varied than you may have thought, but creating and configuring them is not so complicated if you follow the steps outlined in this chapter.

Understand Item Types

QuickBooks needs to categorize the items that you add to your Item List, and it does this by using *item types*. Because it sometimes may not be obvious which type you should use, the following examples are provided as a guide to help you make the right choices:

- **Service** This is a service you provide to a customer. You can create service items that are charged by the job or by the hour and are performed by an employee or an outside contractor.
- **Inventory Part** This is a product you buy for the purpose of reselling. Inventory parts are treated in a special way; you post their cost as you sell them, *not* when you write the check to purchase them. This item type isn't available if you haven't turned on the inventory tracking feature in the Items & Inventory section of the Preferences dialog. Setting up and managing inventory requires that you understand the ground rules and valuation method that QuickBooks uses. Be sure to refer to Chapter 15 if you plan on tracking inventory, as it covers this topic in great detail.
- **Non-inventory Part** This item type is a product you buy and sell but don't track as inventory, such as merchandise that is always drop shipped to a customer, as well as products you buy but don't necessarily sell, such as boxes and bubble wrap for shipping products.
- **Other Charge** You'll use this item type for things like shipping charges or other line items that don't fit into a service or product item.
- **Subtotal** This item type automatically adds up the line items that come immediately before it on a sales transaction. It provides a subtotal before you add other charges or subtract discounts.

- **Group**   This item type can be a big time saver because it's used to enter a group of individual items that you typically sell together, instead of entering each individual item on the sales transaction. For example, if you always have a shipping charge accompanying the sale of a particular item, you can create a group item that includes those two items. To create a group item, each item must first exist on its own in your Item List.
- **Discount**   When entered on a sales transaction, this item allows you to apply either a percentage or dollar discount to the item immediately above it. You may want to create more than one item that falls within this item type—for example, a discount for wholesale customers and a discount for a volume purchase. When you create a discount item, you can indicate a flat dollar value or percentage of the original price.
- **Payment**   If you receive an advance payment from a customer, for either the total of the invoice amount or a partial payment as a deposit, you indicate it as a line item on an invoice using this item type.
- **Sales Tax Item**   Create one of these item types for each sales tax authority for which you collect sales tax. This item type is available to you only if the sales tax preference is enabled. See the section "Collect Sales Tax Using Sales Tax Items" later in this chapter.
- **Sales Tax Group**   This is a way for you to apply (and track) multiple sales tax rates on a customer sales transaction.

Build Your Item List

The information that QuickBooks needs to create an item depends on the type of item you're creating. Although service items are relatively simple to create, inventory items require a bit more planning, which is why they are covered in greater detail in Chapter 15. Let's start by learning how to create a service item.

How to Create a Service Item

Regardless of the type of item you want to create, the process of building your item starts by choosing Lists | Item List from the menu bar. With the Item List open, press CTRL-N. The New Item window opens. The Type field at the top has a drop-down menu that displays a list of available item types (as described in the previous section). Select Service as the type. Figure 5-1 shows an example of the fields used to create a new Service type item called "Design Services."

The Item Name/Number field is the place to insert a unique identifying code for the item. In this case, the Item Name/Number can simply be the service that's being

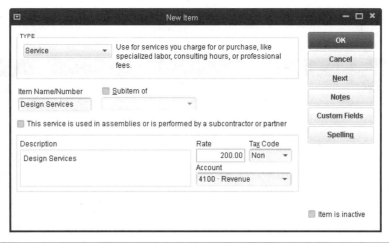

FIGURE 5-1   The fields in the New Item dialog hold the information that QuickBooks needs to take care of all the "behind the scenes" accounting for you.

offered—in our example, it's Design Services. Later, when you are filling out invoices (or other sales or purchasing related transactions), this is the identifier you see in the drop-down list.

Next you see the Subitem Of check box. If you wanted to make Design Services a subitem of another item called Architectural Services, for example, you would check this box. Why would you want to use subitems? First, it gives you the ability to track the sales and purchases of an item at either a summary or detail level. Second, it allows you to organize a complex Item List in a way that makes sense to you and others in your company.

ProAdvisor Tip: Subitems are a convenient way to list your items in your Item List in a logical order. For example, if you're a distributor of lighting fixtures, you might create a parent inventory item called Bath/Vanity fixtures and list the individual items that you sell under that category as the subitems. Creating and using subitems is covered in more detail in Chapter 15.

Next you see the option to tell QuickBooks if this service is used in assemblies (only QuickBooks Premier and Enterprise Editions offer the assembly feature) or is performed by a subcontractor or partner. When you check this box, the item record expands to include fields that allow you to link both the expense side of this item as well as the income side to different accounts in your chart of accounts, as shown next:

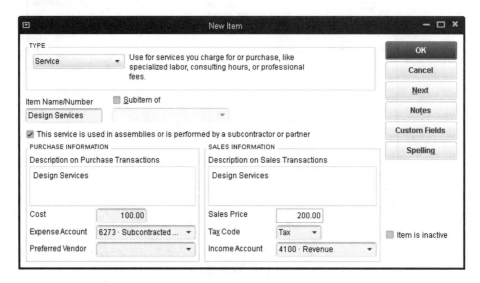

Use the drop-down arrow next to the Expense Account field to select an appropriate expense account from your chart of accounts. You can fill in the Cost field here or leave it at zero if you pay more than one rate for that service to different subcontractors. Later, when you pay the vendor you've hired as a subcontractor for this service, you'll select this item (using the Items tab on either the Write Checks or Enter Bills windows) and fill in a cost.

In the Sales Price field, enter the amount or hourly rate you charge for this service. You can leave this field at zero if your business doesn't have a standard rate for this service and it makes more sense for you to fill it in when you create an invoice or sales receipt. Next, be sure to use the Tax Code drop-down arrow to indicate whether or not this service is taxable, and then choose which income account you want QuickBooks to link this item to. Use the Notes button to open a notepad to record and store any special information that you want to keep track of about this item.

When you're done, click OK to return to the Item List or click Next to create another new item.

Create Custom Fields for Items

With custom fields, you can capture and use unique information about the products and services you sell. For example, you may want to add information about the size or color of an item that you carry in stock or identify the location in your warehouse where a particular part is stored. You can create up to five fields by following these steps:

1. Open the Item List and select an item.
2. Press CTRL-E to edit the item.
3. Click the Custom Fields button. (The first time you create a custom field, a message appears telling you that there are no custom fields yet defined; click OK.)
4. When the Custom Fields dialog appears, click Define Fields.
5. When the Set Up Custom Fields For Items dialog opens, enter a name for each field you want to add:

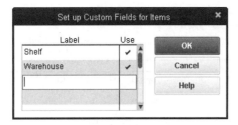

6. Place a check mark in the Use column to use the field.
7. Click OK.

As you create your fields, keep in mind that all fields are shared among all the items in your Item List (with the exception of subtotals, sale tax items, and sales tax groups), whether they're inventory, non-inventory, or service items. In addition, the maximum number of fields available to you is five. Refer to Chapter 24 to learn more about how to add these fields to your invoice and other forms (QuickBooks calls these *templates*).

Creating the Other Items in Your Item List

Although many of the fields in the New Item window are fairly similar, regardless of the type of item you're creating, some fields are particular to the type of item you're creating. The following section covers these other item types while also pointing out any unique fields you should be aware of.

Non-inventory Items

As with service items, you have the option of making a non-inventory item "two-sided," meaning when you check the This Item Is Used In Assemblies Or Is Purchased For A Specific Customer:Job box, you can designate both an income and expense account at the same time (see Figure 5-2). When you enable this function, you're making many of the standard QuickBooks item and job-related reports much more valuable.

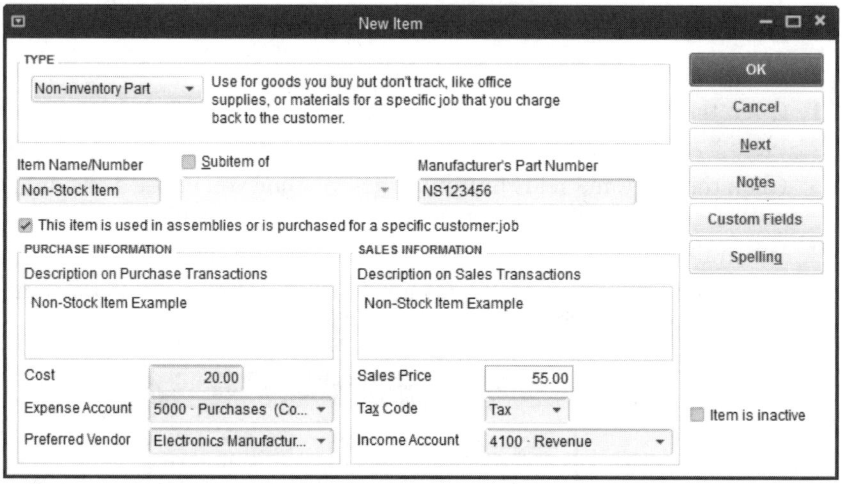

FIGURE 5-2 Create a non-inventory part when you don't need to track on-hand quantities.

If the vendor that you purchase this item from references this non-inventory part using their own unique number, you can store that number in the Manufacturer's Part Number field. This information then becomes available to you when you make purchases from that vendor.

Other Charge Items

Other charge items are generally used to list amounts for things like shipping and handling or any other miscellaneous charges that you want to appear on a sales transaction. A key feature of this item type is that it can also be set up as a percentage of another item by listing it directly below the line item that you want it to refer to.

Subtotal Items

This is a very useful item type because it allows you to add and total groups of items within the body of an invoice or sales receipt. It's very easy to use: simply list the subtotal item immediately after the list of items that you want to display a subtotal for.

Group Items

A group item is an efficient way to list items that you typically sell together on an invoice or sales receipt. For example, you may run a promotion where you bundle discounted installation services with the purchase of a high-end lighting fixture. In this case, you would create a group item that includes the fixture and the installation as a single item (see Figure 5-3).

FIGURE 5-3 When you use a group item, you can choose to show all the items on a sales transaction or show only one description line.

Before you attempt to create a group item, be sure that the individual items have already been entered into your Item List. Then follow these steps:

1. From the Item List, press CTRL-N to open the New Item window.
2. Select Group from the Type drop-down list.
3. Create a name for the new group in the Group Name/Number field.
4. Optionally, enter a description. Note that whether or not you select the Print Items In Group option (which ensures that individual items in the group will appear in the transaction), your entry in the Description field is what will appear on the printed sales transaction—unless you decide to change it.
5. Select each item that is to be part of this group and enter the quantity (if applicable) for each item.
6. Click OK.

Discount Items

A discount item works by affecting the line item immediately preceding it. When you create an item, you can indicate either a flat rate or a percentage discount.

Payment Items

Payment items are used to record the receipt of a partial payment on a sale. When listed on an invoice, a payment item reduces the balance due.

➡ **ProAdvisor Recommends**

The Importance of Items for Job Costing

Because items are most often associated with sales transactions, many QuickBooks users who are service-based are not accustomed to using them in purchase transactions (bills and checks). Make sure that when you're entering a bill (covered in Chapter 11) or check that relates to a purchase you've made for a specific customer job, you click the Items tab (instead of the Expenses tab) and select the service or non-inventory part item that you used on the sales transaction for that customer job (see the example shown here).

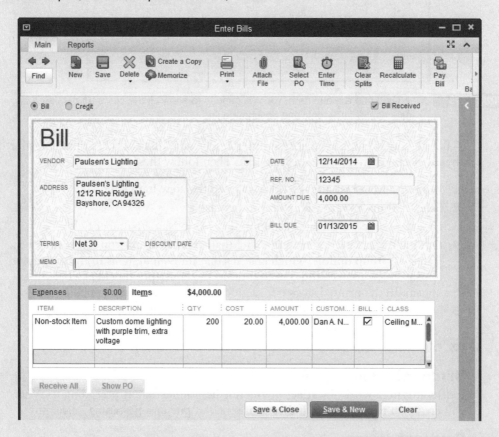

In addition, be sure that this item is "two-sided" (see the "Non-inventory Items" section earlier in this chapter). Following this logic gives you the ability to take full advantage of the many job-related reports that come with QuickBooks Pro. For example, from the Reports menu, select Jobs, Time & Mileage. You'll see several reports designed to give you insight into precisely where you're making (or losing) money on a job and how your original estimate for a job compares to your actual costs and revenues for that job as of a particular date.

Changing Item Prices

If you want to implement a price increase (or decrease) for one or more of the services or products you sell, use the Change Item Prices window.

1. From the Customers menu, select Change Item Prices.
2. In the Change Item Prices window, use the Item Type filter to list only those items of a particular type (Service, Inventory Part, Inventory Assembly, Non-inventory Part, or Other Charge).

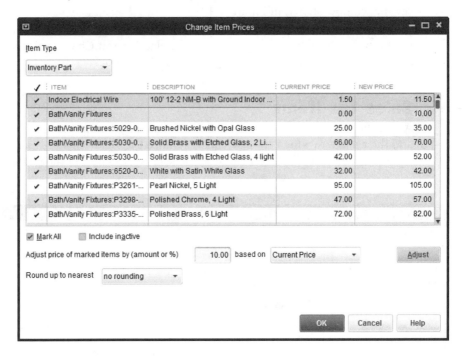

3. Place a check mark next to the items subject to a price change and tell QuickBooks if the price change should be calculated as an amount or as a percentage of the item's cost or its current price.
4. If you'd like QuickBooks to round up the adjustment, use the Round Up To Nearest drop-down menu to choose a rounding option. Otherwise, you can leave this option at its default of No Rounding.
5. Click the Adjust button to effect the change, and then click OK.

Collect Sales Tax Using Sales Tax Items

If you collect and remit sales tax, you need to configure your Sales Tax Preferences and set up tax codes to link to your customers so you know whether a customer is liable for sales tax. You also need to set up tax items so you can set a percentage rate for the sales tax to be collected and link the item to the taxing authority to which you'll be remitting the collected sales tax.

Start your sales tax setup by choosing Edit | Preferences from the menu bar. Click the Sales Tax icon in the left pane and select the Company Preferences tab to see the window shown in Figure 5-4.

If you used Advanced Setup and you didn't enable the sales tax feature, you can do it now by selecting Yes for the option labeled Do You Charge Sales Tax? The following sections cover the other options in this dialog.

Sales Tax Items

A sales tax item is really just a collection of data about a sales tax, including the rate and the agency to which the sales tax is remitted. QuickBooks uses sales tax items to calculate the Tax field at the bottom of sales forms and to prepare reports for you

FIGURE 5-4 Set up your most common sales tax using the Sales Tax Preferences.

so that you can send the correct amounts due each period to your local taxing authority. You can create your first sales tax item here in the Sales Tax Preferences or directly in your Item List (see the section "Creating Sales Tax Items in the Item List" a bit later).

Most Common Sales Tax

The Sales Tax Company Preferences dialog (as shown in Figure 5-4) includes a field named Your Most Common Sales Tax Item, and you must enter a sales tax item in that field. Of course, to do that, you must first create at least one sales tax item. This item becomes the default sales tax item for any customers you create hereafter, but you can change any customer's default sales tax item any time.

Creating Sales Tax Items in the Item List

Once the Sales Tax Preference has been set, you can create a sales tax item directly in your Item List by following these steps:

1. Select Lists | Item List from the main menu to open the Item List.
2. Press CTRL-N to open the New Item dialog.
3. Select Sales Tax Item as the item type.
4. Enter a name for the item. You can use the state's code for the specific sales tax rate and taxing authority. You can also enter a description, although that's optional.
5. Enter the tax rate.
6. Select the tax agency (a vendor) to which you pay the tax from the drop-down list, or add a new vendor by choosing <Add New>.
7. Click OK.

Sales Tax Codes

Sales tax codes are used by QuickBooks to designate an item as taxable or nontaxable when that item is listed on a sales transaction. However, it's not difficult to create codes to track sales tax status in a manner more detailed than taxable and nontaxable: you just add new sales tax codes to fit your needs.

Follow these steps to add a new sales tax code:

1. Select Lists | Sales Tax Code List.
2. Press CTRL-N to open the New Sales Tax Code window.
3. Enter the name of the new code (up to three characters in length).
4. Enter a description.
5. Select Taxable if you're entering a code to track taxable sales.
6. Select Non-taxable if you're entering a code to track nontaxable sales.
7. Click Next to set up another tax code.
8. Click OK when you've finished adding tax codes.

Although you can always use the default nontaxable code that QuickBooks provides, called "Non," you may be required (depending on your state sales tax agency) to provide further definition of your nontaxable sales to identify nonprofit organizations, government agencies, sales to resellers, or out-of-state customers, for example. The same logic may apply to taxable customers as well; some state agencies will require that you provide a breakdown of your company's taxable sales.

C a u t i o n : It's always a good idea to check in with your local taxing authority prior to setting up your sales tax codes and items. This will help ensure that you're capturing the correct sales tax amounts and that the sales tax reports you run in QuickBooks (which are very dependent on how you set up sales tax items and groups) will be accurate.

Sales Tax Payment Basis

There are two ways to remit sales tax to the taxing authorities, and they're listed in the When Do You Owe Sales Tax section of the Sales Tax Preferences dialog:

- As Of Invoice Date, which is accrual-based tax reporting
- Upon Receipt Of Payment, which is cash-based tax reporting

Check with your accountant (and the local taxing authority) to determine the method you need to select. Each state has its own reporting rules.

Sales Tax Payment Dates

You must indicate the frequency of your remittance to the taxing authority in the When Do You Pay Sales Tax section of the Preferences dialog. Your sales tax licensing agency dictates the schedule you must use.

Create and Use Tax Groups

A tax group is a collection of two or more individual tax items that are displayed as one tax to a customer on a sales transaction. For example, you might be required to collect 6.25 percent state sales tax in addition to 5 percent county sales tax because of the county your business operates from. This is especially important in some states where city, county/parish, and state portions are paid to different tax entities.

When you use a sales tax group, QuickBooks keeps track, behind the scenes, of which taxing authority the tax collected is due to, but the customer sees only a 11.25 percent sales tax rate (see Figure 5-5).

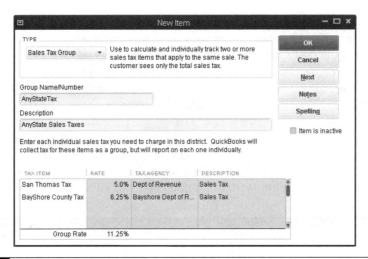

FIGURE 5-5   A sales tax group is made up of sales tax items.

To create a tax group, you must first create the individual tax items and then add those items to the group item. Follow these steps to create a tax group:

1. Open the Item List by choosing Lists | Item List.
2. Press CTRL-N to open the New Item dialog.
3. Select Sales Tax Group as the Type.
4. Enter a name for the group.
5. Enter a description (which appears on your sales forms).
6. In the Tax Item column, choose the individual tax code items you need to create this group. (QuickBooks fills in the rate, tax agency, and description of each tax you already selected.) Notice that the calculated total (the group rate) appears at the bottom of the dialog.
7. When all the required tax code items have been added, click OK.

Assigning Sales Tax Codes and Items to Customers

When you turn on the Sales Tax preference and create your first sales tax item, QuickBooks asks if you want to make all of your customers as well as your inventory and non-inventory parts taxable, as shown next:

If you do not deselect either of these options, QuickBooks will apply the "taxable" tax code to all customers and to your inventory parts as well. You can modify this setting at the customer level in the Sales Tax Settings tab of a customer's record.

If your Customers list is large, opening each record to make this change to several records can be quite tedious and time consuming. Instead, you can use the Add/Edit Multiple List Entries window to assign or change the tax items or codes for multiple customers in a single view.

To utilize this feature, from within the Customer Center, point your mouse anywhere on the Customer:Job list and right-click. Select Add/Edit Multiple Customers:Jobs to open the Add/Edit Multiple List Entries window. You may have to customize the columns in this window to bring these fields into view.

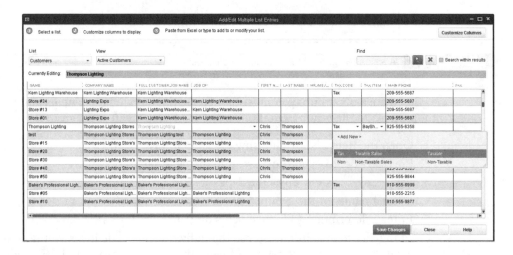

ProAdvisor Tip: You can use the Add/Edit Multiple List Entries window to modify the tax code setting for your items as well. With your Item List open, right-click anywhere in the list and select Add/Edit Multiple Items to open the Add/Edit Multiple List Entries window.

Creating Other Lists You May Need

In this chapter:

- Fixed Asset Item list

- Price Level list

- Currency List

- Class List

- Other Names list

- Customer & Vendor Profile Lists

- Memorized Transaction List

In Chapters 2 through 5, you learned how to set up the key lists that QuickBooks uses in nearly every transaction you enter and how important these lists are. This chapter is about the other lists that you'll find in the Lists menu.

Generally, these lists don't require extensive amounts of data or time to set up, and you may not even use all of them. But those that you do use will not only help make your work in QuickBooks more efficient, but will make it easier to generate more meaningful reports.

Fixed Asset Item List

Use the Fixed Asset Item list to store information about the fixed assets your business owns. Choose Lists | Fixed Asset Item List to open the list that provides a way to track data about the assets you purchase and depreciate. As you can see in Figure 6-1, you can record many details about each asset.

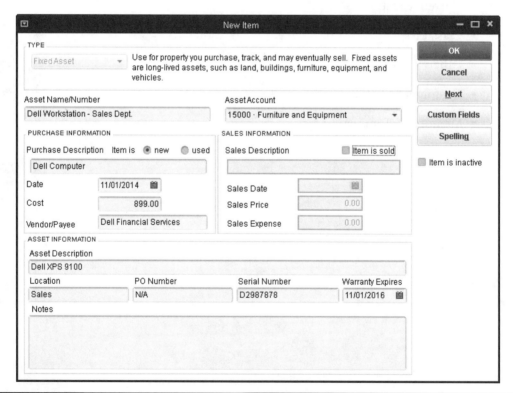

FIGURE 6-1 Store information about your business's assets in the Fixed Asset Item list.

Keep in mind that this is not like your Item List in that it *doesn't* provide links to any financial data in your QuickBooks company file. It does not interact with the chart of accounts, so any values you enter in this list have to be entered in your Fixed Asset accounts separately.

This list does not add any financial information to your company file, nor does it perform any calculations. It's merely a way to use QuickBooks to catalog your fixed assets instead of whatever list you're keeping in Microsoft Word, Microsoft Excel, a legal pad, or a shoebox full of index cards.

C a u t i o n : Be aware that items added to the Fixed Asset Item list will be visible in the drop-down list you see when you create a transaction that involves your regular items (the "regular" items you create to transact business, which are discussed in Chapters 5 and 11), such as an invoice, a cash sale, or a purchase order. If you accidentally select a fixed asset item while creating a sales transaction, for example, your financial records can become confusing. If you use the Fixed Asset Item list, consider making all the items in the list inactive to suppress their display in drop-down lists. To make an item inactive, highlight it while in list view, and then right-click and select Make Item Inactive.

P r o A d v i s o r   T i p : Using the Fixed Asset Item list to track your businesses assets can assist your accountant in the year-end tax-related chores they perform for you. If your accountant is using the Premier Accountant Edition version of QuickBooks, they can open your company file and read from your Fixed Asset Item list using a program call the Fixed Asset Manager (FAM). FAM works by pulling the information it needs from your QuickBooks company file to calculate the depreciation for a given period and then posting a journal entry back to your company file.

Price Level List

The Price Level list is an easy way to apply special pricing to customers and jobs. This list is available only if price levels are enabled in the Sales & Customers section of your Preferences. To turn on this feature, use the following steps:

1. Choose Edit | Preferences and select the Sales & Customers category in the left pane.
2. Move to the Company Preferences tab.
3. Select the option labeled Enable Price Levels.
4. Click OK.

Creating a Price Level

To create a price level, open the Price Level list from the Lists menu and press CTRL-N to open the New Price Level dialog, shown next. Each price level has two components: a name and a formula. The name can be anything you wish, and the formula is a percentage of the price you entered for the items in your Item List (the formula increases or reduces the price by the percentage you specify).

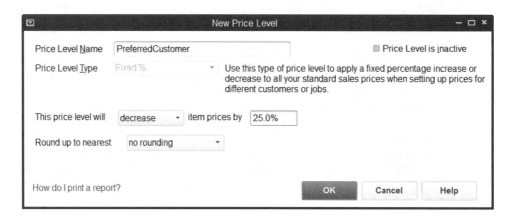

For example, you may want to give your favorite customers a deep discount. Name the price level something like "PreferredCustomer." Then enter a healthy percentage by which to reduce the price of items purchased by this customer. Or you may want to create a discount price level for customers that are nonprofit organizations.

On the other hand, you may want to keep your regular prices steady and increase them for certain customers (perhaps customers who don't pay in a timely manner). You can use price levels to set a price above the standard price, too.

Assigning Price Levels to Customers

After you create price levels, you can apply a price level to customers. Open the Customers & Jobs List in the Customer Center and double-click the customer's listing. Select or create a new price level from the Price Level drop-down list on the Payment Settings tab (see Figure 6-2).

Once a price level is linked to a customer, sales transactions for that customer reflect the price level automatically. See Chapter 9, "Invoicing Your Customers," to learn how to create sales transactions with price levels.

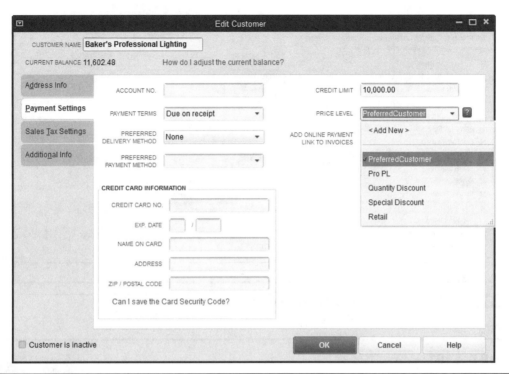

FIGURE 6-2 Assign a price level to a customer.

Currency List

Available only if you've enabled the QuickBooks multiple currencies feature, the Currency List specifies the currencies you want to work with (see Figure 6-3). Multiple currencies can be turned on in the Company Preferences area. From the Edit menu, select Preferences | Multiple Currencies. By default, the majority of currencies are marked Inactive; open this list to activate the currencies you need so they appear in drop-down lists. Refer to Appendix B for more information on how to set up and use the QuickBooks multiple currencies feature.

C a u t i o n : Be sure to make a backup copy of your company file before turning on the multiple currencies feature in your company file. Once it is enabled, it cannot be turned off.

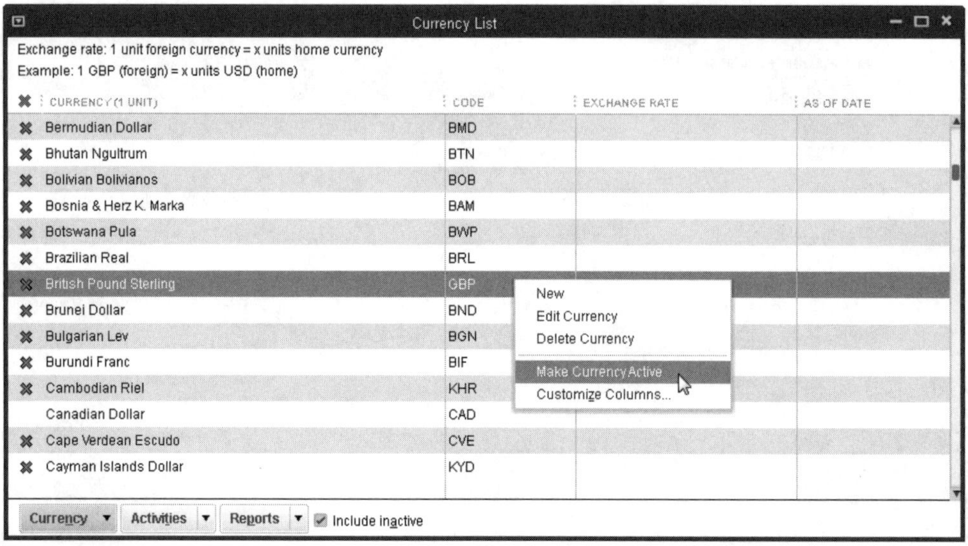

FIGURE 6-3 Activate the currency you need for your customers and vendors.

Class List

Classes provide a method of organizing your company's income and expense transactions by division or department, allowing you to filter many of the standard QuickBooks reports by class. Some of the common reasons to use classes include these:

- Tracking expenses and profitability by location if you have more than one office
- The need for financial reporting by business type—perhaps you manage both a retail and wholesale division

The Class list appears in the Lists menu only if you've enabled the Use Class Tracking feature. From the Edit menu, select Preferences | Accounting | Company Preferences | Use Class Tracking For Transactions.

You should use classes for a single purpose; otherwise, the feature won't work properly. For example, you can use classes to separate your business into locations or by type of business, but don't try to do both. If you need to further define a class or narrow its definition, you can use subclasses.

When you enable classes, QuickBooks adds a Class field to transaction forms so that you can associate a class with a particular transaction (you can assign a class only to a specific transaction and not a customer or vendor). Optionally, you can require that QuickBooks prompt you to assign a class when you enter transactions. For each transaction or each line of any transaction, you can assign one of the classes you created.

P r o A d v i s o r   T i p : When you use class tracking in the Pro version of QuickBooks, you're report choices by class are limited to income and expense accounts. If you find that you need to run a balance sheet report by class, for example, or other reports that show totals by class for an asset or liability account (such as a bank or loan account), consider upgrading to the Premier or Enterprise version of QuickBooks.

Create a Class

To create a class, choose Lists | Class List from the QuickBooks menu bar to display the Class List window. Press CTRL-N to open the New Class dialog, shown next:

Fill in the name of the class, and then click Next to add another class, or click OK if you are finished.

P r o A d v i s o r   T i p : If you decide to use classes, it's a good idea to create a class for general overhead expenses. You can then allocate the amounts accumulated in this overhead class to other classes with a journal entry at a later time if you wish. Using journal entries in QuickBooks is covered in Chapter 17.

Creating a Subclass

Subclasses let you post transactions to specific subcategories of classes, and they work similarly to subaccounts in your chart of accounts. If you set up a subclass, you must post transactions only to the subclass, never to the parent class. However, unlike the chart of accounts, classes have no option to force the display of only the subclass when you're working in a transaction window. As a result, if you're using subclasses you should keep the name of the parent class short, to lessen the need to scroll through the field to see the entire class name.

You create a subclass using the same steps required to create a class. After you enter a name for the subclass in the Class Name field, click the check box next to the option Subclass Of to insert a check mark. Then select the appropriate parent class from the drop-down list.

Other Names List

QuickBooks provides a list called Other Names, which is the list of people whose names are used when you write checks, but who don't fit the definition of vendor because you don't need to track payables and transactions the way you do for a vendor.

The names in the Other Names list appear in the drop-down list when you write checks but are unavailable when you're entering vendor bills, vendor credits, bill payments, purchase orders, or sales transactions.

One of the most common reasons to add a name to the Other Names list is to write checks to owners and partners. Strictly speaking, these people aren't vendors of your company, and they aren't employees. You can also use the Other Names list for cash and use that name when you write checks for cash to fill your petty cash box (covered in Chapter 12).

ProAdvisor Tip: If you reimburse employees for expenses they incur, and you don't want to manage the reimbursement through their paychecks, create Other Name listings for those employees and use those names for reimbursements. QuickBooks does not allow duplicate names, so you'll have to change the name you use in the Employee list slightly to create the Other Name listing (for instance, add an "RE" for "reimbursable expenses" to the end of their names).

To open the Other Names list, choose Lists | Other Names List. To create a new name for the list, press CTRL-N to open a New Name window, as shown next:

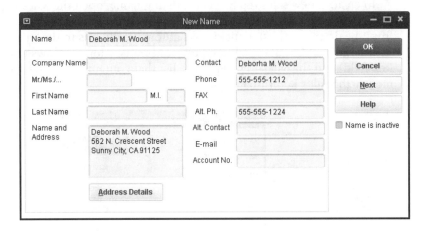

The New Name window provides fields for the address (handy for printing checks you're going to place into window envelopes), telephone numbers, and other contact information.

C a u t i o n : Use the Other Names list only for check payees you don't have to track as vendors. Otherwise, you could end up having to move these names to the Vendors list if you find you need to track their activities as a vendor or issue them a Form 1099.

Customer & Vendor Profile Lists

The Profile lists are those lists that appear in the submenu you see when you choose Customer & Vendor Profile Lists. Most of the lists in the submenu are designed to help you categorize and refine the information you keep about your customers and vendors. Other lists can contain data that is available when you create transactions.

Sales Rep List

By definition, a *sales rep* is a sales person who is connected to a customer, usually because he or she receives a commission on sales to that customer. However, it's quite common to track sales reps who are not necessarily paid commissions as a way to determine who is the primary contact for a customer (some people call this a *service rep*).

To create a sales rep, the rep's name has to exist in your QuickBooks system as a vendor, employee, or a member of the Other Names list.

To create a new sales rep from an existing name, open the Sales Rep list and press CTRL-N to open a New Sales Rep dialog, shown next. Select the person's name from the drop-down list. QuickBooks automatically fills in the Sales Rep Initials field (which is the data used in reports and transaction windows that have a Sales Rep field) and the Sales Rep Type (the list that contains this sales rep). You can modify the Sales Rep Initials field if you wish.

Customer Type List

When you create your Customers list, you may decide to use the Customer Type field as a way to categorize your customers. This gives you the opportunity to sort and select customers in reports, so you can view the total income from specific types of customers.

For example, you may want to use the Customer Type List to track the source of new customer referrals or to separate sales reporting by wholesale and retail customers.

Vendor Type List

When you create your Vendors list, you may decide to use the Vendor Type field as a way to categorize your vendors and suppliers. This will allow you to sort and select vendors in reports so you can then view the total expenses by a category. Examples of useful Vendor Types are reimbursable employee expenses, training and development expenditures, as well as entertainment expenses.

Job Type List

Use the Job Type list to set up categories for jobs. For example, if you're a plumber, you may want to separate new construction from repair work.

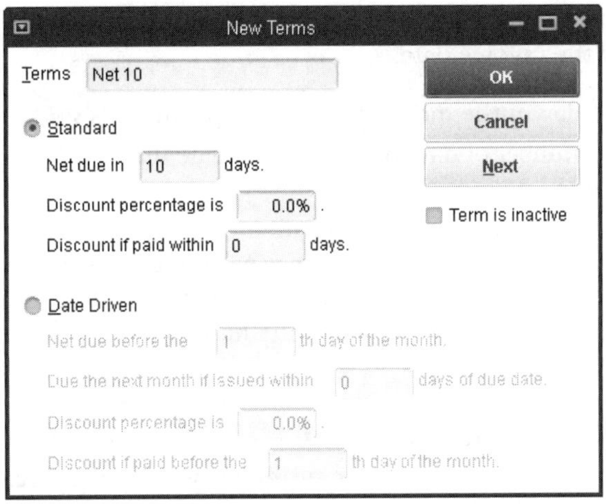

FIGURE 6-4 Set up the terms you need for both customers and vendors.

Terms List

QuickBooks keeps both customer and vendor payment terms in one list, so the terms you need are all available whether you're creating an invoice, entering a vendor bill, or creating a purchase order. To create a terms listing, open the Terms List window and press CTRL-N to open the New Terms window seen in Figure 6-4.

Use the Standard section to create terms that are due at some elapsed time after the invoice date:

- Net Due In is the number of days allowed for payment after the invoice date.
- To create a discount for early payment, enter the discount percentage and the number of days after the invoice date that the discount is in effect. For example, if 30 days are allowed for payment, enter a discount percentage that is in effect for 10 days after the invoice date (such terms are usually referred to as "X percent 10, net 30," substituting the amount of the discount for X).

ProAdvisor Tip: Discounts for early payment are commonly found only in the manufacturing and wholesale distribution industries and are applied to product sales. It would be unusual to receive (or give) such discounts for ordinary business expenses, such as utilities, rent, services rendered, and so on.

Use the Date Driven section to describe terms that are due on a particular date, regardless of the invoice date:

- Enter the day of the month the invoice payment is due.
- Enter the number of days before the due date that invoices are considered payable on the following month.
- To create a discount for early payment, enter the discount percentage and the day of the month at which the discount period ends. For example, if the standard due date is the 15th of the month, you may want to extend a discount to any customer who pays by the 8th of the month.

Customer Message List

If you like to write messages to your customers when you're creating a sales transaction (an invoice or a cash sales receipt), you can enter a bunch of appropriate messages ahead of time and then just select the one you want to use. For example, you may want to insert the message "Thanks for doing business with us" or "Happy Holidays!"

Press CTRL-N to enter a new message to add to the list. You just have to type out the text (which can't be longer than 101 characters, counting spaces)—this is one of the easier lists to create. Keep in mind, however, that once a message is used in a transaction, you can't delete it. However, if it becomes obsolete, you can make it inactive to remove it from your message choices.

Payment Method List

You can accept and track payments from customers in multiple ways. QuickBooks prepopulates the Payment Method list with the most common payment types (such as credit card, check, and cash). If you have a payment method that isn't listed, you can add that method to the list. To do so, select Lists | Customer & Vendor Profile Lists | Payment Method List, and then press CTRL-N to open the New Payment Method window. Name the payment method and select the appropriate payment type.

Maintaining this list not only provides some detail about the payments you receive (in case you're having a conversation with a customer about invoices and payments), but also allows you to print reports on payments that are subtotaled by the method of payment, such as credit card, check, cash, and so on. In addition, your bank may use the same subtotaling method on your monthly statement, which makes it easier to reconcile the bank account.

Ship Via List

Use the Ship Via list to add a description of your shipping method to your invoices (in the field named Via), which many customers appreciate. QuickBooks prepopulates the list with a variety of shipment methods, but you may need to add a shipping method.

To do so, select Lists | Customer & Vendor Profile Lists | Ship Via List, and then press CTRL-N to add a new Shipping Method entry to the list. All you need to do is enter the name—for example, Our Truck or Sam's Delivery Service.

If you use one shipping method more than any other, you can select a default Ship Via entry, which appears automatically on your invoices (you can change it on any invoice if the shipping method is different). The default entry is in the Sales & Customers category of the Preferences dialog, where you can select the Usual Shipping Method entry you want to appear by default on your sales transactions. You can also enter the FOB site you want to appear on invoices, if you want to display this information.

FOB (Free or Freight On Board) is the site from which an order is shipped and is also the point at which transportation and other costs are the buyer's responsibility.

Vehicle List

The Vehicle list lets you create vehicle records in which you track mileage for vehicles used in your business. You can use the mileage information for tax deductions for your vehicles and to bill customers for mileage expenses. However, even if you don't bill customers for mileage or your accountant uses a formula for tax deductions, the Vehicle list is a handy way to track information about the vehicles you use for business purposes. (You can learn how to track mileage and bill customers for mileage in Chapter 19.)

To add a vehicle to the list, select Lists | Customer & Vendor Profile Lists | Vehicle List, and then press CTRL-N to open a New Vehicle dialog. The record has two fields:

- Vehicle, in which you enter a name or code for a specific vehicle. For example, you could enter BlueTruck, 2012 Toyota, Ford Mustang Convertible, or any other recognizable name.
- Description, in which you enter descriptive information about the vehicle. While the Description field is handy for standard description terms (such as black or blue/white truck), take advantage of the field by entering information you really need. For example, the VIN, the license plate number, the expiration date for the plate, the insurance policy number, or other "official" pieces of information are good candidates for inclusion. You can enter up to 256 characters in the Description field.

Templates List

This is a list where QuickBooks stores the many forms (QuickBooks calls them templates) you'll use when creating transactions. More about this list and how to customize templates can be found in Chapter 24.

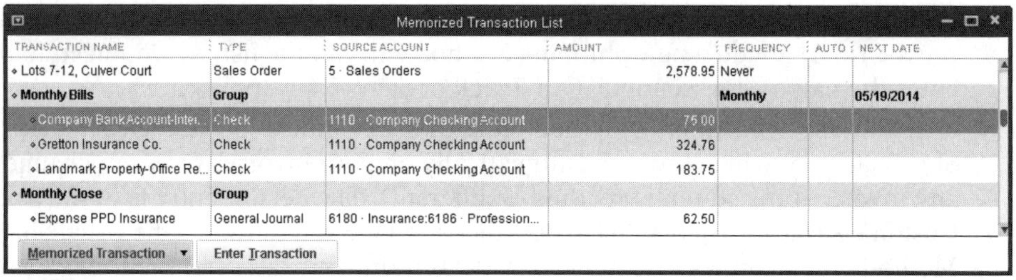

TRANSACTION NAME	TYPE	SOURCE ACCOUNT	AMOUNT	FREQUENCY	AUTO	NEXT DATE
◆ Lots 7-12, Culver Court	Sales Order	5 · Sales Orders	2,578.95	Never		
◆ **Monthly Bills**	**Group**			**Monthly**		**05/19/2014**
◆ Company Bank Account-Inter...	Check	1110 · Company Checking Account	75.00			
◆ Gretton Insurance Co.	Check	1110 · Company Checking Account	324.76			
◆ Landmark Property-Office Re...	Check	1110 · Company Checking Account	183.75			
◆ **Monthly Close**	**Group**					
◆ Expense PPD Insurance	General Journal	6180 · Insurance:6186 · Profession...	62.50			

Memorized Transaction ▼   Enter Transaction

FIGURE 6-5   Use the Memorized Transaction List to edit or post a memorized transaction.

Memorized Transaction List

The Memorize Transaction feature in QuickBooks saves you from having to enter the same transaction multiple times. With few exceptions, the transactions that you enter in QuickBooks can be memorized and set to post automatically on the day and with the frequency you need. "Memorizing" your monthly rent check, for example, can help ensure that this important obligation gets posted and sent out in a timely manner each month. And because the memorized transaction already includes the name of your landlord, the rent amount, and the rent expense account assignment, you have to enter this information only once for it to appear on each monthly check.

The transactions that you memorize (such as invoices, checks, bills, general journal entries, and so on) are all stored in the Memorized Transaction List (see Figure 6-5).

To view or edit a memorized transaction, choose Lists | Memorized Transaction List to open the list. Highlight a transaction name, click the Memorized Transaction button at the bottom of the window, and then choose Edit Memorized Transaction.

Chapter 9 provides a step-by-step example of how to memorize an invoice; follow these same steps to memorize all other transactions.

Entering Your Beginning Balances

In *this chapter:*

- What is an opening trial balance?

- Ten steps to creating an accurate opening trial balance

If you've created your company file, created your lists, and completed all the other setup-related activities covered in the first seven chapters of this book, then you've built about 80 percent of your new QuickBooks file. If these key tasks have not yet been completed, you should return to this chapter when they are.

The last 20 percent of the setup process involves entering your beginning balances and the historical transactions (if any) needed to ensure that your data file accurately reflects your business's financial position on the day you start using your QuickBooks software. Entering accurate beginning balances and the detail behind these balances is perhaps the most important part of the setup process. Why? Because if you start with inaccurate or incomplete starting balances, you'll compromise your ability to rely on the key reports that QuickBooks offers to manage your business. In addition, you'll likely spend more time and money (mostly payable to your accountant) fixing these balances at year end. So it's definitely worth your time and effort to get the numbers right from the start.

What Is an Opening Trial Balance?

Your opening trial balance is simply a detailed listing of the value of your company's assets, liabilities, and equity. If your QuickBooks start date is the beginning of the year (which is the most common start date), your opening trial balance for the first day of the year has no income or expenses to report. It will, however, contain the balances that have accumulated in your Asset, Liability, and Equity accounts since you've been in business. With the help of your accountant, you should prepare what I call a pre-QuickBooks opening trial balance. Your accountant knows that much of the information needed for the pre-QuickBooks trial balance will come directly from the balance sheet he or she prepared for you the previous year end. The pre-QuickBooks opening trial balance doesn't have to be fancy—it can be created in Excel or on a piece of paper—but, of course, it must be accurate. A typical pre-QuickBooks opening trial balance for a business with a QuickBooks start date of January 1, 2014, might look something like Table 7-1.

Your mission is to get these beginning balances into your QuickBooks file. You might want to bookmark this page, as I'll be referring to the numbers in the preceding table throughout the rest of the chapter.

Account Type	Account	Debit	Credit
Assets	Bank	$25,000	
Asset	Accounts Receivable	$15,000	
Asset	Inventory	$30,000	
	Fixed Assets	$15,000	
	Accumulated Depreciation		$2,500
Liabilities	Loan from Bank		$20,000
Liabilities	Accounts Payable		$7,500
Equity	Equity (Capital, Prior Retained Earnings, and so on)		$55,000

TABLE 7-1 Your "Pre-QuickBooks" Balances as of December 31, 2013

Ten Steps to Creating an Accurate Opening Trial Balance

Although there's certainly more than one way to get your beginning balances into your new QuickBooks data file, I have found that the majority of my clients (and their accountants) have had the most success—and the least stress—when they follow the ten simple steps outlined here.

1. Gather All the Information You Need

In Chapter 1, a detailed list of the information that you should have at your fingertips prior to entering your beginning balances was provided. If you haven't already organized these essential records and numbers, or if you don't remember exactly what you need to compile, return to Chapter 1 to refresh your memory.

2. Enter Beginning Balances for Simple Balance Sheet Accounts

For this second step, you'll use a journal entry to enter the beginning balances for accounts *except* bank accounts, accounts receivable, accounts payable, inventory, and sales tax payable. Those balances will be created later when you enter outstanding individual transactions and other adjustments. So what accounts are left to enter? Your fixed assets (including any accumulated depreciation) such as vehicles, furniture, and equipment, as well as any loans payable. You'll want to check in with your accountant for other balances that should also be entered as part of this first step, such as prepaid expenses, unpaid payroll taxes, or employee advances. Your journal entry should be dated as of the closing date of the prior fiscal year. In this example, the fiscal and calendar year are the same.

From the Company menu, select Make General Journal Entries to open the Make General Journal Entries window. Using the trial balance figures in the table shown earlier in this chapter, your journal entry should look like the one shown in Figure 7-1.

You'll see that after the balances for Fixed Assets (in this case Furniture and Fixtures), Accumulated Depreciation, and the Bank Loan have been entered, there's a debit balance of $7,500.00 that needs to be assigned to an account in order for the entry to be in balance. QuickBooks has a special account that's reserved just for that purpose called Opening Balance Equity. Using this account to balance the entry will require that you (or your accountant) zero-out this balance (and any other balances posted to this account during the setup) to a retained earnings account in order to complete the setup. That adds another, often overlooked, journal entry requirement in the setup process. Alternatively, you can post this offsetting balance directly to a retained earnings or owner's equity account (as shown in Figure 7-1). Check with your accountant on the method that works best in your situation.

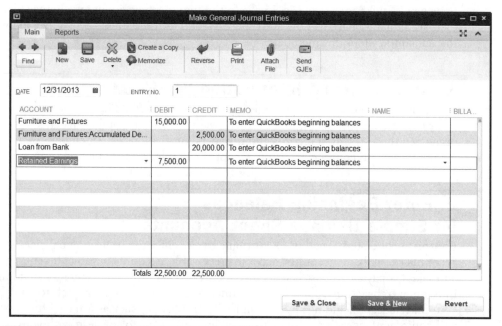

FIGURE 7-1   Use a journal entry to establish some of your beginning balances.

If you choose this alternative method, QuickBooks warns you that you're posting to an account that's intended to track profits from earlier periods. Clicking OK allows you to continue with the posting. Then click Save & Close to save this entry.

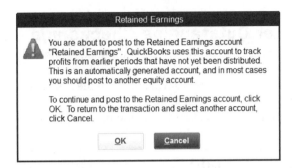

3. Enter Bank Account Balances

The next step is to establish the bank balance. Use the bank register to do this. Select Banking | Use Register to open the register for your bank account. Enter the ending balance as it appears on the bank statement from the last month of the previous year in the Deposit side of the register. Be sure to put a note in the memo field (as shown in Figure 7-2) that will help remind you what this entry was for

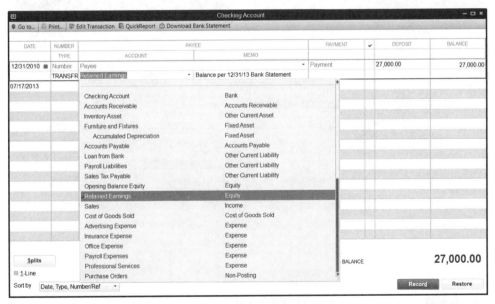

FIGURE 7-2   Post the offsetting balance to the Opening Balance Equity Account or a retained earnings account.

later on. Again, you can choose to post the offsetting balance to the Opening Balance Equity Account or directly to a retained earnings account (see Figure 7-2). Click the Record button to save your entry.

4. Enter Outstanding Checks and Deposits

With your register still open, enter all outstanding transactions—checks and deposits—that occurred prior to the QuickBooks start date (see Figure 7-3). This step ensures that these items will appear in the first bank reconciliation you perform in QuickBooks. In the example, there are two checks outstanding from November 2013. Be sure to use the *original* transaction date to post these outstanding transactions.

5. Enter Unpaid Accounts Receivable and Accounts Payable Transactions

To establish your accounts receivable balance, create an invoice for each customer invoice that was still open as of the end of the previous fiscal year using the original transaction date and all other invoice details (customer name, item(s) purchased, terms, and so on). Don't forget to enter any unused customer credits as well. In our example, the total Accounts Receivable balance (refer to Table 7-1) is actually made

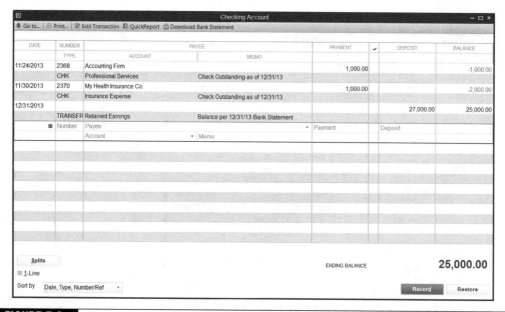

FIGURE 7-3 Use the bank register to enter outstanding checks and deposits.

up of two outstanding customer invoices that together total $15,000.00. For more information on how create an invoice, refer to Chapter 9.

Likewise, to establish your accounts payable balance, create a bill for each unpaid vendor bill as well as any unused vendor credits. Use the original transaction date and all other bill details. In our example, the total Accounts Payable balance (refer to Table 7-1) is made up of just one unpaid bill for $7,500.00. For more information on how to enter vendor bills and credits, refer to Chapter 11.

6. Enter Nonposting Transactions

You should record all open purchase orders and estimates, again with their original dates and details. Although this step is optional because these "nonposting" transactions have no effect on your opening balances, you'll then be able to, in the case of a PO, for example, receive these items through QuickBooks or, in the case of an estimate, generate an invoice when you're awarded the job. Estimates are covered in Chapter 9 and purchase orders in Chapter 11.

7. Enter Mid-year Income and Expenses (if Applicable)

If your QuickBooks start date is a mid-year date, enter a journal entry that summarizes the year-to-date balances in all income and expense accounts as of the QuickBooks start date. You may also want to enter monthly totals rather than one lump sum to give yourself the ability to run monthly Profit and Loss Statements for your entire fiscal year. Post the difference in debits and credits either to the Opening Balance Equity Account or directly to a retained earnings/equity account.

8. Adjust Sales Tax Payable

If you collect sales tax, you may need to adjust the Sales Tax Payable account to be sure that it is in sync with the amount (if any) listed on your pre-QuickBooks opening trial balance. This adjustment should be made after all open invoices are entered, since recording open invoices can affect the Sales Tax Payable account in QuickBooks. Use the Sales Tax Adjustment window to do this: select Vendors | Sales Tax | Adjust Sales Tax Due. For more information on how to use the Sales Tax Adjustment window, refer to Chapter 11.

9. Establish Inventory Balances

If your business carries inventory, you have to tell QuickBooks about the on-hand quantities of each of your inventory items as of your QuickBooks start date. This step assumes that you've already entered your Item List (minus any on-hand quantity information) and that each item has a cost associated with it. If this is not the case, you'll want to update your inventory list with that information prior to completing this step. Chapter 15 covers the details of how to set up an inventory item.

On-hand quantities are added using the Adjust Quantity/Value On Hand window. Select Vendors | Inventory Activities | Adjust Quantity/Value On Hand. Be sure that Quantity appears in the Adjustment Type drop-down menu field. In my simple example, this business carries only a single inventory item that has a cost of $300.00. As of December 31, 2013, I had 100 units in inventory (see Figure 7-4), so I added that quantity in the New Quantity column. The Qty Difference column populates automatically.

Note that QuickBooks requires you to select an offsetting Adjustment Account in order to add the on-hand quantities to inventory. Like the other beginning balance entries, you can choose to post the offsetting balance that the software requires either to Opening Balance Equity or directly to a retained earnings/equity account. You'll

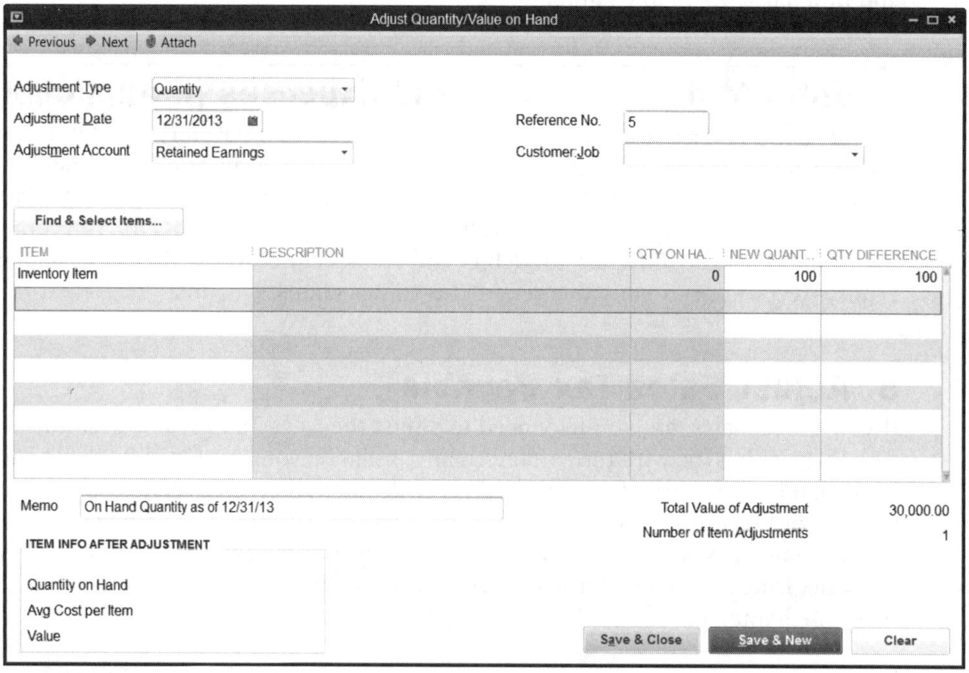

FIGURE 7-4   Use the Adjust Quantity/Value On Hand window to establish your opening inventory balance.

see a message telling you that QuickBooks is expecting you to use an expense account as the adjustment account.

This statement is true for most of your future adjustments—when you'll be using the Adjust Quantity/Value On Hand window to record obsolescence and shrinkage, for example. But in this instance, go ahead and post to one of your equity accounts.

C a u t i o n : Using the Adjust Quantity/Value On Hand (aka Inventory Adjustment) window to establish beginning on-hand inventory quantities is an acceptable method for a business with an existing inventory that has been paid for as of the business's QuickBooks start date. For all other situations, you should "receive" items as normal into your inventory using the steps outlined in Chapter 11.

---

10. Zero-Out the Opening Balance Equity Account

If you've elected to use the Opening Balance Equity account to establish your opening balances, you'll need to zero-out this account in order to complete your setup.

Use a journal entry dated with the QuickBooks start date and an offsetting entry to a retained earnings account (or another account of your accountant's choosing).

Run Your QuickBooks Trial Balance Report as of Your Start Date

You'll want to run your QuickBooks Opening trial balance to be sure that it's in sync with your pre-QuickBooks opening trial balance. Figure 7-5 shows my Trial Balance report in QuickBooks of January 1, 2014, my QuickBooks start date (note that you can run this report as of 12/31/13). Also note that it exactly matches the figures and totals shown in the table at the beginning of this chapter.

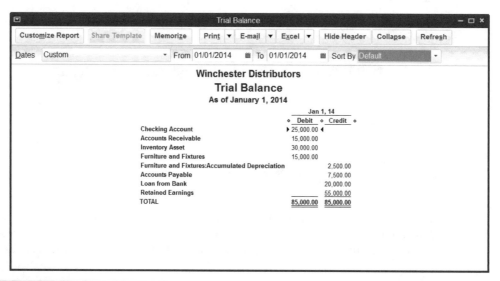

FIGURE 7-5   Drum roll please...the Trial Balance report as of January 1, 2014

If you follow the steps outlined in this chapter and work closely with your accountant, establishing accurate opening balances can be a surprisingly straightforward process.

Good luck!

Setting Up Users
and Permissions

In this chapter:

- Why user logins are important

- Learn about the QuickBooks administrator

- Create QuickBooks users

- Set permissions for users

In many businesses, multiple users have access to the QuickBooks company file, either taking turns accessing the file on the same computer or accessing the file from other computers on a network. (Refer to Appendix A for help with installing QuickBooks on a network.) If this is the case with your business, you should create a user name and password for each of these users. This will help you keep track of who is making what changes to your company file. Even if you're the only one using QuickBooks, you should make sure that you log in with a password to ensure the security of the company file.

Why User Logins Are Important

If you run QuickBooks on a network with multiple users accessing a company file from other computers on the network, QuickBooks requires user logins. What's more, you can't use multi-user mode, which allows simultaneous access by others in your business, until you set up users.

If you're the only QuickBooks user, it's tempting to avoid the extra step of logging in and remembering a password. Don't yield to that temptation, however, because without a login and password, if anyone else wanders into your office and accesses your computer, it's possible for him or her to open QuickBooks and view your financial information. Even worse, it's possible for someone to create, delete, or modify transactions that you might not notice for a very long time.

If you have only one computer running QuickBooks but more than one user who shares that computer to work in QuickBooks, you may need to know who did what. Without creating and requiring separate login names, that information won't be available to you when you need it. The QuickBooks Audit Trail report—which tracks activities with a time and date stamp—displays the name of the logged-in user for every transaction it tracks, but if you and your staff are using "Admin" as the login name each time you use QuickBooks, the value of this report will be greatly diminished. You can learn more about the Audit Trail report in Chapter 25.

User names are linked to permission levels, which means that if you choose, you can limit the parts of QuickBooks that certain users can access to create or view transactions and reports. For example, you can keep users from seeing payroll information or sensitive reports that contain information about your company's profits, debts, and so on.

A Word About Passwords

Most of us who use computers and the Internet on a regular basis know that passwords are very important when it comes to protecting our personal and business information. You shouldn't use passwords that are based on information that someone else may know, such as your child's name, your dog's name, your nickname, your license plate, or your birth date, because many computers have been attacked by hackers who have successfully guessed a password.

Creating Complex Passwords

If you've enabled the credit card protection feature in QuickBooks (covered in Chapter 3), you must create a complex password (also sometimes called a strong password) if you're the Admin or a user who has permission to view customer credit card information. The rules for the complex password are

- A minimum of seven characters is required.
- At least one character must be a number.
- At least one letter must be uppercase.

However, even if you're not using the credit card protection feature, you should still consider using a complex password; after all, if you're going to use passwords, you might as well be serious about security.

Of course, the longer the password and the more complicated it is, the harder it is for someone else to guess. For example, Xyyu86RDa is a great password, but it would be very difficult for a user to remember. Try to strike a balance between complexity and your ability to remember the password.

The QuickBooks Admin

The person who creates the company file becomes the Admin (administrator) user automatically, because she is the first person to open the file. The Admin is in charge of all QuickBooks users and is the only user who can set up additional users, set period closing dates, and complete other sensitive activities in the company file. QuickBooks lets you change the name "Admin" to any other name without losing the administrator power.

As previously mentioned, it is never a good idea to use QuickBooks without the security of having users log in to a company file with a user name and a password. Even if you're the only person who works in QuickBooks, and therefore you're automatically the administrator, be sure the user named Admin has a password.

ProAdvisor Tip: The administrator's (Admin) privileges in QuickBooks are totally unrelated to your Windows logon name and privileges. Even if you're an ordinary user in Windows and can't install software or manage users on the computer, you can be a QuickBooks administrator.

Adding or Changing the Administrator Password

If you didn't create a password for the user named Admin when you set up the company file, you can create a password at any time. If you did create a password and you think the existing password may have been discovered by someone else, you can create a new password.

To add or change the password for the user named Admin, log in to QuickBooks as Admin and choose Company | Set Up Users And Passwords | Change Your Password to open the Change QuickBooks Password dialog seen in Figure 8-1. If the Admin account is already password-protected and you're merely changing the password, you have to enter the current password to complete the process. Enter the new password, enter it again in the Confirm New Password field, and select a challenge question (and the answer).

Creating a Challenge Question for the Admin Account

If you don't remember your Admin password, you can't get into your company file. If Admin is the only user, that means you can't use QuickBooks. If there are other users, they can open the company file, but they can't perform administrative tasks in the file (many QuickBooks functions can be performed only by the Admin user). Essentially, this brings your QuickBooks work to a screeching halt.

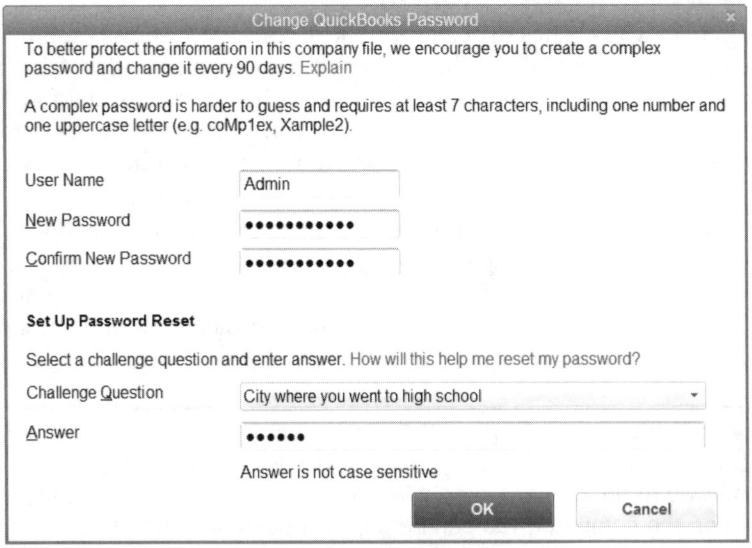

To better protect the information in this company file, we encourage you to create a complex password and change it every 90 days. Explain

A complex password is harder to guess and requires at least 7 characters, including one number and one uppercase letter (e.g. coMp1ex, Xample2).

User Name   Admin
New Password   ••••••••••••
Confirm New Password ••••••••••••

Set Up Password Reset

Select a challenge question and enter answer. How will this help me reset my password?

Challenge Question   City where you went to high school
Answer   ••••••
                      Answer is not case sensitive

OK   Cancel

FIGURE 8-1   You can easily add or change an Admin password.

To prevent this inconvenience, QuickBooks gives the Admin user the opportunity to create a reminder about the password.

Select a question from the drop-down list in the Challenge Question field and then enter the answer to that question in the Answer field. You cannot see what you're typing in the Answer field, so type carefully. (QuickBooks treats this the same way it treats password entry; you see bullet characters instead of the characters you're typing.)

Resetting the Admin Password When You Forget It

If you forget your Admin password, you can reset it using the challenge question you created. In the QuickBooks Login dialog, click the "I forgot my password" link.

The challenge question is displayed in the Reset QuickBooks Administrator Password dialog. Enter the answer you recorded in the Answer field (this time you can see what you're typing).

When you answer the question correctly, all of your password information is removed from the company file and you can start all over with a new password (and a new challenge question and answer).

If you can't remember your challenge question, click the "I forgot my answer" link. The Reset QuickBooks Administrator Password window opens, where you'll have to enter your QuickBooks license number, your name, address, and e-mail. Once this information is completely filled in, Click OK. The Reset QuickBooks Administrator Password window opens, notifying you that a password reset code was sent to the e-mail address provided. Enter the reset code sent to you and click OK. In the next window, you'll be asked to enter and confirm your new password and create a challenge question. Click OK and your password will be reset.

Add Users

Only the Admin user can add QuickBooks users. To add a new user to your company file, choose Company | Set Up Users And Passwords | Set Up Users. QuickBooks asks you to enter your Admin password to proceed, and it then opens the User List dialog. Click Add User to open the Set Up User Password And Access wizard that assists you in setting up the new user.

Use the following guidelines to create a new user:

- The user name is the name this user must type to log in to QuickBooks.
- A password is optional, but it's much less secure to omit passwords. Enter the same password in both password fields. (Later, the user can change the password—see the section "Users Can Change Their Own Passwords" later in the chapter.)
- Assign permissions for this user to access QuickBooks features. See "Setting User Permissions" later in the chapter.

Deleting a User

If you want to remove a user from the User list, select the user name and then click the Delete User button. QuickBooks asks you to confirm your decision. Note that you can't delete the Admin user.

Editing User Information

You can change the user settings for any user. Select the user name in the User List window and click Edit User. This launches a wizard similar to the Set Up User Password And Access Wizard, and you can change the user name, password, and permissions.

The Edit User feature is handy when one of your QuickBooks users comes to you because he cannot remember his password—and you don't have it handy either. You can create a new password for the user, who will then have the option to change the password to something of his own liking. See the section "Users Can Change Their Own Passwords" later in this chapter for more details.

Setting User Permissions

When you're adding a new user or editing an existing user, the wizard walks you through the steps for configuring the user's permissions. Click Next on each wizard window after you've supplied the necessary information.

The first permissions window (see Figure 8-2) asks if you want this user to have access to selected areas of QuickBooks or all areas. If you give the user access to all areas of QuickBooks, or you select the option to make this user an External Accountant, when you click Next you're asked to confirm your decision, and there's no further work to do in the wizard. Click Finish to return to the User List window. (See Chapter 25 to learn about the External Accountant user type.)

If you want to limit the user's access to selected areas of QuickBooks, select that option and click Next. The windows that follow take you through all the QuickBooks features (Sales and Accounts Receivable, Check Writing, Payroll, and so on) so you can establish permissions on a feature-by-feature basis for this user. You should configure permissions for every component of QuickBooks. Any component not configured is set as No Access for this user (which means the user cannot work in that part of QuickBooks). For each QuickBooks component, you can select one of the following permission options:

- **No Access**   The user is denied permission to open any windows in that section of QuickBooks.
- **Full Access**   The user can open all windows and perform all tasks in that section of QuickBooks.
- **Selective Access**   The user will be permitted to perform tasks as you see fit.

FIGURE 8-2 The Set Up User Password And Access window gives you control over a user's access to your QuickBooks data.

If you choose to give selective access permissions, you're asked to specify the rights this user should have. Those rights vary slightly from component to component, but generally you're asked to choose one of these permission levels:

- Create transactions only
- Create and print transactions
- Create transactions and create reports

You can select only one of the three levels, so if you need to give the user rights to more than one of these choices, you must select Full Access instead of configuring Selective Access.

Special Permissions Needed for Customer Credit Card Data

If you provide Full or Selective Access permissions to a user for the Sales And Accounts Receivable area, by default, the user is not able to view customer credit card data. A separate option for this permission appears on the wizard window.

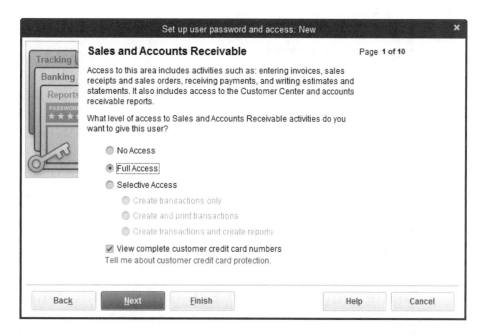

- If you've enabled the Customer Credit Card Security feature (explained in Chapter 3), the next time this user logs in to the company file, he will be asked to create a strong password.
- If you haven't enabled the Customer Credit Card Security feature, this user, and any other user you configure to have access to customer credit card information, does not have to set up a strong password and can view credit card numbers you store in your customers' records.

Configuring Special Areas of QuickBooks

Two wizard windows are used for setting permissions that are not directly related to any specific area of the software: sensitive accounting activities and sensitive accounting reports.

Sensitive accounting activities are those tasks that aren't directly related to QuickBooks transactions, such as the following:

- Making changes to the chart of accounts
- Manipulating the register for any balance sheet account
- Using online banking
- Transferring funds between banks

- Reconciling bank accounts
- Creating journal entries
- Working with budgets

Sensitive financial reporting provides important financial information about your company, such as the following:

- Profit & Loss reports
- Balance Sheet reports
- Budget reports
- Cash flow reports
- Income tax reports
- Trial balance reports
- Audit trail reports

Configuring Rights for Existing Transactions

If a user has permissions for certain areas of QuickBooks, you can limit her ability to manipulate existing transactions within those areas. This means the user can't change or delete a transaction, even if she created it in the first place.

You can also prevent the user from changing transactions that occurred prior to the closing date you set (even if the user knows the password to access transactions that were created before the closing date). See Chapter 18 to learn about setting a closing date and password-protecting access to transactions that predate the closing date.

When you have finished configuring user permissions, the last wizard page presents a list of the permissions you've granted and refused. If everything is correct, click Finish. If there's something you want to change, use the Back button to return to the appropriate page.

Users Can Change Their Own Passwords

Any user can change her password by choosing Company | Set Up Users And Passwords | Change Your Password to open the Change QuickBooks Password dialog. The dialog opens with the name of the current logged in user in the User Name field, and that text cannot be changed.

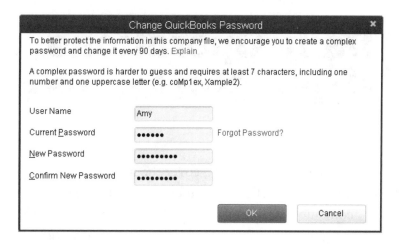

To change the password, the user must enter the old password and then enter the new password (twice). That's an excellent security device, because it prevents other users from changing a user's password (which can happen if a user leaves the computer without logging out of QuickBooks).

Theoretically, it's a good idea for the QuickBooks administrator to know all user passwords and to ask users to notify the administrator when a password is changed. However, tracking passwords can be burdensome if more than just a couple of users are involved. It's perfectly acceptable to decide that you don't want to know user passwords, because if a user forgets a password, you can edit the user's record to create a new one (as described earlier in this chapter) and tell the user her new password.

QuickBooks Login Dialog

The QuickBooks Login dialog appears whenever you open a company file, unless you have not configured any users in addition to the built-in administrator named Admin, and the Admin user has not been assigned a password.

The Login dialog displays the name of the last user who logged in to this company file on this computer. If the same user is opening the file, entering the correct password opens the file.

If a different user is opening the file, replace the text in the User Name field with the login name of the new user, enter the password, and click OK.

Daily Operations Using QuickBooks

The chapters in Part Two cover the most common day-to-day bookkeeping chores you'll be performing in QuickBooks. They contain instructions and tips that will help you complete your most routine tasks in QuickBooks efficiently and accurately. From time to time, there will also be information that you can pass along to your accountant, who may want to know how QuickBooks is handling the tasks you're performing.

Specifically, in Chapters 9 and 10 you'll learn what you need to know about sending invoices to your customers, recording the payments you receive from them, and creating transactions that provide job-costing data. Chapter 11 covers how to track and pay the bills you receive from vendors. Printing, sending, and managing these and other related documents is covered in Chapter 14.

In Chapters 12 and 13, you'll gain an understanding of how to manage your bank and credit card accounts using QuickBooks.

Invoicing Your Customers

n this chapter:

- Create invoices

- Use price levels, discounts, and subtotals

- Edit and memorize invoices

- Issue credit memos

- Create and work with estimates and progress billing

- Invoice customers for reimbursable expenses

For many businesses, the only way to get money in is to send an invoice to a customer. Creating an invoice in QuickBooks is easy once you understand what all the parts of the invoice do and how to modify these parts to reflect the way you do business.

In addition to invoices, you may have to issue credits, print packing slips, and create estimates. These and other sales-related transactions are covered in this chapter.

Create Invoices

QuickBooks gives you multiple ways to open the Create Invoices window. You can select Customers | Create Invoices from the menu bar, press CTRL-I, or click the Create Invoices icon in the Customers section of the Home page.

A blank invoice form will open, and at the top of the window you'll see four tabs: Main, Formatting, Send/Ship, and Reports. If you take a moment to open each tab and review its contents, you'll see that they each contain a set of buttons that allow you to complete any and all tasks for creating and working with an invoice. Clicking the Full Screen icon (see Figure 9-1) at the top right of the Create Invoices window hides these buttons (as well the Icon Bar), making the Invoice template larger and easier to work with.

The Create Invoices window also displays an informational panel that will initially be blank. When you select a customer for invoicing, this panel will show information

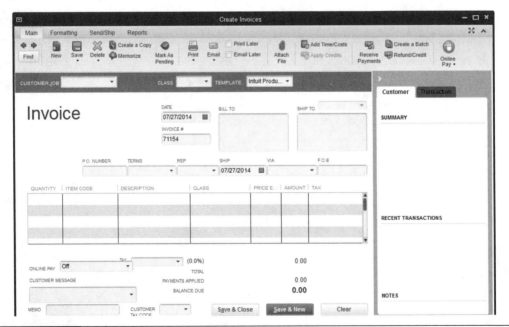

FIGURE 9-1 The Create Invoices window has all the fields you need to track sales and manage all the information that relates to a sale.

about the customer, such as open balance, recent transactions, or notes—if any exist. To close this panel, simply click the Hide History arrowhead to the immediate left of the customer's name. Clicking the Full Screen icon will also close the panel.

Several invoice templates are built into QuickBooks, and you can use any of them as well as create your own (covered in Chapter 24). The first thing to do is decide whether the displayed template suits you—keeping in mind that the prebuilt templates available to you may vary depending on the version of QuickBooks that you're working in and the industry you choose during the QuickBooks setup. You should probably look at each of the templates available in your version before settling on the one you want to use. To do that, click the arrow next to the Template field (located in the upper-right corner of the window) and select another invoice template from the drop-down list. The most common templates that QuickBooks includes for you are outlined here:

- **Finance Charge** This template appears the first time you use the Assess Finance Charges feature. Information about finance charges is in Chapter 10.
- **Intuit Packing Slip** This template is discussed in the section "Print Packing Slips," later in this chapter.
- **Intuit Product** This template has more fields and different columns because it's designed for product sales, including inventory items.
- **Intuit Professional and Service** These two templates are almost identical. There's a difference in the order of the columns, and the Service template has a field for a purchase order number.
- **Progress** This template is covered later in this chapter in the "Create Progress Billing Invoices" section. It is designed specifically for progress billing against a job estimate. It doesn't appear in the Template list unless you have specified Progress Invoicing in the Company Preferences tab of the Jobs & Estimates category of the Preferences dialog.

For this discussion, we'll use the Intuit Product invoice template. If you're using any other template, you'll still be able to follow along, even though your invoice form may lack some of the fields related to products.

The top portion of the invoice is for the basic information and is called the *invoice header*. The middle section, where the billing items are placed, is called the *line item* section. The bottom section, called the *footer*, holds the totals and other details (such as customer messages). Each section of the invoice has fields into which you enter data.

Entering Basic Information in the Invoice Header

To create an invoice, start with the customer or the job. Click the arrow to the right of the Customer:Job field to see a list of all your customers. If you've attached jobs to any customers, those jobs are listed under the customer name. Select the customer or job for this invoice.

If the customer isn't in the system, choose <Add New> to open a new customer window and enter all the data required for setting up a customer. Read Chapter 3 for information on creating customers and jobs.

If you've charged reimbursable expenses or assigned time to this customer, QuickBooks displays a message reminding you to add those charges to this invoice. You'll learn how to charge customers for reimbursable expenses in Chapter 11.

In the Date field, the current date shows by default, but if you want to change the date, you can either type in a new date or click the calendar icon at the right side of the field to select a date. If you change the date, the new date appears automatically in each invoice you create during this session of QuickBooks (the current date returns after you close and then reopen the software). If you want QuickBooks to use the current date on the next invoice you create during this session, see the ProAdvisor Tip that follows.

ProAdvisor Tip: If you want QuickBooks to use the current date as the default date when creating a new invoice, you can set this option from the Edit menu. Choose Edit | Preferences, and in the General category of the Preferences window (in the My Preferences tab) select the option Use Today's Date As Default instead of the default option, Use The Last Entered Date As Default. The first time you enter an invoice, fill in the invoice number you want to use as a starting point. Hereafter, QuickBooks will increment that number for each ensuing invoice.

➥ ProAdvisor Recommends

Using Multiple Invoice Number Sequences

QuickBooks is smart enough to work with alphanumeric invoice numbers. So, for example, if the previously saved invoice number is R-0001, the next invoice number will be R-0002. But suppose you run a contracting business and you'd like your residential invoices to have the numbering scheme "R-0001" and your commercial invoices to use "C-0001," and you don't want to change the numbering scheme manually each time? Consider creating another accounts receivable (A/R) account (refer to Chapter 2 to learn how to create a new account). This will allow you to maintain the different numbering schemes easily when creating an invoice.

If you do decide to use more than one A/R account, the top of the Invoice window has a field to select the A/R account you want to use to post this transaction. Keep in mind that you must select the same A/R account when it comes time to receive payment for the invoice.

The Bill To address is taken from the customer record, as is the Ship To address that's available on the Product invoice template (using the Ship To address you configured to be the default Ship To address). You can select another Ship To address from the drop-down list or add a new Ship To address by choosing <Add New> from the list. Learn more about defining a default Ship To address for a customer in Chapter 3.

ProAdvisor Tip: If you enter or change any information about a customer (such as a change to the customer's Bill To address, for example) while you're creating an invoice, QuickBooks offers to add the information to the customer record when you save the invoice. If the change is permanent, click the Yes button in the dialog that displays the offer. This saves you the trouble of going back to the customer record to make the changes. If the change is for this invoice only, click the No button. If you never make permanent changes, you can tell QuickBooks to turn off this feature by changing the option in the Company Preferences tab in the General category of the Preferences dialog. Select the option Never Update Name Information When Saving Transactions.

If you have a purchase order from this customer, enter the PO number in the P.O. Number field. Optionally, you can click the Attach File icon, located at the top of the Invoice window, to scan and store an online copy of the customer's PO (or any other document that you'd like to associate with this transaction) that relates to this sale so you can easily retrieve it at a later date if the need arises.

The Terms field is filled in automatically with the terms you initially entered for this customer. You can change the terms for this invoice if you wish. If terms don't automatically appear, it means you didn't enter that information in the customer record. If you enter it now, when you save the invoice QuickBooks offers to make the entry the new default for this customer by adding it to the customer record.

The Rep field (available by default in the Product template, but it can be added to any template) will automatically fill in the salesperson attached to this customer. If you didn't link a salesperson when you filled out the customer record, you can click the arrow next to the field and choose a name from the drop-down list. If the rep you want to use doesn't exist in the list, you can select <Add New> to add the rep on the fly. See Chapter 6 to learn how to add reps to your system.

The Ship field (available only in the Product and Packing Slip templates) is for the ship date, and the date defaults to the invoice date. You can change the date if you're not shipping until a later date.

The Via field (available only in the Product and Packing Slip templates) is for the method of shipping. Click the arrow next to the field to see the available shipping choices or select <Add New>. (See Chapter 6 for information about adding to this list.)

The F.O.B. field (available only in the Product and Packing Slip templates) is used by some companies to indicate the point at which the shipping costs are transferred to the buyer and the assumption of a completed sale takes place. If you use Free On Board (FOB), you can enter the applicable data in the field; it has no impact on your QuickBooks financial records and is there for your convenience only.

Entering Line Items

You can now begin to enter the items for which you are invoicing this customer. Click in the first column of the line item section.

If you're using the Product invoice template, that column is Quantity. (If you're using the Professional or Service invoice template, the first column is Item.) Enter the quantity of the first item you're invoicing.

An arrow appears on the right edge of the Item Code column. Click it to see a list of the items you sell (see Chapter 5 to learn how to enter items) and select the item you need. The description and price are filled in automatically using the information you provided when you created the item. If you didn't include description and/or price information when you created the item, you can enter it manually now.

QuickBooks does the math, and the Amount column displays the total of the quantity times the price. If the item and the customer are both liable for tax, the Tax column displays "Tax."

Repeat this process to add all the items that should appear on this invoice. You can add as many rows of items as you need; if you run out of room, QuickBooks automatically adds pages to your invoice.

For line items that are inventory items, QuickBooks checks the quantity on hand (QOH) and warns you if you don't have enough inventory to fill the sale. It's a warning only; QuickBooks lets you complete the sale anyway, but it's never a good idea to sell into negative QOH, as it can affect the average cost of that item.

Applying Price Levels

If you've enabled price levels in QuickBooks Preferences and created entries in your Price Level list (explained in Chapter 6), you can change the amount of any line item by applying a price level. Most of the time, your price levels are a percentage by which to lower (discount) the price, but you may also have created price levels that increase the price.

If you have already assigned a price level to this customer, the appropriate price shows up automatically. If not, to assign a price level, click within the Price Each column to display an arrow. Click the arrow to see a drop-down list of price level items, and select the one you want to apply to this item. As you can see in Figure 9-2,

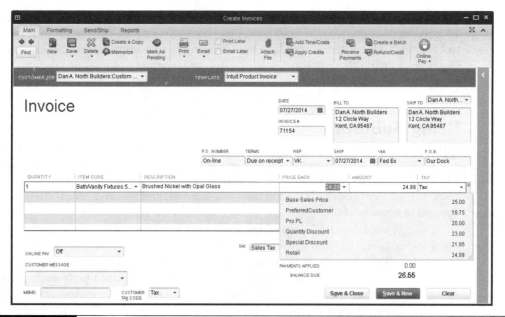

FIGURE 9-2 Assign a predefined price level to the price of any item.

QuickBooks has already performed the math, so you not only see the name of your price level, but you also see the resulting item price for each price level. After you select a price level, QuickBooks changes the amount you're charging the customer for the item and adjusts the amount of the total for this item.

The customer sees only the price on the invoice; there's no indication that you've adjusted the price. This is different from applying a discount to a price (covered in the next section), where a discrete line item exists to identify the discount.

Using Discounts

You can also adjust the invoice by applying discounts. Discounts are entered as line items, so the discount item has to first exist in your Item List.

When you enter a discount, its amount (usually a percentage) is applied to the line item *immediately* above it. For example, suppose you have already entered the following line items:

- Line 1: Qty of 1 for Some Item with a price of $100.00 for a total line item price of $100.00
- Line 2: Qty of 2 for Some Other Item with a price of $40.00 for a total line item price of $80.00

Now you want to give the customer a 10-percent discount, so you've created a 10-percent discount item in your Item List (if you're not sure how to do this, refer to Chapter 5). If you enter the discount item on the line immediately after line 2, QuickBooks will calculate the discount value as 10 percent of the *last* line you entered—for an $8.00 discount.

Using Subtotals

If you want to apply the discount against multiple (or all) line items, you must first enter a line item that creates a subtotal of items you want to discount. To do this, use a subtotal item type that you've created in your Item List. Then enter the discount item as the next line item *after the subtotal*, and the discount is then applied to the subtotal.

Subtotals work by adding up all the line items that have been entered after the last subtotal item (the first subtotal item adds up all line items starting at the first line item on the invoice). This gives you the added benefit of offering a discount to some line items but not others and to apply a different discount rate to each group of subtotaled items. And because discounts are displayed on the invoice, your "generous" discounts are clearly communicated to the customer!

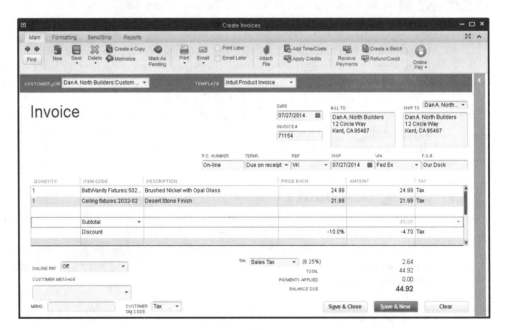

Checking the Footer Section

When you're finished entering all the line items and any discounts, you'll see that QuickBooks has kept a running total, including taxes, in the footer section of the invoice (see Figure 9-3).

Adding a Message

If you want to add a message to the invoice, click the arrow in the Customer Message field to see the messages you created in the Customer Message list (described in Chapter 6). You can create a new message if you don't want to use any of the existing text by choosing <Add New> from the message drop-down list and entering your text in the New Customer Message window. Click OK to enter the message in the invoice. QuickBooks automatically saves the message in the Customer Message list so you can use it again. You can also type the message directly in the Customer Message field and press the TAB key, which opens a Customer Message Not Found dialog that offers you the chance to do a QuickAdd to put your new message in the Customer Message list.

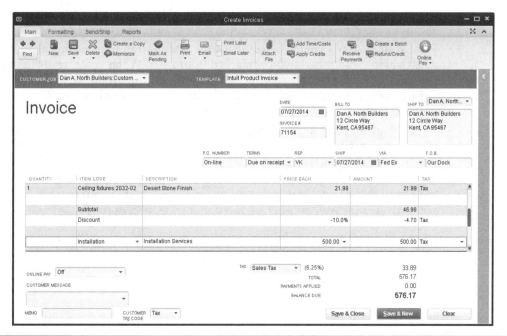

FIGURE 9-3 The invoice is complete, and all the items and discounts are accounted for in the Balance Due field.

Adding a Memo

You can add text to the Memo field at the bottom of the invoice. This text doesn't print on the invoice—it appears only on the screen (you'll see it if you reopen this invoice to view or edit it). However, the memo text *does* appear on statements next to the listing for this invoice. Therefore, be careful about the text you use—don't enter anything you wouldn't want the customer to see (unless you never send statements).

Choosing the Method of Sending the Invoice

There are several ways to get an invoice into the hands of your customer:

- **Print each invoice as it's completed.** Click the Print button on the Main tab of the Create Invoices window. This will open the Print One Invoice window from which you can select your printer, set additional print options, and print a single invoice.
- **E-mail each invoice as it's completed.** Click the Email button on the Main tab of the Create Invoices window. The way your invoice is sent will depend on the send method and template you selected in Company Preferences. In addition, if a document or file has been "attached" to this invoice, you'll see an option to send that as well, along with the invoice, via e-mail. You'll learn more about how to e-mail forms and the attach file feature in Chapter 14.
- **Print your invoices later.** Select the Print Later option to print this invoice in a batch along with other invoices marked Print Later. When you're ready to print the batch, click the down arrow below the Print button on the Main tab of the Create Invoices window and select Batch. Read more about batch printing your invoices (as well as other transaction forms) in Chapter 14.
- **E-mail your invoices later.** Select the Email Later option to add this invoice to a batch of other invoices that you'll send via e-mail to your customers. When you're ready to e-mail the batch, click the down arrow below the Email button and select Batch. The Send Forms window will open, where you can also edit the e-mail that will accompany your invoices. Read more about batch e-mailing your invoices (as well as other transaction forms) in Chapter 14.

You can also configure QuickBooks to allow your customers to pay their invoices online. If you're interested in accepting online payments for invoices, click the Online Pay button on the Main tab to learn more about or to configure your payment settings. Once you're set up to receive online payments, you can designate which online payment methods you'll accept—your choices are bank account only or from a credit card and bank account. Additional fees may apply. Read more about receiving customer payments in Chapter 10.

Saving an Invoice

Click Save & New to save this invoice and move on to the next blank invoice form. If this is the last invoice you're creating, click Save & Close to save this invoice and close the Create Invoices window.

P r o A d v i s o r   T i p : In the General section of the Preferences window is a default setting that automatically saves a transaction (such as an invoice or check) before printing. I recommend that you don't turn off this default setting—it's not only a good business practice to save a transaction before you print it, but it's also a way to protect your business from dishonest users.

Edit an Invoice

If you want to correct an invoice (perhaps you charged the wrong amount or forgot you'd promised a different amount to a particular customer), you can do so quite easily.

Open the Create Invoices window and click the left-pointing blue arrow button located on the Main tab to move back through all the previous invoices in your file. However, if you have a large number of invoices to sort through, it's faster to click the Find button located just below the blue arrows. In the Find Invoices window, you can search by the customer, date, invoice number, or amount.

Use the following guidelines when you're editing a previously entered invoice:

- If a previously entered invoice has been paid, don't change anything, unless you want to edit the text in the Memo field.
- If a previously entered invoice has not been paid but has been mailed, you shouldn't edit anything, although it's probably safe to enter or modify text in the Memo field if necessary.
- If the previously entered invoice has not yet been sent to the customer, you can make any changes you wish.

When you click Save & Close, QuickBooks displays a message dialog asking whether you want to save the changes you made. Click Yes.

Mark an Invoice as Pending

Marking an invoice as "pending" makes it *nonposting*, meaning that it does not affect your account balances or reports. If, for example, you require a final approval for invoices before they are sent out to customers, marking them as pending is a great way to make them available to the appropriate person for review, editing, and final approval.

To mark an invoice as pending, click the Mark As Pending button on the Main tab in the Create Invoices window. A watermark will appear indicating that the invoice is now Pending/Non-Posting. Similarly, to mark an invoice as final, click the Mark As Final button.

The Pending Sales report lists all invoices currently marked as pending as well as the accounts that will be affected once the pending status is removed and the invoice is considered final. To run this report from the Reports menu, you can choose Sales | Pending Sales.

Void and Delete Invoices

There's an important difference between voiding and deleting an invoice. Voiding an invoice makes it nonexistent to your accounting and customer balances. However, the invoice number continues to exist (it's marked "VOID" on reports) so you can account for it. To void an invoice, open it, and on the Main tab in the Create Invoices window, select the Void option from the drop-down arrow below the Delete button. Then click Save. When QuickBooks asks if you want to record your change, click Yes.

Deleting an invoice, on the other hand, removes all traces of it from your transaction registers and most reports (with the exception of the Audit Trail report). To delete an invoice, open it and click the Delete button on the Main tab in the Create Invoices window. Then click Save. When QuickBooks asks if you want to record your change, click Yes.

ProAdvisor Tip: QuickBooks tracks transactions that you void, unvoid (a voided transaction that you decide to re-enter into QuickBooks), or delete, and it displays them in two reports: the Voided/Deleted Transactions Summary report and the Voided/Deleted Transactions Detail reports. Both reports show transactions that have been voided, unvoided, or deleted in the date range selected for the report. These reports can be accessed by selecting Reports | Accountant & Taxes | Voided/Deleted Transactions Summary (or Detail).

Print Packing Slips

QuickBooks provides a template for a packing slip, which is basically an invoice that doesn't display prices. Product prices are not necessarily something that warehouse personnel who manage, pack, and unpack products need to know.

Printing the Default Packing Slip

To print the default packing slip, complete the invoice. Then click the arrow below the Print icon at the top of the Create Invoices window and select Packing Slip from the drop-down list. The Print Packing Slip dialog opens so you can select your printing options (see Figure 9-4).

Changing the Default Packing Slip

If you create your own customized packing slip template, you can select it each time you print a packing slip, or you can make that new form the default packing slip by choosing Edit | Preferences to open the Preferences dialog.

Go to the Sales & Customers category and click the Company Preferences tab. In the Choose Template For Invoice Packing Slip field, select your new packing slip form from the drop-down list and click OK. If you have multiple packing slips, you can choose any of them for printing. Instead of selecting Print Packing Slip from the Print button's drop-down list in the Create Invoices window, select a packing slip template from the drop-down list in the Template field. The Create Invoices window changes to display the packing slip, as shown in Figure 9-5.

FIGURE 9-4 Select the appropriate options for printing the packing slip.

FIGURE 9-5 View a packing slip before you print it.

I know I just told you that a packing slip doesn't display any amounts, and there they are! Confused? Don't be! The packing slip in Figure 9-5 is the Intuit Packing Slip, which has one set of configuration options for the screen and another set of configuration options for the printed version. In this case, the amounts are visible on the screen but will not appear on the printed version. This is true for any packing slip template you create as a customized template. It's a handy feature, as you'll learn when you read the section on customizing templates in Chapter 24.

To see what the printed version of the packing slip looks like, click the arrow below the Print icon on the Create Invoices window toolbar and choose Preview. Satisfied? Close the Preview window and return to the Create Invoices window. Now you can print the packing slip.

Batch Invoicing

Suppose you own a landscaping company and you charge the same monthly maintenance fee to several of your customers. Batch invoicing gives you an easy way to create and send the same invoice to these customers. You can also choose to create a billing group and add customer names to that group if those customers will need to be invoiced for a similar service in the future.

1. From the Main tab on the Create Invoices window or from the Customers menu, click the Create A Batch button. You'll see a reminder about updating your customer information. Review and click OK.

2. From the Batch Invoice window (refer to Figure 9-6), individually select the names of customers for whom you want to create an invoice (you can also hold down the SHIFT key and select multiple, contiguous customer names), and click the Add button to include them in this batch. Alternatively, you can create a billing group (by selecting <Add New> from the Billing Group drop-down list) to which you can add customers in the same manner. Click Next.

3. Select the items for your batch invoice, add a customer message, and update the invoice date and template if necessary. Click Next.

4. Review the list of batch invoices to be created. You can deselect a customer to prevent them from receiving an invoice in this batch by clicking the check mark next to their name in the Select column. Click the Create Invoices button.

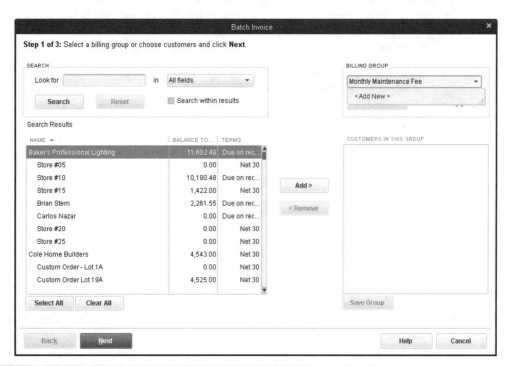

FIGURE 9-6 Choose the customers to invoice in this batch or create a new billing group.

5. Review the Batch Invoice Summary window to confirm and execute the send methods (either Print or Email) of the invoices in the batch. Click Close when finished or to send any unmarked (meaning there's no send method in the customer record) invoices later.

ProAdvisor Tip: This invoicing method relies on the details you've entered for your customers (such as mailing address, terms, and send method), so to get the full benefit from using this feature, you'll want to be sure that this information is up to date and complete.

Use Memorized Invoices

If you have a recurring invoice (common if you collect rent from tenants, for example), you can automate the process of creating it. Recurring invoices are those that are posted to QuickBooks at regular intervals, usually for the same amount.

Create the first invoice, filling out all the fields. If there are any fields that will change, leave those fields blank and fill them out each time you send the invoice. Then press CTRL-M to open the Memorize Transaction dialog, shown next:

Fill in the fields using the following guidelines:

- Change the title in the Name box to reflect what you've done. It's easiest to add a word or phrase to the default title (which is the customer or job name), such as Retainer. You can use up to 31 characters, including spaces.
- Choose Add To My Reminders List. Then specify how and when you want to be reminded in the How Often and Next Date fields. The reminder will appear in the automatic QuickBooks Reminder window.
- Choose Do Not Remind Me if you have a great memory, or if you use this memorized invoice only for special occasions.

- Choose Automate Transaction Entry if you want QuickBooks to issue this invoice automatically. If you opt for automatic issuing of this invoice, you must fill in the fields so that QuickBooks performs the task accurately, as follows:
  - The How Often field is where you specify the interval for this invoice, such as monthly, weekly, or so on. Click the arrow to see the drop-down list and choose the option you need.
  - The Next Date field is the place to note the next instance of this invoice.
  - The Number Remaining field is a place to start a countdown for a specified number of invoices. This is useful if you're billing a customer for a finite number of months because you only have a one-year contract, for example.
  - The Days In Advance To Enter field is for specifying the number of days in advance of the Next Date you want QuickBooks to create the invoice.

Click OK when you have finished filling out the dialog. Then click Save & Close in the Invoice window to save the transaction. Later, if you want to view, edit, or remove the transaction, you can select it from the Memorized Transaction List, which you open by pressing CTRL-T.

Creating Memorized Invoice Groups

Let's say you have a lot of invoices that you've memorized but they need to be created and sent out on a particular day of the month. You can create a separate Memorized Transaction Group and QuickBooks will automatically take action on every invoice in the group on the day that you specify. To use this feature, follow these steps:

1. Press CTRL-T to display the Memorized Transaction List.
2. Right-click any blank spot in the Memorized Transaction window and choose New Group from the shortcut menu.
3. In the New Memorized Transaction Group window, give this group a name (such as 1st Of Month or 15th Of Month).
4. Fill out the fields to specify the way you want the invoices in this group to be handled.
5. Click OK to save this group.

Adding Memorized Invoices to Groups

After you create the group, you can add memorized transactions to it as follows:

1. In the Memorized Transaction List window, select the first memorized invoice transaction you want to add to the group.
2. Right-click and choose Edit Memorized Transaction from the shortcut menu.

3. When the Schedule Memorized Transaction window opens with this transaction displayed, select the option named Add To Group.
4. Select the group from the list that appears when you click the arrow next to the Group Name field and click OK.

Repeat this process for each invoice you want to add to the group. As you create future memorized invoices, just select the Add To Group option to add each invoice to the appropriate group.

Issue Credits and Refunds

Sometimes you have to give money back to a customer. You can do this in the form of a credit against current or future balances, or you can write a check and refund money you received from the customer. Neither is a lot of fun, but it's a fact of business life.

Creating a credit memo is similar to creating an invoice. You can use the credit memo either to reduce a customer's balance or issue a cash refund to them. What's more, QuickBooks makes it easy for you to issue a credit against a particular invoice or retain it as an available credit to be used on a future date. (Information about applying the credit memo against the customer's account when you're entering customer payments is in Chapter 10.)

Creating a Credit Memo Against an Invoice

Suppose you've sold merchandise to a customer on an invoice and later they return some or all of the items. You can issue a credit memo directly from the original invoice, saving you the time of having to research the particulars of the original sale (such as price and quantity sold). This feature also saves you from having to re-enter the item information a second time on the credit memo.

To issue a credit memo, locate and open the original invoice. Click the Refund/Credit button on the Main tab (see Figure 9-7) to create a return receipt for this invoice. All items from the invoice are automatically listed on the newly created credit memo. From here, you can edit the line items as needed to account for what is being returned. When you save the credit memo, QuickBooks asks you to specify the way you want to apply the credit amount. See the section "Applying Credit Memos" later in this chapter for information on how to do this.

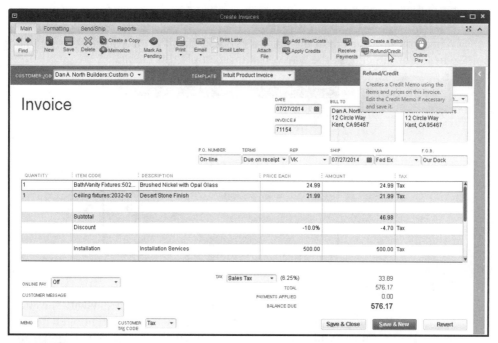

FIGURE 9-7 Creating a credit memo from the original invoice will save you time and ensure accuracy.

Creating a Credit Memo Without a Previous Invoice

To create a credit memo (also referred to as a return receipt) that is not attached to a particular invoice, choose Customers | Create Credit Memos/Refunds from the menu bar to open a blank Create Credit Memos/Refunds window.

Select the appropriate customer or job, and then fill out the rest of the heading. Move to the line item section and enter the item, the quantity, and the rate for the items in this credit memo. Do *not* use a minus sign—QuickBooks knows what a credit is.

On the Main tab, you can use one of two buttons to designate how to use this credit—Use Credit To Give Refund or Use Credit To Apply To Invoice. Alternatively, when you click Save & Close to save the credit memo, QuickBooks asks you to specify the way you want to apply the credit amount. See the next section, "Applying Credit Memos."

Applying Credit Memos

When you save the credit memo, QuickBooks displays an Available Credit dialog where you can choose the way you want to apply this credit:

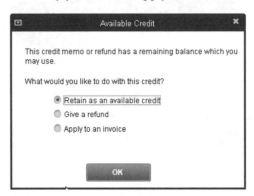

Retaining the Credit

Choose Retain As An Available Credit to let the credit amount stay with the customer. You can apply the credit to a future invoice or apply it to a current open invoice later if the customer sends a payment that deducts the credit. When you create new invoices or apply customer payments to existing invoices, the credit is available.

If the credit is for a job and the job doesn't have any outstanding invoices, you should retain the credit, because you can re-assign and then apply it against a different job for the same customer.

Giving a Refund for the Credit

Choose Give A Refund to give money back to the customer. When you click OK, the Issue A Refund window opens (see Figure 9-8). Use the following guidelines to configure the Issue A Refund window:

- In the Issue This Refund Via field, select the method for the refund from the drop-down list (Cash, Check, or Credit Card).
- If you choose Cash or Check, be sure to select the appropriate bank account in the Account field.
- If you choose Check, the dialog adds an option labeled To Be Printed, which is selected by default.
- If you print checks, leave the check mark in the check box, and click OK. The check is added to the list of checks to be printed when you choose File | Print Forms | Checks. (The check also appears in the bank account register with the notation "To Print.")

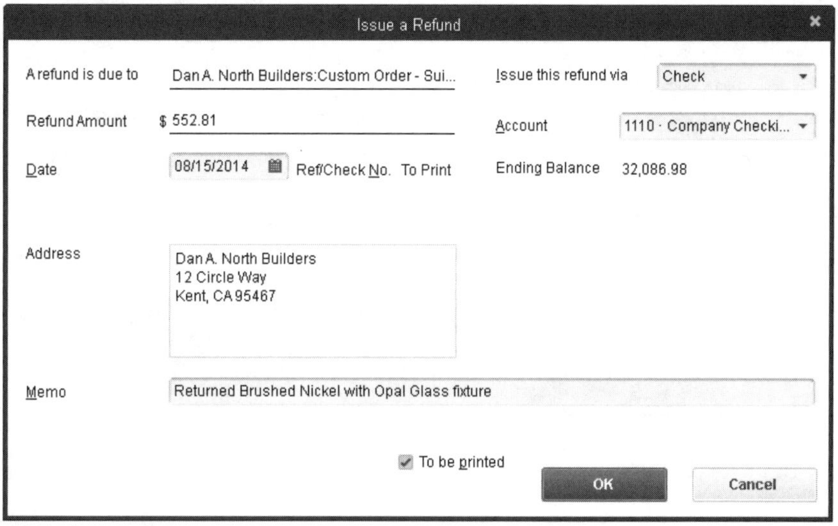

FIGURE 9-8 Tell QuickBooks how to manage the refund you want to send to the customer.

- If you write checks manually, deselect the check mark in the To Be Printed check box, enter the check number you'll be using, and click OK. The check is added to your bank account register, using the next available check number.
- If you choose Credit Card, follow the usual procedure for creating a credit card transaction.

Applying the Credit to an Invoice

Choose Apply To An Invoice to apply the credit to a current invoice. When you click OK, QuickBooks displays a list of open invoices for this customer or job and automatically applies the credit against the oldest invoice (see Figure 9-9).

If the credit is larger than the oldest invoice, QuickBooks applies the remaining amount of the credit to the next oldest invoice. If there are no additional invoices, the remaining amount of the credit is held in the customer's record and is treated as a retained credit. Click Done to save the transaction.

Using Estimates

Certain customers or certain types of jobs may require you to create an estimate. An estimate isn't an invoice, but it can be used as the basis of an invoice (or multiple invoices if you choose to send invoices as the job progresses). Estimates are also a great way for you to create a "budget" for the job on which you're bidding, since there are some comprehensive job reports in QuickBooks that help you keep track of actual job income and costs versus what was initially estimated.

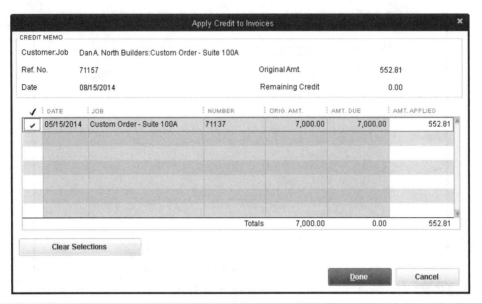

Apply Credit to Invoices

CREDIT MEMO

Customer:Job	Dan A. North Builders:Custom Order - Suite 100A				
Ref. No.	71157		Original Amt.		552.81
Date	08/15/2014		Remaining Credit		0.00

✓	DATE	JOB	NUMBER	ORIG. AMT.	AMT. DUE	AMT. APPLIED
✓	05/15/2014	Custom Order - Suite 100A	71137	7,000.00	7,000.00	552.81
			Totals	7,000.00	0.00	552.81

Clear Selections

Done   Cancel

FIGURE 9-9 Select the invoice against which you want to apply the credit.

ProAdvisor Tip: Estimates are available only if you enable them in the Jobs & Estimates section of the Preferences dialog (Edit | Preferences).

Creating an Estimate

The first (and most important) thing to understand is that creating an estimate doesn't affect your financial records. No amounts in the estimate post to income, accounts receivable, or any other general ledger account.

To create an estimate, choose Customers | Create Estimates from the menu bar. As you can see in Figure 9-10, the Create Estimates transaction window has virtually the same navigation and task buttons as the Create Invoices window—including an informational panel to the right.

You'll notice that once you've selected an existing customer or job, this panel will display their most recent transactions, including the current balance if one exists. To close this panel, simply click the Hide History arrowhead to the immediate left of the customer's name as it appears in the pane. Clicking the Full Screen icon at the top-right of the window will also close the panel. Fill out the fields the same way you would for invoices.

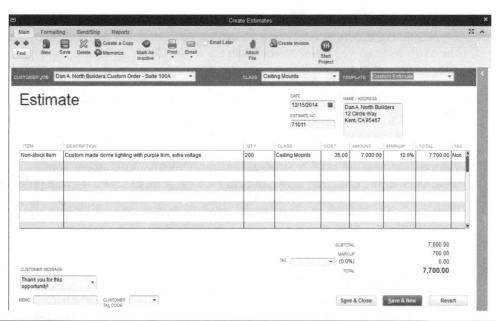

FIGURE 9-10 Estimates provide a way to bid for a job and then track your progress.

Some estimate templates permit you to invoice customers with a markup over cost (such as the built-in Custom Estimate template). This is often the approach used for time and materials on bids. Just enter the cost and indicate the markup in dollars or percentage. If you decide to change the total of the item, QuickBooks will change the markup to make sure the math is correct.

If the item you use has been set up with both a cost and price, the Custom Estimate template displays both the cost and the price and automatically calculates the markup percentage for you. You can change the markup (as either a percentage or dollar amount) if you wish and the new price will appear in the Total column. If the item you use has only a price associated with it, the estimate uses that price as the cost on which the markup is calculated.

The Markup field is displayed only on the screen version of the estimate—this column doesn't appear on the printed version. And if you've created price levels, they'll appear in the Markup field for easy selection.

Creating Multiple Estimates for a Job

You can create multiple estimates for a customer or a job—a very handy feature. You can create an estimate for each phase of the job or create multiple estimates with different prices. Of course, that means each estimate has different contents.

When you create multiple estimates for the same job, they remain active (or open) by default. If a customer rejects any estimates, you can either delete them or click the Mark As Inactive button on the Main tab of the Create Estimates window—effectively closing the estimate.

Copying Estimates

A quick way to create multiple estimates with slightly different contents is to make copies of the original. Click the Create A Copy button on the Main tab while the estimate you want to copy is displayed in your QuickBooks window. You can also right-click in the estimate header and choose Duplicate Estimate from the shortcut menu to accomplish the same thing. The Estimate # field changes to the next number, while everything else remains the same. Make the required changes, and then click Save & Close.

Memorizing Estimates

If you frequently present the same estimated items to multiple customers, you can use the Memorize feature to create boilerplate estimates for future use. QuickBooks removes the name when memorizing the document so you can easily use it for other jobs.

First, create an estimate, filling in the items that belong in it. Don't fill in amounts that usually change (such as quantities, or even prices). Then click the Memorize button on the Main tab (or press CTRL-M) to memorize the estimate. Use the following guidelines to fill out the Memorize Transaction dialog:

1. Give the estimate a name that reminds you of its contents.
2. Select the option Do Not Remind Me.
3. Click OK.

To use this boilerplate estimate, press CTRL-T or choose Lists | Memorized Transaction List to open the Memorized Transaction List. Double-click the estimate, fill in the Customer:Job information and any pricing information that's not automatically included, and then save it. The memorized estimate isn't changed; only the new estimate is saved.

Create Progress Billing Invoices

If you've enabled estimates and progress billing in the Jobs & Estimates category of the Preferences dialog (reached by choosing Edit | Preferences), you can use the Progress Invoice template to invoice your customers as each invoicing milestone arrives.

Choosing the Estimated Job

Progress invoices are invoices that are connected to an estimate for a customer or job. Open the Create Invoices window, select Progress Invoice from the Template drop-down list, and choose the customer or job for which you're creating the progress invoice. Because you've enabled estimates in your QuickBooks Preferences, the system always checks the customer record to see if you've recorded any estimates for this customer or job, and if so, presents them:

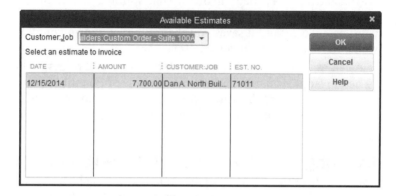

Select the estimate you're invoicing against and click OK. QuickBooks then asks you to specify what to include on the invoice.

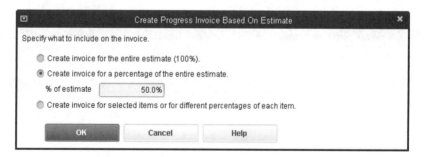

Fill out the dialog using the following guidelines:

- You can create an invoice for the whole job, 100 percent of the estimate. When the line items appear, you can edit individual items.
- You can create an invoice for a specific percentage of the estimate. The percentage usually depends upon the agreement you have with your customer. For example, you could have an agreement that you'll invoice the job in a certain number of equal installments, or you could invoice a percentage that's equal to the percentage of the work that's been finished.

- You can create an invoice that covers only certain items on the estimate, or you can create an invoice that has a different percentage for each item on the estimate. This is the approach to use if you're billing for completed work on a job that has a number of distinct tasks. Some of the work listed on the estimate may be finished and other work not started, and the various items listed on the estimate may be at different points of completion.

After you've created the first progress billing invoice for an estimate, a new option is available for subsequent invoices. That option is to bill for all remaining amounts in the estimate (it replaces the 100 percent option). This is generally reserved for your last invoice, and it saves you the trouble of figuring out which percentages of which items have been invoiced previously.

As far as QuickBooks is concerned, the items and prices in the estimate are not etched in stone; you can change any amounts or quantities you wish while you're creating the invoice. Ultimately, however, your ability to invoice for amounts that differ from the estimate depends on your agreement with the customer.

Entering Progress Invoice Line Items

After you choose your progress billing method and click OK, QuickBooks automatically fills in the line item section of the invoice based on the method you selected. Figure 9-11 shows an example of a progress bill for 50 percent of the estimate to reflect the fact that half of the work was done.

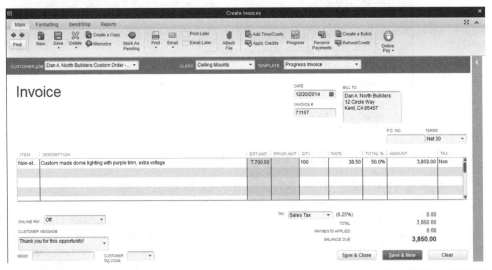

FIGURE 9-11 Progress invoices are automatically filled in using the information in the estimate.

Changing Line Items

If you chose to invoice a percentage of the estimate's total, the amount of every line item on the estimate reflects that percentage. This doesn't work very well for those lines that have products (it's hard to sell a percentage of a physical product). You can leave the invoice as is, because the customer will probably understand that this is a progress invoice, or you can make changes to the invoice.

In addition, the line items for services rendered may not be totally accurate. For example, some of the line items may contain service categories that aren't at the same percentage of completion as others.

To change the invoice and keep a history of the changes against the estimate, don't just make changes to the line items on the invoice. Instead, click the Progress icon on the Main tab of the Create Invoices window. This opens a dialog (see Figure 9-12) that allows reconfiguration of the line items. You can change the quantity, rate, or percentage of completion for any individual line item.

If you select Show Quantity And Rate, the columns in the dialog display the columns from the estimate, and you can make changes to any of them. Click the Qty column for any line item to highlight the number that's been used to calculate the invoice. Replace the number with the amount you want to use for the invoice. You can also change the rate as agreed to by you and the customer.

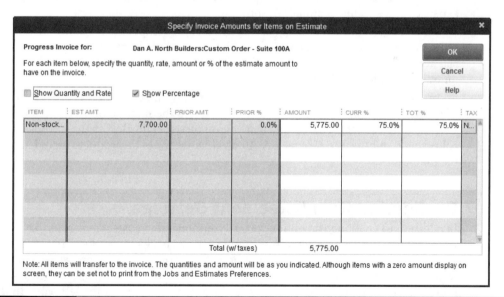

FIGURE 9-12 You can make changes to the data that QuickBooks automatically inserted in the invoice.

If you select Show Percentage, the dialog displays the Curr % column, which shows the percentage of completion for this and previous billings. The percentages compare the dollar amounts for invoices against the estimated total. You can change the percentage for any line item.

Select both options if you need to make changes to one type of progress on one line item and another type of progress on another line item. All the columns (and all the previous billings, if any exist) appear in the window.

Click OK when you have finished making your adjustments. You return to the invoice form, where the amounts on the line items have changed to match the adjustments you made. Click Save & New to save this invoice and move on to the next invoice, or click Save & Close to save this invoice and close the Create Invoices window.

Using this method to change a line item keeps the history of your estimate and invoices intact, as opposed to making changes in the amounts directly on the invoice form, which does not create a good audit trail.

Invoice Customers for Reimbursable Expenses

When you pay vendors, some purchases may be made on behalf of a customer, or they may be purchases needed to complete a job. When you create a vendor bill or write a check to a vendor, you can specify expenses as reimbursable and link those expenses to a specific customer or job.

You can automatically invoice customers for those expenses. In addition, you can link mileage costs and time costs (for employees or subcontractors) to customers and automatically invoice customers for those expenses. (Chapter 19 has information on tracking mileage and time.)

Any amounts you link to a customer are saved in the customer record, and you can collect the money by adding those amounts to the next invoice you create for that customer. In fact, you could create an invoice specifically for the purpose of collecting reimbursable expenses, with no other services or products included on the invoice.

Configuring Reimbursement Settings

In addition to enabling the option to track reimbursable costs when entering transactions for vendors (vendor bills and writing checks to vendors are covered in Chapter 11), QuickBooks gives you options for invoicing customers when you want to recover your reimbursable expenses. To set your own preference, choose Edit | Preferences and select the Sales & Customers category in the left pane. In the My Preferences tab, select one of the available options.

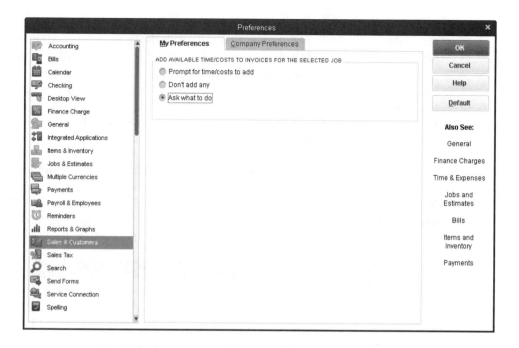

- **Prompt For Time/Costs To Add** Choosing this option tells QuickBooks to open the Choose Billable Time And Costs dialog, which displays the current reimbursable expenses whenever you create an invoice or sales receipt for a customer with outstanding reimbursable costs. This is the option to select if you always (or almost always) collect reimbursable costs from customers.
- **Don't Add Any** Selecting this option prevents the automatic display of the Choose Billable Time And Costs dialog. Choose this option if you collect reimbursable expenses periodically on separate invoices. When you're ready to create an invoice for these expenses, click the Add Time/Costs button on the sales transaction form.
- **Ask What To Do** Select this option to tell QuickBooks to ask you what you want to do whenever you create a sales transaction for a customer with outstanding reimbursable costs. Depending on your selection in that dialog (discussed in the next section), you can add the costs to the sales transaction or omit them.

Creating a Transaction for Reimbursable Expenses

When you're creating a sales transaction (an invoice or a sales receipt) for a customer that has outstanding reimbursable costs, QuickBooks uses the preference you set to determine how to manage those costs.

If you selected the preference Prompt For Time/Costs To Add, when you select the customer, QuickBooks automatically displays the current reimbursable expenses so you can select those you want to include in the current transaction.

If you selected the preference Don't Add Any, the invoice or sales receipt transaction window opens as usual. If you want to check for reimbursable costs for this customer and then decide whether you want to recover any of them, click the Add Time/Costs button on the Main tab above the transaction form. When the Choose Billable Time And Costs dialog opens, you can see if there are any reimbursable expenses you want to collect from your customer. If you do, follow the steps in the next section, "Adding Expenses to the Sales Transaction."

If you selected the preference Ask What To Do, when you select a customer that has unpaid reimbursable costs in the transaction window, QuickBooks displays a dialog asking how you want to handle those amounts. Your response determines whether the Choose Billable Time And Costs dialog opens automatically.

Adding Expenses to the Sales Transaction

To collect expenses, also called *reimbursable costs,* from a customer, select those costs from the Choose Billable Time And Costs dialog (see Figure 9-13). Each type of expense is displayed in its own tab, and you'll need to review each tab to see if any amounts exist. Unfortunately, the amount displayed on each tab doesn't help you head for the appropriate tab—all the amounts are set at $0.00 until you actually select amounts to add to the sales transaction. So start clicking each tab to find reimbursable expenses to transfer to the transaction.

When you find a tab that has contents, click in the leftmost column to place a check mark next to the expense(s) you want to include (see Figure 9-13).

Click OK to move the item(s) to the transaction window to join any other items you're entering in that transaction. You may find reimbursable expenses on more than one tab—for example, you may have expenses on the Expenses tab and expense items on the Items tab—so you have to check each tab. QuickBooks automatically transfers the selected reimbursable costs to the invoice. The description of the reimbursable expenses that appears on the invoice is taken from the text you

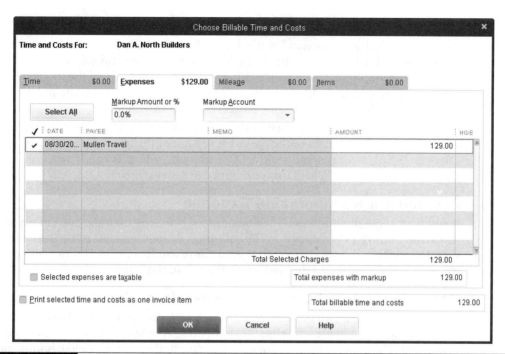

FIGURE 9-13 Select the reimbursable time, expenses, mileage, or items you want to add to the transaction you're preparing.

entered in the Memo column when you entered a bill or created a check for this vendor. If you didn't use the Memo column on the Enter Bills or Write Check window, you'll have to enter text manually in the Description column of the invoice. Otherwise, the customer sees only an amount and no explanation of what it's for. (The description of mileage or item costs is taken from the Description field of the item you configured.)

Adding Taxes to Reimbursable Expenses

If an expense is taxable and the customer is not tax exempt, choose the option Selected Expenses Are Taxable. When the expenses are passed to the invoice, the appropriate taxes are applied. If you select the taxable option and the customer is tax exempt, QuickBooks won't add the sales tax to the invoice.

If some expenses are taxable and others aren't, you have to separate the process of moving items to the invoice. First, deselect each nontaxable expense by clicking its check mark to remove it (it's a toggle). Click OK to put those expenses on the invoice. Then return to the Choose Billable Time And Costs window, put a check mark next to each nontaxable expense, deselect the Selected Expenses Are Taxable option, and click OK.

Omitting the Details on the Invoice

Each of the tabs has the option Print Selected Time And Costs As One Invoice Item. When you click OK and view the results in the invoice, you still see each individual item. Don't panic—you're not seeing things. The screen version of the invoice continues to display the individual items. However, when you print the invoice, you'll see a single line item with the correct total in the Amount column.

QuickBooks changes the format of the printed invoice to eliminate the details but doesn't change the data in the onscreen version of the invoice. This means you can open the invoice later and see the detailed items, which is handy when the customer calls to ask, "What's this reimbursable expense item on my bill?"

Excluding a Reimbursable Expense

If you have some reason to exclude one or more expenses from the current invoice, just avoid putting a check mark in the column. The item remains in the system and shows up on the Choose Billable Time And Costs window the next time you open it. You can add the item to the customer's invoice in the future.

Removing a Reimbursable Expense from the List

Suppose when it's time to invoice the customer, you decide that you don't want to ask the customer to pay an expense you marked as reimbursable; you've changed your mind. The Choose Billable Time And Costs window has no Delete button and no method of selecting an item and choosing a delete function. You could deselect the check mark that tells QuickBooks to move the item to the sales transaction, but afterward, every time you open the window, the item will, strangely enough, still be there.

The solution lies in the Hide column. If you place a check mark in the Hide column, the item is effectively deleted from the list of reimbursable expenses that you see when you're preparing invoices but the amount is still in your system. This means you won't accidentally invoice the customer for the item, but the link to this expense for this customer continues to appear in reports about this customer's activity, which is helpful for job costing. In effect, by selecting the Hide option, you've marked the expense as "nonbillable," and it's not available in the future.

Changing the Amount of a Reimbursable Expense

You're free to change the amount of a reimbursable expense. To accomplish this, select the amount in the Amount column of the Choose Billable Time And Costs window on the Expenses tab, and enter the new figure.

If you reduce the amount, QuickBooks does not keep the remaining amount on the Choose Billable Time And Costs window. You won't see it again because QuickBooks makes the assumption you're not planning to pass the remaining amount to your customer in the future.

You may want to increase the charge for some reason. If you're increasing all the charges, you'll find it's easier to apply a markup (covered next) than to change each individual item.

Marking Up Reimbursable Expenses

You can mark up any expenses you're invoicing, which many companies do to cover any additional costs incurred, such as handling, time, or general aggravation. To apply a markup, select the items you want to mark up by placing a check mark in the Use column in the Expenses tab of the Choose Billable Time And Costs window. Then enter a markup in the Markup Amount Or % field in either of the following ways:

- Enter an amount.
- Enter a percentage (a number followed by the percent sign).

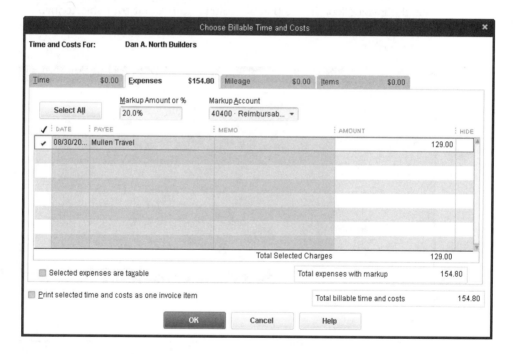

Specify the account to which you're posting markups. You can create an account specifically for markups or use an existing income account.

When you click OK to transfer the reimbursable expenses to the customer's invoice, you'll see the reimbursable expenses and the markup as separate items.

Although it would be unusual for you to be marking up expenses without having discussed this with your customer, if you don't want your customer to see the markup amounts, select the Print Selected Time And Costs As One Invoice Item option. You'll see the breakdown on the screen version of the invoice, but the printed invoice will contain only the grand total.

One big difference between using the markup function and just changing the amount of the reimbursable expense in the Amount column is the way the amounts are posted to your general ledger. If you use the markup function, the difference between the actual expense and the charge to your customer is posted to the markup account. If you change the amount of the expense, the entire amount is posted to the income account you linked to the reimbursable expense account.

ProAdvisor Tip: If you void or delete a saved sales transaction that contains reimbursable expenses, these expenses are not automatically made "billable" again. You'll need to go to the original expense transaction and click the Invoice icon in the Billable column to make it available to invoice again.

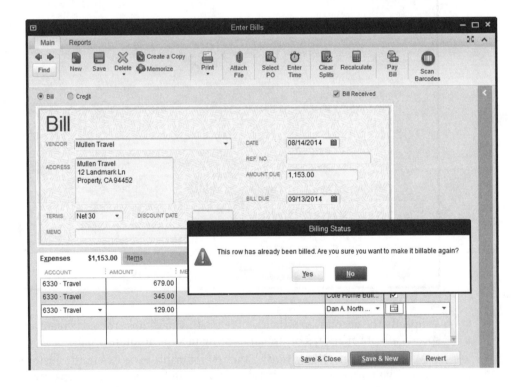

Managing Your Accounts Receivable

n this chapter:

- Apply customer payments

- Apply credits and discounts to invoices

- Handle cash sales

- Deposit customer payments into your bank account

- Track receivables

- Impose finance charges

- Send statements to customers

As you create invoices and send them to your customers, there's an expectation that money will eventually arrive to pay off those invoices. In fact, for most businesses, the most rewarding QuickBooks task is receiving a payment from a customer. QuickBooks gives you the tools you need to make sure that you apply customer payments the way your customer intended so that you both have the same information in your records.

Your Options for Receiving Customer Payments

In QuickBooks, payments are applied to specific invoices, not to a general balance forward. You can, however, change how QuickBooks applies payments with just a mouse click or two, using the following steps:

1. Choose Edit | Preferences and click the Payments icon in the left pane.
2. Move to the Company Preferences tab.
3. In the Receive Payments section, select or deselect options to match your needs:
   - Automatically Apply Payments means that when you enter the amount you've received from the customer, QuickBooks will automatically pay off matching invoices, first by amount, then by the oldest due date.
   - Automatically Calculate Payments tells QuickBooks to let you omit the amount of the customer's payment in the transaction window and select invoices to pay off. QuickBooks adds up the invoice amounts and applies the total as the customer's payment. (This assumes the customer has sent a payment that matches the total.)
   - Use Undeposited Funds As A Default Deposit To Account automatically posts the payments you receive to the Undeposited Funds account, and from there you'll deposit the funds into a bank account.

Recording the Payment

When a payment arrives from a customer, choose Customers | Receive Payments to open a blank Receive Payments window, as shown in Figure 10-1. Note the ribbon bar at the top of the window that contains three tabs: Main, Reports, and Payments. Each of these tabs contains buttons that give you easy access to important payment related tasks (such as processing credit payments) as well as reports where you can find customer balance information.

Click the arrow to the right of the Received From field and select the customer or job from the drop-down list using the following guidelines:

1. Select the customer. The details for the open invoice balance(s) for this customer are displayed. If the payment is for a job, select the job. The details for the open invoice balance(s) for this specific job are displayed. If the payment covers multiple jobs, select the main customer name to see all invoices for all jobs. The details for the open invoice balance(s) for this customer and jobs are displayed.

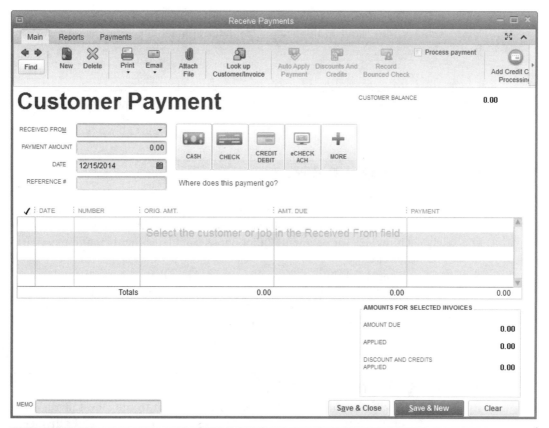

FIGURE 10-1 The Receive Payments window has everything you need to apply payments accurately and to choose QuickBooks customer payment options.

2. In the Payment Amount field, enter the amount of this payment. To select the payment method, click one of the payment method buttons to the right of the Payment Amount field. If the payment method is a check, enter the check number in the Check # field that appears. If the payment method is a credit card, complete the Card No. and Exp. Date fields for your records. If you have a merchant account with the QuickBooks Merchant Account Service, check the Process Payment check box on the Main tab on the Icon Bar.

3. The Memo field at the bottom of the window is optional, and you can use it if you want to link a note to this payment record.

If the Deposit To field is displayed, select the bank account for depositing the payment, or select Undeposited Funds if you're using that account to receive payments. If the Deposit To field is not displayed, it means your Payments Preferences are configured to deposit payments to the Undeposited Funds account automatically, which is the most often used setting. See the section "Depositing Payments into Your Bank Account" later in this chapter to determine which setting would work best for you.

ProAdvisor Tip: You can add any additional payment methods you need by choosing <Add New> in the Pmt. Method drop-down list.

Calculating the Payment

If you've enabled the Automatically Calculate Payments option in the Payments category of the Preferences dialog (the default setting), you can skip the Amount field and move directly to the list of invoices in the Receive Payments window. As you select each invoice for payment, QuickBooks calculates the total and places it in the Amount field.

If you *haven't* enabled the option to calculate payments automatically and you select an invoice listing without entering the amount of the payment first, QuickBooks issues an error message, telling you that the amount of the payment you're applying is higher than the amount you entered in the Amount field. In that case, enter the amount of the payment in the Amount field at the top of the Receive Payments window.

Applying Payments to Invoices

By default, QuickBooks automatically applies the payment to the oldest invoice(s), unless the amount of the payment exactly matches the amount of another invoice, as seen in Figure 10-2.

In situations where the customer's intention isn't clear, the smart thing to do is to call and ask how the payment should be applied. You must, of course, apply the entire amount of the customer's payment. If you are not tracking the customer balance by invoice and are instead using a balance forward system, just let QuickBooks continue to apply payments against the oldest invoices.

If the customer payment doesn't match the amount of any invoice, check to see whether the customer indicated a specific invoice number for the payment. If so, apply the payment against that invoice; if not, let the automatic selection of the oldest invoice stand.

Depositing Payments into Your Bank Account

If you don't see the Deposit To field in the Receive Payments window when recording payments from customers, it means your Payments Preferences setting is set to post payments automatically to the Undeposited Funds account. This is the default setting in QuickBooks and is almost always the best way to handle money you receive.

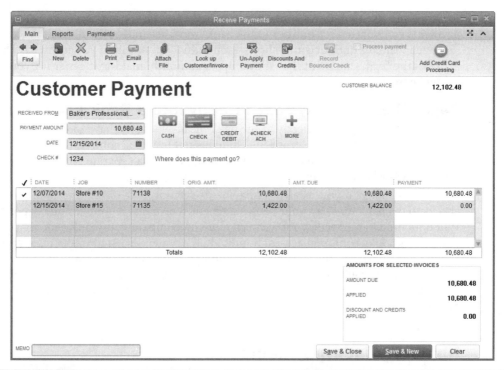

FIGURE 10-2   QuickBooks has applied the payment to an invoice that exactly matches the payment.

To confirm this, select Edit | Preferences | Payments and look on the Company Preferences tab.

If you decide to change this setting, you'll use the Deposit To field in the Receive Payments window to select an account for depositing the payments. You can select a bank account or select the Undeposited Funds account. Read the following two sections carefully before deciding which setting is the best for you.

Depositing Cash Receipts into the Undeposited Funds Account

When you enable the automatic use of the Undeposited Funds account (or manually select that account in the transaction window), each payment you receive is entered into the account named Undeposited Funds (QuickBooks establishes this account automatically). It's an account type of Other Current Asset.

When you finish applying customer payments in QuickBooks, and you're ready to make your bank deposit, you move the money from the Undeposited Funds account into a bank account by choosing Banking | Make Deposits from the menu bar. (See the section "Recording Bank Deposits from the Undeposited Funds Account" later in this chapter for the rest of the details.)

While the bank account shows only the total amount of each bank deposit (the payments you selected for transfer to the bank from the Undeposited Funds account), the Undeposited Funds account shows each individual payment you received. This matches the bank statement that shows up each month, making it easier for you to reconcile the account.

Depositing Each Payment Directly into a Bank Account

Depositing each payment directly to the bank means you don't have to take the extra step of moving cash receipts from the Undeposited Funds account into the bank account. However, each payment you receive appears as a separate entry when you reconcile your bank account.

So, for instance, if you receive six payments totaling $10,450.25 and take the checks to the bank that day, your bank statement shows that amount as one deposit. When it's time to reconcile your account and you compare your bank statement to your QuickBooks bank register, each individual payment is listed in the register. When added together, these payments should all equal that same amount of $10,450.25, but you'll have to select each payment individually, mark it as cleared, and make sure it matches the bank statement. (See Chapter 13 for detailed instructions on reconciling bank accounts.)

Handling Underpayments

After you apply the customer's payment, if it isn't enough to pay off an existing invoice, the lower-left corner of the Receive Payments window displays a message that asks whether you want to leave the underpaid amount as an underpayment or write it off.

To make it easy for you to contact the customer to ask about the reason for the underpayment, QuickBooks adds a button labeled View Customer Contact Information that opens to the customer record when clicked.

If you opt to retain the underpayment, the invoice you selected for payment remains as a receivable, with a new balance (the original balance less the payment you applied). When you click Save & Close (or Save & New), QuickBooks makes the appropriate postings.

If you select the option to write off the underpayment, when you click Save & Close or Save & New, QuickBooks opens the Write Off Amount dialog so you can choose the posting account, and, if applicable, apply a class to the transaction.

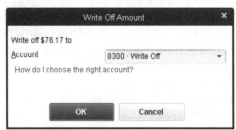

Discuss the account to use for a write-off with your accountant. You can create an Income or Expense account for this purpose, depending on the way your accountant wants to track receivables you've decided to forgive.

Applying Credits to Invoices

You can apply any existing credits to an open invoice, in addition to applying the payment that arrived. If credits exist, customers usually let you know how they want credits applied, and it's not unusual to find a note written on the copy of the invoice that the customer sent along with the check that probably represents the net due when the credit is applied.

When credits exist for the customer or job you select in the Receive Payments transaction window, QuickBooks displays the credit balance in the Available Credits field at the bottom of the window (see Figure 10-3).

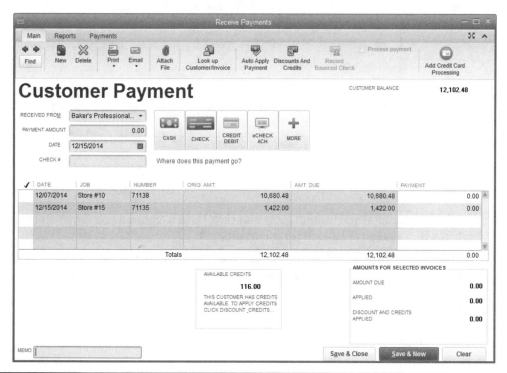

FIGURE 10-3   This customer has a credit balance that can be applied to the invoice along with the payment the customer sent.

To apply a credit balance to an invoice, click the Discount And Credits button at the top of the Receive Payments window, which opens the Discount And Credits dialog.

Select the credit(s) you want to apply and click Done. Depending on the circumstances, here's how QuickBooks handles the credits:

The Credit Total Is Equal to or Less Than the Unpaid Amount of the Oldest Invoice
This reduces the balance due on that invoice. If the customer sent a payment that reflects his net balance due (balance minus unused credits), the invoice has no remaining balance.

If applying the existing credit along with the payment doesn't pay off the invoice, the balance due on the invoice is reduced by the total of the payment and the credit.

The amount of the credit is added to the postings for the invoice. Don't worry—this change affects only the invoice balance and the accounts receivable posting; it doesn't change the amount of the payment that's posted to your bank account.

The Credit Total Is Larger Than the Amount Required to Pay Off an Invoice

If the customer payment is smaller than the amount of the invoice, but the amount of credit is larger than the amount needed to pay off the invoice, the balance of the credit remains available for posting to another invoice.

To apply the unapplied credit balance to another invoice, click Done and select the next invoice in the Receive Payments window. Then click the Discount And Credits button and apply the credit balance (or as much of it as you need) against the invoice. Any unused credits remain for the future.

You should send a statement to the customer to reflect the current, new invoice balances as a result of applying the payments and the credits to make sure your records and your customer's records match.

Applying Credits to a Different Job

You may encounter a situation in which a customer has already paid the invoices for a job when the credit is created or has paid for part of the job, exceeding the amount of the credit. If the customer tells you to apply the entire credit balance to another job or to float the credit and apply it against the next job, open the credit transaction and change the job (because a credit can be applied to an invoice for that same job only). Then apply the credit to an invoice for the job you specified, or tell QuickBooks to retain it as an available credit that you'll apply when payment arrives.

Applying Discounts for On-Time Payments

If you offer your customers terms that include a discount if they pay their bills promptly (for instance, 2%10 Net30), you should apply the discount to the payment if it's applicable.

Figure 10-4 shows the Receive Payments window for a customer who has an invoice that is eligible for a discount for timely payment. QuickBooks has displayed a message that discounts are available. However, if multiple invoices are listed in the transaction window, the only clue you have to recognize an invoice with such a discount is the fact that the Disc. Date column shows the date by which the invoice must be paid to receive the discount. For invoices without discount terms, that column is blank in the Receive Payments window—in fact, if there are no invoices with available discounts for a customer, the Disc. Date column does not appear at all.

QuickBooks doesn't apply the discount automatically. Instead, you must select the invoice (unless QuickBooks automatically selected it in order to apply the payment) and click the Discount And Credits button to see the Discount And Credits dialog connected to this invoice.

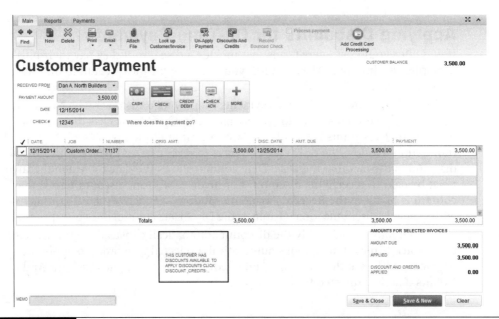

FIGURE 10-4 A discount date appears for invoices that are eligible for a discount.

If the payment arrived by the discount date, QuickBooks inserts the amount of the discount to use. Accept the amount of discount and enter a Discount Account (see "Posting Discounts to a Sales Discount Account" later in this chapter). If the payment did not arrive by the discount date, QuickBooks displays 0.00 as the discount amount, which can be changed at your discretion. Click Done to return to the Receive Payments window. You'll see that QuickBooks has added a discount column and displayed the discount amount in that column. If the net amount and the customer payment amount are the same, the invoice is now paid off.

Applying Discounts for Untimely Payments

Sometimes customers expect to take the discount even if the payment arrives after the discount date. You can apply the payment to the invoice and leave a balance due for the discount amount deducted by the customer. Or, as a goodwill gesture, you can give the customer the discount even though the payment is late.

When you click the Discount And Credits button in that case, QuickBooks does not automatically fill in the discount amount, because the discount period has now passed. To preserve your goodwill with that customer, simply enter the amount of the discount manually, select the posting account, and then click Done to apply the discount to the invoice.

Posting Discounts to a Sales Discount Account

You should create a specific account in your chart of accounts to track the discount amounts you allow your customers to take. You could post the amounts taken to your regular sales account, which would have the effect of reducing the total sales reported in that account. A better approach would be to create a separate account, such as "Discounts on Sales" (account type should be Income), so you can easily track the discounts you're allowing your customers to take over time.

> **C a u t i o n :** If there's an account named Discounts in the part of your chart of accounts that's devoted to expenses or cost of goods, don't use that account for your customer discounts, because it's there to track the discounts you take with your vendors.

Printing a Receipt for an Invoice Payment

You can print a receipt for an invoice payment by clicking the Print icon at the top of the Receive Payments window. Most customers don't expect printed receipts for invoice payments, but you may have a customer who requests one.

Handling Cash Sales

In QuickBooks, a *cash sale* is handled via a transaction called a Sales Receipt. When entering a sale using a Sales Receipt, the payment you take can be in the form of cash, check, e-check, or credit/debit card. This means you have no accounts receivable as a result of the transaction. Most restaurants and retail businesses that use QuickBooks use Sales Receipts to record their sales.

There are two methods for handling cash sales in QuickBooks:

- Record each cash sale as a separate record. This is useful for tracking sales of products or services to customers. It provides a way to maintain historical records about those customers in addition to tracking income and inventory.
- Record sales in batches (usually one batch for each business day). This method tracks income and inventory when you have no desire to maintain historical information about each customer that pays cash.

To record a cash sale, choose Customers | Enter Sales Receipts from the menu bar, which opens the Enter Sales Receipts window shown in Figure 10-5.

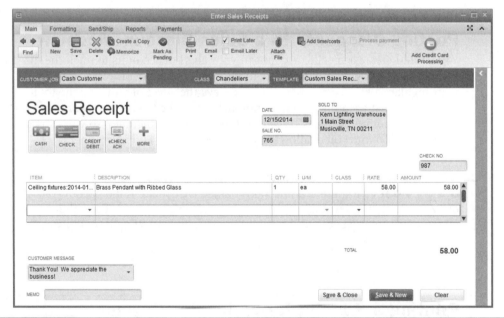

FIGURE 10-5 A Sales Receipt form is like an invoice, a receive payment form, and a printable customer receipt, all rolled into one transaction window.

➠ ProAdvisor Recommends

Is It Time for a Dedicated Point of Sale System?

If you're running a retail store, the Sales Receipt feature in QuickBooks isn't necessarily the most efficient way to handle your transactions and manage your inventory. You should consider using specialized retail software, such as QuickBooks Point of Sale, which makes it easy to process the payment at the end of a sale, tracks your inventory, and helps you better manage your cash. If you want to learn more about the QuickBooks Point of Sale product, visit the website: payments.intuit.com.

Entering Cash Sale Data

If you want to track customer information, enter a name in the Customer:Job field or select the name from the drop-down list. If the customer doesn't exist, you can add a new customer by choosing <Add New>.

If you don't want to track customers, create a customer for cash sales, such as "Cash Customer." Even if you use a generic customer name, you can still type in the actual customer name and address in the Sold To field. (You'll have to add this field to the default Sales Receipt template—see Chapter 24 to learn more about customizing transaction templates.) In the future, you can run the Sales by Ship To Address Report (Reports | Sales | Sales By Ship To Address) to view a report that shows the transactions for this generic "cash sale" customer that includes the information you've entered in the Sold To field. You can use this report for this purpose, because behind the scenes QuickBooks tracks Sold To and Ship To as the same field type.

Use the payment buttons (as shown in Figure 10-5) on the Sales Receipt form to indicate the type of payment being received. From there, the Enter Sales Receipts window works exactly the way it works for invoices and payments—just fill in the information. To save the record, click the Save button on the Main tab of the Enter Sales Receipts ribbon bar. You can also select Save & New to open a new blank record or click Save & Close if you're finished.

> **ProAdvisor Tip:** Some fields are missing from the default QuickBooks cash receipts template (named Custom Sales Receipt) that you might find useful when recording a cash sale. For example, there's no place for a sales rep, which is needed if you're paying commissions on cash sales or you just want to track the person who made the sale. There's also no Ship To address if the customer pays cash and wants delivery, nor is there a Ship Via field. You can learn more about customizing templates in general in Chapter 24.

Handling Batches of Cash Sales

If you operate a restaurant, you can batch and enter your cash transactions on a daily basis. This works only if you don't care about maintaining information about the customers and no customer expects a printed receipt from QuickBooks. This technique also works if you have a business in which sales and service personnel return to the office each day with customer payments in hand.

Create a customized template using the steps described in Chapter 24, with the following guidelines:

- Name the template, for example, "Batch Sales."
- On the Header tab, keep only the Date and Sale Number fields in the header part of the template.
- On the Columns tab, deselect all the optional fields, leaving only the Item, Description, and Amount columns selected.
- On the Footer tab, remove the Message field.

To batch-process cash sales, use the new template just described with the following procedures:

- Use a customer named "Cash" or "DailySales."
- Create a Service type or Other Charge type item called "Daily Sales."
- In the line item section of the Sales Receipt, you can either use a separate line for each sale that day or enter the item once to capture the total for the day.
- Click the Save & Close button at the end of the day. If you need to close the window during the day, you can reopen the Sales Receipt window and click the Previous button to find that day's receipt and add to it as needed.

Tracking Your Cash Drawer in QuickBooks

If you deal in real cash, have a cash register, and are not using QuickBooks Point of Sale (see "ProAdvisor Recommends: Is It Time for a Dedicated Point of Sale System?" in the previous section), consider these suggested steps for keeping track of your cash drawer.

There are two basic ways to track receipts from cash sales separate from customer payments; choose the one that best suits your needs:

- Post the cash receipts to the Undeposited Funds account but deposit those funds separately from noncash payments when you work in the QuickBooks Payments To Deposit window.
- Post the cash receipts directly to a new bank account called "Cash in Drawer" (or something similar). Then, when you empty the drawer and deposit the cash into your bank account, you can record it in QuickBooks by making a Transfer (Banking | Transfer Funds) from the cash drawer account into the appropriate bank account.

The advantage of having a Cash in Drawer account is that you can match the contents of the physical till of your cash register to an account in QuickBooks. In a perfect world, you'll open the register for the Cash in Drawer account in QuickBooks and see that it matches your actual drawer count. The world isn't perfect, however, and sometimes the two amounts will not be equal. To resolve this, refer to the next section, "Handling the Over and Short Problem."

Handling the Over and Short Problem

If you literally take cash for cash sales, when you count the money in the till at the end of the day, you may find that the sales total recorded doesn't match the cash you expected to find in the till. Or you may find that the money you posted to deposit to the bank doesn't match the amount of money you put into the little brown bag you took to the bank.

One of the problems you face is how to handle this in QuickBooks. If you post $100.00 in cash sales but have only $99.50 in cash to take to the bank, how do you handle the missing 50 cents? You can't just post $100.00 to your bank account (well, you could, but your bank account won't reconcile).

You can easily account for the over/short dilemma in your bookkeeping procedures. In many cases, by the way, the Overs and Shorts balance out—short one day, over another.

Creating Over and Short Accounts

To track over/short, you need to have some place to post the discrepancies, which means you have to create some new accounts in your chart of accounts, as follows:

- Create an account named "Over," using the account type Income.
- Create an account named "Short," using the account type Income.

If you want to see a net number for over/short (a good idea), create three accounts. Create the parent account first and name it "Over/Short," and then make the Over and Short accounts subaccounts of the parent account. If you use account numbers, make the three numbers sequential—for instance:

- Over/Short (parent account)
- Over (subaccount)
- Short (subaccount)

Creating Over and Short Items

If you track cash sales by tracking batches of sales in a Sales Receipt transaction, you need items for your overages and shortages (in QuickBooks, you need items for everything that's connected with entering sales data in a transaction window). Create items for overages and shortages as follows:

- Create two Other Charge items, one named "Overage," the other named "Shortage."
- Don't assign a price.
- Make the items nontaxable.
- Link each item to the appropriate account (or subaccount) that you just created for Over/Short.

Now that you have the necessary accounts and items, use the Over and Short items right in the Enter Sales Receipts window to adjust the difference between the amount of money you've accumulated in the cash-sale transactions and the amount of money you're actually depositing to the bank. It's your last transaction of the day. Remember to use a minus sign before the figure when you use the Short item.

Recording Bank Deposits from the Undeposited Funds Account

When you receive a customer payment or save a Sales Receipt, by default, QuickBooks posts the offsetting total on that receipt to the Undeposited Funds account. Then when it's time to go to the bank, you have to tell QuickBooks about your bank deposit.

Choosing the Payments to Deposit

As you've been completing the receive payment and cash sales forms, QuickBooks has been keeping a list of these transactions in the Undeposited Funds account. These transactions remain in Undeposited Funds until you clear them by depositing them into your bank account.

To tell QuickBooks about the details of your bank deposit, choose Banking | Make Deposits from the menu bar, which brings up the Payments To Deposit window, shown in Figure 10-6.

ProAdvisor Tip: You may have other deposits to make, perhaps refunds, loan proceeds, capital infusion, or some other type of deposit. Don't worry—you can tell QuickBooks about them in the next transaction window. This window is displaying only the payments you've entered into QuickBooks through customer-based transaction windows.

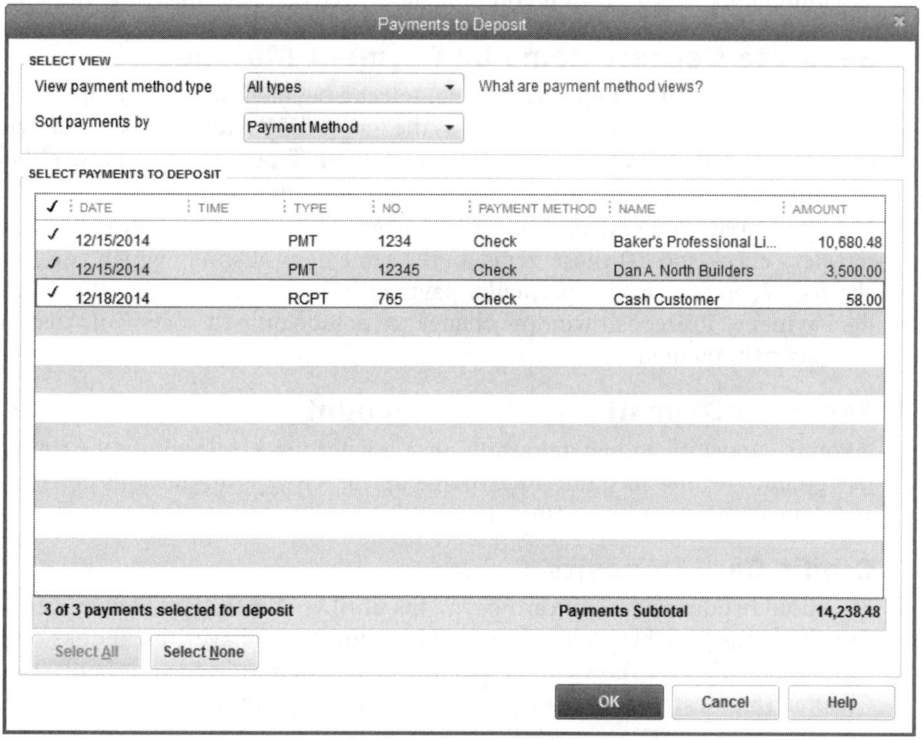

FIGURE 10-6 All the income you've collected since the last bank deposit is waiting to be deposited.

Notice the following about the Payments To Deposit window:

- The Type column displays information about the payment type for each transaction—PMT for payment of an invoice and RCPT for a cash sale (as shown in Figure 10-6).
- The Payment Method column displays the specific payment method for each transaction, such as cash, check, a specific credit card, and so on.

This information is important because you should match it to the way your bank records deposits; otherwise, bank reconciliation becomes much more complicated.

For example, your bank probably lists credit card deposits separately from a deposit total for cash and checks, even if all the money was deposited the same day. That's because your credit card deposits are probably made directly to your bank account by your merchant account bank.

Select Deposit Items

If you have only a few transactions to deposit, select those you just deposited (when you went to the bank) by clicking their listings to place a check mark in the left column. Click Select All if you took all the payments to the bank for deposit.

Separate Deposit Items by Payment Method

If you have to separate deposits by type, select a payment method from the View Payment Method Type drop-down list at the top of the Payments To Deposit window. Choose Selected Types to open the Select Payment Types list and choose either individual or multiple payment types to include in the same deposit.

For example, you may use the Other category to signify a money order or a traveler's check and list those items on the same deposit slip in which you listed checks. When you select a particular payment method from the list, the listings on the Payments To Deposit window change to include only the payments that match that payment method.

Separate Deposits by Bank Account

If you're depositing money into multiple bank accounts, select only the transactions that go into the first account. After you complete the deposit, start this process again and deposit the remaining transactions into the other account(s).

Credit Card Deposits

You shouldn't deposit credit card payments until your merchant bank notifies you that the funds have been placed in your account. If you have QuickBooks online banking, the deposit shows up in the downloaded report from your bank (see Chapter 16 to learn about managing online banking transactions).

- If you have online access to your merchant card account, the transfer will appear on the activities report on the bank's website.

- If you don't have any form of online access, you'll have to wait for the monthly statement to arrive (or contact the bank periodically to see if anything showed up in your account).

If your merchant bank deducts fees before transferring funds, learn how to deposit the net amount in the section "Calculating Merchant Card Fees," later in this chapter.

Working in the Make Deposits Window

After you select the appropriate payment method (or select all payments), click OK in the Payments To Deposit window to bring up the Make Deposits window shown in Figure 10-7.

Select the bank account you're using for this deposit. Then make sure the date matches the day you physically deposit the money.

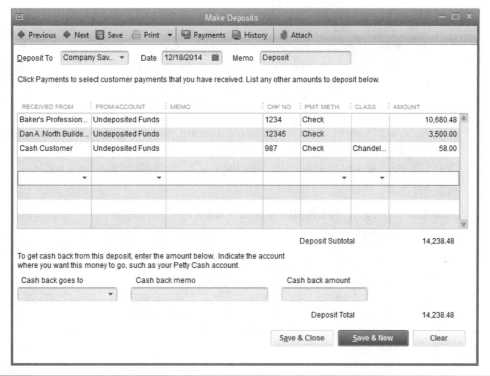

FIGURE 10-7   The Make Deposits form looks a lot like a bank deposit slip.

Adding Items to the Deposit

If you want to add deposit items that weren't in the Payments To Deposit window, click anywhere in the Received From column to make it accessible and select an existing name by clicking the arrow, or click <Add New> to enter a name that isn't in your system. If the source of the check is any entity that isn't a customer or vendor (perhaps you're depositing your own check to put additional capital into the company, or you have a check representing a bank loan), you can either skip the Received From column or add the name to the Other Names List. (If you don't need to track the entity as a customer or vendor, it's fine to skip the name.)

Press TAB to move to the From Account column and enter the account to which you're posting this transaction. Here are examples and basic instructions on how to enter the most common deposits (that are not customer payments):

- If the check you're depositing represents a bank loan, use the liability account for that bank loan (you can create it here by choosing <Add New> if you didn't think to set up the account earlier). The bank should be in your Vendors list, because you have to write checks to repay the loan.
- If the check you're depositing represents an infusion of capital from you, use the owner's capital account in the Equity section of your chart of accounts.
- If the check is a refund for an expense (perhaps you overpaid someone, and they're returning money to you), use the vendor's name and post the deposit to the same expense account you used for the original transaction.
- If the check is a rebate from a manufacturer instead of the vendor, skip the Received From column and post the amount to the original expense account you used when you purchased the item.
- Use the TAB key to move through the rest of the columns, which are self-explanatory.

Calculating Merchant Card Fees

If your merchant card bank deposits the gross amount of each transaction and charges your bank account for the total fees due at the end of the month, you don't have to do anything special to deposit credit card payments. You can deal with the fees when your bank statement arrives by entering the fee directly in the bank account register, posting the amount to the merchant card fee expense account.

If your merchant card bank deducts fees from transactions and deposits the net proceeds to your account, it takes a few extra steps to track credit card transactions and deposit the correct amount.

1. Select the credit card transactions in the Payments To Deposit window—these are gross amounts, representing the sales price you charged (and the customer paid). Then click OK to move the payments to the Make Deposits window.

2. In the first empty line below the transactions that were transferred to the Make Deposits window, click the From Account column and select the account to which you post merchant card fees.

3. Move to the Amount column and enter the fee as a negative number. Now, the net matches the amount that the merchant card company deposited in your bank account, and your merchant card expense has been posted to the general ledger.

> **ProAdvisor Tip:** Using the QuickBooks Merchant Service can make it easier to track and account for customer credit card payments. With this service, your customer's credit card charges are processed directly through QuickBooks and you can download the fees directly into your check register. They appear the way they do in your bank statement, which can prevent data entry errors and reduce the time it takes to reconcile your bank account. Learn more about Intuit's Merchant Service options at www.payments.intuit.com.

Getting Cash Back from Deposits

If you're getting cash back from your deposit, you can tell QuickBooks about it directly on the Make Deposits window, instead of making a journal entry to adjust the total of collected payments against the total of the bank deposit.

Enter the account to which you're posting the cash (usually a petty cash or draw account), and then enter the amount of cash you want to get back from this deposit. Even though you can put the cash in your pocket, you should account for it. As you spend the cash for business expenses, you can post the expenses directly in the same petty cash account register.

Printing Deposit Slips

If you want to print a deposit slip or a deposit summary, click the Print button at the top of the Make Deposits window. QuickBooks asks whether you want to print a deposit slip and summary or just a deposit summary.

If you want to print a deposit slip that your bank will accept, you must order printable deposit slips from QuickBooks. The QuickBooks deposit slips are guaranteed to be acceptable to your bank. You must have a laser printer or inkjet printer to use them. When you print the deposit slip, a tear-off section at the bottom of the page has a deposit summary. Keep that section for your own records and take the rest of the page to the bank along with your money.

If you don't have QuickBooks deposit slips, select Deposit Summary Only and fill out your bank deposit slip manually. Be sure to fill out the payment method field (cash or check), or QuickBooks won't print the deposit slip. A Print Lists dialog appears so you can change printers, adjust margins, and even print in color. Choose Print to send the deposit information to the printer. When you return to the Make Deposits window, click Save & Close to save the deposit.

Keeping Track of Accounts Receivable

Collecting the money owed to you is likely one of your most important tasks when running a business. You have to track what's owed and who owes it, and then devote time and effort to collect it. QuickBooks offers several tools and reports that give you what you need to manage your Accounts Receivable efficiently.

Getting the Most from the Customer Center

In Chapter 3, you were introduced to the Customer Center, where you access and work with your customers and jobs as well as view all the transactions associated with them. The Customer Center also contains links that give you quick access to accounts receivable reports and the Income Tracker, a tool that will help you keep your client balances in check.

The Income Tracker

The Income Tracker provides a comprehensive view of all the customer-related transactions you've entered into your QuickBooks file. From this list, you can review the details of any transaction by double-clicking it.

Use the Income Tracker to take follow-up action on past-due transactions or outstanding estimates, or just to send an e-mail to stay in touch with a valued customer. You can access the Income Tracker from the Customer Center.

1. Open the Customer Center by choosing Customers | Customer Center or by clicking the Customers icon on the Icon Bar.
2. Click the Income Tracker button located at the top of the window. The Income Tracker opens, displaying all of your customer's transactions.

At the top of the Income Tracker window, you'll find totals for Unbilled (open) estimates, Unpaid invoices, Overdue invoices, and Paid receipts received in the last 30 days. Clicking the boxes that contain these totals will quickly filter the list of transactions displayed below. In our example, there are two overdue invoices totaling $1547.01.

Another way to control which transactions appear in the list is by using one or all of the Customer:Job, Type, Status, or Date filters located at the top of the Income Tracker window. In addition, the list of transactions displayed can be re-sorted by clicking any one of the column headings.

Use the Select drop-down menu (in the Action column) to take an action on a specific transaction. For example, if you're ready to create an invoice for an open estimate, you can use the Select menu for that purpose. If you want to print multiple transactions at once, you can click the Batch Actions button located at the bottom of the window. Maybe you want to create a new sales-related transaction while working in the Income Tracker—if so, you can click the Manage Transactions button at the bottom of the window.

The Collections Center

The Collections Center is an optional feature that has to be turned on by you. When enabled, it's located within the Customer Center. Its purpose is to help you keep track of past-due and almost past-due customer balances while giving you an easy way to send e-mail reminders to the customers that are listed there.

To enable the Collection Center feature, choose Edit | Preferences | Sales & Customers | Company Preferences | Enable Collections Center. A Collections

Center button will appear in the Customer Center. Follow these steps to open both the Customer Center and Collections Center:

1. Open the Customer Center by choosing Customers | Customer Center or by clicking the Customers icon on the Icon Bar.
2. Click the Collections Center button located at the top of the window. The Collections Center opens to the Overdue tab.

From this list, you can review the details of individual invoices in question by double-clicking an invoice. The list can also be sorted by balance or days overdue by clicking the appropriate column heading. If you've entered an e-mail address in the customer's record, you can also send a reminder e-mail to one or all of the customers on this list. Just click Select And Send Email at the top of the Overdue tab window. You'll see a yellow alert icon in the Notes/Warnings column if an e-mail address is missing. Clicking this icon allows you to add an e-mail address to the customer's record if you choose.

The Notes icon next to the customer name lets you document your collections activities or view previous entries. To see a list of customers that have upcoming invoices due, select the Almost Due tab.

Reports You Can Run from the Customer Center

You can run some key reports on individual customers right from the Customer Center. Simply highlight the customer or job and click the Reports links located in the upper-right corner of the customer information pane. The following reports are available:

- **Quick Report**   Displays all transactions related to that customer within a specified date range.
- **Open Balance**   Displays the transactions (invoices, payments, and credit memos) that make up a customer's current balance.
- **Show Estimates**   Displays all estimates created for the customer within a specified date range.
- **Customer Snapshot**   Displays a dashboard-like view of a customer's relationship with you (including what they buy, how they pay, and how long they've been doing business with you).

Running A/R Aging Reports

A/R aging reports are lists of the money owed you by your customers, and they're available in quite a few formats. They're designed for you, not for your customers. You run them whenever you need to know the extent of your receivables. Many companies run an aging report every morning, just to keep an eye on the amount of money due them on a particular day.

➠ ProAdvisor Recommends

Accounts Receivable (A/R) Totals

The total amount of A/R is the value of your A/R asset. It can be an important asset—in fact, banks give lines of credit and loans using the A/R balance as part of the collateral.

When you look at your balance sheet, the general ledger A/R balance and the total on the A/R aging report should be the same (for the same date)—not close, not almost, but exactly the same.

If your A/R account balance doesn't match your A/R report for the same date, it likely means that the A/R account balance was changed using a journal entry (versus via a transaction such as an invoice or a customer payment).

The quickest way to find a journal entry (or entries) posted directly to the A/R account is to run a Quick Report for this account. With the chart of accounts open, highlight your A/R account. Click the Reports button at the bottom of the window and select Quick Report. By default, this report will show every transaction ever posted to this account. Your job is to find journal transactions in this report, and you can do that either by sorting the report by transaction type or filtering it to show only the "journal" transactions (Chapter 26 covers customizing reports).

If you find journal transactions, they should be reviewed and either replaced with a transactional document or removed altogether. Consult with your accountant if you're not sure how to handle a particular transaction.

A couple of aging reports are available in QuickBooks, and you can also customize any built-in reports so they report data exactly the way you want it. To see an aging report, choose Reports | Customers & Receivables, and then choose either A/R Aging Summary or A/R Aging Detail (these reports are explained in the upcoming sections).

A/R Aging Summary Reports

The quickest way to see how much of the money is owed to you is current or past due is to run the A/R Aging Summary (see Figure 10-8). This report produces a listing of customer balances by aging period (such as 31–60, or 61–90 days).

A/R Aging Detail Reports

If you choose Aging Detail from the Customers & Receivables reports menu, you see a much more comprehensive report, such as the one shown in Figure 10-9. The report is not only sorted by aging period, but it also shows individual invoice, finance charge, and credit memo transactions for each aging period.

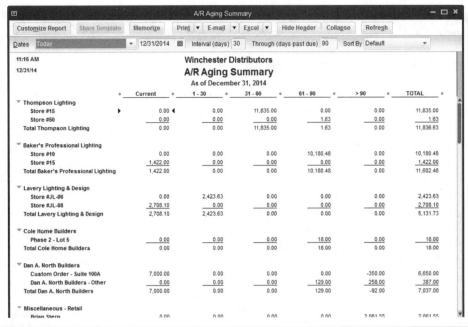

FIGURE 10-8 An A/R Aging Summary report provides totals for each customer, broken down by aging periods.

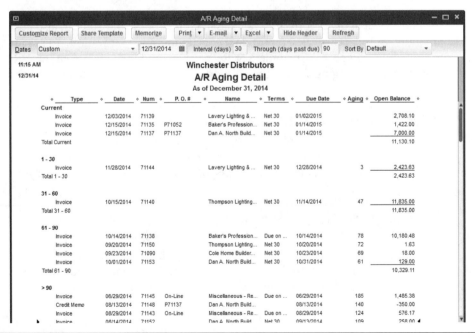

FIGURE 10-9 A/R Aging Detail reports display information about every transaction that's involved in each customer's A/R balance.

Customizing Aging Reports

If you don't need to see all of the columns in the A/R Aging Detail report, or you'd prefer to see the information displayed in a different manner, you can customize the report. Start by clicking the Customize Report button at the top of the window to open the Modify Report window shown in Figure 10-10.

Customizing the Columns

The most common customization is to get rid of any column you don't care about. For example, if you use the Classes feature but don't care about that information in your aging report, you can get rid of the column. Or you might want to get rid of the Terms column since it doesn't impact the totals. To remove a column, scroll through the Columns list and click to remove the check mark, and then click OK to accept your changes. The column disappears from the report.

While you're looking at the list of column names, you may find a column heading that's not currently selected but that contains information you'd like to include in your report. If so, click that column listing to place a check mark next to it and then click OK. The column will appear on the report and the data linked to it is displayed.

FIGURE 10-10 Customize an A/R aging report in the Modify Report window to get exactly the information you need.

FIGURE 10-11 Filters let you specify criteria for displaying data.

Filtering Information

If you want to produce an aging report for a special purpose, you can easily filter the information so it meets criteria important to you. To filter your aging report, click the Filters tab (see Figure 10-11).

Select a filter and then set the conditions for it. (Each filter has its own specific type of criteria.) For example, you can use this feature if you want to see only those customers with receivables higher than a certain figure or older than a certain aging period.

> **Caution:** If you filter the report in a way that affects the amounts, your report total will not match your A/R account balance. Use this type of filter only to get certain types of information for yourself, not for an "official" aging report.

Configuring Header/Footer Data

You can customize the text that appears in the header and footer of the report by making changes in the Header/Footer tab shown in Figure 10-12.

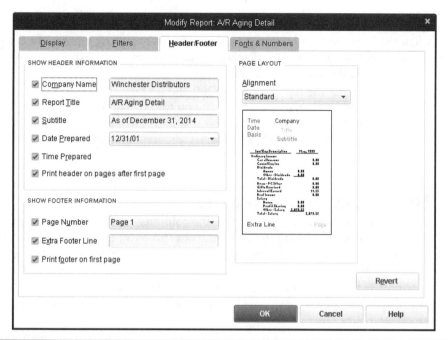

FIGURE 10-12 Specify the text you want to display on the top and bottom of the report.

You'll probably find that your decisions about the contents of the header and footer depend on whether you're viewing the report or printing it. And, if you're printing it, some stuff is more important if an outsider (a banker or your accountant) will be the recipient of the report, rather than your credit manager.

For example, the date and time of preparation is more important for outsiders than for you. Incidentally, on the Header/Footer tab, the Date Prepared field has a meaningless date—don't panic, your computer hasn't lost track of the date. That date is a format, not today's date. Click the arrow to the right of the field to see the other formats for inserting the date. The Page Number field also has a variety of formats to choose from.

You can eliminate a Header/Footer field by removing the check mark from the field's check box. For fields you want to print, you can change the text. You can also change the layout by choosing a different Alignment option from the drop-down list.

Customizing the Appearance

Click the Fonts & Numbers tab to change the format of the report. You can change the way negative numbers are displayed, and you can change the fonts for any or all of the individual elements in the report.

When you close the report window, QuickBooks may ask if you want to memorize the report with the changes you made (if you told QuickBooks to stop asking this, you won't see the message). Click Yes so you don't have to go through all the modifications again. If QuickBooks doesn't ask, memorize the report using the instructions in the next section.

Memorizing Aging Reports

If you've customized a report and have the columns, data, and formatting you need, there's no reason to reinvent the wheel the next time you need the same information. Instead of going through the customization process again next month, memorize the report as you designed it. Then you can fetch it whenever you need it.

Click the Memorize button in the report window. When the Memorize Report dialog appears, enter a new name for the report, optionally save it within a report group, and click OK.

From now on, this report name will be on the list of memorized reports you can select from when you choose Reports | Memorized Reports from the menu bar.

ProAdvisor Tip: When you use a memorized report, only the criteria and formatting is memorized. Each time you open the report, the data is generated from the QuickBooks transaction records, so you get current, accurate information.

Printing Reports

Whether you're using the standard format or one you've customized, you'll probably want to print the report. When you're in a report window, click the Print button at the top of the window and select Report to bring up the Print Reports dialog. If the report is wide, use the Margins tab to set new margins, and use the options on the Settings tab to customize other printing options. You can also use the Fit Report To options to fit all the columns or rows on your report to a page.

Running Customer and Job Reports

Customer and job reports are designed to give you information about the selected customers/jobs instead of providing information on the totals for your business. Plenty of customer reports are available from the menu that appears when you choose Reports | Customers & Receivables, including but not limited to the following:

- **Customer Balance Summary Report**   Lists the current total balance owed for each customer.
- **Customer Balance Detail Report**   Lists every transaction for each customer with a net subtotal for each customer and job.
- **Open Invoices Report**   Lists all unpaid invoices, sorted and subtotaled by customer and job.
- **Collections Report**   Includes the contact name and telephone number, along with details about invoices with balances due. With this report in hand, you're all set to call the customer and have a conversation, and you can answer any questions about invoice details.
- **Accounts Receivable Graph**   Shows a graphic representation of the accounts receivable. For a quick overview, there's nothing like a graph.
- **Unbilled Costs By Job**   Tracks job expenses that were linked to customers or jobs that you haven't yet invoiced.
- **Transaction List By Customer**   Displays individual transactions of all types for each customer.
- **Customer Contact List**   Displays an alphabetical list of customers along with the contact, telephone numbers, billing address, and current open balance for each. Give this list to the person in charge of collections.
- **Item Price List**   Lists all your items with their prices and preferred vendors.

Assessing Finance Charges

The amount of time spent tracking, analyzing, and chasing receivables can be substantial. Imposing finance charges can be a way to help offset the time and resources needed to collect past-due balances and can act as an incentive to get your customers to pay on time!

Configuring Finance Charges

Your company's finance charges are configured as part of your company preferences. It's from here that you'll establish the rate and parameters that QuickBooks uses to create a finance charge invoice for your customers with past-due balances. Choose Edit | Preferences to open the Preferences dialog. Then click the Finance Charge icon in the left pane and select the Company Preferences tab (see Figure 10-13).

Here are some guidelines for filling out this dialog:

- In the Annual Interest Rate field, replacing the default data (0.00%) with any positive number automatically enables the Finance Charges feature (the dialog has no Yes/No check box to enable or disable finance charges).
- Notice that the interest rate is annual. So, for example, if you want to charge 1.5 percent a month, enter 18% in the Annual Interest Rate field.
- You can assess a Minimum Finance Charge for overdue balances. QuickBooks will calculate the finance charge, and if it's less than the minimum, the amount will be rolled up to the minimum charge you specify here.

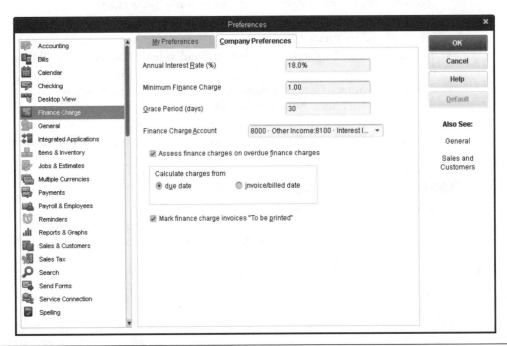

FIGURE 10-13 Configure the way in which you'll impose finance charges on overdue balances.

- Use the Grace Period field to enter the number of days of lateness you permit before finance charges are assessed.

- During setup, QuickBooks probably created an account for finance charges. If so, select it in the Finance Charge Account field. If not, enter (or create) the account you want to use to post finance charges (it's an income account).

- The issue of assessing finance charges on overdue finance charges is a sticky one. In fact, this calculation method may be illegal in your state, so check with the appropriate agency before implementing it. Selecting the Assess Finance Charges On Overdue Finance Charges option means, for example, that a customer who owed $100.00 last month and had a finance charge assessed of $2.00 now owes $102.00. As a result, the next finance charge is assessed on a balance of $102.00 (instead of on the original overdue balance of $100.00).

- In the Calculate Charges From area, specify whether to calculate the finance charge from the due date or the invoice/billed date (it's common to use the due date).

- QuickBooks creates an invoice automatically when finance charges are assessed in order to have a permanent record of the transaction. By default, these invoices aren't printed; they're just accumulated along with the overdue invoices so they'll print as a line item on a monthly statement. You can opt to have the finance charge invoices printed by adding a check mark to Mark Finance Charge Invoices "To Be Printed," which you should do only if you're planning to mail invoices to nudge your customers for payment.

Click OK to save your settings after you've filled out the Preferences window.

Assessing Finance Charges

You should assess finance charges just before you create customer statements, which is commonly a monthly chore. Choose Customers | Assess Finance Charges from the menu bar. The Assess Finance Charges window opens (see Figure 10-14) with a list of all the customers with overdue balances.

If you have any customers that have made payments that you haven't yet applied to an invoice, or if any customers have credits that you haven't yet applied to an invoice, an asterisk (*) appears to the left of the customer or job name. Close the Assess Finance Charges window and correct the situation, and then return to this window.

Choosing the Assessment Date

Change the Assessment Date field (which displays the current date) to the date on which you actually want to impose the charge—this date appears on customer statements. It's common to assess finance charges on the last day of the month. When you press TAB to move out of the date field, the finance charges are recalculated to reflect the new date.

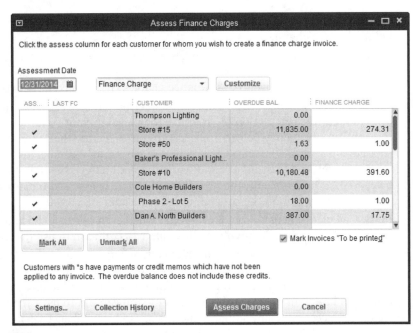

FIGURE 10-14 QuickBooks automatically assesses finance charges as of the assessment date you specify.

Selecting the Customers

You can eliminate a customer from the process by clicking in the Assess column to remove the check mark. QuickBooks does not have a finance charge assessment option on each customer record, so all customers with overdue balances are included when you assess finance charges. This means you have to know off the top of your head which customers are liable for finance charges and which aren't—or you have to keep a list near your desk.

It can be time consuming to deselect each customer, so if you have only a few customers for whom you reserve this process, choose Unmark All, and then reselect the customers you want to include.

Changing the Amounts

You can change the calculated total if you wish (a good idea if there are credit memos floating around that you're not ready to apply against any invoices). Just click the amount displayed in the Finance Charge column to activate that column for that customer. Then enter a new finance charge amount. If you need to calculate the new figure (perhaps you're giving credit for a floating credit memo), press the equal sign (=) on your keyboard to use the QuickBooks built-in calculator.

Checking the History

To make sure you don't assess a charge that isn't really due (or fair), you can double-check by viewing a customer's history from the Assess Finance Charges window. Highlight a customer listing and click the Collection History button to see a Collections Report for the selected customer (see Figure 10-15). Your mouse pointer turns into a magnifying glass with the letter "z" (for "zoom") in it when you position it over a line item. Double-click any line item to display the original transaction window if you need to examine the details.

Saving the Finance Charge Invoices

If you're sure all the calculations and figures are correct, click Assess Charges in the Assess Finance Charges window. When you create your customer statements, the finance charges will appear. If you've opted to skip printing the finance charge assessments as invoices, there's nothing more to do. If you're printing the finance charges, see the next paragraph.

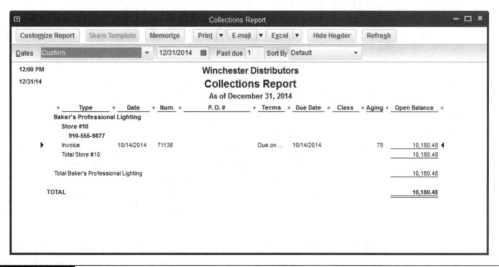

FIGURE 10-15 You can check a customer's history to make sure the finance charges are legitimate and fair.

Selecting Printing Options

If you want to print the finance charge invoices, be sure to select the Mark Invoices "To Be Printed" check box on the Assess Finance Charges window. You can send the printed copies to your customers as a nagging reminder. If you only care about having the finance charge on the monthly statement (the common method for most businesses), deselect the printing option.

To print the finance charge invoices, choose File | Print Forms | Invoices. The list of unprinted invoices appears, and unless you have regular invoices you didn't print yet, the list includes only the finance charge invoices. If the list is correct, click OK to continue on to the printing process.

Sending Statements

On a periodic basis, you should send statements to your customers. (Most businesses send statements monthly.) They serve a couple of purposes: they remind customers of outstanding balances, and they provide detailed documentation of your records, which your customers can match against their own records.

If you're coming to QuickBooks from a manual system or a system in which you tracked invoices and payments in a spreadsheet, these statements will seem like a miraculous tool. Creating statements from customer cards maintained manually in a word processing document or in a spreadsheet is a nightmare. As a result, companies without real accounting software generally don't even bother to try.

Entering Statement Charges

Before creating statements, you should create any transactions that should appear on the statements. Invoices and payments appear automatically, but you may want to add statement charges. A *statement charge* is a charge you want to pass on to a customer for which you don't create an invoice. You can use statement charges for special charges for certain customers, such as a general overhead charge, or a charge you apply for your own out-of-pocket expenses (instead of using the reimbursable expenses feature for expenses incurred on behalf of the customer). Some companies use statement charges instead of invoices for invoicing regular retainer payments.

You must add statement charges before you create the statements (or else the charges won't show up on the statements). Statement charges use items from your Item List, but you cannot use any of the following types of items:

- Items that are taxable, because the statement charge can't apply the tax
- Items that have percentage discounts (instead of discounts with specific amounts), because the statement charge can't look up the discount percentage (and therefore can't apply it)
- Items that represent a payment transaction, because those are negative charges, which a statement charge doesn't understand

Statement charges are recorded directly in a customer's register or in the register for a specific job. To create a statement charge, choose Customers | Enter Statement Charges from the menu bar to open the customer register, which looks like Figure 10-16. By default, QuickBooks opens the register for the first customer in your Customers & Jobs List; you can use the drop-down list at the top of the window to select a different customer. Then follow these steps to add statement charges (use the TAB key to move through the register's fields):

1. Select the appropriate customer or job from the drop-down list in the Customer:Job field at the top of the register.
2. Enter the date on which the statement charge is being assessed.
3. In the Item field, select the item for the statement charge from the drop-down list.
4. Enter a quantity in the Qty field if the item is invoiced by quantity.
5. Enter a rate (or accept the default rate if one exists) if you're using the Qty field.
6. Enter the amount charged if the Qty and Rate fields aren't used (if they are, the total amount is entered automatically).
7. Optionally, edit the item description.
8. Optionally, enter the billed date, which does not have to match the transaction date in the first column of the register. Postdating or predating this field determines which statement it appears on.
9. Optionally, enter the due date, which affects your aging reports and your finance charge calculations.
10. When all the fields you want to use are filled in, click Record to save the transaction.

Continue to select customers and/or jobs to enter additional statement charges.

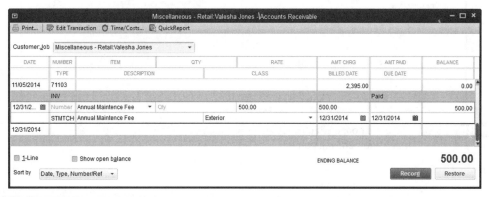

FIGURE 10-16 Statement charges are entered directly in a customer or job register.

Creating Statements

Before you start creating your statements, be sure that all the transactions that should be included on the statements have been entered into the system. Did you forget anything? Applying credit memos? Applying payments? Assessing finance charges? Entering statement charges?

When all customer accounts are up-to-date, choose Customers | Create Statements to open the Create Statements dialog, shown in Figure 10-17.

Selecting the Date Range

The Statement Period determines which transactions appear on the statement. The printed statement displays the previous balance (the total due before the From date) and includes all transactions that were created within the date range specified for that Statement Period. The starting date should be the day after the last date of your last statement run. If you send monthly statements, choose the first and last days of the current month; if you send statements quarterly, enter the first and last dates of the current quarter—and so on.

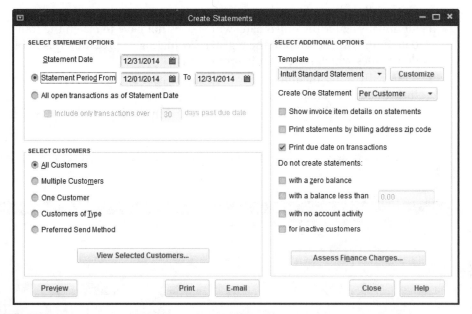

FIGURE 10-17 You can choose which customers will receive a statement and what information that statement will contain.

If you choose All Open Transactions As Of Statement Date, the printed statement just shows unpaid invoices and charges and unapplied credits. You can narrow the criteria by selecting the option to include only transactions overdue by a certain number of days (which you specify). However, this makes the printed statement more like a list than a standard statement.

Selecting the Customers

You can send statements to all or some of your customers. If you want to send statements only to a select group of customers, click the Multiple Customers option to display a Choose button next to the option. Click the Choose button to bring up a list of customers, and then select each customer you want to include. You can manually select each customer, or select Automatic and then enter text to tell QuickBooks to match that text against all customer names and select the matching customers. (The Automatic match option isn't efficient for multiple customers because it matches only exact text, not partial text, and therefore matches only one customer at a time.) Click OK when all the appropriate customers are selected.

If you're sending a statement to one customer only, select One Customer, and then click the arrow next to the text box to scroll through the list of your customers and select the one you want.

To send statements to customers who are designated with a specific customer type, select the Customers Of Type option, and then select the customer type you want to include from the drop-down list. This works, of course, only if you created and used customer types as part of your QuickBooks setup.

P r o A d v i s o r   T i p : If you want to send statements to certain customers only, create a customer type for statement recipients, such as "Statements." Refer to Chapter 3 to learn how to create a new customer type.

Filtering for Send Methods

If the way you send statements varies by customer (the option you selected in the Preferred Delivery Method field of the customer record), you can opt to handle your statement delivery in batches, using one delivery method per batch. To do this, select the Preferred Send Method option, and then select the send method for this batch from the drop-down list that appears:

- **E-mail**   Sends the statements by e-mail using a compatible e-mail application.
- **Mail**   Sends the statements to QuickBooks Billing Solutions, where the invoice is created with a tear-off slip that the customer can use to pay the invoice. QuickBooks mails the invoice. (Additional fees may apply.)
- **None**   Means no special handling. You print the statements, put them in envelopes, and mail them.

Specifying the Printing Options

You can specify the way you want the statements to print using the following criteria and options in the Select Additional Options section:

- You can print one statement for each customer, which lists all transactions for all that customer's jobs, or you can print a separate statement for each job.
- You can opt to show invoice item details instead of just listing the invoice on the statement. If your invoices have a lot of line items, this could make your statements very long. However, this option can speed up collections since the customer won't have to call you with questions like, "What makes up this balance?" or "What was that charge for again?" So, if customers often call you after you send less detailed statements, consider this alternative.
- Printing statements in order by ZIP code is handy if you're printing labels that are sorted by ZIP code. This option is also important if you have a bulk mail permit, because the post office requires bulk mail to be sorted by ZIP code.
- By default, the original due date for each transaction listed on the statement is displayed on the statement. If you have some reason to hide this information from your customers, QuickBooks offers the opportunity to deselect the option.

Specifying the Statements to Skip

You may want to skip statement creation for customers that meet the criteria you set in the Do Not Create Statements section of the dialog. If statements are the only documents you send to customers (you don't send the individual invoices and credits you create), selecting any of these options makes sense.

If, however, you use statements to make sure you and your customers have matching accounting records, you should create statements for all customers except inactive customers.

Last Call for Finance Charges

If you haven't assessed finance charges and you want them to appear on the statements, click the Assess Finance Charges button. The Assess Finance Charges window opens, showing customers that have been selected for finance charges.

If you've already assessed finance charges, QuickBooks will warn you (when you click the Assess Charges button) that finance charges have already been assessed as of the selected date. If you ignore the message, another round of finance charges is imposed (and you'll have a lot of angry and distrustful customers). Therefore, this window is useful only if you don't assess finance charges as described earlier in this chapter.

Previewing the Statements

Before you commit the statements to paper, you can click the Preview button to get an advance look. This is not just to see what the printed output will look like; it's also a way to look at the selected customer records and to make sure that all the customers you selected are included.

Use the Zoom In button to see the statement and its contents close up. Click the Next Page button to move through all the statements. Click Close to return to the Create Statements window.

Printing the Statements

When everything is just the way it should be, print the statements by clicking the Print button in the Create Statements window. The Print Statements window opens. Here, you can designate the printer you want to use and adjust printer settings.

If you want to first take a look at what will be sent to the printer, click the Preview button. If you like what you see, you can select Print from this window. Keep in mind that clicking the Print button from the Preview window will send the entire statement print job to the default printer (with no additional opportunity to change the print settings).

Customizing Statements

You don't have to use the standard statement form—you can design your own. The instructions for creating a template with customized fields and columns are in Chapter 24. If you want to create a customized template for statements, think about adding the Terms field to the statement (which is not selected by default). It doesn't seem fair to tell a customer of amounts past due without reminding the customer of the terms.

Tracking and Paying Your Bills

Chapter 11

In *this chapter:*

- Enter bills from your vendors

- Use purchase orders

- Receive inventory purchases

- Enter credit memos from your vendors

- Use the Memorize feature to enter recurring bills

- Track reimbursable expenses

- Pay your bills

- Write a check without entering a bill first

- Track and pay sales tax

There are two ways to pay your vendors in QuickBooks: You can enter the bill you receive from them into QuickBooks and then pay it later, or you can simply write a check without entering a bill. This chapter covers the process of entering and paying bills and also shows you how to link expenses on those bills to customers, so you can later send an invoice to the customer to be reimbursed for the expense. The process of writing a check to a vendor without entering a bill first is covered in this chapter, too.

Entering your bills into QuickBooks and then paying them in separate transactions is called *accrual accounting*. That means an expense is recognized by QuickBooks when you enter the bill, not when you actually pay the bill. Your Accounts Payable account should always equal the total of unpaid bills in your company file.

However, if your taxes are filed on a cash basis—where an expense isn't recognized until you actually *pay* the bill—be assured that QuickBooks understands how to report your financial picture on a cash basis.

Record Vendor Bills

To enter your bills, choose Vendors | Enter Bills from the menu bar. When the Enter Bills window opens (see Figure 11-1), fill out as much information as you can from the bill you've just received.

ProAdvisor Tip: If you're using multiple currencies, the Amount Due field uses the currency of the vendor you select, along with the appropriate amount in your currency (the multiple currencies feature covered in Appendix B).

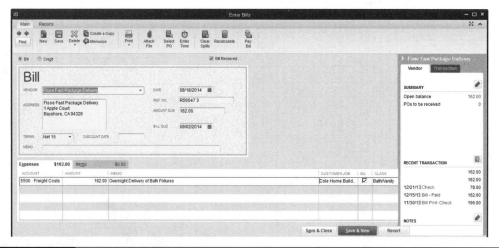

FIGURE 11-1 The Enter Bills window has four distinct areas.

The window has four distinct areas: the ribbon bar at the top, where you'll find tabs and buttons for most bill payment tasks; the form section, which contains information about the vendor and the bill; the details section (at the bottom), in which you record the data related to your general ledger accounts; and a History pane on the right-hand side of the form. When you create a new bill for a vendor that you've done business with before, this pane will be filled with information about them, including their most recent transactions. To close this pane, simply click the arrow at the top-left corner.

The details area of the Enter Bills window has two tabs: Expenses and Items. In this section, bills that are posted directly to an Expense account are covered; assigning items to a bill is covered a bit later in this chapter with the discussion of handling the purchase of inventory items.

> **ProAdvisor Tip:** An A/P Account field (and accompanying drop-down list) appears at the top of the Enter Bills window only if you have multiple Accounts Payable accounts. For example, some manufacturers and distributors separate payables for overhead expenses from payables to suppliers of inventory parts (usually called Accounts Payable—Trade).

Depending on the bill, you may be able to assign the entire bill to one expense account, or you may need to split the bill among multiple expense accounts. For example, your utility bills are usually posted to a single utility account (electric, heat, and so on). However, credit card bills may need to be split among numerous expense accounts, while loan payments are split between interest and principal.

Filling in the Details

In the Vendor field, click the arrow to choose the vendor from the list that appears. If the vendor isn't on the list, choose <Add New> to add this vendor to your QuickBooks Vendors list. Then fill out the rest of the Enter Bills window as follows:

1. In the Date field, enter the bill date. The due date then fills in automatically in the Bill Due field, depending on the terms you have with this vendor.
2. Enter the vendor's invoice number in the Ref. No. field.
3. Enter the amount of the bill in the Amount Due field.
4. In the Terms field, if the displayed data doesn't reflect your terms with this vendor, click the arrow to display a list of terms and select the one you need. If the terms you have with this vendor aren't available, choose <Add New> to create a new Terms entry. The Bill Due date changes to reflect the terms.

5. To enter the expense account information, click in the Account column on the Expenses tab, and then click the arrow to display your chart of accounts. Select the account to which this bill should be posted. QuickBooks automatically assigns the amount you entered in the Amount Due field to the Amount column. (See Chapter 4 to learn how to configure vendors so the posting account is automatically filled in.)

6. If you wish, enter a note in the Memo column.

7. In the Customer:Job column, enter a customer or job if you're paying a bill that you want to track for job costing, or if this bill is a reimbursable expense. If you do select a Customer, you'll see a check box that includes a check mark in the Billable column. You can uncheck the box with a mouse click to make the expense nonbillable while still keeping it associated with that customer for job costing purposes. (You'll read more about tracking and charging customers for reimbursable expenses later in this chapter and in Chapter 9.)

8. If you're tracking classes, a Class column appears; enter the appropriate class.

9. When you're finished, click Save & New to save this bill and bring up another blank Enter Bills window. When you've entered all your bills, click Save & Close.

ProAdvisor Tip: If you don't set up terms for a vendor, the due date is automatically filled out using the default number of days for paying bills. QuickBooks sets this default at ten days, but you can change the default by choosing Edit | Preferences and going to the Company Preferences tab of the Bills category.

Splitting Expenses Among Multiple Accounts

Some bills aren't neatly assigned to one account in your general ledger; instead, they're split among multiple accounts. The most common examples are a loan repayment where you post the interest to your Interest expense account and the principal to the liability account for the loan, or a credit card bill that covers multiple categories of expenses (see Figure 11-2). Learn more about your options for tracking credit card expenses in Chapter 12.

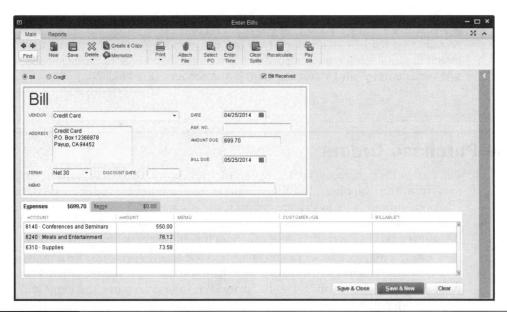

FIGURE 11-2 QuickBooks keeps recalculating, so the last account posting entry automatically has the correct amount.

Entering a vendor bill with split expenses is basically the same as entering a vendor bill that's assigned to one expense, until you begin assigning the expense accounts and amounts in the details section of the Enter Bills window. When you enter the first account in the Account column, QuickBooks automatically applies the entire amount of the bill in the Amount column. Replace that amount with the total you want to assign to the account you selected.

Then, on the next row, select the next account. As you add each additional account to the column, QuickBooks assumes that the unallocated amount is assigned to that account (see Figure 11-2). Repeat the process of changing the amount and adding another account until the total amount assigned to accounts equals the amount of the vendor bill.

> **ProAdvisor Tip:** If you don't fill in an amount for the bill in the Amount Due field, or you make a typo and the amounts in the line items don't match the total, click the Recalculate button on the ribbon bar to have QuickBooks add the line items and insert the total in the Amount Due field.

Use Purchase Orders

Purchase orders are most often used to order inventory items or manufacturing parts from your suppliers. But if you want to issue a purchase order for services or other non-inventory items that are not for resale, such as office supplies or professional services, you can create non-inventory or service items in QuickBooks and link them to an expense account (rather than an income account) for use on a PO.

Creating a purchase order has no effect on your financial records. No amounts are posted because purchase orders exist only to help you track what you've ordered against what you've received. You create the financial transactions when the items and the vendor's bill are received.

When you enable the Inventory and Purchase Order features, QuickBooks creates a nonposting account named Purchase Orders the first time you open the Create Purchase Order window. You can double-click the account's listing to view and drill down into the purchase orders you've entered, but the data in the register has no effect on your finances and doesn't appear in financial reports.

Create a Purchase Order

Use the following steps to create a purchase order:

1. Choose Vendors | Create Purchase Orders from the menu bar to open a blank Create Purchase Orders window.
2. Fill in the purchase order fields, which are easy and self-explanatory (see Figure 11-3).
3. Click Save & New to save the purchase order and move on to the next blank purchase order form, or click Save & Close if you have created all the purchase orders you need right now.

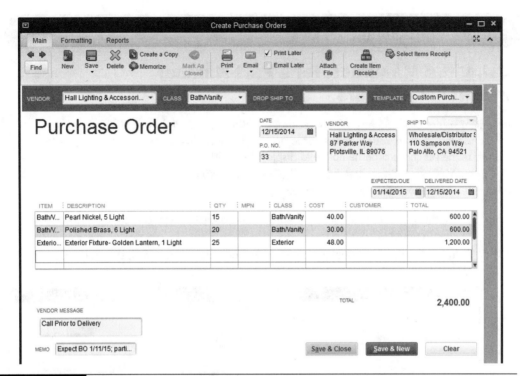

FIGURE 11-3 Creating a purchase order in QuickBooks has no effect on your financial records.

You can print the purchase orders as you complete them by clicking the Print icon on the ribbon bar in the Create Purchase Orders window. Or, if you'd prefer, you can print them all in a batch by placing a check mark next to the Print Later option on the Main tab before saving each purchase order. When you're ready to print the batch, click the arrow below the Print button and select Batch.

You can also e-mail the purchase orders as you create them, or e-mail them as a batch by selecting Batch from the drop-down list below the E-mail icon on the transaction window's Main tab.

When the items and the bill for them are received, you can use the purchase order to automate the receipt of these items (covered later in this chapter) as well as the entry of the vendor's bill.

➡ **ProAdvisor Recommends**

Using the Manufacturer's Part Number in Purchase Orders

If the item you're ordering has a manufacturer's part number (MPN) in the item record, you should use that data in your purchase order to avoid any confusion. However, you have to customize the purchase order template to display the MPN data.

Choose Vendors | Create Purchase Orders to open a PO transaction window. Then use the following steps to customize the PO template:

1. On the Formatting tab on the Create Purchase Orders window, click the Customize Data Layout button.

2. In the Additional Customization window, open the Columns tab, shown here:

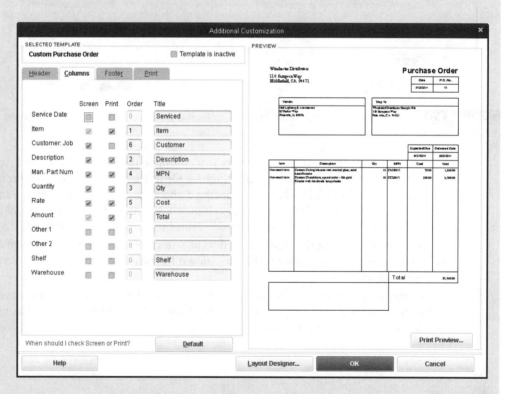

(Continued)

➤➤ ProAdvisor Recommends

3. Add the Man. Part Num field to the screen, print, or both by clicking the appropriate check boxes to add a check mark (adding the field to both the screen and print versions is best).

4. Enter the column number for this column, working from left to right across the columns. For example, entering 4 puts the MPN in the fourth column. When you press TAB, QuickBooks automatically renumbers the column order to accommodate your selection.

5. Optionally, change the text that appears as the column title. By default, the title is MPN, but you might want to change it to something like Part # or Part No.

Check the Preview pane on the right side of the dialog to make sure the layout works. QuickBooks will also prompt you if the template needs additional adjustments to the layout. Adding this column doesn't overcrowd the template, but if you previously customized the template to add columns or fields, you may have to rework your changes (see Chapter 24 to learn everything about customizing templates). If the layout looks presentable, click OK to save your changes.

Hereafter, when you create a PO for an item that has the MPN stored in its record, the data appears automatically in the MPN column.

Purchase Inventory Items

If the vendor bill you're recording is for inventory items, there are some additional factors to consider, because the accounting issues (the way you post amounts) are different. Frequently, two transactions are involved when you buy items for inventory:

- You receive the shipment first (with a packing slip).
- You receive the bill for the items that were shipped.

Sometimes the bill comes before the products, oftentimes the items arrive first, and sometimes both events occur at the same time (the bill is in an envelope pasted to the carton or included inside the carton). If you created a purchase order for these items, you can use it to automate the receiving and vendor bill entry processes when the items and the bill arrive.

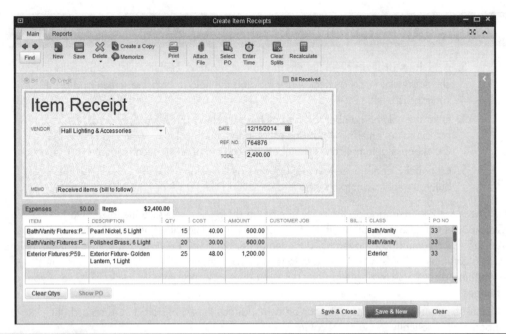

Receiving Inventory Items Without a Bill

If the inventory items arrive before you receive a bill from the vendor, you must use the Create Items Receipts window to tell QuickBooks about the new inventory. This form brings the items into inventory so they become available for resale. Use the following steps to receive inventory in this scenario:

1. Choose Vendors | Receive Items from the menu bar to open a blank Create Item Receipts window (see Figure 11-4).

2. Select the vendor name, and if open purchase orders exist for this vendor, QuickBooks notifies you:

3. If you know there isn't a purchase order for this particular shipment, click No, and just fill out the Create Item Receipts window manually.

4. If you know a purchase order exists for this shipment, or if you're not sure, click Yes. QuickBooks displays all the open purchase orders for this vendor so you can put a check mark next to the appropriate PO (or multiple POs if the shipment that arrived covers more than one PO). If no PO matching this shipment is listed on the Open Purchase Orders list for this vendor, click Cancel on the Open Purchase Orders window to return to the receipts window and fill in the data manually.

5. If a PO exists, QuickBooks fills out the Create Item Receipts window using the information in the PO. Check the shipment against the PO and change any quantities that don't match.

6. Click Save & New to receive the next shipment into inventory, or click Save & Close if this takes care of all the receipts of goods.

QuickBooks posts the amounts in the purchase order to your Accounts Payable account as an Item Receipt type. When the bill arrives with the actual costs, the Accounts Payable account will be updated accordingly and the transaction type changed to Bill. (See the "ProAdvisor Recommends: How QuickBooks Posts Inventory Receipts and Bills.")

➡ ProAdvisor Recommends

How QuickBooks Posts Inventory Receipts and Bills

Technically, an Accounts Payable liability should be connected only to a bill and not an Item Receipt (receipt of goods without a corresponding bill). In most cases, the bill you eventually receive for these goods will have the same unit cost as the Item Receipt. Sometimes, however, the cost per item listed on the Item Receipt may not be the same as the cost per item on the final bill. Whatever the reason, the bill that arrives will presumably have the correct costs, and those costs are the amounts that should be posted to the Accounts Payable account.

If this situation occurs, QuickBooks allows you to adjust the initial posting you made to A/P when you received the items, so that the new amounts match the bill. This means that on one date your Accounts Payable total and inventory valuation may show one amount, but a few days later, the amount shown is different, even though no additional transactions are displayed in reports. If the interval between those days crosses the month, or even worse, the year, your accountant might have a problem trying to figure out what happened. But now that you understand what happens, you can explain the logic behind the change.

Recording Bills for Items Already Received

After you receive the items, eventually the bill comes from the vendor. To enter the bill, do *not* use the regular Enter Bills window, which would cause another posting to Accounts Payable. Instead, do the following:

1. Choose Vendors | Enter Bill For Received Items to open the Select Item Receipt dialog.
2. Select the vendor, and you'll see the current items receipt information for that vendor.

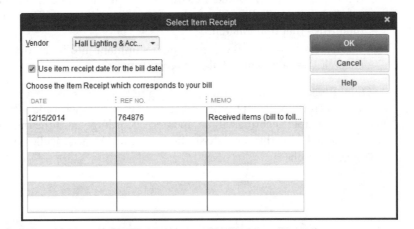

3. If you want the date of the bill to be the same as the date you received the item, place a check mark next to the Use Item Receipt Date For The Bill Date option.
4. Select the appropriate listing and click OK to open an Enter Bills window. The information from the Item Receipt is used to fill in the bill information.
5. Change anything in the Items tab that needs to be changed, such as a different cost per unit.
6. To add any shipping or handling charges, move to the Expenses tab and enter the appropriate accounts and amounts.
7. If you made any changes, you must click the Recalculate button so QuickBooks can match the total in the Amount Due field to the changed line item data.
8. Click Save & Close.

Even if you didn't make any changes and the bill matches the receipts transaction, QuickBooks displays a message asking if you're sure you want to save the changes. Click Yes. The message appears because you've changed the transaction from a receipt of goods transaction to a vendor bill transaction and QuickBooks overwrites the original postings that were made when you received the items. If you look at the Accounts Payable register (or the Inventory Assets register) after you receive the items, the transaction type is ITEM RCPT. When you save this transaction, QuickBooks overwrites the entire transaction, changing the transaction type to BILL (and also uses the new amounts if you made changes).

Receiving Items and Bills Simultaneously

If the items and the bill arrive at the same time, you can enter both into QuickBooks at the same time. To do this, choose Vendors | Receive Items And Enter Bill. The standard Enter Bills window opens, and when you enter the vendor's name you may see a message telling you an open PO exists for the vendor. The message dialog asks if you want to receive these goods (and the bill) against an open PO.

Click Yes to see the open POs for this vendor and select the appropriate PO. The line items on the bill are filled in automatically, and you can correct any quantity or price difference between your original PO and the actuals. When you save the transaction, QuickBooks receives the items into inventory in addition to posting the bill to your Accounts Payable account.

If no PO exists, enter the item quantities and amounts. When you save the transaction, QuickBooks receives the items into inventory in addition to posting the bill to Accounts Payable.

Recording Vendor Credits

If you receive a credit from a vendor and record it in QuickBooks, you can apply it against an existing open bill or keep it unapplied so you can apply it to a future bill from that vendor.

QuickBooks doesn't provide a separate Enter Credit window; instead, you can change a vendor bill form to a credit form with a click of the mouse by following these steps:

1. Choose Vendors | Enter Bills to open a blank Enter Bills window.
2. Select the Credit option near the top of the window, which automatically deselects Bill and changes the fields on the form (see Figure 11-5).
3. Choose the vendor from the drop-down list that appears when you click the arrow in the Vendor field.
4. Enter the date of the credit memo.
5. In the Ref. No. field, enter the vendor's credit memo number.
6. Enter the amount of the credit memo.
7. If the credit is not for inventory items, use the Expenses tab to assign an account and amount to this credit.

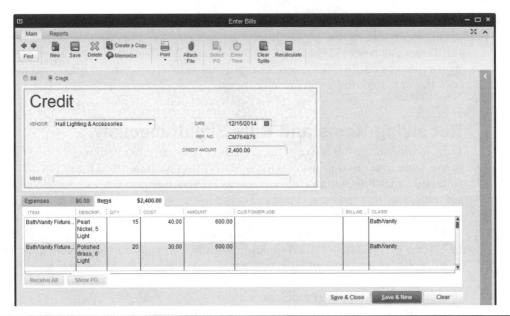

FIGURE 11-5 When you select the Credit option, the Enter Bills transaction window changes and the fields for terms and due date disappear.

8. If the credit is for inventory items, use the Items tab to enter the items, along with the quantity and cost, for which you are receiving this credit.

9. Click Save & Close to save the credit (unless you have more credits to enter—in which case, click Save & New).

ProAdvisor Tip: You can temporarily use the return authorization (RA) number you received on the telephone as the Ref. No. for your credit. This can help you keep track of when (or if) the actual credit memo is issued by the vendor. When the credit memo arrives, you can replace the QuickBooks Ref. No. with the actual credit memo number. Enter the original RA number in the Memo field for future reference in case there are any disputes.

Enter Recurring Bills

Most businesses have at least a few recurring bills that need to be paid every month. Typically, the list includes the rent or mortgage payment, loan payments, or a retainer fee (for an attorney, accountant, or subcontractor).

You can make it easy to pay those bills every month without entering a bill each time. QuickBooks provides a feature called *memorized transactions*, which you can put to work to make sure your recurring bills are covered.

Creating a Memorized Bill

To create a memorized transaction for a recurring bill, first open the Enter Bills window and fill out the information as you normally would. If the amount of a recurring bill isn't always exactly the same, it's okay to leave the Amount Due field blank. You can fill in the amount each time you use the memorized bill.

Before you save the transaction, click the Memorize button on the Enter Bills Main tab. The Memorize Transaction dialog opens. Use these guidelines to fill out the required information:

- In the Name field, enter a name for the transaction. QuickBooks automatically enters the vendor name, but you can change it. Use a name that describes the transaction so you don't have to rely on your memory.
- Select Add To My Reminders List (the default) to tell QuickBooks to issue a reminder that this bill must be put into the system to be paid.
- Select Do Not Remind Me if you want to forego getting a reminder and enter the bill yourself.
- Select Automate Transaction Entry to have QuickBooks enter this bill as a payable automatically, without reminders. Specify the number of Days In Advance To Enter this bill into the system. At the appropriate time, the bill appears in the Select Bills To Be Paid section of the Pay Bills window.
- Select the interval for this bill from the drop-down list in the How Often field.
- Enter the Next Date this bill is due.
- If this payment is finite, such as a loan that has a specific number of payments, use the Number Remaining field to specify how many times this bill must be paid.

Click OK in the Memorize Transaction dialog to save the information, and then click Save & Close in the Enter Bills window to save the bill. If you want to use the bill only to create a memorized version of it, you can cancel the transaction itself before saving it.

Caution: When you select the reminders options for the memorized bill, the reminders appear only if you're using reminders in QuickBooks. Choose Edit | Preferences and click the Reminders category icon to view or change reminders options.

Using a Memorized Bill

If you've opted to enter the memorized bill manually instead of having it automatically added to the Select Bills To Be Paid section, you must open it to make it a current payable. To open a memorized bill, use the following steps:

1. Press CTRL-T to open the Memorized Transaction List window or, from the Lists menu, select Memorized Transaction List.
2. Double-click the appropriate listing to open the bill in the usual Enter Bills window with the next due date showing.
3. If the Amount Due field is blank, fill it in.
4. Click Save & Close to save this bill so it becomes a current payable and is listed as a bill that must be paid when you write checks to pay your bills.

Creating Memorized Bill Groups

If you have a whole bunch of memorized transactions to cover all the bills that are due the first of the month (rent, mortgage, utilities, car payments), you don't have to select them for payment one at a time. You can create a group and QuickBooks will automatically take action on every bill in the group. To use this feature, follow these steps:

1. Press CTRL-T to display the Memorized Transaction List.
2. Right-click any blank spot in the Memorized Transaction window and choose New Group from the shortcut menu.
3. In the New Memorized Transaction Group window, give this group a name (such as 1st Of Month or 15th Of Month).
4. Fill out the fields to specify the way you want the bills in this group to be handled.
5. Click OK to save this group.

Adding Memorized Bills to Groups

After you create the group, you can add memorized transactions to it as follows:

1. In the Memorized Transaction List window, select the first memorized transaction you want to add to the group.
2. Right-click and choose Edit Memorized Transaction from the shortcut menu.
3. When the Schedule Memorized Transaction dialog opens with this transaction displayed, select the option named Add To Group.
4. Select the group from the list that appears when you click the arrow next to the Group Name field and click OK.

Repeat this process for each bill you want to add to the group. As you create future memorized bills, just select the Add To Group option to add each bill to the appropriate group.

If you have other recurring bills with different criteria (perhaps they're due on a different day of the month, or they're due annually), create groups for them and add the individual transactions to the group.

Reimbursable Expenses

A reimbursable expense is one that you incurred on behalf of a customer. Even though you pay the vendor bill, there's an agreement with your customer that you'll send an invoice to recover your costs. There are two common types of reimbursable expenses:

- General expenses, such as long-distance telephone charges, parking and tolls, and other incidental expenses, might be incurred on behalf of a client. Those portions of the bill that apply to customer agreements for reimbursement are split out when you enter the bill.
- Specific goods or services that are purchased on behalf of the customer.

Options for Managing Reimbursable Expenses

There are two ways to manage reimbursable expenses:

- Enter and pay a bill (or you could enter a check), and then let QuickBooks automatically post the customer's reimbursement to the same expense account selected when the bill (or check) was created. This cancels the original expense and reduces the expense total in your Profit & Loss statements, so that the expense amount reflects the net between what you paid and what you collected for reimbursement.
- Enter and pay a bill (or you could enter a check), and then let QuickBooks automatically post the customer's reimbursement to an income account that's created specifically for the purpose of tracking reimbursements. This lets you track totals for both expenses and reimbursements.

You may want to discuss these choices with your accountant. Many businesses prefer and use the second option—tracking the expenses and reimbursements separately—because it makes it easier to determine whether you've rebilled your customers correctly. The steps for this second approach are outlined in detail in the following section.

But if you prefer to reduce your expense totals by posting reimbursements to the expense account used when you entered a bill, set the Time & Expense Preference as follows:

1. Choose Edit | Preferences to open the Preferences dialog.
2. Select the Time & Expenses icon in the left pane.
3. Click the Company Preferences tab.
4. In the Invoicing Options section of the dialog, uncheck the check box next to the option Track Reimbursed Expenses As Income.
5. Click OK.

Configuring Reimbursement Tracking

To track reimbursed costs from customers, you need to enable reimbursement tracking in QuickBooks, and you must also create income accounts that are used for collecting reimbursements.

Enabling Reimbursement Tracking

To tell QuickBooks that you want to track reimbursable costs, you must enable the feature in the Preferences dialog, using the following steps:

1. Choose Edit | Preferences to open the Preferences dialog.
2. Select the Time & Expenses icon in the left pane.
3. Click the Company Preferences tab.

4. In the Invoicing Options section of the dialog, click the check box next to the Track Reimbursed Expenses As Income option to put a check mark in the box.
5. Click OK.

Applying Automatic Markups

The Time & Expenses Preferences window also has an option for setting a default markup percentage. You can use this feature to have QuickBooks automatically mark up expenses you're linking to a customer for reimbursement. Be sure to select (or create) the default account that you want to use to track the income generated by the markup. Most businesses use something like "markup income."

The default markup percentage is unrelated to the option to track reimbursed expenses as income. You can apply this markup whether you're tracking reimbursed expenses as income or posting the reimbursements to the original expense account.

You can also override any automatic markup that QuickBooks applies, so filling in a percentage in this field doesn't prevent you from setting up your own pricing formula for any individual item.

ProAdvisor Tip: The markup percentage that you designate in the Time & Expenses Preference can also be applied to the products and services that you sell. Specifically, when you enter an amount in the Cost field when you're creating a new item or editing an existing one, QuickBooks will automatically fill in the item's Price field by marking up the cost with this percentage.

Setting Up Income Accounts for Reimbursement

When you enable the reimbursement tracking option, QuickBooks adds a new field to the dialog you use when you create or edit an expense account. As you can see in Figure 11-6, you can configure an expense account so that reimbursements for the expense are posted to an income account.

Whenever you post a vendor expense to this account and also indicate that the expense is reimbursable, the amount you charge to the customer when you create an invoice for that customer is automatically posted to the income account that's linked to this expense account.

You may have numerous expense accounts that you want to use for reimbursable expenses; in fact, that's the common scenario. Portions of telephone bills, travel expenses, subcontractor expenses, and so on are frequently passed on to customers for reimbursement.

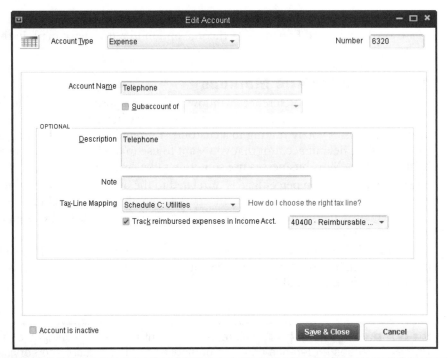

FIGURE 11-6 Configure expense accounts to post reimbursements to an income account.

The easiest way to manage all of this is to enable those expense accounts to track reimbursements and post the income from customers to one account named Reimbursed Expenses. However, QuickBooks requires a one-to-one relationship between a reimbursable expense and the reimbursement income from that expense. As a result, if you have multiple expense accounts for which you may receive reimbursement (which is fairly common), you must also create multiple income accounts for accepting reimbursed expenses.

This is a one-time chore, however, so when you've finished setting up the accounts, you can just enter transactions, knowing QuickBooks will automatically post reimbursed expenses to your new income accounts.

The best way to set up the income accounts you'll need for reimbursement is to use subaccounts, as shown next in the Chart of Accounts window. That way, your reports will show the total amount of income due to reimbursed expenses, and you have individual account totals if you have some reason to audit a total.

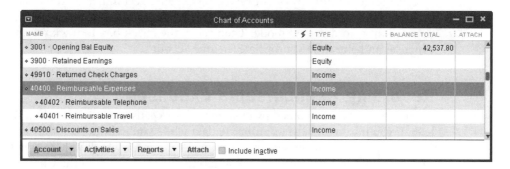

Depending on the company type you selected when you created your company file, QuickBooks may have already created a Reimbursed Expenses account in the Income section of your chart of accounts. If so, you already have a parent account, and you only have to set up subaccounts.

If you don't already have an income account named Reimbursed Expenses, follow these steps to create the parent account:

- Open the chart of accounts by pressing CTRL-A or by clicking the Chart of Accounts icon on the Home page.
- Press CTRL-N to open the Add New Account: Choose Account Type dialog.
- Select Income as the account type and click Continue.
- In the Add New Account dialog, enter an account number (if you use numbers) and name the account Reimbursed Expenses (or something similar).
- Click Save & New.

Now that you've created the parent account, you can create all the subaccounts you need, using the same steps you used to create the parent account, with the following changes:

- If you're using numbered accounts, use the next sequential number after the number you used for the parent account.
- Name the account for the type of expense you're tracking, such as Telephone Reimbursements.
- Select the Subaccount Of check box and link it to the parent account you created.

Repeat this process as many times as necessary. Your reports show the individual account postings as well as a total for all postings for the parent account.

Don't forget to edit any of your existing expense accounts that you'll use to invoice customers for reimbursements. Select the account and press CTRL-E to open the account record in Edit mode. Then select the check box to track reimbursed expenses and enter the appropriate income account.

Recording Reimbursable Expenses

If you want to be reimbursed by customers for expenses you incurred on their behalf, you must enter the appropriate data while you're filling out the vendor's bill (or writing a direct disbursement check to a vendor for which you don't enter bills). After you enter the account and the amount, click the arrow in the Customer:Job column and select the appropriate customer or job from the drop-down list (see Figure 11-7).

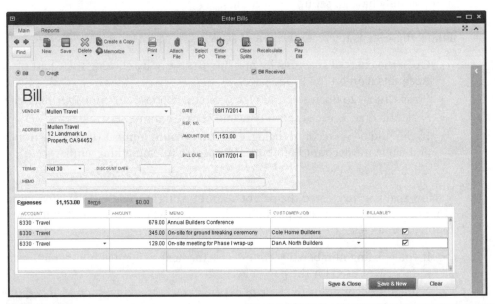

FIGURE 11-7 Charge portions of an expense to one or more customers by splitting the total expense among customers when you enter the vendor bill.

Entering data in the Customer:Job column automatically places a check box with a check mark inserted in the Billable? column. The expense is charged to the customer, and you can pass the charge along to the customer when you create an invoice (covered in Chapter 9).

ProAdvisor Tip: You can click the check box to remove the check mark if you don't want to bill the customer for the expense but you still want to track what you're spending for the customer or the job. This disables the reimbursement feature, but the expense is still associated with the customer/job so that you can track job costs.

Sometimes a vendor's bill is for an amount that's not entirely chargeable to a customer. Some of the amount may be your own responsibility, and it may also be that multiple customers owe you reimbursement for the amount. (This is often the case with telephone expenses when your customers reimburse you for long-distance charges.)

Follow these steps to create a vendor bill (or a direct disbursement check if you're not entering vendor bills) that splits expenses between you and a customer or multiple customers:

1. Select the vendor and enter the amount, date, reference number, and a memo if you wish.
2. Select the expense account, and then enter the portion of the bill that is your own responsibility.
3. In the next line, select the same account, and then enter the portion of the bill you are charging back to a customer.
4. Enter an explanation of the charge in the Memo column. When you create the invoice, the text in the Memo column is the only description the customer sees.
5. In the Customer:Job column, choose the appropriate customer or job (be sure that the Billable box next to the customer or job name is checked).
6. Optionally, assign the expense to a class.
7. Repeat steps 3 through 6 to include any additional customers for this expense account.

When you're finished, the total amount entered should match the amount on the vendor's bill.

Pay Your Bills

When it's time to pay your bills, you may find that you don't have the cash or credit available to pay every bill that's entered, or even to pay the entire amount due for each bill.

There are plenty of opinions about how to decide what to pay when money is tight, and the term "essential vendors" is used quite often. "Essential" can be a very subjective term, since having electricity can be just as important as buying inventory items. Having worked with hundreds of clients over the years, however, I can offer you these insights:

- The government (taxes) comes first.
- Never use payroll withholding money to pay bills.
- When feasible, it's better to send multiple vendors small checks than to send a large payment only to a couple of vendors who have been applying pressure. Vendors dislike being ignored much more than they dislike small payments on account.

Viewing Your Unpaid Bills

To see a list of each unpaid bill, totaled by vendor, choose Reports | Vendors & Payables | Unpaid Bills Detail. By default, the report is sorted by vendor name, but you can re-sort the list (using the drop-down list in the Sort By field) by bill date, due date, or open balance—to name just a few of the sort options. You may find that choosing to sort by Due Date or Aging is helpful in deciding which bills need urgent attention (see Figure 11-8).

Double-click any entry if you want to see the original bill you entered, including all line items and notes you made in the Memo column.

You can filter the report to display only certain bills by clicking Customize Report and selecting the Filters tab in the Modify Report dialog. Use the filters to change what's displayed in the report. For example, you might want to filter for bills that are more than a certain number of days overdue for "essential" vendors only. If you're short on cash, this type of information can help you decide who gets paid so you can work out a payment plan that will maintain good relationships with your vendors.

Selecting the Bills to Pay

When you're ready to tell QuickBooks which bills you want to pay, choose Vendors | Pay Bills. The Pay Bills window appears (see Figure 11-9), and you can make your selections

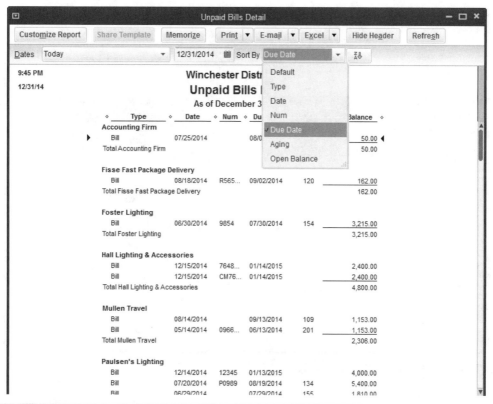

FIGURE 11-8 See the details for all your unpaid bills.

by placing a check mark next to the bills you want to pay. You can also choose which open bills to work with in this window by using the filters, as described next.

• **Due On Or Before** Selecting this option displays all the bills due on or before the date displayed. Note that the default date that's automatically inserted in this field is ten days from the current date, but you can change the date to display more or fewer bills. If you have discounts for timely payments with any vendors, this selection is more important than it seems. The due date isn't the same as the discount date. Therefore, if you have terms of 2% 10 Net 30, a bill that arrived on April 2 is due on May 2 and won't appear on the list if the due date filter you select is April 30. In this case, unfortunately, the discount date is April 12, but you won't know this because the bill won't appear. If you want to use a due date filter, go out at least 30 days. (See "ProAdvisor Recommends: Applying Discounts for Timely Payments" later in this chapter.)

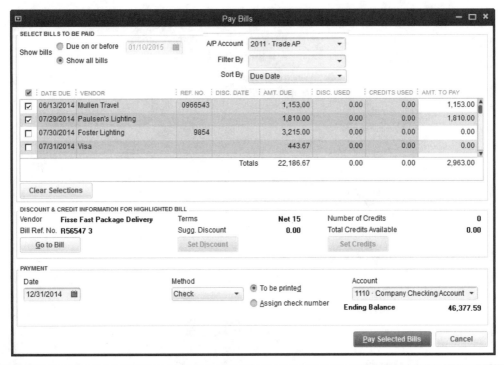

FIGURE 11-9 Paying bills starts in the Pay Bills window.

- **Show All Bills**   Shows all the bills in your system, regardless of when they're due. This is the safest option (and it's selected by default), because you won't accidentally miss a discount date. On the other hand, the list can be rather long.

- **A/P Account**   If you have multiple Accounts Payable accounts, you'll see an A/P Account drop-down menu. Select the Accounts Payable account that the bills you want to pay were originally posted to. You have to repeat this process for each of your Accounts Payable accounts. If you don't have multiple Accounts Payable accounts, this field doesn't appear in the window.

- **Filter By**   This filter lets you choose to see open bills for a particular vendor or all vendors (the default filter).

- **Sort By**   Determines the manner in which your bills are displayed in the Pay Bills window. The choices are

  - Due Date (the default)
  - Discount Date
  - Vendor
  - Amount Due

In the Payment section of the Pay Bills window are the following fields:

- **Date** This is the date that appears on your checks. By default, the current date appears in the field, but if you want to predate or postdate your checks, you can change that date. You can also tell QuickBooks to date checks on the day of printing by changing the Checking Preferences. If you merely select the bills today and wait until tomorrow (or later) to print the checks, the payment date set here still appears on the checks.
- **Method** The Method drop-down list displays the available methods of payment: Check and Credit Card are listed by default, but if you've signed up for QuickBooks online bill payment services, that payment method also appears in the list (see Chapter 16 to learn about using QuickBooks for online banking, including online bill payments).

  If you are paying by check and QuickBooks prints your checks, be sure the To Be Printed option is selected. When you finish selecting payments, click the Pay Selected Bills button, and QuickBooks opens the Payment Summary dialog, where you can choose to print the checks now or wait until later. (See Chapter 14 to learn how to set up and configure check printing.)

  If you prepare checks manually, select Assign Check Number, and when you click the Pay Selected Bills button, QuickBooks opens the Assign Check Numbers dialog so you can specify the starting check number for this bill-paying session.
- **Account** The Account drop-down list displays the checking or credit card account you want to use for these payments.

If you made changes to the selection fields (perhaps you changed the Sort By option to Discount Date), your list of bills to be paid may change. If all the bills displayed are to be paid either in full or in part, you're ready to move to the next step. If there are still some bills on the list that you're not going to pay, you can just select those you do want to pay. Selecting a bill is simple—just click the leftmost column to place a check mark in it. You can also click Select All Bills to select all of them and click the leftmost column to toggle off the check mark of any bills you don't want to pay in this bill-paying session.

Paying Bills in Full

The easiest bills to pay (if you have enough cash in the bank or credit on your credit cards) are those you want to pay in full, when none of them have credits or discounts to worry about. Select the bills, and then click Pay Selected Bills.

Making Partial Payments

If you don't want to pay a bill in full, you can easily adjust the amount by clicking the check mark column on the bill's listing to select the bill for payment. Then move to the Amt. To Pay column and replace the amount that's displayed with the amount you want to pay. When you press TAB, the total at the bottom of the column is recalculated (and QuickBooks reserves the unpaid balance for your next bill payment session).

Using Discounts and Credits

QuickBooks has a preference you can set to determine whether you make the decision about applying discounts and credits at the time you select the bill for payment or you let QuickBooks apply the amounts automatically to bills that you select for payment.

To set your default options, choose Edit | Preferences and select the Bills category in the left pane. In the Company Preferences tab, select either or both of the options Automatically Use Credits or Automatically Use Discounts and enter the account to which you want to post the discounts.

The account for the discounts you take (sometimes called *earned discounts*) can be either an income or expense account. Although there's no absolute right and wrong here, my vote would be to recognize it as a reduction in an expense—and if that expense account is a Cost Of Goods Sold account, it means you'll show a higher gross profit as a result of paying your bills promptly. So if you think of the discount as income—money you've earned by paying your bill—make the account an income account. If you think of the discount as a reverse expense—that is, money you've saved by paying your bills promptly—make the account an expense account. In this case it posts as a minus amount, which means it reduces your total expenses.

▶▶ ProAdvisor Recommends

Applying Discounts for Timely Payments

In many cases, early payment discounts are offered by those vendors from whom you buy inventory items. Consider putting the discount account in the section of your chart of accounts that holds the Cost Of Goods Sold accounts. For example, let's say you have a parent account called Cost Of Goods Sold. You can then create two subaccounts:

- Cost Of Goods
- Discounts Taken

Post only to the subaccounts (make sure your inventory items are linked to the Cost Of Goods subaccount). You'll be able to see the individual amounts on your financial reports, and the parent account (Cost of Goods Sold) will report the net COGS.

QuickBooks may have created a Cost Of Goods Sold account automatically for you during your company setup. If not, you can create it and the subaccounts now.

Applying Discounts

Bills that have terms for discounts for timely payment will have a Discount Date in the Disc. Date column. If you enabled automatic application of discounts and credits, when you select the bill by clicking the check mark column, the discount is automatically applied. You can see the amount in the Disc. Used column; the Amt. To Pay column also adjusts accordingly.

If the discount isn't applied automatically, it's probably because today's date is later than the discount cutoff date. Don't worry; you can choose to take the discount anyway—see the next section, "Taking Discounts After the Discount Date."

If you're making a partial payment and want to adjust the discount, click the Set Discount button to open the Discount And Credits window and enter the amount of the discount you want to take. Click Done, and when you return to the Pay Bills window, the discount is applied and the Amt. To Pay column has the correct amount.

Taking Discounts After the Discount Date

Some vendors will accept a payment with the discount applied if the payment is received within a few business days of the discount period. You'll quickly learn which vendors will accept a discounted payment and which won't. Seeing that the discount you took has been added back in the next statement you receive is a pretty good hint that you're not going to be allowed to take the discount the next time!

To take a discount after the discount date, select the bill for payment, and then click the Set Discount button to open the Discount And Credits window. The amount showing for the discount is zero. Enter the discount you would be entitled to if you paid the bill in a timely fashion and click Done.

Applying Credits

If you set the Preference for QuickBooks to take credits automatically (covered in the prior section "Using Discounts and Credits), when you select a bill for payment for which vendor credits exist, the amount of the credit appears in the Credits Used column, and the Amt. To Pay column is adjusted. If credits are applied automatically and you don't want to take the credit against this bill (perhaps you want to save it for another bill), click Set Credits to open the Discount And Credits window. Deselect the credit and click Done.

If you didn't enable automatic credit application, when you select the bill, the amount of existing credits appears below the list of bills (see Figure 11-10). Click Set Credits to open the Discount And Credits window. Make the appropriate selections of credit amounts, and click Done to change the Amt. To Pay column to reflect your adjustments.

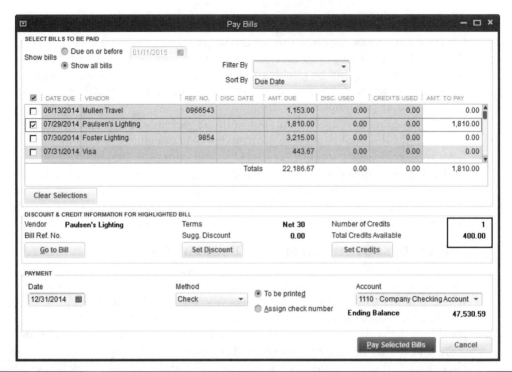

FIGURE 11-10 You can choose when and how to apply a vendor credit to an open bill.

If your total credits with the vendor are equal to or exceed the bill you select, QuickBooks does not create a check, because the bill is paid in its entirety with credits (the Payment Summary window that displays indicates an Amount Paid of $0.00).

Printing and Sending Bill Payments

When you finish selecting the bills to pay, click Pay Selected Bills. If you chose the option to print checks, QuickBooks displays a Payment Summary dialog (see Figure 11-11) that offers three choices for your next step:

- Choose Pay More Bills to return to the Pay Bills window and select other bills to pay (you'll print these checks later). Use this choice to pay bills without printing checks, such as sending payments to vendors you've configured for online payments.
- Choose Print Checks to print your checks now.
- Click Done to close the Payment Summary dialog, close the Pay Bills window, and print your checks later.

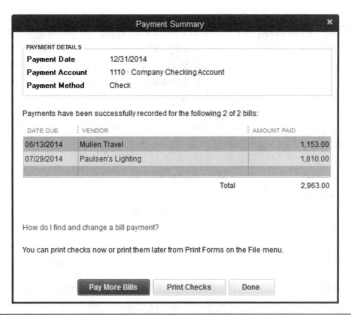

FIGURE 11-11   You can print checks now, or wait until later.

When you defer check printing, the bill payment checks are posted to the bank account register with the notation "To Print." Choose File | Print Forms | Checks to print your checks.

If you selected the Assign Check Number option because you manually write checks, QuickBooks displays the Assign Check Numbers dialog.

- If you select the option Let QuickBooks Assign Check Numbers, QuickBooks looks at the last check number used in the bank register and begins numbering with the next available number.
- If you select the option Let Me Assign The Check Numbers Below, enter the check numbers in the dialog.

When you click OK, QuickBooks opens the Payment Summary dialog that displays the payments. Click Pay More Bills if you want to return to the Pay Bills window, or click Done if you're finished paying bills.

If you're paying bills online, select the Online Payment option when you select those bills. QuickBooks retains the information until you go online. (See Chapter 16 to learn about online banking.)

Check Writing Without Entering a Bill

You can record and print a check in QuickBooks without first entering a bill. In fact, if you've decided not to enter vendor bills, this is how you'll always pay your vendors. However, even if you are entering vendor bills on a regular basis, you sometimes need to write a quick check without going through the process of first entering the bill, selecting it, paying it, and printing the check—for example, when a delivery person is standing in front of you waiting for a COD check and doesn't have time for you to go through all those steps.

Manual Checks

If you use manual checks, you can write your checks and then tell QuickBooks about it later, or you can bring your checkbook to your computer and enter the checks in QuickBooks as you write them. You have two ways to enter your checks in QuickBooks: directly in the bank register or in the Write Checks window.

Entering Manual Checks in the Bank Register

To use the bank register, open the bank account register and enter the check directly in a transaction line, as follows:

1. Enter the date.
2. Press TAB to move to the Number field. QuickBooks automatically fills in the next available check number.
3. Press TAB to move through the rest of the fields, filling in the name of the payee, the amount of the payment, and the expense account you're assigning to the transaction.
4. Click the Record button to save the transaction.

Repeat the steps for the next check and continue until all the manual checks you've written are entered into the register.

> **Caution:** You can't use the check register to purchase items: you must use the Write Checks transaction window. There, you can use the Items tab to tell QuickBooks exactly which items you're purchasing.

Using the Write Checks Window

You can also use the Write Checks window to tell QuickBooks about a check you manually prepared. To get there, press CTRL-W. When the Write Checks transaction window opens (see Figure 11-12), select the bank account you're using to write the checks.

The next available check number is already filled in unless the Print Later option box is checked (if it is, click it to remove the check mark so that QuickBooks can add the check number or leave it checked and type in the number yourself). QuickBooks warns you if you enter a check number that's already been used. It's worth noting that the warning doesn't appear until you fill in all the data and attempt to save the check.

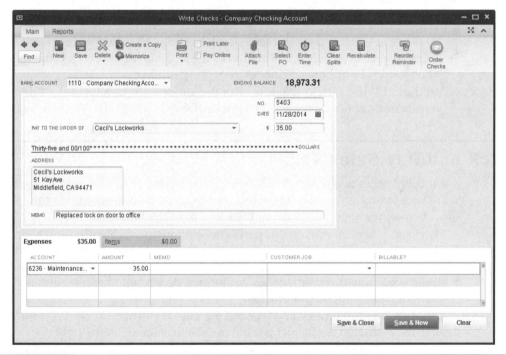

FIGURE 11-12 Fill out the onscreen check the same way you'd fill out a paper check—they look the same.

Fill out the check, posting amounts to the appropriate accounts. If the check is for inventory items, use the Items tab to make sure the items are placed into inventory. When you finish, click Save & New to open a new blank check. When you're through writing checks, click Save & Close to close the Write Checks transaction window. All the checks you wrote are recorded in the bank account register.

Printing Checks in a Batch

If you pay your bills by printing checks from the Write Checks window, by default QuickBooks saves the checks you prepare and then prints them in a batch instead of one at a time.

Open the Write Checks window and make sure the Print Later option, located on the toolbar, is selected. Fill out all the fields for the first check and click Save & New to move to the next blank Write Checks window. Continue to fill out checks, until every check you need to print is ready. Then print the checks using one of the following methods:

- Click Save & Close when you are finished filling out all the checks, and then choose File | Print Forms | Checks from the menu bar.
- In the last Write Checks window, click the arrow at the bottom of the Print button, located on the toolbar, and choose Batch.

Track and Pay Sales Tax

If you collect sales tax from your customers, you have to turn that money over to your state's taxing authorities. Instead of using the Pay Bills feature to do this, QuickBooks uses a special system to track and pay sales taxes.

Many states have county, city, or parish tax authorities, each with its own rate. Businesses in those states may have to remit the sales tax they collect both to the state and the local sales tax authority, and the sales tax a customer pays is the total of all the taxes from these various tax authorities. As a result, tracking sales tax properly can be a complicated process.

This discussion assumes you've created the sales tax items you need (creating these items is covered in Chapter 5), and each item is linked to the right tax authority as a vendor.

Managing Sales Tax

QuickBooks provides a feature called Manage Sales Tax that acts as a "home page" for information and help, and offers links to reports and payment forms covered in this section. You can open the Manage Sales Tax window (see Figure 11-13) by choosing Vendors | Sales Tax | Manage Sales Tax.

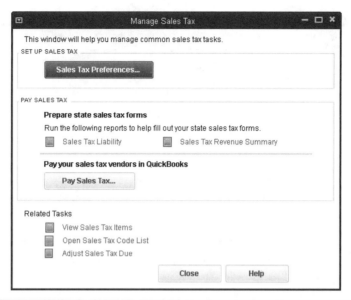

FIGURE 11-13 The Manage Sales Tax window has links to sales tax functions.

The menu commands needed to access features and functions are provided in the following sections, but you can also use the links on the Manage Sales Tax window for some of those chores.

Running Sales Tax Reports

At some interval determined by your taxing authority, you need to report your total sales, your nontaxable sales, and your taxable sales, along with any other required breakdowns. And, of course, you also have to write a sales tax payment check (or multiple checks) to remit the taxes.

Sales Tax Liability Report

QuickBooks has reports to help you fill out your sales tax forms. Choose Vendors | Sales Tax | Sales Tax Liability. Use the Dates drop-down list to select an interval that matches the way you report to the taxing authorities. By default, QuickBooks chooses the interval you configured in the Preferences dialog, but that interval may apply to your primary sales tax only. If you collect multiple taxes due at different intervals, you must create a separate report with the appropriate interval to display those figures. Figure 11-14 shows a Sales Tax Liability report for a monthly filer.

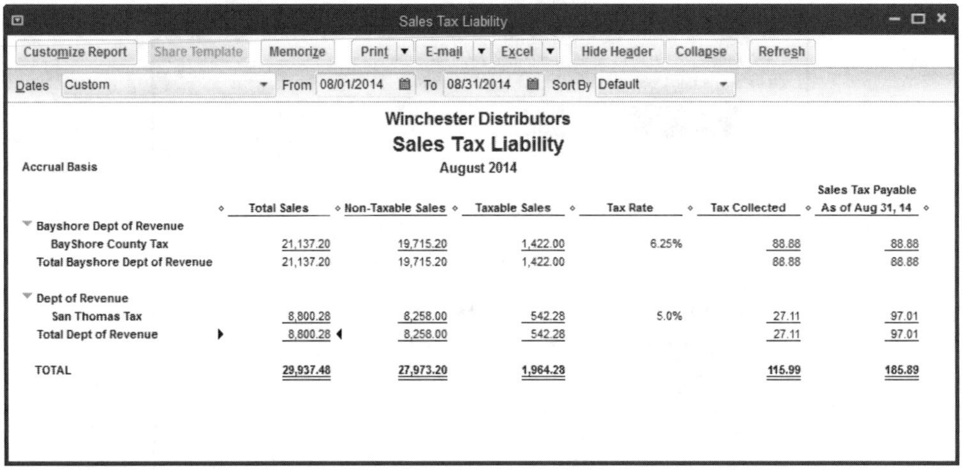

Winchester Distributors
Sales Tax Liability
Accrual Basis
August 2014

	Total Sales	Non-Taxable Sales	Taxable Sales	Tax Rate	Tax Collected	Sales Tax Payable As of Aug 31, 14
Bayshore Dept of Revenue						
BayShore County Tax	21,137.20	19,715.20	1,422.00	6.25%	88.88	88.88
Total Bayshore Dept of Revenue	21,137.20	19,715.20	1,422.00		88.88	88.88
Dept of Revenue						
San Thomas Tax	8,800.28	8,258.00	542.28	5.0%	27.11	97.01
Total Dept of Revenue	8,800.28	8,258.00	542.28		27.11	97.01
TOTAL	29,937.48	27,973.20	1,964.28		115.99	185.89

FIGURE 11-14 The Sales Tax Liability report displays taxable and nontaxable sales for each tax code.

Tax Code Reports

If you have to report specific types of taxable or nontaxable sales, you can obtain that information by creating a report on the tax code you created to track that information. Choose Lists | Sales Tax Code List and select (highlight) the tax code for which you need a report. Press CTRL-Q to see a report on the sales activity with this tax code. Change the date range to match your reporting interval with the sales tax authority (this isn't a sales tax report, so QuickBooks doesn't automatically match the settings in the Sales Tax Preferences dialog).

You don't have to create these reports one sales tax code at a time; you can modify the report so it reports all of your sales tax codes or just those you need for a specific tax authority's report.

Click the Customize Report button on the report window. In the Display tab, use the Columns list to deselect any items you don't require for the report (for example, the Type, Date, and Number of an invoice/sales receipt, and the contents of the Memo field).

In the Filters tab, choose Sales Tax Code from the Current Filter Choices list. Click the arrow to the right of the Sales Tax Code field and from the drop-down list, choose one of the following options:

- **All Sales Tax Codes** Displays total activity for the period for every code
- **Multiple Sales Tax Codes** Opens the Select Sales Tax Code window, listing all codes, so you can select the specific codes you want to report on
- **All Taxable Codes** Displays total activity for the period for each taxable code
- **All Non-Taxable Codes** Displays total activity for the period for each nontaxable code

Click OK to return to the report window, where your selections are reflected. Unless you want to take all these steps again when you need this report, click the Memorize button to memorize the report.

Pay the Sales Tax

After you check the figures (or calculate them, if you have multiple reports with different standards of calculation), it's time to pay the tax, using the following steps:

1. Choose Vendors | Sales Tax | Pay Sales Tax to open the Pay Sales Tax dialog.

2. In the Pay From Account drop-down, select the bank account to use.
3. Check the date that's displayed in the Show Sales Tax Due Through field. It must match the end date of your current reporting period (for instance, monthly or quarterly).
4. Click in the Pay column to insert a check mark next to those items you're paying now. If you're lucky enough to have the same reporting interval for all taxing authorities, just click the Pay All Tax button (the label changes to Clear Selections).
5. If you're going to print the check, be sure to select the To Be Printed check box at the bottom of the dialog. If you write the check manually, or if you remit sales tax online using an electronic transfer from your bank, deselect the To Be Printed check box. Then, if you're writing a manual check, insert the check number, and if you're remitting online, either remove the check number entirely or enter EFT (for Electronic Funds Transfer) in the Starting Check No. field.
6. Click OK when you've finished filling out the information.

C a u t i o n : Don't use the bank account register or Write Checks window to pay sales taxes. Such payments won't be applied to your sales tax reports correctly. Instead, use the Pay Sales Tax method described in this section.

Adjusting Sales Tax Amounts

If you need to adjust the amount of sales tax due, select the appropriate sales tax item in the Pay Sales Tax window and click the Adjust button to open the Sales Tax Adjustment dialog (Figure 11-15).

Specify the amount by which to reduce the amount due—maybe for an overpayment made the previous period or to take an early payment discount offered by the taxing authority. You may also need to increase the amount due to pay a fine or penalty for a late payment. Specify an Adjustment Account and click OK to return to the Pay Sales Tax dialog, where the amount has been changed to reflect your adjustment.

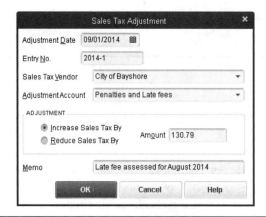

FIGURE 11-15 You can adjust the amount of sales tax due at any time.

Working with Bank and Credit Card Accounts

In this chapter:

- Make deposits that aren't customer payments

- Transfer funds between accounts

- Manage petty cash

- Maintain and track credit card balances

Most deposits and withdrawals are easy to enter in bank accounts, because the routine transaction windows you use take care of adding or removing funds automatically. But there are times when money is deposited or withdrawn outside of the usual transaction windows. This chapter covers what you need to know about how to account for these situations in QuickBooks.

Deposit Money That Isn't from Customers

Even though QuickBooks takes care of recording the deposits into your bank account when you receive money from customers (covered in Chapter 10), there are times when you receive money that's unconnected to a customer payment. Some of the most common of these deposits are

- Rebate checks from manufacturers or stores
- Checks from vendors with whom you have a credit balance and requested a check
- Infusion of capital from an owner or partner
- Loan from an owner, partner, officer, or bank

You can use one of two ways to deposit noncustomer payments into your bank account. If the deposit is the only deposit you're making and it will appear on your statement as an individual deposit, you can record the deposit directly in the bank account register. If you're going to deposit the check along with other checks, use the Make Deposits window.

Using the Account Register for Deposits

To work directly in the bank account register, open the register by choosing Banking | Use Register, and then select the appropriate bank account. When the account register window opens, the next available transaction line is highlighted and the current date is displayed. Follow these steps to record the deposit directly into the bank account:

1. Change the date if necessary, and then press TAB to move to the Number field.
2. Delete the check number if one automatically appears (or wait until you enter the amount in the Deposit column, at which point QuickBooks deletes the check number).
3. Press TAB to move past the next three columns to get to the Deposit column, or click in the Deposit column to move there immediately. (See "Assigning a Payee to a Noncustomer Deposit" later in this section to learn about your options when tracking a payee for this type of deposit.)
4. Enter the amount of the deposit.

5. Move to the next field (Account) and assign the deposit to the appropriate account. (See "Assigning Accounts to Noncustomer Deposits" later in this section for guidelines.)
6. Use the Memo field to enter an explanation in case your accountant asks you about the deposit.
7. Click the Record button.

Using the Make Deposits Window

Sometimes it's better to use the Make Deposits window for a deposit that's not related to a customer payment (such as a rebate from a vendor), because you're planning to deposit the check along with other checks, and you want your deposit records to match the bank statement. In this case, follow these steps:

1. Choose Banking | Make Deposits to open the Payments To Deposit window.
2. Select the deposits you're taking to the bank. Note that the check you want to deposit (for a noncustomer payment) is not listed here, because the window shows only the money you've received through customer payment transactions.
3. Click OK to move to the Make Deposits window.
4. Click either in the From Account column of the blank line under the last entry or in the Received From column if you need to track the payee (which is optional).
5. Select the account to which you want this deposit to be posted (in Figure 12-1, it's Office Equipment).
6. Optionally, enter data in the Memo, Chk No., and Pmt Meth. columns. (Don't forget the Class field if you're tracking classes.)
7. Enter the amount.

Your check is added to the total of the deposit you're making (see Figure 12-1).

Assigning a Payee to a Noncustomer Deposit

You can, if necessary, enter a payee name in the Received From column, but QuickBooks doesn't require that. Most of the time, a payee isn't needed. For example, if you're depositing a rebate on a purchase you made, there's a good chance the company that wrote the check doesn't exist in your QuickBooks system, and there's no point in adding a name you don't need to produce reports about.

If the money is from an owner or partner, the name should exist in your system in the Other Names list. If the money is from a corporate officer, that officer probably exists as an employee, but you should not use the employee name for this transaction. Instead, create the name in the Other Names list to track this deposit. Because you can't have duplicate names in QuickBooks, most users will append an extra letter or symbol to the existing name.

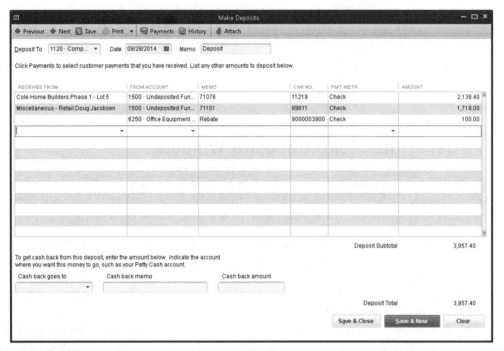

FIGURE 12-1 Record the deposit of a rebate check, along with a customer payment.

If you're depositing the proceeds of a bank loan, you'll need a vendor, because you'll be writing checks to pay back the principal and interest.

If you type a payee name that doesn't exist in any of your name lists, QuickBooks displays a Name Not Found message offering you the following selections:

- **Quick Add**   Lets you enter the name only after choosing a Name Type (Vendor, Customer, or Employee, for example)
- **Set Up**   Lets you create a new name using the regular New Name window
- **Cancel**   Returns you to the original window you were working in so you can either choose another name or delete the name of the nonexistent payee

If you select Quick Add or Set Up, you're asked which type of name you're adding: Vendor, Customer, Employee, or Other. Unless this payee will become a vendor or customer, choose Other.

Assigning Accounts to Noncustomer Deposits

If you're depositing your own money into the business and the business is a proprietorship or partnership, that's capital and you should post the deposit from a capital account, which is an equity account. If you're depositing the proceeds of a loan—from either yourself as a corporate officer or from a bank—post the deposit from the liability account for the loan. Keep in mind that you may have to create this liability account. If you're making a deposit that's a refund from a vendor, you can post the amount to the expense account that was used for the original expense.

When in doubt, post the amount to the most logical place and ask your accountant for verification, or post the amount to the Ask My Accountant account (if you have one) or some other "suspense" account. You can always edit the transaction later or make a journal entry to post the amount to the appropriate account.

Transfer Funds Between Accounts

Moving money between bank accounts is a common practice in business. If you have a bank account for payroll, you have to move money out of your operating account into your payroll account every payday. Some people deposit all the customer payments into an interest-bearing money market or savings account and then transfer the necessary funds to an operating account when it's time to pay bills. Others do it the other way around, moving money not immediately needed from the business operating account to a money market account. Lawyers, agents, real estate brokers, and other professionals have to maintain escrow accounts and move money between them and the operating account.

You can use either of two methods to transfer funds between bank accounts:

- Use the QuickBooks Transfer Funds Between Accounts transaction window.
- Post a check from the sending bank to a transfer account and then bring the funds into the receiving account from the funds transfer account.

Both methods are quite easy and are covered in the following section.

Using the Transfer Funds Transaction Window

QuickBooks offers a Transfer Funds feature, which is the best solution to record a "noncheck" transfer of funds between bank accounts that are held either by the same or different banks. But the Transfer Funds feature also works if you prefer to write a check, either because the bank accounts are in separate banks or because you want to have a check as a record of the transfer. If you don't mind the fact that a check number from one bank account appears in the deposit column of another bank account, then the Transfer Funds feature is still an easy method for transferring funds.

To transfer money between accounts using the Transfer Funds transaction window, follow these steps:

1. Choose Banking | Transfer Funds from the menu bar to open the Transfer Funds Between Accounts dialog.
2. Fill out the fields.

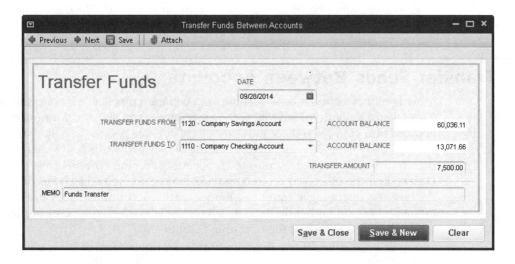

3. Click Save & Close (or Save & New if you have another transfer to make).

QuickBooks posts the transaction (you'll see it marked as TRANSFR in both bank accounts if you open their registers) without affecting any totals in your financial reports. All the work is done on the balance sheet, but the bottom line of your balance sheet doesn't change because money was neither added nor removed from your company.

If you wrote a check from one account and took it to the bank to effect the transfer, open the register of the sending bank, select the transaction line, enter the check number in the Number field, and click Record. QuickBooks displays a dialog asking you to confirm the fact that you're changing the transaction (click Yes). That number is also recorded on the transaction line in the receiving bank register, and you cannot remove it.

Handle a Returned Check

When you receive and deposit a check from a customer for payment on an open invoice, QuickBooks performs two tasks for you. First, it reduces your accounts receivable account (on the day you post that check), and second, it increases your bank account in the same amount. A week later, when your bank notifies you that your customer's check has been returned, you also need to record that event in QuickBooks to keep both your accounts receivable and bank balances up to date.

You may also need to record a returned check taken on a sales receipt (cash sale) or for a deposit that was recorded directly in your bank account register. QuickBooks handles the recording of these events differently, and each method is covered in this section.

Recording a Returned Customer Invoice Payment

When you receive notification of a returned customer payment (a "bounced" payment), your first step (after you call the customer to notify him or her of that fact) is to locate the original Receive Payments transaction in QuickBooks. If it is a fairly recent transaction, you could open the Receive Payments window by selecting Customers | Receive Payments and click the left-pointing blue arrow until you see the payment. Or you can use the Find button located on the Main tab of the Receive Payments window and search for the payment by customer name, payment amount, or date.

Once you've located the bounced payment, follow these steps:

1. Click the Record Bounced Check button located on the Main tab to open The Manage Bounced Check dialog:

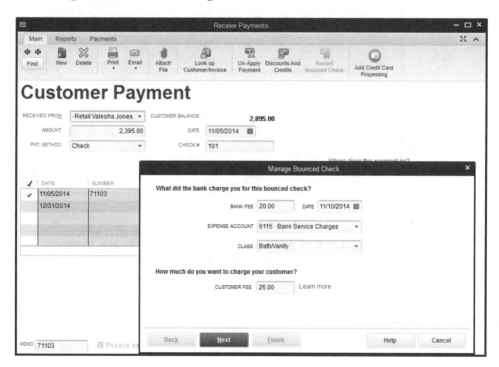

2. Enter the date and the fee that your bank has assessed you for the returned check.

3. Confirm the expense account to which QuickBooks will post the bank fee.

4. If you're using class tracking, you can assign a class (which should be the same class that was used on the invoice transaction that this payment relates to).

5. Enter the fee that you want to charge your customer. When determining this fee, consider the extra time and effort you or your staff are expending on behalf of this customer. Then click Next.

6. Review the Bounced Check Summary that confirms the following for you:

   • The original invoice(s) that will now be marked as unpaid

   • The amounts that QuickBooks will deduct from your bank account to account for both the amount of the bounced check and the returned check fee your bank assessed you

   • That an invoice will be created by QuickBooks for the amount of the returned check fee you want to charge your customer

7. Click Finish to accept the transactions and complete the process. The original customer payment window will now have a "Bounced Check!" watermark.

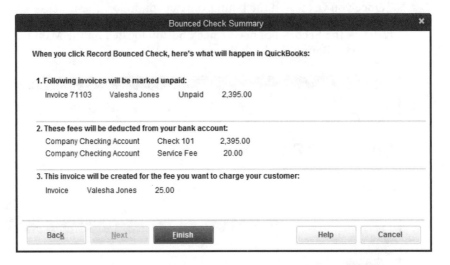

ProAdvisor Tip: If your customer directs you to redeposit the original check, you should create a new Receive Payments transaction (with the date of the redeposit) so that you're treating it the same way as if it were a new replacement check. This method will help you keep your record keeping straight and maintain better detail when running customer statements and balance detail reports.

Recording a Returned Cash Receipt Payment

Recording a returned check taken on a sales receipt (cash sale) or for a deposit that was recorded directly in your bank account register or in the Make Deposits window requires a different approach. For these transactions, you'll need to create special items and then manually create a new invoice transaction to record the amount of the bounced check as well as the fees you owe your bank and those you want to charge to your customer.

1. Create a new item and name it "NSF Check." This should be an Other Charge type that's used to capture the amount of the check that bounced. Leave the Amount Or % field blank, select Non for the Tax Code, and link this item to your bank account (whichever account you deposit your checks into).

2. Create a new item for Your NSF Charge to Your Customer (name it "NSF Service Charge," for example). Again using the Other Charge type, this will be a nontaxable item, and you can either fill in the amount that you want to charge when you create the item or you can leave the amount field blank and enter the charge amount when you list it on an invoice. This item can be linked to your bank service charge expense account.

3. Create an invoice that includes the special items you just created to handle bounced checks (see Figure 12-2). Be sure the date reflects the date that your customer's payment was returned. When (or if) the payment arrives, you'll use the Receive Payments window to record the customer's payment.

When you enter the NSF item on the invoice, it credits the bank account, which, in effect, reverses the amount of the original deposit of the check. It also provides both transactions in the Reconcile window when your statement arrives so you can reconcile each entry.

Recording Your Bank's NSF Charge to You

As a final step, don't forget to record the fee that your bank is charging you for your customer's bounced check. The easiest way to record this fee is directly in your bank account register. Simply enter the date and the amount of the fee in the Payment column with a note about the NSF charge in the Memo field. And although you don't need to designate a check number or payee, you'll want to be sure you

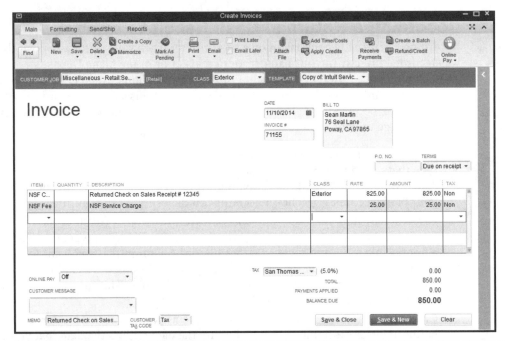

FIGURE 12-2 Use special items on an invoice to take care of all the entries you need to account for a bounced check accepted on a sales receipt or recorded directly into your bank account.

attribute this fee to your customer. To do this while in the register, click the Splits button to open additional fields for the transaction.

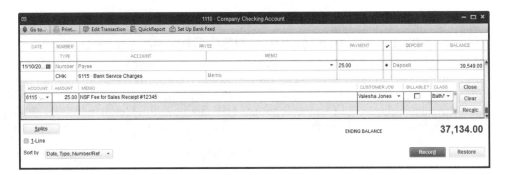

Then, in the Customer:Job column, use the drop-down arrow to select the customer to whom the NSF fee applies.

Void a Check

Sometimes you have to void a check that you've written. Perhaps you decided not to send it for some reason, or perhaps it was lost in the mail. Whatever the reason, if a check isn't going to clear your bank, you should void it. Deleting (versus voiding) a check removes all history of the transaction from your register. This is not a good way to keep financial records—especially in the event of an audit. Voiding a check keeps the check number but sets the amount to zero.

The way QuickBooks completes the process of voiding a check can differ based on whether the check was used to record an expense or it was used to record the purchase of an asset, such as new inventory or furniture for your office. The process starts the same way, however, by opening the bank account register and selecting the disbursement that you want to void. Next, right-click to open the shortcut menu and choose Void Check. In the first case—when you record the voiding of an expense-related check from a closed period—QuickBooks will give you the option of allowing the program to automatically create two journal entries for you. Selecting Yes will ensure that the voiding of this check does not affect any of your prior accounting periods. If the check to be voided is *not from a closed period*, the offer for the automatic journal entries is not made.

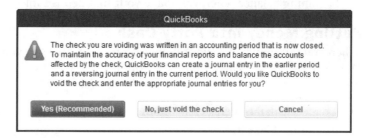

Selecting No keeps the check number along with its current date and then simply sets the amount of the check to zero without making any adjustments to a prior period.

In the second case—when you're voiding a check that is posted to an asset or liability account—the offer for the automatic journal entries is not made. The check is simply adjusted to zero along with the amounts posted to the other balance sheet accounts. Click Record to save the transaction.

Track Cash Disbursements

Virtually every business, whether large or small, makes purchases with cash. Because the amount of the expense is usually small (or "petty"), these minor expenses are often difficult to keep track of. In fact, it's not uncommon for receipts to get lost or for cash that the business has on hand to disappear, unaccounted for.

Whether the cash you use in your business is from a petty cash box or from an ATM machine, QuickBooks can help you keep track of every penny of it.

Keeping a Petty Cash Box

Many businesses keep a petty cash box (or even cash in a desk drawer) in order to have money on hand to cover such things as buying lunch for employees or a quick trip to the office supply store. If you decide to keep cash on hand, the first thing you'll do is put money in to fund your petty cash. Next, you'll need to keep track of how the cash that's taken is spent. And, last, you'll have to put more money into the box to replace what's been spent.

When you put money in the cash box, you tell QuickBooks about it by recording a deposit transaction into your petty cash account. If you don't yet have a petty cash account in your chart of accounts, create one using the following guidelines:

- The account type is Bank.
- If you number your accounts, use a number that places your new petty cash account among the other bank accounts in your chart of accounts.
- Leave the opening balance of the petty cash account at zero. You'll record the beginning balance when you make your first deposit into this account.

Putting Money into Petty Cash

When you put money into your petty cash box (or drawer), you have to tell QuickBooks where it came from. Most of the time, you'll write a check for petty cash from your bank account. Use these steps as a guideline:

1. Create the name "Petty Cash" in the Other Names list (which you can open from the Lists menu).
2. Write a check from your bank account and post it to the petty cash account. You can use the Write Checks window to do this, or enter the deposit directly in the petty cash account register. Be sure to enter the check number you used in the number field.

Recording Petty Cash Expenses

Next, you'll need to tell QuickBooks about what you (or your employees) bought with the cash taken from petty cash. Open the Write Checks window and select the petty cash bank account. You can delete the check number QuickBooks automatically places in the Number field, or you can leave the number there (you'll never get a statement that you have to reconcile, so it doesn't matter). You can also skip the Payee field or you can just use Petty Cash as the payee.

The advantage of using the Write Checks window (and not the petty cash register) is that you can use the fields at the bottom of the window to tie an expense to a customer or a class for job-costing purposes if you need to.

It's important to note that the steps described in this section allow you to record accurately the money being *spent* from petty cash, which is not always the same amount as the money being *taken* from petty cash. If you spend less than the amount of cash taken out, it's a good idea to put what's left over back into the box so it's available the next time cash is needed. It's also a really good idea to keep a log of who has taken out cash (and when) and to require that all employees turn in a receipt for each and every cash purchase they make.

> **ProAdvisor Tip:** When you open the Write Checks window, QuickBooks uses the same bank account that you worked in the last time you wrote a check. A common mistake is not noticing that when you are trying to write a real check you're using the petty cash account instead of your actual checking account. To help prevent you or a member of your staff from inadvertently posting a check to the wrong bank account, consider changing the onscreen account color of the petty cash account so it has a different color than your regular checking account. To do this, with your petty cash account check register open, choose Edit | Change Account Color. Choose a standard color or create one of your own.

Replacing the Cash Spent

As you take or spend money from petty cash, you need to replace it. The usual method is to bring it back to its original balance. Use the same steps you used to write the first check to petty cash, and use the total amount of funds spent thus far as the amount of the check.

Tracking Other Cash Withdrawals

Many businesses use ATM and debit cards in their day-to-day transactions. Recording these transactions is essentially the same as recording a check. However, ATM/debit card transactions can differ from checks in that often the amount withdrawn doesn't have a specific expense attached to it at the time it's withdrawn. To track these amounts, use your petty cash account (bank account type) to post to when recording the withdrawal from your bank account. Then, as the person who made the withdrawal begins handing in receipts, you can debit the appropriate expense account directly from this account's register.

Manage Credit Card Transactions

When you use a credit card to make purchases for your business, you have two choices about the way you can enter and manage those transactions in QuickBooks: create a credit card account or treat the credit card as a bill.

Create a Credit Card Account

With this option, you create a credit card account on your balance sheet that has its own register and to which you'll post individual transactions. The advantage of this method is that, as with your bank account, you can perform a reconciliation of this account (refer to Chapter 13 for details on how to reconcile a bank account) and use online banking to download transactions from your credit card company.

To create a credit card account, follow these steps:

1. With the chart of accounts list open, press CTRL-N to open the Add New Account window.
2. Select Credit Card as the account type and click Continue.
3. Enter the name of the credit card (usually the issuer's name).
4. Enter an account number if you're using account numbers.
5. Optionally, enter a credit card number (this is required if you'll be using online banking, which is covered in Chapter 16).
6. Click Save & Close.

You can now enter individual transactions into your account in one of two ways: select Banking | Enter Credit Card Charges to enter your transactions in the Enter Credit Card Charges window (see Figure 12-3), or you can enter them directly into the credit card account register.

There are several fields to fill out when you use the Enter Credit Card Charges window.

1. Use the drop-down menu in the Credit Card field to select the credit card to which you want to post transactions.
2. Select either the Purchase/Charge or Refund/Credit option.
3. In the Purchased From field, you can enter the name of the establishment where the card was used. If it's not important for you to track that information, you can leave that field blank, which can help keep your Vendors list from growing too large.
4. Enter the date of the transaction.
5. Optionally, fill in the Ref No. field with the reference number found on the credit card statement.
6. Fill in the amount of the charge.

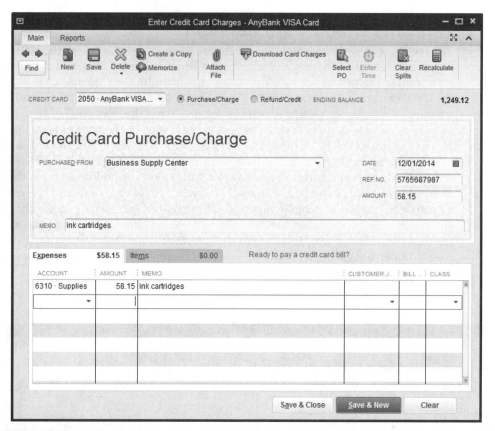

FIGURE 12-3   Use the Enter Credit Card Charges window to track individual credit card charges.

7. Use the Expenses tab for general expenses, or use the Items tab if the transaction was for the purchase of an item for inventory or for a customer.

8. If you track classes, assign the transaction to the appropriate class.

When it's time to make a payment on this card, you'll use the Write Checks window and fill in the Pay To The Order Of field with the credit card company name. In the Account column (on the Expenses tab), select the *credit card account* from your chart of accounts.

Treat the Credit Card as a Bill

The second way to manage your credit card is to enter the charges on the statement just as you would a bill from a vendor. Select Vendors | Enter Bills, and then list each transaction that appears on the statement (including any finance charges) in the Expenses tab for general expenses (see Figure 12-4), or use the Items tab if the transaction was for the purchase of an inventory item. The advantage of this method is that in addition to your charges being posted to the appropriate expense account as you enter the bill, any amount outstanding on the card is included as part of your accounts payable and listed on your reports as such. The drawback of this method, however, is that if you wait for your credit card bill to come in the mail, you could be posting these individual credit card charges a month or even two months after they were actually incurred. This may become an issue if the charges you made were in December, for example, and your statement arrives in January, the start of a new tax year. Be aware of the timing of when these expenses show on your Profit & Loss statement, and be sure to consult with your accountant if you choose to employ this method.

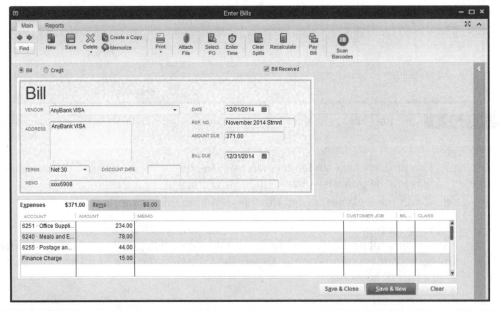

FIGURE 12-4 You can enter your credit card statement just as you would any other vendor bill.

Balancing Your Bank Accounts

In *this chapter:*

- Work in the QuickBooks reconciliation windows

- Find and fix discrepancies

Reconciling a bank account is one of the most important tasks connected with financial record keeping—but ironically, it's also one of the most avoided tasks. When you use QuickBooks, however, the job of reconciling your accounts becomes a very manageable one.

Reconcile in QuickBooks

Most of the time, performing a bank reconciliation in QuickBooks is easy and straightforward. If you've been keeping your QuickBooks up to date, you shouldn't have to make a lot of "catch-up" entries because most of the data you need is already in your bank register.

The following sections explain the steps involved in a reconciliation in the order that you'll be performing them. By the way, these same steps apply to reconciling a credit card account.

The Begin Reconciliation Window

Reconciling your bank account starts with the Begin Reconciliation window, which you open by choosing Banking | Reconcile (see Figure 13-1). If you have more than one bank account, or you have credit card accounts you reconcile in addition to bank accounts, select the account you want to reconcile from the drop-down list in the Account field.

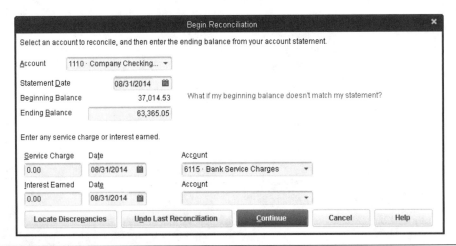

FIGURE 13-1 Enter your ending balance and confirm your starting balance in the Begin Reconciliation window.

Enter the statement date from your bank statement and then check the Beginning Balance field in the window against the beginning balance on the bank statement. (Your bank may call it the *starting balance.*) If your beginning balances match, enter the ending balance from your statement in the Ending Balance field. If this is the *first* time you're reconciling the bank account in QuickBooks, your Beginning Balance field in QuickBooks will automatically be zero. Enter the ending balance from your statement in the Ending Balance field in QuickBooks.

If the beginning balances don't match and this is not the first time you're reconciling the bank account in QuickBooks, read "Troubleshooting Differences in the Beginning Balance" later in this chapter, and then return to this section of the chapter to perform the reconciliation.

Entering Interest Income and Service Charges

Your bank statement lists interest earned and bank service charges if either or both are applicable to your account. Enter those numbers in the Begin Reconciliation window and choose the appropriate accounts for posting.

If you use the Bank Feeds feature (aka online banking) and the interest payments and bank charges have already been entered into your register as a result of downloading transactions, do *not* enter them again in the Begin Reconciliation window—they'll be in the register list you see in the next window, and you can clear them the way you clear checks and deposits. More about working with Bank Feeds in Chapter 16.

Use the Service Charge field to enter a standard monthly charge. Standard bank charges typically do not include special charges for bounced checks, fees for electronic bank transfers, or any purchases you made that are charged to your account, such as the purchase of checks or deposit slips. Those should be entered in your bank register as individual transactions, and you can use the Memo field to explain the transaction. This will make them easier to find in case you have to talk to the bank about your account.

Working in the Reconcile Window

After you've filled out the information in the Begin Reconciliation window, click Continue to open the Reconcile window, shown in Figure 13-2. You can arrange the way transactions are displayed to make it easier to work in the window.

Sorting the Data

By default, QuickBooks sorts transactions first by date, and then by transaction number. For example, in the Checks And Payments pane, if multiple checks have the same date, those checks are sorted in numerical order.

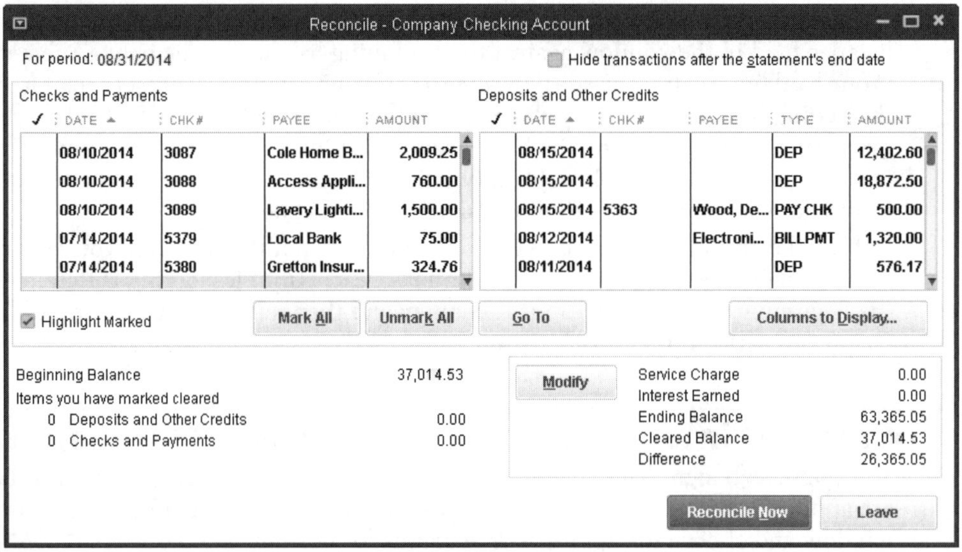

FIGURE 13-2 Uncleared transactions appear in the Reconcile window.

Reconciling is easier if you sort the data to match the way your bank arranges the statement. For instance, if you have a lot of electronic payments in addition to checks, and your bank lists the electronic payments separately from checks, click the CHK # column header to list withdrawals without check numbers separately from checks.

Eliminating Future Transactions

If the list is long, you can shorten it by selecting the option Hide Transactions After The Statement's End Date. Theoretically, transactions that weren't created before the ending date couldn't have cleared the bank. Removing them from the window leaves only those transactions likely to have cleared. If you select this option and your reconciliation doesn't balance, deselect the option so you can clear the transactions in case one of the following scenarios applies:

- You issued a postdated check and the recipient cashed it early. Since occasionally a bank won't enforce the date, this is a real possibility.
- You made a mistake when you entered the date of the original transaction. You may have entered a wrong month or even a wrong year, which resulted in moving the transaction date into the future.

Clearing Transactions

Now you must tell QuickBooks which transactions have cleared. If this is your first bank reconciliation in QuickBooks, on the Deposits And Other Credits side of the Reconcile window you'll see a deposit transaction that represents the beginning bank balance you (or your accountant) entered either via a journal entry (read Chapter 17 to learn more about journal entries) or directly in the check register when you set up your QuickBooks data file. You'll need to "clear" this transaction during your first reconciliation. When you clear a transaction in the Reconcile window, a check mark appears in the leftmost (Cleared) column to indicate that the transaction has cleared the bank. If you clear a transaction in error, click again to remove the check mark—it's a toggle.

Use the following shortcuts to speed your work:

- If all, or almost all, of the transactions have cleared, click Mark All. Then deselect the transactions that didn't clear.
- Mark multiple, contiguous transactions by dragging down the Cleared column.
- Click the Highlight Marked check box so that the items you mark as cleared have a shaded background, making them easier to distinguish from those that haven't cleared.
- If the account you're reconciling is enabled for online access (using the QuickBooks Bank Feed feature), click Matched to automatically clear all transactions that were downloaded and matched. QuickBooks asks for the ending date on the statement and clears each previously matched transaction up to that date. See Chapter 16 for more information about using the Bank Feeds feature.

As you check each cleared transaction, the Difference amount in the lower-right corner of the Reconcile window changes. The goal is to get that figure to 0.00.

Adding Transactions During Reconciliation

While you're working in the Reconcile window, if you find a transaction on the statement that you haven't entered into your QuickBooks software—such as one of those ATM transactions you forgot to enter—you don't have to leave the Reconcile window to remedy the situation. You can just enter the transaction into your register.

To open the bank account register, right-click anywhere in the Reconcile window and choose Use Register from the shortcut menu. When the account register opens, record the transaction. Return to the Reconcile window, where that transaction is now conveniently waiting for you to check it off as cleared.

Adding Undeposited Funds During Reconciliation

If the statement shows a deposit that doesn't appear in your reconcile window, don't add the deposit to your register until you check the Payments To Deposit window (choose Banking | Make Deposits). Most of the time, you'll find the payments listed there, still awaiting deposit, even though you already may have gone to the bank and deposited those checks.

Select the payments that match the total shown on the bank statement and go through the Make Deposits function. When you're finished, the deposit appears in the Reconcile window. If the deposit isn't in the Payments To Deposit window, then you forgot to enter a transaction. Enter the transaction now, using the appropriate transaction window. Make sure you deposit it into the bank account to have it appear in the Reconcile window.

Voiding or Deleting Transactions During Reconciliation

Sometimes you find a transaction in the Reconcile window that shouldn't be there. This commonly occurs if you mistakenly entered an ATM withdrawal twice, for example. Or perhaps you forgot that you'd entered a deposit, and a couple of days later you entered it again. QuickBooks offers you two ways to remedy the situation: you can either delete or void the transaction.

To delete a transaction, double-click its listing in the Reconcile window to open the original transaction. Then right-click and select Delete. QuickBooks asks you to confirm the deletion. The transaction disappears from the Reconcile window and the bank register.

To void a transaction, double-click its listing in the Reconcile window to open the original transaction. Then right-click and select Void, which changes the amount to zero.

Voiding a transaction is almost always the preferred method of removing a transaction, because QuickBooks retains most all the details of the transaction and allows you to add a note for future reference. Deleting removes a transaction completely, making it more difficult for your accountant or you to track down a change in an account balance or report that occurred as a result of the deletion.

Editing Transactions During Reconciliation

Sometimes you'll want to change some of the information in a transaction. For example, when you see the real check, you realize the amount you entered in QuickBooks is wrong. You might even have the wrong date on a check.

Whatever the problem, you can correct it by editing the transaction. Double-click the transaction's listing in the Reconcile window to open the original transaction window. Enter the necessary changes and close the window. Answer Yes when QuickBooks asks if you want to record the changes, and you're returned to the Reconcile window where the changes are reflected.

Resolving Missing Check Numbers

Most banks list your checks in order and indicate a missing number with an asterisk on the bank statement. For instance, you may see check number 5003 followed by check number *5007 or 5007*. When a check number is missing, it means one of three things:

- The check is still outstanding.
- The check number is unused and is probably literally missing.
- The check cleared in a previous reconciliation.

If a missing check number on your bank statement is puzzling, you can check its status. To see if the check cleared in the last reconciliation, open the Previous Reconciliation report (discussed later in this chapter) by choosing Reports | Banking | Previous Reconciliation.

To investigate further, right-click anywhere in the Reconcile window and choose Missing Checks Report from the shortcut menu. When the Missing Checks dialog opens, select the appropriate account (if you have multiple bank accounts). You'll see asterisks indicating missing check numbers, as seen in Figure 13-3.

If a check number is listed in your Missing Checks report, it doesn't exist in the register. Here are some of the most common reasons why it may be missing:

- You deleted the check that was assigned that number.
- The check is physically missing (usually because somebody grabbed one or more checks to carry around).
- Checks jammed while printing and you restarted the print run with the number of the first available check. QuickBooks doesn't mark checks as void in that case; it just omits the numbers in the register so they show up in the Missing Checks report.

Finishing the Reconciliation

If this isn't the first reconciliation you're performing, there's a good chance that the Difference figure at the bottom of the Reconcile window displays 0.00. If there is a difference, refer to "Troubleshooting Differences in the Beginning Balance" later in this chapter.

Type	Date	Num	Name	Memo	Account	Split	Amount
Check	01/01/2014	5001	Kuver Property	Janaury Rent	1110 · Company C...	6295 · Rent	-583.75
Check	01/05/2014	5002	Deborah Wood (O...	Petty Cash	1110 · Company C...	1140 · Petty C...	-500.00
Check	01/08/2014	5003	Gas & Electic Com...	ACCT# 0987...	1110 · Company C...	6970 · Utilities	-65.08
*** Missing numbers here ***							
Check	01/15/2014	5007	Automobile Loan C...	Car lease	1110 · Company C...	6131 · Car Le...	-563.00
Check	01/22/2014	5008	Cell Phone Company	Cell	1110 · Company C...	6320 · Teleph...	-101.18
Check	01/22/2014	5009	Fisse Fast Packag...	ACCT# 2560...	1110 · Company C...	6255 · Postag...	-78.00
Check	01/22/2014	5010	Local Phone Comp...	6503221414	1110 · Company C...	6320 · Teleph...	-253.00
Check	01/22/2014	5011	Office Supply Store	Acct# 27804	1110 · Company C...	6310 · Supplies	-634.21
Check	01/25/2014	5012	King, Vicki		1110 · Company C...	6240 · Meals...	-55.00
Check	01/25/2014	5013	Gretton Insurance...	WC Policy #...	1110 · Company C...	-SPLIT-	-231.84
Check	01/25/2014	5014	Payroll Service Co.	Payroll	1110 · Company C...	6278 · Payro...	-127.08
Check	01/25/2014	5015	Pace Shipping Sup...	Acct# 45980	1110 · Company C...	6250 · Office...	-25.00
Check	01/25/2014	5016	Deborah Wood (O...	13103 Exp R...	1110 · Company C...	6330 · Travel	-55.23
Check	01/25/2014	5017	Health Insurance Co.	Employee He...	1110 · Company C...	-SPLIT-	-543.83
Check	01/25/2014	5018	Novello Lights Mag...	Q1 07 Ad	1110 · Company C...	6100 · Adver...	-500.00
Check	01/26/2014	5019	Deborah Wood (O...	Owners Draw	1110 · Company C...	3120 · Debor...	-10,500.00
Check	01/29/2014	5020	Credit Card	ACCT# 3786...	1110 · Company C...	2050 · QuickB...	-95.71
Check	01/29/2014	5021	Gretton Insurance...	Liability Ins. ...	1110 · Company C...	1255 · Prepa...	-6,875.00
Check	01/31/2014	5022	Automobile Insuran...	Auto Insuran...	1110 · Company C...	6138 · Insura...	-120.00
Check	01/31/2014	5023	Jonathan Graham ...	13103 Expe...	1110 · Company C...	-SPLIT-	-223.15
Check	01/31/2014	5024	Jeff's Janitorial		1110 · Company C...	6237 · Outsid...	-200.00
Check	01/31/2014	5025	Lawson Professio...	Spring Semi...	1110 · Company C...	6140 · Confe...	-1,000.00
Check	01/31/2014	5026	Gretton Insurance...	Policy # 14B...	1110 · Company C...	6188 · Gener...	-230.00
Check	01/31/2014	5027	Professional Asso...	07 Annual d...	1110 · Company C...	6155 · Dues ...	-500.00
Check	01/31/2014	5028	Professional Asso...	07 Annual d...	1110 · Company C...	6155 · Dues ...	-350.00
Check	02/01/2014	5029	Kuver Property	February Rent	1110 · Company C...	6295 · Rent	-583.75
Check	02/05/2014	5030	Gretton Insurance...	Feb 07 WC P...	1110 · Company C...	-SPLIT-	-461.84
Check	02/05/2014	5031	Local Bank	Interest on L...	1110 · Company C...	9100 · Interes...	-100.13

FIGURE 13-3   A few checks are missing from the QuickBooks bank register.

Click Reconcile Now and then print either a summary or detail (or both) reconciliation report.

Printing the Reconciliation Report

When you have a balanced reconciliation (even if it results from an adjusting entry), QuickBooks offers congratulations and also offers to print a reconciliation report.

The dialog has a Close button to skip the report, but it's a good practice to print and keep a copy of the Reconciliation Detail report with your bank statement.

Whether you print, view, or cancel, QuickBooks saves the reports and you can view them in the future by choosing Reports | Banking | Previous Reconciliation.

Deciding on the Type of Report

QuickBooks offers two reconciliation reports: Detail and Summary. Here are the differences between them:

- The Detail Report shows all the transactions that are cleared and all the transactions that haven't yet cleared as of the statement closing date. Any transactions dated after the statement closing date are listed as *New Transactions*.
- The Summary Report breaks down your transactions in the same way, but it doesn't list the individual transactions; it shows only the totals for each category: Cleared, Uncleared, and New.

Selecting the Detail report makes it easier to resolve problems in the future, since you have a list of every check and deposit and when it cleared.

Printing a Reconciliation Report

If you opt to print one or both reports, the Print Reports dialog opens so you can select the printer. The Print Reports dialog offers the following options:

- Print the report to the selected printer. You can file the printed report with that month's bank statement in case you ever need to refer to it.
- Print the report to a file—ASCII text, comma delimited, or tab delimited (this option is not available if you decide to print both reports).

Viewing the Last Reconciliation Report

Even if you don't display or print a reconciliation report after you reconcile an account, QuickBooks saves the report and stores it for you as a Previous Reconciliation report. This can be extremely helpful when you're trying to track down a discrepancy in your beginning bank balance the next time you do a reconciliation.

Click Reports | Banking | Previous Reconciliation to open the Select Previous Reconciliation Report dialog. You're given the option of running the Summary, Detail, or both reports in one of two ways:

- Include transactions cleared at the time of the reconciliation—essentially giving you a snapshot of what the reconciliation looked like at the time it was completed. This report will print only as a PDF file.
- Include transactions cleared at the time of the original reconciliation *plus* any changes made to the transactions since original reconciliation. I find that this report is the most effective in tracking down a discrepancy. Once it's displayed, you can export this report to Excel by clicking the Excel button at the top of the reconciliation report window.

If You Don't Balance

If the account doesn't reconcile (the Difference figure isn't 0.00), and you don't have the time, energy, or emotional fortitude to track down the problem at the moment, you can stop the reconciliation process without losing all the transactions you cleared.

Click the Leave button in the Reconcile window and do something else for a while. Have dinner, play with the cat, go to the movies, clear your mind. When you restart the reconciliation process, all the entries you made are still there.

Finding and Correcting Problems

When you're ready to investigate the cause of a difference between the ending balance and the cleared balance, follow the guidelines presented here to find the problem.

Count the number of transactions on the bank statement. Then look in the lower-left corner of the Reconcile window, where the number of items you have marked cleared is displayed. Mentally add another item to that number for each of the following:

- A service charge you entered in the Begin Reconciliation window
- An interest amount you entered in the Begin Reconciliation window

If the numbers differ, the problem is in your QuickBooks records; there's a transaction you should have cleared but didn't or a transaction you cleared that you shouldn't have.

If you're sure you didn't make any mistakes clearing transactions, do the following:

- Check the amount of each transaction against the amount in the bank statement.
- Check your transactions and make sure a deposit wasn't inadvertently entered as a payment (or vice versa). A clue for this is a transaction that's half the difference. For example, if the difference is $220.00, find a transaction that has an amount of $110.00 and make sure it's a deduction if it's supposed to be a deduction (or the other way around).
- Check for transposed figures. Maybe you entered a figure incorrectly in the register, such as $549.00 when the bank clears the transaction as $594.00. A clue that a transposed number is the problem is that the reconciliation difference can be divided by nine.

If you find the problem, correct it. When the Difference figure is 0.00, click Reconcile Now.

ProAdvisor Tip: Consider having somebody else check over the statement and the register, because sometimes you can't see your own mistakes.

Making an Adjusting Entry

You may not be able to find a reason for the difference in the beginning balances. If you've reached the point where it isn't worth your time to keep looking, go ahead and click the Reconcile Now button. QuickBooks will present you with an option to make an adjusting transaction at the end of the reconciliation process that will post to an expense account that is automatically created for you, called Reconciliation Discrepancies. If you ever learn the reason for the difference, you can void the adjustment made in this account post and then clear the correct transaction.

Troubleshooting Differences in the Beginning Balance

If this isn't the first time you've reconciled the bank account, the beginning balance that's displayed on the Begin Reconciliation window should match the beginning balance on the bank statement. That beginning balance is simply the ending balance arrived at from the last reconciliation you did.

If the beginning balance doesn't match the statement, it means that you or someone else working in your QuickBooks file did one (or more) of the following:

- You changed the amount on a transaction that had previously cleared.
- You voided a transaction that had previously cleared.
- You deleted a transaction that had previously cleared.
- You removed the cleared check mark from a transaction that had previously cleared.
- You manually entered a cleared check mark on a transaction that had not cleared.

You have to figure out which one of those actions you took after you last reconciled the account, and luckily, QuickBooks has a tool to help you. Click the Locate Discrepancies button on the Begin Reconciliation window to open the Locate Discrepancies dialog seen here:

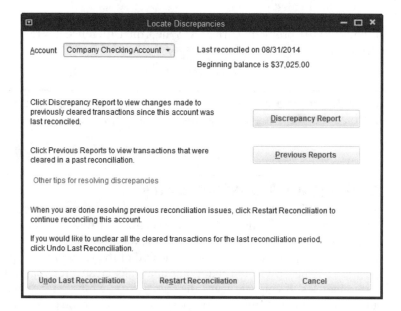

Viewing the Discrepancy Report

Click Discrepancy Report in the Locate Discrepancies dialog to see if any transactions that were cleared during a past reconciliation were later changed or deleted (see Figure 13-4).

This report shows you the details of the transactions that cleared during a previous reconciliation if any changes were made to those transactions since that reconciliation. If the Reconciled Amount column shows a positive number, the original cleared transaction was a deposit; a negative number indicates a disbursement.

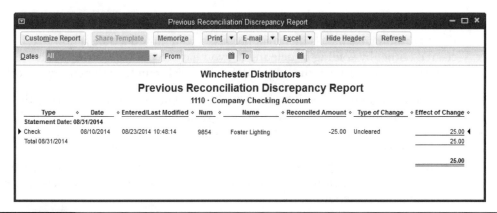

FIGURE 13-4 Someone uncleared a transaction that was cleared during a previous reconciliation.

The Type Of Change column provides a clue about the action you must take to correct the unmatched beginning balances:

- **Uncleared** The check mark was removed in the Cleared column of the register.
- **Deleted** You deleted the transaction.
- **Amount** You changed the amount of the transaction. The difference between the amount in the Reconciled Amount column and the amount in the Effect Of Change column is the amount of the change.

This report doesn't offer a Type Of Change named Void, so a voided transaction is merely marked as changed, and the text in the Type Of Change column is Amount. A transaction with a changed amount equal to and opposite of the original amount was almost certainly a transaction you voided after it cleared.

Correcting Opening Balance Differences

Use the information in the Discrepancy Report to correct the problems you created by changing previously cleared transactions.

Correcting Changed Transactions

If you cleared or uncleared a transaction manually, open the bank register and undo this action by clicking in the Cleared column (designated by a check mark) until a check mark appears next to the transaction. If you changed the amount of a transaction that had cleared and the transaction still exists in the register with an amount, change the amount back to the original amount for that transaction.

Replacing Voided or Deleted Cleared Transactions

If the beginning balance is incorrect because you removed a transaction that had cleared (either by voiding or deleting it), you have to put the transaction back into your register. You can get the information you need from the Discrepancy report.

- If a transaction is there but marked VOID, re-enter it, using the data in the reconciliation report. That transaction wasn't void when you performed the last reconciliation; it had cleared. Therefore, it doesn't meet any of the reasons to void a transaction.
- If a transaction appears in the reconciliation report but is not in the register, it was deleted. If it cleared, it can't be deleted. Re-enter it, using the data in the reconciliation report.
- Check the amounts on the printed check reconciliation report against the data in the register to see if any amount was changed after the account was reconciled. If so, restore the original amount.

If you re-enter a transaction that was voided or deleted after it cleared, and you put a check mark into the Cleared Column, QuickBooks adds it to your Reconcile window with a check mark already in place. This action doesn't adjust your opening balance on the Begin Reconciliation window, but it does readjust the math so the current reconciliation works and next month's opening balance will be correct.

Undoing the Last Reconciliation

QuickBooks lets you undo the last reconciliation, which means that all transactions cleared during the reconciliation are uncleared. This is a good way to start over if you're "stuck" with the current reconciliation and the problems seem to stem from the previous reconciliation (especially if you forced the previous reconciliation by having QuickBooks make an adjusting entry).

Click the Undo Last Reconciliation button on the Begin Reconciliation window. QuickBooks suggests you click Cancel and back up your company file before continuing. Backing up is an excellent idea, because you can restore the data back to its reconciled state in case you don't get the results you were expecting. Then, begin reconciling again, click Undo Last Reconciliation, and click Continue.

QuickBooks performs the following actions:

- Removes the cleared status of all transactions you cleared during the last reconciliation
- Leaves the amounts you entered for interest and bank charges so you don't need to re-enter them

When the process completes, QuickBooks displays a message to confirm that fact. Click OK to clear the message and return to the Begin Reconciliation window.

If QuickBooks made an adjustment entry during the last reconciliation, click Cancel to close the Begin Reconciliation window. Open the account's register and delete the adjustment entry—it's the entry posted to the Reconciliation Adjustment account. Hopefully, this time the reconciliation will work and you won't need another adjusting entry.

Start the reconciliation process again for the same month you just "undid." When the Begin Reconciliation window opens, the data that appears is the same data that appeared when you started the last reconciliation—the last reconciliation date, the statement date, and the beginning balance are back.

Enter the ending balance from the bank statement. Do *not* enter the interest and bank charges again since they were *not* removed when QuickBooks undid the last reconciliation. Instead, find them in the Reconcile window and clear them.

Good luck!

Printing, E-mailing, and Managing Documents in QuickBooks

n this chapter:

- Set up your printers for use with QuickBooks

- Print forms and checks

- E-mail forms

- Manage QuickBooks documents

Many of the transactions that you create in QuickBooks need to be delivered to your customers, vendors, or employees. In some cases, the delivery method is in the form of a printed document; in other cases, transactions are sent electronically. This chapter covers your options for both sending and storing the forms and documents that are critical to running your business.

QuickBooks Printer Setup

If you choose to send printed versions of your documents, you have to link each type of document you print to a specific printer and then configure the way the printer processes each document type.

Choose File | Printer Setup to begin. The Printer Setup dialog opens with the drop-down list of the Form Name field displayed. Select the form you want to print, as shown in Figure 14-1.

FIGURE 14-1   Start by selecting the form you want to print.

The form type you select determines the contents of the Printer Setup dialog; the tabs, fields, and options vary depending on the form. Many of the forms you print come out of the printer perfectly with little or no adjustment; however, some forms (such as checks) should be tweaked to make sure the output is what you want it to be. If you use multiple printers, you can assign specific printers to specific types of forms, and QuickBooks will always select the appropriate printer when you print those forms.

Choosing Form Printing Settings

This section covers setting up forms, with the exception of checks. See the section "Using QuickBooks to Print Checks" later in this chapter to learn how to set up check printing.

You must assign a printer and assign settings for the forms you print. Start by selecting the appropriate form in the Form Name field at the top of the Printer Setup dialog; the fields in the dialog change to match the needs of the form you selected. For example, Figure 14-2 shows the setup options for an invoice; other forms have different—and sometimes fewer—options available.

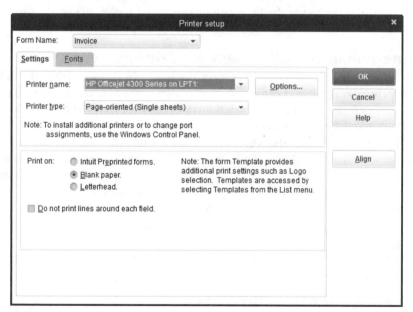

FIGURE 14-2 Choose your settings for printing an invoice.

Choosing a Printer for a Form

The drop-down list in the Printer Name field displays the printers installed on your computer. Select the appropriate printer for this form.

Selecting the Paper for Printing a Form

For transaction forms, the setup offers three types of paper: Intuit preprinted forms, blank paper, and letterhead.

- **Intuit Preprinted Forms** You can order these forms from Intuit or your favorite supplier that carries forms specifically designed for QuickBooks. All the fields are preprinted and aligned to match the way QuickBooks prints the form. When you print, only the data prints, not the field names.
- **Blank Paper** If you use blank paper to print transaction forms, QuickBooks prints your company name and address at the top of the paper and prints the field names in addition to the data. Lines to separate fields and columns are also printed. You can select the option not to print the lines, but without the column and field lines, the invoice may be difficult to read or understand.
- **Letterhead** This setting is the same as the Blank Paper setting, except QuickBooks does not print the company name and address information at the top, and the top of the form begins printing 2 inches below the top of the paper to make sure the data doesn't print over your preprinted letterhead text.

Fine-tuning the Alignment for Printing Forms

To make sure that everything prints in the right place or to change the position of the printed output, you can fine-tune the alignment of text. Although it's important to do this if you're using preprinted forms, it doesn't hurt to check the way the printout looks on blank paper or letterhead.

Click Align to open the Align Printer dialog. Choose the template that you want to work with and click OK. This opens the Fine Alignment dialog in which you can print a sample and then move text up, down, left, or right to make adjustments to the sample printout. Continue to print a sample and make adjustments until the printout looks the way you want it to.

Adjustments affect all the text as a block. You cannot adjust individual fields, rows, or other elements in the printed form. So if you adjust the alignment by moving a field up 14/100th of an inch, for example, everything that prints on the form moves up 14/100th of an inch.

Printing Forms as PDF Files

QuickBooks automatically installs a PDF printer driver when you install the software. The printer driver is used by QuickBooks when, for example, you send an invoice or purchase order via e-mail to customers or vendors (covered later in this chapter in the section, "E-mail Forms and Reports"). If you want to print your forms as PDF documents, with the form open choose File | Save As PDF.

Using QuickBooks to Print Checks

If you want to print your checks from within QuickBooks instead of creating checks manually, you must use checks that are designed specifically for QuickBooks.

Purchasing Checks That Work with QuickBooks

QuickBooks checks come in a wide range of colors and designs and in several varieties. You can order any of the following check types directly from Intuit by choosing Banking | Order Checks & Envelopes | Order Checks:

- Voucher checks
- Standard business checks
- Wallet-sized checks

Setting Up Your Printer for Checks

To configure your printer to manage check printing, choose File | Printer Setup from the menu bar. Select Check/PayCheck as the form, and then select the printer you're using for checks. Your Printer Setup window should look similar to Figure 14-3.

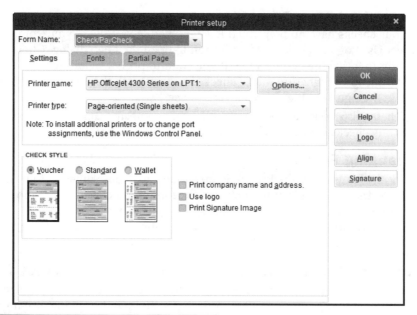

FIGURE 14-3   Set up your printer for check printing.

Choosing a Check Style

You have to select a check style, and it has to match the check style you purchased, of course. Three styles are available for QuickBooks checks, and a sample of each style appears in the dialog to show you what the style looks like.

- **Voucher checks**   These have a detachable section on the check form. QuickBooks prints voucher information if you have voucher checks, including the name of the payee, the date, and the individual amounts of the bills being paid by this check. The voucher is attached to the bottom of the check. The check is the width of a regular business envelope.
- **Standard checks**   These are just basic checks. They're the width of a regular business envelope (usually called a *#10 envelope*). If you have a laser or inkjet printer, three checks fit on each page. Continuous (dot-matrix) feed printers just keep rolling, since the checks are printed on a continuous sheet with perforations separating the checks.
- **Wallet checks**   These are narrower than the other two check styles so they fit in your wallet. The paper size is the same as the other checks (otherwise, you'd have a problem with your printer), but there's a perforation on the left edge of the check so you can tear the ledger portion off the check.

Adding a Logo and Signature

If your checks have no preprinted logo and you have a file of your company logo, select Use Logo or click the Logo button to open the Logo dialog. Click the File button to locate the graphics file. If you want to print a signature on your checks, select the Print Signature Image check box; then click the Signature button and locate the signature file that you want to use.

There's also a selection box for printing your company name and address, but when you buy checks, you should have that information preprinted.

Changing Fonts

Click the Fonts tab in the Printer Setup window to choose different fonts for printed checks. Use the Font button to change the font for all check information, with the exception of your company's name and address. To change the font for this information, click the Address Font button. Click the appropriate button and then choose a font, a font style, and a size from the dialog that opens.

Handling Partial Check Pages on Laser and Inkjet Printers

If you're printing to a laser or inkjet printer, you don't have the advantage that a continuous feed printer provides—printing a check and stopping, leaving the next blank check waiting in the printer for the next time you print checks. QuickBooks offers a handy solution for this problem on the Partial Page tab (see Figure 14-4). The solution that matches your printer's capabilities is preselected.

FIGURE 14-4 Partial page printing allows you to print one check on a full page of checks.

Aligning the Printout

Click the Align button to print a sample check and see where the printing lines up on the physical check. You can move the starting points for printing up/down or left/right to make sure everything prints where it's supposed to. When you're finished, click OK in the Printer Setup window to save the configuration data.

Printer Settings vs. Printer Options

When you assign a printer to a specific form and customize the printing setup for that form, QuickBooks memorizes that selection. If you change printers when you're ready to print, the next time you print the same form, QuickBooks returns to the original printer and printer settings linked to that form type, unless you reconfigure the setup to change printers.

Every printer has its own set of options to control the way printing occurs. And when you're ready to print a document, such as an invoice, you can set the printing options when you print. On the Print dialog is an Options button that you can click to open an additional dialog for selecting options for the selected printer. You can change the tray (or select manual feed), change the resolution of the printing, and perform other tweaks.

▶▶ ProAdvisor Recommends

Print Settings May Not Work for Multiple Companies

QuickBooks printer settings are applied to the software, not to the company file that's open when you set up printers. That means that if you work in multiple company files and they require different print settings, you'll need to set up the printer and the printing options each time you change the company file.

So, for example, if one company file has payroll and buys voucher checks for all their check printing, but the other company uses wallet-size checks, you must go through a complete printer setup every time you switch company files and want to print checks. In addition, QuickBooks doesn't let you perform separate setups for payroll checks (with vouchers) and vendor checks (without vouchers). You can solve that problem for a single company by buying voucher checks for both types of check printing. If you've repositioned printing with the Align feature, you should write down your saved settings so you can enter them again each time you switch between companies.

QuickBooks does not memorize these options; it uses the printer's defaults the next time you print the form type. If you want to make printer options permanent, you must change the printer configuration in the Windows Printers folder.

Print Checks

If you print checks in QuickBooks, you can print each check as you enter and save it in the Write Checks window, or you can wait until you've finished entering all your checks and then print them in a batch.

Printing Each Check As You Create It

If you use the Write Checks window to create a check, when you've finished entering all the data, you can click the Print icon at the top of the window. The Print Check dialog opens, and the next printed check number is entered as the default.

Peek at the checks in your printer to make sure this is actually the next check number; if it's not, change the number in the dialog. Then click OK to open the Print Checks dialog and click Print. After sending the check to the printer, QuickBooks displays the Print Checks – Confirmation dialog.

	Print Checks - Confirmation		✖

If your checks printed correctly, click OK.

What if my checks printed in reverse order?

If you need to reprint any checks, select them and click OK. Then return to the Select Checks to Print window to reprint them.

REPRINT	CHECK NO.	PAYEE	AMOUNT
	3090	Kuver Property	183.75

Select All

What if my checks printed incorrectly?   **Cancel**   **OK**

If the check printed properly, click OK. If not, click Cancel to fix the problem and print the check again; see "Reprinting Checks After a Problem," later in this section. If you want to create additional checks in the Write Checks window, you can repeat these steps. However, if you're creating multiple checks, it's faster to create all the checks and then print them in a batch.

➤➤ **ProAdvisor Recommends**

How QuickBooks Numbers Checks

QuickBooks tracks two sets of check numbers for each checking account:

- **Numbers for checks that are entered manually**   The next available number is automatically inserted when you enter checks in the check register or deselect the Print Later option in the Write Checks or Pay Bills window.
- **Numbers for checks that are printed in QuickBooks**   The next available number is used automatically when you print checks.

This is a useful feature if you have preprinted checks in the office for printing checks and a checkbook you carry around so you can write checks when you're not in the office.

Printing Checks in Batches

You can print all your checks in a batch after you've completed the task of creating them. If you've been working in the Write Checks window, click the Save & New button to continue to create checks. When you're finished, use one of the following options to print all the checks you've prepared:

- On the last check, click Save, and then click the arrow below the Print icon on the check window and select Batch.
- Click Save & Close when you create the last check, and then choose File | Print Forms | Checks to print the batch.

Either option opens the Select Checks To Print dialog.

By default, all the unprinted checks are selected for printing, which is almost always what you want to do, but you can deselect checks if there's a reason to do so (they remain in the batch and will be waiting for you the next time you print checks). Click OK to open the Print Checks window.

If your checks were written on different bank accounts, the Select Checks To Print window displays only the checks ready for printing from a specific bank account. After you print those checks, use the same steps to get to the Select Checks To Print window and change the bank account to see those checks. Don't forget to put the correct checks in your printer.

If you use the Pay Bills window to create checks for vendors, when you finish selecting the bills and amounts to pay, click Pay Selected Bills. If you selected the To Be Printed option, QuickBooks displays a Payment Summary window with a Print Checks button. If you selected the Assign Check Number option, you're asked to assign a check number in the Assign Check Numbers dialog before you see the summary.

- If these are the only checks you're creating at the moment, click Print Checks.
- If you have additional checks to print, you can click Done and print all your checks at once from the File menu, as described earlier in this section.

In the Print Checks dialog, click Print to begin printing your checks. When all the checks have been sent to the printer, QuickBooks displays the Print Checks – Confirmation window. If all the checks printed correctly, click OK.

Reprinting Checks After a Problem

Sometimes things go awry when you're printing. The paper jams, you run out of toner, or an ink cartridge is empty.

If there is a problem, select the check(s) that didn't print properly in the Print Checks – Confirmation window, click OK, and put more checks into the printer.

Then click OK and choose File | Print Forms | Checks. Your unprinted checks are listed in the Select Checks To Print dialog, and the first check number should be the next available check number—if it's not, you can change it.

Ways to Print Transaction Forms

All of the forms that you create in QuickBooks (such as invoices and checks, for example) can be printed one at a time, as you create them, or together in a batch.

Printing Transactions As You Create Them

For your security and the integrity of your QuickBooks file, it's best to save the transaction before printing; that way, you have a record of the transaction in your QuickBooks file. In fact, QuickBooks has a default Preference setting that will automatically save the transaction for you before printing. You can find this option by selecting Edit | Preferences | General. On the Company Preferences tab, select the Save Transactions Before Printing option. You can deselect this option setting if you want the ability to print the current transaction before saving it.

To print the current transaction, click the Print button at the top of the transaction window. QuickBooks opens the Print dialog (Figure 14-5 displays the Print One Invoice dialog). Click Print to send the transaction form to the selected printer.

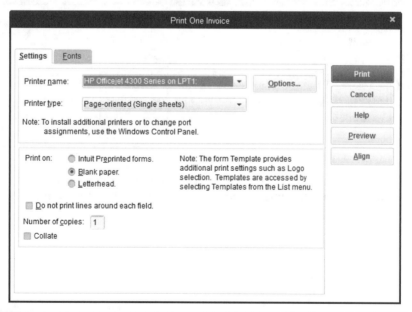

FIGURE 14-5 Printing a single invoice transaction is quick and easy.

Previewing Form Printouts

If you want to see what the printed document looks like, click the arrow below the Print icon at the top of the document window and select Preview.

Often, the printed form differs from the form shown onscreen. For example, if you're creating a packing slip, the onscreen form shows prices, but the printed form doesn't. If you create custom fields for lists or items, the custom field data may appear only in the onscreen form to help you prepare the transaction (such as backorder preferences for customers, advance payment requirements for vendors, and so on).

To learn how to customize transaction forms and decide which fields are seen only onscreen, only on the printed form, or on both, read Chapter 24.

Printing Transaction Forms in Batches

To print transactions in batches, make sure the Print Later check box is selected on each transaction you create. Then follow these steps to batch-print the documents:

1. Choose File | Print Forms | *<Transaction Type>* (substitute your transaction type).
2. In the Select *<Transaction Type>* To Print window, all your unprinted transaction forms are selected with a check mark. Click the check marks to remove them from any forms you don't want to print at this time (it's a toggle).

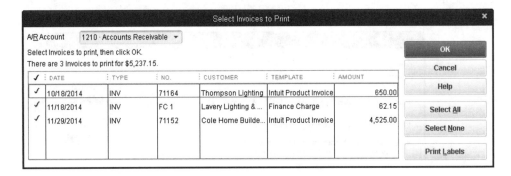

3. Click OK to print. A Print *<Transaction Type>* dialog appears, where you can change or select printing options. Click Print to begin printing. After sending

the documents to the printer, QuickBooks asks you to confirm that all the documents printed properly.

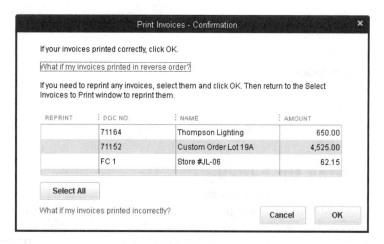

4. If everything printed properly, click OK; if not, in the Confirmation dialog, select the forms that need to be reprinted and click OK. Now return to the Print Forms *<Transaction Type>* dialog, where the forms you selected for reprinting are listed, so you can continue printing your batch. Of course, before taking this step, you'll need to unjam the printer, put in a new ink cartridge, or correct any other problem that caused the original print job to fail.

E-mail Forms and Reports

You can e-mail documents and reports directly from QuickBooks as PDF attachments to e-mail messages. E-mailing works exactly the same as printing forms and reports, as described earlier in this chapter. That is, you can e-mail each individual transaction as you create it or save the transactions and e-mail them in a batch.

If you're using Outlook or a compatible web-based e-mail service, QuickBooks can send e-mail to your customers either directly through your e-mail software or your e-mail service. If you use e-mail software other than the supported software, you can use QuickBooks E-mail, which provides a server-based e-mail service. This is a service that you have to sign up for, and additional fees may apply.

You can e-mail any report (either as a PDF file or as an Excel file), and you can also e-mail all of the following QuickBooks transaction forms:

- Invoices
- Estimates
- Sales receipts
- Credit memos
- Statements
- Purchase orders
- Pay stubs (if you use QuickBooks payroll and have signed up for direct deposit)

Setting Up E-mail

Your e-mail setup options can be found by selecting Edit | Preferences | Send Forms. If QuickBooks finds a copy of one of the supported e-mail software applications (such as Outlook) on your computer with an active profile installed (an *active profile* is an e-mail account established in the software, and the software is the default e-mail software on your computer), the Send Forms category on the My Preferences tab shows this as the default e-mail method, as shown in Figure 14-6. If these options aren't displayed, you must use the QuickBooks E-mail service to send transaction forms and reports.

The My Preferences tab also shows an option, Auto-check The "Email Later" Checkbox If Customer's Preferred Delivery Method Is E-mail, to instruct QuickBooks to select Email Later automatically on every transaction linked to a customer that has e-mail set as their preferred delivery method (set on the Payment Settings tab of the customer record). If you configure a customer's delivery method as e-mail, make sure you enter the customer's e-mail address as well.

When creating Purchase Orders, you'll also have the option to Email Later if you want to send those transactions in a batch. This option works only if you've entered an e-mail address for the vendor on their Address Info tab in their record.

On the Company Preferences tab (Figure 14-7), you can use e-mail templates to design multiple versions of the message that accompanies an e-mailed form (such as invoices, purchase orders, and estimates, to name a few).

Click the Add, Edit, or Delete buttons to create, modify, or delete an e-mail template.

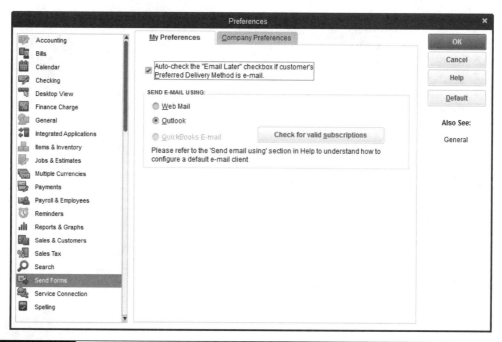

FIGURE 14-6 QuickBooks selects your installed e-mail software by default.

Sending E-mail

To send a single transaction form by e-mail, click the Email button at the top of the transaction form. Or select Email Later (located next to the Email button), before saving the transaction to send the e-mail in a batch.

Using Your E-mail Software

If QuickBooks is using Outlook to send transaction forms (or reports), the standard Create Message window appears.

- If the customer's or vendor's e-mail address is stored in QuickBooks, it's automatically inserted into the To: field.
- If the customer's or vendor's e-mail address is not available, QuickBooks searches your e-mail software address book. If the name/e-mail is found, the entry in the To: field is underlined to indicate the name has been matched to an existing address book entry.
- If the customer's or vendor's e-mail address is not available in either place, you'll need to add the customer's e-mail address to your QuickBooks file.

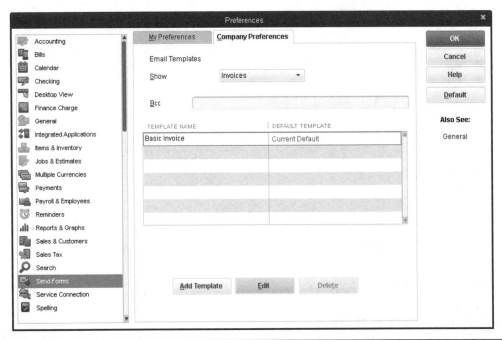

FIGURE 14-7 Use e-mail templates to create a customized e-mail message when sending a form from QuickBooks

The Subject field is prefilled with *<Transaction Number>* from *<YourCompanyName>*. The Attachment field is prefilled with the name of the PDF file of the transaction form. The text of the message is prefilled by QuickBooks, using the text in the Send Forms Preferences dialog, discussed in the previous section.

Using QuickBooks E-mail

If you're not using one of the supported e-mail applications and you've activated the QuickBooks E-mail service, QuickBooks fills out the message and attaches the document in the same way it does when you're using your own e-mail software.

When you click Send Now, QuickBooks opens a browser window and takes you to the QuickBooks Billing Solutions website. If this is the first time you're e-mailing invoices, follow the prompts to complete the sign-up process, and then QuickBooks will send the e-mail. Thereafter, your e-mail is sent automatically. An additional feature of this Billing Solutions service is the ability to accept online payments from your customers that receive an invoice from you via this service (additional fees may apply).

ProAdvisor Tip: If you use the QuickBooks Billing Solutions, enter your own e-mail address in the CC: or BCC: field of the message window so you have a record of the e-mail. (If you use your own software, you have a copy in the Sent Messages folder.)

Document Management: Using the Attach File Feature

The Attach File feature allows you to attach files of any type to a QuickBooks list record or transaction. You'll see an Attach File icon at the top of all transaction windows as well as in all QuickBooks centers.

Once you've attached a file or scanned image, it is easily accessible via the Doc Center (which you can open by clicking the Docs button on the Icon Bar). For example, you might want to attach a scanned copy of a customer's purchase order to the invoice that you generate for them in QuickBooks, or maybe you'll need to attach an e-mailed copy of a vendor's bill when you enter the bill into QuickBooks. Or you might want to attach a file or image to a vendor record.

To attach a file or image to a transaction (such as an invoice or estimate), open the transaction and click the Attach File button. To attach a document to a customer or vendor record, highlight the record's name in the appropriate Center, and then click the Attach (paper clip) icon.

The Attachments window opens, giving you the option of attaching a document directly from your computer, your scanner, or the Doc Center.

A QuickBooks transaction or record that has an attachment will display a blue icon (a paper clip attached to a piece of paper), indicating that an attached file or image exists. Click this icon to open the Doc Center to view this and other files and documents stored there.

Other Tasks You May Need to Complete in QuickBooks

Part Three covers features and tasks in QuickBooks that are either optional or used less frequently than those covered in the previous two parts. Tracking inventory, for example, is something that not all QuickBooks users need to do—but for businesses that need to keep track of the on-hand quantities of the products that they sell, Chapter 15 is required reading.

Using Bank Feeds (aka Online Banking) can be a big time saver and can also help you keep accurate bank balances in QuickBooks. Learn more about this feature in Chapter 16.

The last two chapters of Part Three cover tasks that you won't necessarily be doing every day, but they are nonetheless very important. Journal entries, covered in Chapter 17, are special transactions that are used to make changes directly to an account without using a regular transaction (such as an invoice or check). Chapter 18 tells you what you can do to prepare your QuickBooks data for year end and for your accountant.

Using QuickBooks to Manage Your Inventory

n this chapter:

- Create inventory items
- Complete a physical inventory
- Adjust inventory quantities and costs
- Run inventory reports

Accurately keeping track of the inventory items that you sell is no easy task. In fact, for many businesses, the warehouse can be a source of frustration and erroneous information. (The term "warehouse" is used generically here to indicate the place where you store inventory, but it may be your basement or garage instead of a real warehouse.) This chapter covers how to set up and make adjustments to your inventory. Chapter 11 covers what you need to know to purchase, receive, and manage your inventory.

What Is an Inventory Item?

An inventory item is a product you manufacture, assemble, or purchase for the purpose of selling to a customer. Items that you store to use in the normal course of business that are resold to customers as part of other services being involved are also inventory. But if you're a plumber and you store valves, pipes, and other plumbing parts to use when you perform a job, you may choose to track those items as non-inventory items (especially if they are low-value items). If you're a consultant who uses consumables or supplies in the course of your consulting work and you keep those products on hand to sell to customers, you can also choose not to track those supplies as inventory.

> **ProAdvisor Tip:** QuickBooks provides an item type called a non-inventory part that you can use to indicate products you used on a job when you invoice customers. You can create reports on those items to track quantity and revenue amounts. These item types don't require you to attend to the kinds of details and tax reports that inventory items do.

In general, the types of businesses that typically track inventory are manufacturers (who may use inventory parts to create other inventory parts), wholesale distributors, and retailers.

Set Up QuickBooks for Inventory Tracking

To track inventory, you must first enable the inventory feature. Choose Edit | Preferences and select the Items & Inventory category in the left pane. Move to the Company Preferences tab (see Figure 15-1) to see the inventory options.

FIGURE 15-1 Enable inventory and set the features to use for inventory tracking.

When you turn on the inventory feature, you also turn on the purchase order feature (although you don't have to use purchase orders to use the inventory feature). In addition, the dialog offers two options that help you keep your inventory records accurately:

- **Warn About Duplicate Purchase Order Numbers** When enabled, if you use a PO number that's already in use, QuickBooks will display a message warning you of that fact. (The system doesn't prevent you from using the duplicate number, but it's a good idea to heed the warning to avoid problems.)
- **Warn If Not Enough Inventory Quantity On Hand (QOH) To Sell** When enabled, QuickBooks flashes a warning if you fill out a sales transaction that has a quantity greater than the current available units of that product. You can continue the sale if you wish and track the unfilled quantity as a backorder (covered later in this chapter).

ProAdvisor Tip: The Company Preferences tab of the Items & Inventory Preferences dialog shows an Advanced Inventory Settings button and an Enable button for Unit of Measure. The Advanced Inventory feature, available only in QuickBooks Enterprise Solutions, allows you to track inventory across multiple locations. Click the Learn About Serial #/Lots, FIFO And Multi-Location Inventory link to see if it's a fit for your business and learn how to upgrade to QuickBooks Enterprise Solutions. The Unit of Measure feature is available in most Premier editions and all Enterprise editions of QuickBooks.

Accounts Required for Inventory Are Automatically Created

After you've enabled inventory tracking and created your first inventory item, QuickBooks adds the following accounts to your chart of accounts:

- An Other Current Asset account named Inventory Asset
- A cost of goods sold account named Cost Of Goods Sold

You'll learn how QuickBooks posts amounts to these accounts in this chapter.

Create Inventory Items

Now you're ready to create your first inventory item. Open the Item List (choose Lists | Item List from the menu bar) to open the Item List window. Then press CTRL-N to open the New Item dialog and select Inventory Part from the drop-down list as the item type.

Fill in the information using the guidelines that follow (Figure 15-2 is an example of a blank inventory item record):

- The Item Name/Number is the way you will reference the item in the software—which is not necessarily the same way you'll want to describe this item to your customers in sales transactions. This field must be unique in your Item List.
- The Manufacturer's Part Number (useful if you're a distributor or retailer) lets you include the manufacturer's part number on your purchase orders. If you purchase from a distributor instead of a manufacturer, enter the distributor's part number. This makes creating an accurate purchase order much easier.
- The text you enter in the Description On Purchase Transactions field automatically appears when you create a purchase order. The text you enter in the Description On Sales Transactions field automatically appears in sales transaction forms, such as invoices, estimates, and sales receipts.
- You can enter a cost, but it's really a convenience for creating purchase orders (the cost appears automatically in the PO, which is useful if the cost doesn't change often). QuickBooks does not use this figure for posting cost of goods

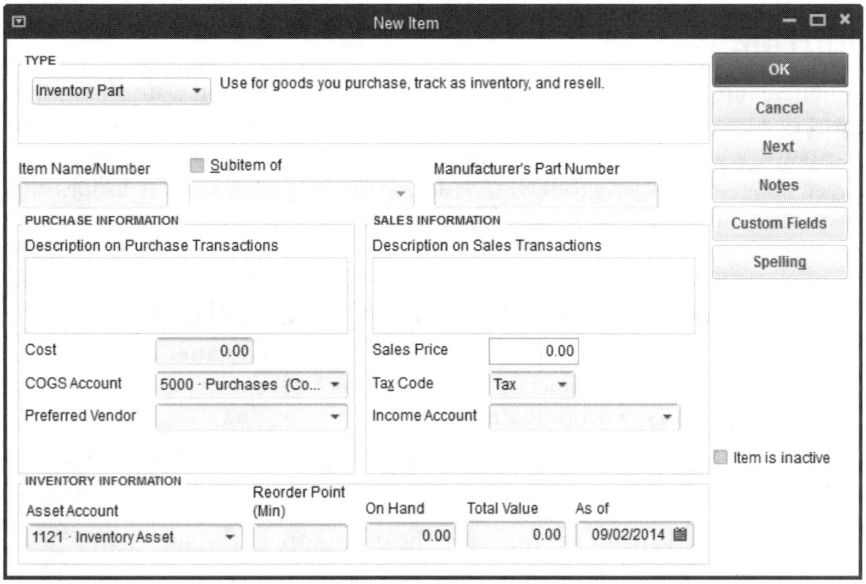

FIGURE 15-2 An inventory item record contains all the information you need to use it in transactions.

sold; instead, it uses the average cost of this item based on your item receipt and inventory adjustment transactions (all covered later in this chapter).

- If you enter a Sales Price, that amount is automatically entered when you create sales transactions (but you can change the price on an individual sales transaction).
- Choose the Tax Code for this item, which indicates whether the item is taxable to customers.
- Select the appropriate posting accounts for Cost Of Goods Sold (COGS) and Income.
- Enter a number in the Reorder Point field that reflects the minimum quantity you want to have in stock. When this quantity is reached, QuickBooks will issue a reminder about reordering if you've enabled the Reminders feature. To turn on the Reminders feature, choose Edit | Preferences and click the Reminders category. On the My Preferences tab, check the Show Reminders List When Opening A Company File check box. On the Company Preferences tab, choose either Show Summary or Show List for the Inventory To Reorder option.
- Do *not* enter anything in the On Hand or Total Value fields. Instead, let QuickBooks track these values as you receive items into inventory (covered in Chapter 11) and/or use the inventory adjustment feature. Inventory adjustments are covered later in this chapter.

Chapter 5 covers the Notes and Custom Fields buttons found on the New and Edit Item windows.

Use Subitems

Subitems are useful when there are choices for items and you want all the choices to be part of a larger hierarchy so you can sell them easily and track them efficiently. For instance, if you sell widgets in a variety of colors, you may want to create a subitem for each color: red widget, green widget, and so on. Or perhaps you sell shoes and want to separate your products by type, such as sandals, sneakers, boots, and so on.

Creating the Parent Item for a Subitem

To have a subitem, you must first create a parent item. Figure 15-3 shows the record of an item that has been specifically created as a parent item, using the Inventory Part type in the Type drop-down list.

Here are some guidelines for creating an inventory item that's designed to be a parent item:

- Use a generic name for the item; the details are in the subitem names.
- Use uppercase to make the item easier to see (especially in a long list of items).
- Don't enter a description; save that for the subitems.
- Don't enter the cost.
- Don't enter the price.
- Don't enter a reorder point.

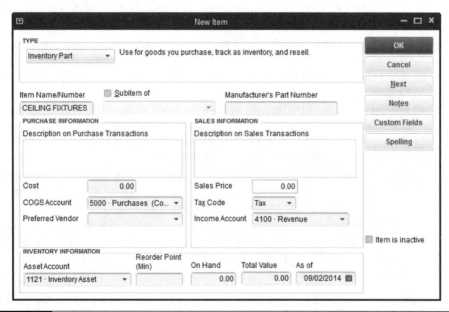

FIGURE 15-3 This item isn't sold to customers—it exists only as a parent item to define a category of items that you sell.

- Don't enter the quantity on hand.
- Enter the Inventory Asset, COG, and Income accounts because they are required fields for all inventory items.

Creating Subitems

Having created the parent item, subitems are easy to create. Open a blank New Item window (press CTRL-N) and follow these steps:

1. In the Item Name/Number field, enter the code for this item. It can be a color, a size, a manufacturer name, or any other code that makes this subitem unique when compared to other subitems under the same parent item (see Figure 15-4).
2. Check the Subitem Of box, and then select the parent item from the drop-down list that appears when you click the arrow to the right of the field.
3. Enter the Manufacturer's Part Number (for creating purchase orders).
4. Optionally, enter any descriptions you want to appear on purchase orders and sales transactions.
5. Optionally, enter the cost that you expect to pay for this item and a preferred vendor.
6. Optionally, enter the sales price.
7. Enter the general ledger account information (Inventory Asset, Cost Of Goods, and Income accounts).

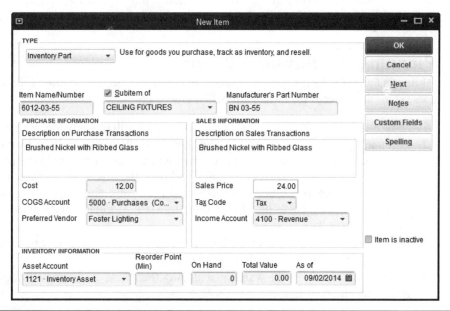

FIGURE 15-4 Creating inventory subitems makes it easier to identify items in your item list.

8. Enter the reorder point if you're using that feature.

9. *Do not* enter anything in the On Hand or Total Value fields. Instead, let QuickBooks track these values as you receive items into inventory (covered in Chapter 11) and/or use the inventory adjustment feature. Inventory adjustments are covered later in this chapter.

10. Click Next to enter another inventory item, or click OK if you're finished.

Count Inventory

For some business owners, there's nothing more dreaded than doing a physical inventory. However, no matter how careful you are with QuickBooks transactions, no matter how strict your internal controls are for making sure everything that comes and goes is accounted for, you'll often find that your physical inventory does not match your QuickBooks figures. Don't worry; you're not alone.

Printing the Physical Inventory Worksheet

If it's time to count your inventory, start by printing a Physical Inventory Worksheet (see Figure 15-5). To open the worksheet, select Reports | Inventory | Physical Inventory Worksheet. This report lists your inventory items and subitems in alphabetical order, along with the current quantity on hand, which is calculated from your QuickBooks transactions. In addition, a column is set up to record the actual count as you walk around your warehouse with this printout (and a pen) in hand. Click the Print button in the worksheet window to bring up the Print Reports window. In the Number Of Copies box, enter as many copies as you need.

Planning the Physical Count

Although QuickBooks doesn't have a built-in automatic "freeze" feature, following these steps during your physical count will allow you to perform this process manually:

1. Print the Physical Inventory worksheet *only* when you're ready to start counting.

2. Enter and print invoices as usual, and then mark them as pending (by clicking the Mark As Pending button on the Create Invoice ribbon bar) until your physical inventory is complete. (Also, don't pick and pack the inventory for these invoices until after the count.) Once you're finished with your counting, you'll mark these pending invoices as final by clicking the Mark As Final button on the Create Invoice ribbon bar.

3. Don't receive inventory in QuickBooks, using a Receive Items or Enter Bill For Received Items form, until after the count.

4. If inventory arrives in the warehouse during the count, don't unpack the boxes until after the count.

Item	Description	Preferred Vendor	Quantity On Hand	Physical Count
Indoor Electri...	100' 12-2 NM-B with Gr...		600	
Bath/Vanity F...			0	
Bath/Vanity F...	Brushed Nickel with Op...	Foster Lighting	74	
Bath/Vanity F...	Solid Brass with Etched...	Foster Lighting	0	
Bath/Vanity F...	Solid Brass with Etched...	Foster Lighting	70	
Bath/Vanity F...	White with Satin White G...	Foster Lighting	6	
Bath/Vanity F...	Pearl Nickel, 5 Light	Paulsen's Lighting	52	
Bath/Vanity F...	Polished Chrome, 4 Light	Paulsen's Lighting	73	
Bath/Vanity F...	Polished Brass, 6 Light	Paulsen's Lighting	35	
Bath/Vanity F...	Beveled Mirror with Etc...	Hall Lighting & Acc...	13	
Ceiling fixtures			11	
Ceiling fixture...	Brass Pendant with Rib...	Foster Lighting	79	
Ceiling fixture...	Desert Stone Finish	Foster Lighting	63	
Ceiling fixture...	Brushed Nickel Pendant...	Foster Lighting	71	
Ceiling fixture...	Tapestry with Etched G...	Foster Lighting	131	
Ceiling fixture...	Brushed Nickel with Rib...	Foster Lighting	88	
Ceiling fixture...	Steel Colonial with Opal...	Hall Lighting & Acc...	111	
Ceiling fixture...	Gold Colonial	Hall Lighting & Acc...	83	
Ceiling fixture...	Millstone Finish, 1 light	Paulsen's Lighting	20	
Ceiling fixture...	Copper Verde, Seeded ...	Paulsen's Lighting	52	
Ceiling fixture...	Textured White Pendant	Paulsen's Lighting	104	
Ceiling fixture...	Cobblestone Pendant w...	Paulsen's Lighting	64	
Ceiling fixture...	Flat Glass, Polished Bra...	Paulsen's Lighting	44	
Ceiling fixture...	White Dome	Paulsen's Lighting	41	
Ceiling fixture...	Polished Brass with Wh...	Paulsen's Lighting	95	
Ceiling fixture...	Cobblestone Pendant Bar	Paulsen's Lighting	9	
Ceiling fixture...	Textured White Pendan...	Paulsen's Lighting	9	
Chandeliers			0	
Chandeliers:2...	Tapestry with Faux Ala...	Foster Lighting	21	
Chandeliers:2...	River Rock with Faux A...	Foster Lighting	17	
Chandeliers:2...	Frosted Taupe with Mar...	Foster Lighting	13	
Chandeliers:7...	Chestnut with Marble G...	Foster Lighting	31	
Chandeliers:P...	Golden Umber, 6 Light	Paulsen's Lighting	10	
Chandeliers:P...	Brass with Golden Umb...	Paulsen's Lighting	18	
Exterior Fixtu...			0	

FIGURE 15-5 The Physical Inventory Worksheet comes with blank lines so you can record your counts, but it can be customized to fit your needs.

It is a good idea to *have somebody in charge*—one person who knows who is counting what. When each counter is finished, their sheet should be handed to the person in charge, who ideally will be the person who enters the counts into QuickBooks.

After the count, bring in any inventory that's arrived during the count. Then start picking and packing the orders that were placed during your physical inventory.

Making Inventory Adjustments

After you've finished counting the inventory, you may find that the numbers on the worksheet don't match the physical count. In fact, it's almost a sure bet that the numbers won't match.

➡➡ **ProAdvisor Recommends**

Customize the Physical Inventory Worksheet

When first opened, the Physical Inventory Worksheet displays only basic information about the inventory that you carry. But depending on the way you plan on carrying out your physical inventory, you may find that you need more information.

For example, by default, only the inventory items that have an active status are displayed. So if you made any inventory items inactive and you think (or know) there are still units in stock of that item, consider filtering the report to show the inactive items so you can identify any on-hand quantities for these items. Also, if any items are obsolete or discontinued, be sure to adjust their quantities or value to zero. If you think they may have a resale value, consider making them active again.

It might make sense, for example, for you to print separate worksheets by vendor, because you want to divide up and assign the counting process to your staff accordingly. In that case, you'd filter the report by Preferred Vendor. Or maybe you want to start your physical inventory by targeting your highest value items first. In that case, you could either add a column for Cost (or Price) and re-sort your report by that column—with the highest value items at the top—or you could filter the report to display items with a cost above a certain dollar amount.

You can find all customization options by clicking the Customize Report button at the top of the Physical Inventory Worksheet window. This action opens the Modify Report window which contains four tabs. Use the Display tab to add or remove columns and the Filters tab to set one of the multiple filters available that allow you to control the items that are displayed. The Header/Footer tab is where you can customize the name of the report and the appearance of other titles that appear on the report, whereas the Fonts & Numbers tab lets you change the font size and color.

To learn more about how to work with and customize QuickBooks Reports in general, check out Chapter 26.

In many cases, the physical count is lower than the QuickBooks figures. This is called *shrinkage*. Shrinkage is a way of describing unexplained missing inventory.

Adjusting the Count

You'll use the Adjust Quantity/Value On Hand window to tell QuickBooks about the results of your physical count. Choose Vendors | Inventory Activities | Adjust Quantity/Value On Hand to open the Adjust Quantity/Value On Hand window shown in Figure 15-6.

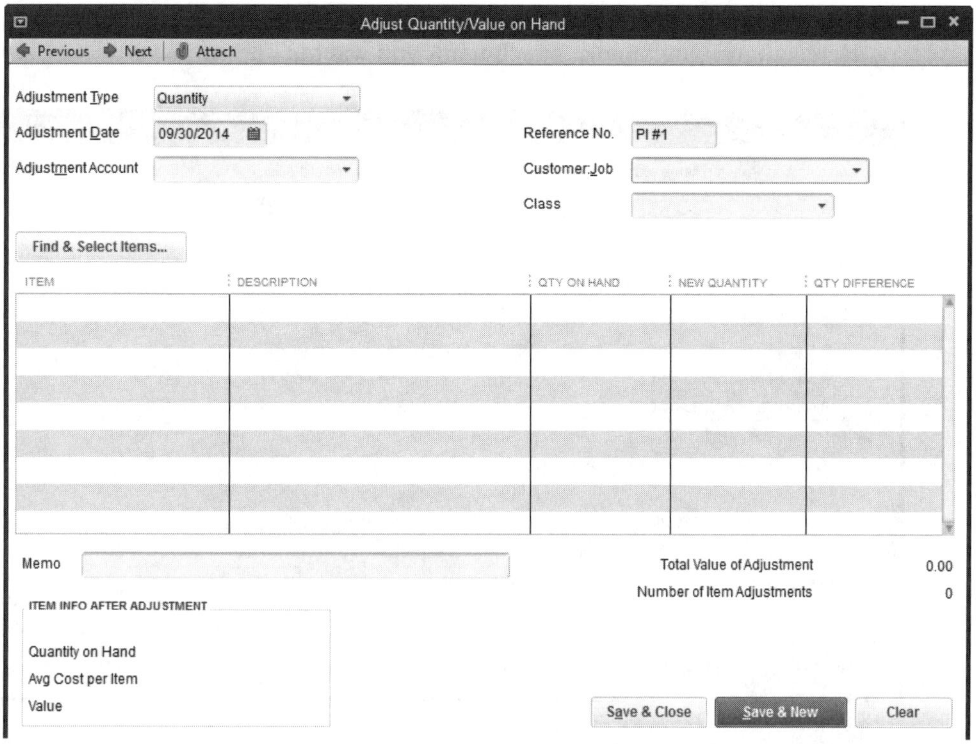

FIGURE 15-6 Adjust for shrinkage in the Adjust Quantity/Value On Hand window.

Here are the steps for filling out this window:

1. From the Adjustment Type drop-down menu, select Quantity.
2. Enter the date. Inventory adjustments are usually dated at the end of the month, quarter, or year.
3. In the Adjustment Account field, enter the inventory adjustment account in your chart of accounts. (See the section "About the Inventory Adjustment Account" for important information about which account you should use.)
4. Use an optional reference number to track the adjustment.

5. Click the Find & Select Items button to open the Find & Select Items window. Here you tell QuickBooks which items you want to adjust.

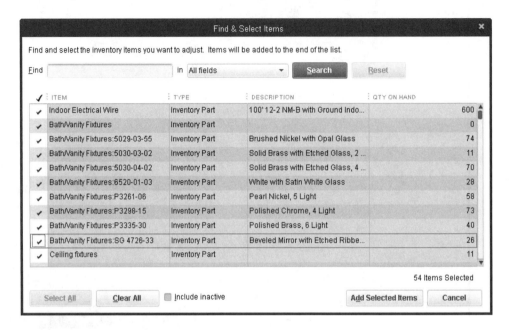

6. Click the Add Selected Items button to add the items you've selected to the adjustment window. Notice the Include Inactive check box at the bottom of the Find & Select Items window.

7. In the Adjust Quantity/Value On Hand window, the Customer:Job field appears in case you're sending items to a customer but didn't include the items on any invoices for that customer or job. This is a way to effect a transfer of the inventory where the inventory count is changed and the cost is posted to the customer or job.

8. If you've enabled the class tracking feature, a Class field appears if the adjustment can be assigned to a class.

9. Use either the New Quantity column or the Qty Difference column to enter the count. Whichever column you use, QuickBooks fills in the other column automatically.

10. Anything you enter in the Memo field appears on your Profit & Loss Detail report, which prevents the question, "What's this figure?" from your accountant.

When you complete the entries, the total value of the adjustment you made is displayed below the Qty Difference column. That value is calculated by using the average cost of your inventory. For example, if you received ten widgets into inventory at a cost of $10.00 each and later received ten more at a cost of $12.00 each, your average cost for widgets is $11.00 each. If your adjustment is for minus one widget and you didn't sell any of that item in the interim, your inventory asset value is decreased by $11.00.

Adjusting the Value

You can be more precise about your inventory valuation; in fact, you can override the average cost calculation and enter a true value when you fill out this transaction window.

Select Total Value from the Adjustment Type drop-down menu. Two new columns named Total Value and New Value appear in the window (see Figure 15-7).

The value of the total adjusted count is displayed for each item, and you can change the current value of the item to eliminate the effects of averaging costs up to this point (although as you continue to receive inventory items, QuickBooks continues to use average costing).

Return to the Adjust Quantity/Value On Hand window and enter the data. When you've finished making your changes, click Save & Close to save your new inventory numbers.

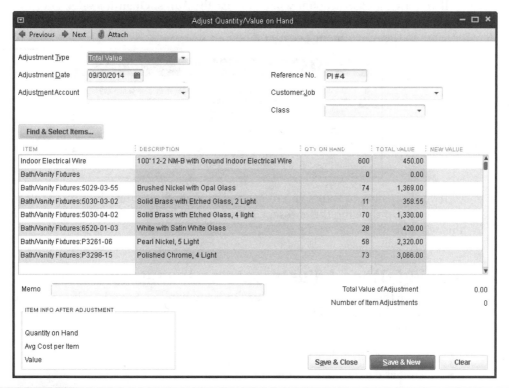

FIGURE 15-7 Adjust the costs of inventory to reflect actual value.

Understanding the Effects of an Adjustment

When you adjust the inventory count, you're changing the value of your inventory asset. After you save the adjustment, the inventory asset account register reflects the differences for each item. Because QuickBooks is a double-entry bookkeeping system, there has to be an equal and opposite entry made to another account.

For example, when you sell items via customer invoices, your inventory asset decreases while at the same time your cost of goods sold increases. When you're adjusting inventory, however, there is no sale or purchase involved. In most cases, the offsetting entry is made to an Inventory Adjustment account created specifically for this purpose.

About the Inventory Adjustment Account

Before you can make adjustments to your inventory, you should first create an account to receive that adjustment. Most users name it the Inventory Adjustment account, and it can either be a Cost Of Goods Sold or an Expense type of account. Check with your accountant on what account type works best for your situation.

If you use a COGS account when you use the Adjust Quantity/Value On Hand window, QuickBooks issues a warning message when you enter your adjustment account in the Adjustment Account field:

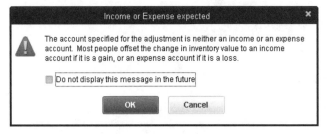

If your accountant wants you to use a cost of goods account, be sure to select the option to stop showing this message before you click OK to continue working in this window.

Making Other Adjustments to Inventory

You can use the Adjust Quantity/Value On Hand window to make adjustments to inventory at any time and for a variety of reasons unconnected to the periodic physical count:

- Breakage or other damage
- Customer demo/sample units
- Gifts or bonuses for customers or employees
- Removal of inventory parts to create built or preassembled inventory items

The important thing to remember is that tracking and periodically adjusting inventory isn't done just to make sure that you have sufficient items on hand to sell to customers. Equally important is the fact that your inventory is a significant asset, just like your cash, equipment, and other assets. As such, it can affect your company's worth in a substantial way.

Running Inventory Reports

You'll probably find that you run reports on your inventory status quite often. For many inventory-based businesses, inventory status reports are likely the second most important set of reports—second only to reports about the current accounts receivable balances.

QuickBooks provides several useful inventory reports, which you can access by choosing Reports | Inventory. These reports are discussed in the following sections.

Inventory Valuation Summary Report

This report gives you a quick assessment of the value of your inventory. By default, the date range is the current month to date, but you can change that to suit your needs. Each item is listed with the following information displayed in columns:

- **Item Description** The description of the item, if you entered a description for purchase transactions.
- **On Hand** The current quantity on hand, which is the net number of received items and sold items. Because QuickBooks permits you to sell items you don't have in stock (a very bad idea, which can wreak havoc with your financials), it's possible to have a negative number in this column.
- **Avg Cost** QuickBooks calculates the average cost of an item each time you record the purchase of more units of the item. It adds the cost of the new items to the cost of the old stock that's left and then divides by the total number of new and old items.
- **Asset Value** The value posted to your Inventory account in the general ledger. The value is calculated by multiplying the number on hand by the average cost.
- **% Of Tot Asset** The percentage of your total inventory assets that this item represents.
- **Sales Price** The price you've set for this item. This figure is obtained by looking at the item's configuration window. If you entered a price when you set up the item, that price is displayed. If you didn't enter a price (because you chose to determine the price at the time of sale), $0.00 displays. QuickBooks does not check the sales records for this item to determine this number, so if you routinely change the price when you're filling out a customer invoice, those changes aren't reflected in this report.

- **Retail Value**   The current retail value of the item, which is calculated by multiplying the number on hand by the sales price (if the sales price is set).
- **% Of Tot Retail**   The percentage of the total retail value of your inventory that this item represents.

Inventory Valuation Detail Report

This report lists all the transactions that affect the on-hand value of each item in your inventory—including sales and purchases. The report shows no financial information about the price charged to customers, because your inventory value is based on cost. You can double-click any transaction line to see the details of that transaction.

Inventory Stock Status Report

There are two Stock Status reports: Inventory Stock Status By Item and Inventory Stock Status By Vendor. The information is the same in both reports, but the order in which information is arranged and subtotaled is different. You can use these Stock Status reports to get quick numbers about inventory items, including the following information:

- The preferred vendor
- The reorder point
- The number currently on hand
- A reminder (a check mark) for ordering items that are below the reorder point
- The number currently on order (a purchase order exists, but the order has not yet been received)
- The next delivery date (according to the data in the purchase orders)
- The average number of units sold per week

Pending Builds Report

If you're using the Premier or Enterprise edition of QuickBooks and you build and track *assembly items*, this report details the current state of items you assemble from existing inventory items (called *builds*). If you find that you need this feature, consider upgrading to either of these editions: go to www.quickbooks.intuit.com.

Inventory QuickReport

QuickBooks provides a reporting feature called QuickReports that provides detailed sales and purchase information about an individual item. QuickReports are available from the Item List window and are the fastest way to take a look at all the transactions for an item.

In the Item List window, select an item and click the Reports button (at the bottom of the list) to open a drop-down menu from which you can select the QuickReport for that item. You can change the date range for the report, and you can double-click any transaction line to drill down to the transaction details.

Using Bank Feeds

In this chapter:

- Set up Bank Feed options

- Set up online accounts

- Download account activity into QuickBooks

- Use renaming rules to match payee names

- Create online payments to vendors

- Transfer funds between banks electronically

With QuickBooks Bank Feeds (referred to as Online Banking in previous versions of the software), you use the Internet to connect to and download your bank and credit card account information into your QuickBooks file. Throughout this chapter, when you see the word "bank" or "financial institution," keep in mind that I'm also referring to your credit card company as well.

Many of the financial institutions that you have accounts with offer one of the following two methods to allow you to connect with and download this information:

- **Direct Connect**   With this method, your financial institution exchanges data interactively with QuickBooks. This allows you to take advantage of additional Bank Feeds features, such as transaction data downloads directly into your QuickBooks bank register, transfers between bank accounts, electronic messages between you and the financial institution, and online bill payments (optional at some financial institutions). Some financial institutions charge a fee for some or all of the services available through Direct Connect.
- **Web Connect**   This is a manual import method you use when your financial institution doesn't provide a way to connect your QuickBooks data directly to the data on its own server. Instead, you'll access a page on the bank's website where you can view and download your transactions and import the downloaded file into QuickBooks.

Set Up Bank Feeds

To use Bank Feeds, your bank must support at least one of the following services:

- Transaction downloads
- Online bill paying

If your bank supports only online account access and doesn't support online bill paying, you can still work directly with the QuickBooks Bank Feeds to automate your bill payment process. See "Use QuickBooks to Pay Your Bills Online" later in this chapter.

Finding Your Bank Online

If you haven't signed up for online services with your bank and you're not sure if your bank has online services, choose Banking | Bank Feeds | Participating Financial Institutions to see the Financial Institutions Directory web page (see Figure 16-1).

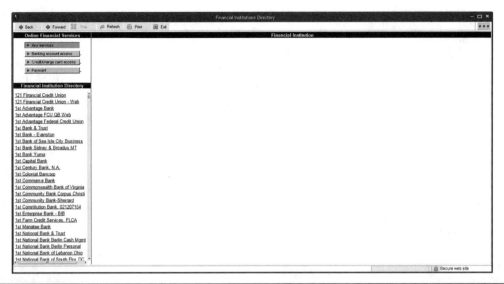

FIGURE 16-1 Select the type of online service you want, and then scroll through the list to see if your bank is included.

The four choices at the top of the left pane determine the contents of the Financial Institutions Directory list that QuickBooks displays. The window opens with the choice labeled Any Services preselected, and all the banks listed provide some type of online service. If you're interested in a particular online service (for example, you want to know about Bank Account Access to download transactions), select that option, and the list of banks changes to those banks that offer the selected service.

Scroll through the list to find your bank and click its listing. The right pane of the Financial Institutions Directory window displays information about your bank's online services. Figure 16-2 shows an example of a bank that offers Direct Connect. If your bank isn't listed, you cannot utilize the Bank Feeds feature.

Click the Apply Now button if you want to start the application process here and now. If no Apply Now button appears, follow the instructions for setting up online services at the bank—usually the bank displays a phone number. If online applications are available, fill out the form and submit the information. Your bank will send you information about using its online service, a login name, and a PIN or a password. This is the information you'll need to enable the bank account for Bank Feeds in QuickBooks.

After you receive your login ID and a PIN or a password from your bank, QuickBooks walks you through the process of enabling Band Feeds for your bank account in QuickBooks.

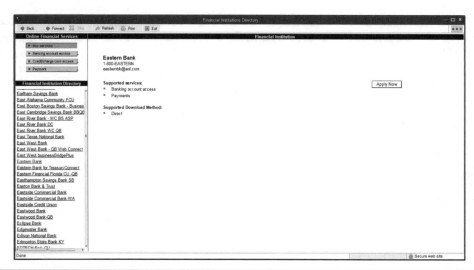

FIGURE 16-2 This bank has Direct Connect.

Those steps differ depending on whether your bank uses Direct Connect or Web Connect. The following sections cover both scenarios.

Enabling Bank Feeds Using Direct Connect

After you receive your ID and PIN or password, you can enable a bank account for online access with Direct Connect:

1. Choose Banking | Bank Feeds | Set Up Bank Feed For An Account. The Bank Feed Setup window opens. Enter the name of your financial institution. If QuickBooks displays matching names, you can select one from the list offered (see Figure 16-3).

2. In the next window, enter the User ID and Password that your financial institution provided to you, and then click Connect.

3. In the next window, link your account with the bank (or credit card) account that you created in QuickBooks. If you have not already created this account in QuickBooks, select Create New Account from the QuickBooks Accounts drop-down list. Then click Connect.

4. The Bank Feed Setup window confirms that you've successfully enabled your account to receive Bank Feeds. Click the link Download Your Transactions From Bank Feeds at the bottom of the window to initiate your first download from the Bank Feeds Center.

Refer to the section "Work with Transactions in the Bank Feeds Center" to learn more about how to view and match downloaded transactions.

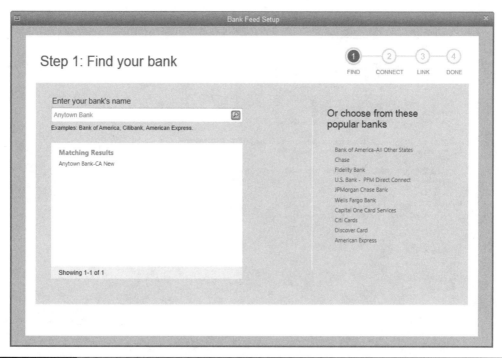

FIGURE 16-3 Select the financial institution from which you want to receive Bank Feeds.

Enabling Bank Feeds Using Web Connect (Manual Import)

After you receive your login information from your bank (as described in the previous section), you can enable a bank account to download as a Web Connect file as follows:

1. Choose Banking | Bank Feeds | Setup Bank Feed For An Account. QuickBooks displays a dialog indicating that it's updating branding files. When that process is complete, enter the name of your financial institution. If QuickBooks displays matching names, you can select one from the list offered.

2. Once a financial institution is selected, the Manually Import Transactions window opens, listing the steps required to download and import the transaction file (see Figure 16-4).

3. Click the link provided in the dialog in Step 1 to be re-directed to your bank's login page. If you don't want to download your transactions at this time, click Close.

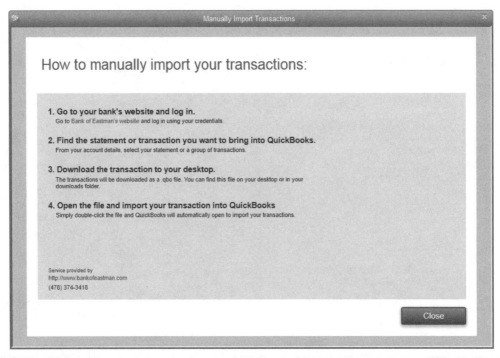

How to manually import your transactions:

1. **Go to your bank's website and log in.**
   Go to Bank of Eastman's website and log in using your credentials.

2. **Find the statement or transaction you want to bring into QuickBooks.**
   From your account details, select your statement or a group of transactions.

3. **Download the transaction to your desktop.**
   The transactions will be downloaded as a .qbo file. You can find this file on your desktop or in your downloads folder.

4. **Open the file and import your transaction into QuickBooks**
   Simply double-click the file and QuickBooks will automatically open to import your transactions.

Service provided by
http://www.bankofeastman.com
(478) 374-3418

Close

FIGURE 16-4   Follow these steps to import transactions from your bank manually.

4. Log in, and then find the transactions that you want to import into QuickBooks. Your bank probably displays criteria selections for a date range (yesterday, today, or a range of dates) and may also offer an option labeled "Since Last Download" (which you can select after this initial download).

5. After you make your selections, your bank generates a file (it should have the extension .qbo) and displays a File Download dialog asking whether you want to open the file or save it to your computer.

   • If you click Open, QuickBooks asks if you want to import the file into your bank account now or save it and import later.

   • If you click Save, you should save the file to your desktop or your download folder. When you're ready to import the file, choose Banking | Bank Feeds | Import Web Connect Files and select the file you saved. You can also simply double-click the filename and it will automatically import the transactions into your QuickBooks file. These transactions will now be available to you in the Bank Feeds Center.

Work with Transactions in the Bank Feeds Center

If you've just enabled an account for Bank Feeds and downloaded transactions for the first time, the Bank Feeds Center opens automatically. From now on, however, if you're using the Direct Connect method, you'll both download and view transactions right from the Bank Feeds Center. If you're using the Manual (Web Connect) method, you'll start by logging into your bank to download your transactions.

Viewing the Downloaded Transactions

When transactions have been downloaded, the Bank Feeds Center (shown in Figure 16-5) displays a summary of the status of the transactions that need to be reviewed or that require action for each of the accounts listed in the Bank Accounts area.

If you are receiving feeds from more than one financial institution (for example, you may have online bank account access at one financial institution and online credit card access at another), select the appropriate account from the list in the Bank Accounts area on the left side of the Bank Feeds window.

If there are no new transactions to review when you select an account from this list, click the Download Transactions button to get the latest transactions from your financial institution. If QuickBooks indicates that downloaded transactions are waiting to be added, click the Transaction List button to begin the process of reviewing and adding these transactions to your account register.

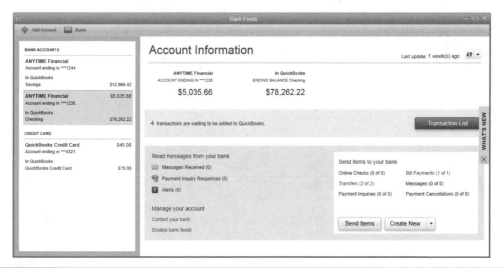

FIGURE 16-5 All the downloaded transactions are available in the Bank Feeds Center.

> **ProAdvisor Tip:** You can view and enter transactions in two ways: via Express Mode, which is the default view, or via Classic Mode. Both modes offer the same functionality, with the exception that the renaming rules created in Express Mode are not available in Classic Mode. Likewise, aliases created in Classic Mode are not available in Express Mode. To switch between modes, choose Banking I Bank Feeds I Change Bank Feeds Mode.

Adding Transactions to the Account Register in QuickBooks

Clicking the Transaction List button in the Bank Feeds Center opens the Transactions List window. From here, you tell QuickBooks how to handle each downloaded transaction. You can work directly in this list to assign/change the account, customer, or vendor name for each transaction listed. You can also filter the list of transactions that appear by their status. For example, in Figure 16-6, the Status filter is set to All, but you can also filter the list to view transactions that need reviewing, those changed by renaming rules (see "ProAdvisor Recommends: Renaming Rules"), and those that have been matched automatically.

FIGURE 16-6   Add transactions to your register from the Bank Feeds Transactions list.

Start with Matched Transactions

QuickBooks automatically tries to match downloaded transactions to transactions already entered in your register. When you filter your Bank Feeds Transactions list to show Auto Matched transactions, the word "Auto" appears in the Status column, indicating that the transaction listed was already entered directly in the bank register. Notice in the example shown in Figure 16-6 that a match was found for one of the downloaded transactions.

- If you have multiple matched transactions and you don't need to review them further, click the check box next to each one, click the Batch Actions drop-down menu (at the bottom of the Transactions List window), and select Add/Approve to add them to your QuickBooks register.
- If you want to work with just one matched transaction at a time, use the Select drop-down menu in the Action column, where you'll see four options:
  - **Approve** Selecting this option adds this transaction to your register.
  - **View Details** Select this option to see more transaction detail to confirm that it's a match. You can also change the status to Not A Match.
  - **Not A Match** Selecting this option lets you manually match this transaction to another one in your register.
  - **Ignore** Select this option to delete the transaction from the Bank Feeds Transactions list.

Add Renamed Transactions

Renamed transactions have been changed by QuickBooks based on a *renaming rule* that you created (see "ProAdvisor Recommends: Renaming Rules"). Filter your Transactions list to show renamed transactions. The letters "Cha" appears in the Status column in the Transactions List window for these transactions.

- If you have multiple renamed transactions and you don't need to review them further, click the check box next to each one, click the Batch Actions button (at the bottom of the Transactions List window), and select Add/Approve to add them to your QuickBooks register.
- If you want to work with just one renamed transaction at a time, use the Select drop-down menu in the Action column, where you'll see four options:
  - **Quick Add** Selecting this option will add this transaction to your register.
  - **Add More Details** This option allows you to add more transaction detail before adding the transaction to your register. You can also add a new customer, vendor, or account if it doesn't already exist in your QuickBooks file.
  - **Match To Existing Transaction** Selecting this option lets you manually match this transaction to one already in your register.
  - **Ignore** Selecting this option deletes the transaction from the Bank Feeds Transactions list.

➡ **ProAdvisor Recommends**

Renaming Rules

When the designation "Cha" appears in the Status column in the Transactions List window, it means that a downloaded transaction was changed by a renaming rule.

You use a *renaming rule* to tell QuickBooks that you want to use a particular name for a vendor or payee when a transaction is downloaded into the Bank Feeds Center. QuickBooks automatically creates a renaming rule the first time you assign a payee to a downloaded payment transaction and there is no matching entry in your register. You can also create your own renaming rules by clicking the Rules link located at the top-left of the Bank Feeds or Transactions List window. This opens the Rules List window, where you'll use the Manage Rules drop-down menu at the bottom of the window to create, edit, or delete a rule.

When you create a new rule, in the Add Rules Details dialog, you can choose to rename the vendor or payee based on whether the name associated with the downloaded transaction contains, starts with, ends with, exactly matches, or does not contain the text or characters that you enter.

(Continued)

➤ ProAdvisor Recommends

Why are renaming rules useful? If you use a credit card to purchase gas for your car at four different Exxon stations, for example, these four transactions can be presented as four different payees when downloaded via the Online Banking Center: ExxonStation #100001, ExxonStation#1000002, ExxonStation#1000003, and ExxonStation#1000004. In QuickBooks, you probably want to refer to that vendor as Exxon. When you download your credit card transactions and there is no matching vendor in your register, QuickBooks will assign it the name you designate (rather than create four new vendors) and will post it in your register to the category you intended.

Add Unmatched Transactions

Unmatched transactions usually require a review and more detail before they can be added to a register. Filter the Status list in the Transactions List window to show unmatched transactions. The letters "Rev" appear in the Status column in the Transactions List window for these transactions.

Use the Select drop-down menu in the Action column to take one of the four following actions for each of these transactions:

- **Quick Add**   Select this option to add this transaction to your register.
- **Add More Details**   Select this option to add more transaction detail before adding the transaction to your register. You can also add a new customer, vendor, or account if it doesn't already exist in your QuickBooks file.
- **Match To Existing Transaction**   Selecting this option lets you manually match this transaction to one already in your register.
- **Ignore**   Selecting this option deletes the transaction from the Bank Feeds Transactions list.

Adding a Downloaded Payment to the Register

When you select a downloaded payment transaction to add to your QuickBooks register, in addition to the four options listed in the previous section for unmatched transactions, the Select drop-down menu in the Action column gives you the choice Select Bills To Mark As Paid, which opens the Transaction Details - Select Bills To Mark As Paid dialog, where you can apply this payment to an outstanding vendor bill (see Figure 16-7).

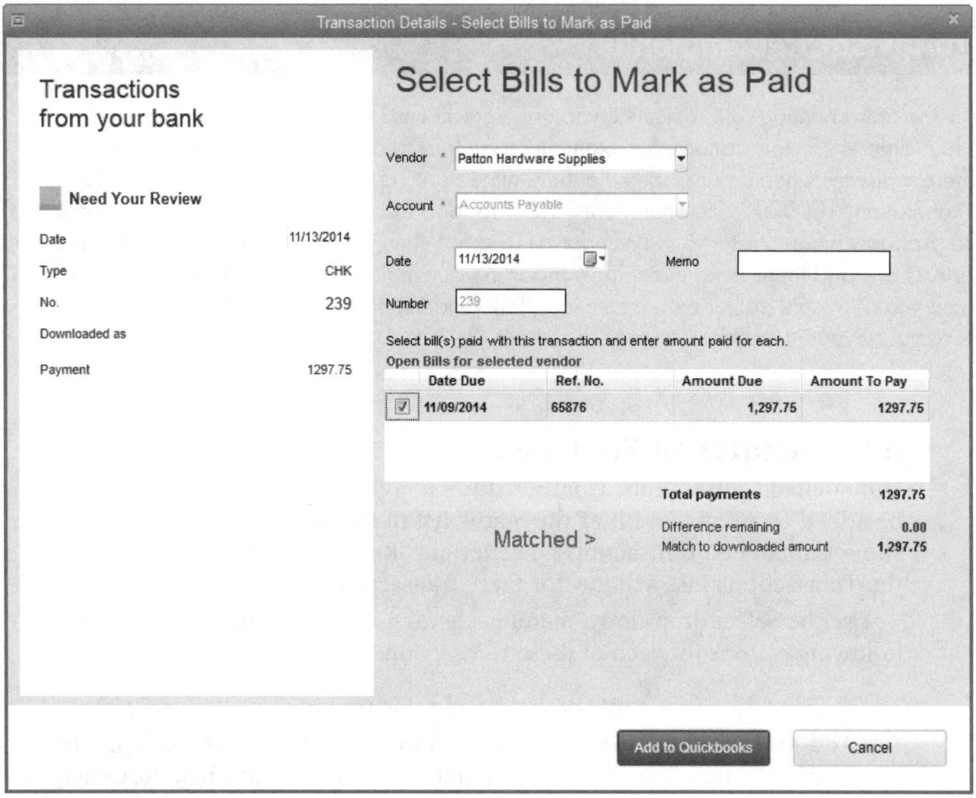

FIGURE 16-7 Use a downloaded payment to mark a vendor bill as paid.

In the Vendor field, select the vendor with an open A/P bill to which this downloaded payment is linked. QuickBooks displays the open bills for the vendor.

Select the bill to pay with this transaction, and change the Amount To Pay if the transaction represented a partial payment. You can also select multiple bills for this vendor if you paid more than one bill with this payment.

Adding a Downloaded Deposit to the Register

A downloaded bank deposit may need to be applied to more than one existing QuickBooks transaction (such as open invoices, for example).

When you use the Select drop-down menu in the Actions column for a downloaded deposit transaction, QuickBooks gives you the same four options listed in the previous section for unmatched transactions. However, when you select the option to Add More Details, you can do the following in the Add More Details window:

- Match this deposit to an existing customer payment already received in QuickBooks by finding and selecting it on the Undeposited Funds tab, which contains all the current transactions waiting for deposit. You will then see these transactions in the Payments To Deposit window (click the Record Deposits button on the Home page to open this window).
- Apply that payment now by finding and selecting the open invoice(s) on the Open Invoices tab, which lists all the current open invoices in your company file (see Figure 16-8).

Choose the appropriate tab, and then choose the matching transaction—or multiple transactions that total up to the amount of the downloaded transaction.

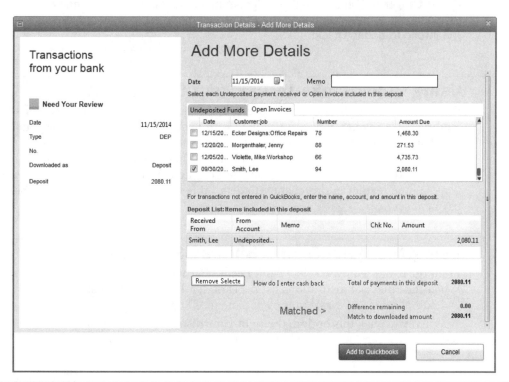

FIGURE 16-8 Apply a payment to an open invoice or match it to an amount.

Ignoring (Deleting) Unmatched Transactions

Sometimes the downloaded file contains transactions that can't be matched. This usually occurs when you don't download transactions frequently and some of the transactions you download have already been cleared during a reconciliation. You can't match transactions that have already been reconciled within QuickBooks.

You should delete these transactions; otherwise, they'll be there waiting for you every time you download new transactions. Here's how to delete them:

- To delete multiple transactions, check the check box next to each one in the Transactions List window, click the Batch Actions button (at the bottom of the Transactions List window), and select Ignore.
- To delete individual transactions, use the Select drop-down menu in the Action column and select Ignore.

Caution: You can apply the Ignore action to matched and renamed transactions, so pay attention to the Status column to avoid deleting transactions you intend to add to QuickBooks.

Using QuickBooks to Pay Your Bills Online

When you pay your bills or write checks, QuickBooks gives you the option of sending these payments electronically to your vendors. You can either use your own bank to transmit these payments to your vendors (if it offers online bill payment services or Direct Connect) or use the QuickBooks Bill Pay Service and have QuickBooks send these payments for you. Refer to the section "Finding Your Bank Online" earlier in this chapter to determine whether your bank offers a bill payment service.

Using the QuickBooks Bill Pay Service

From the Banking menu, select Bank Feeds | Participating Financial Institutions. When the Financial Institutions list appears, scroll through the list to find QuickBooks Bill Pay–New! in the left pane (see Figure 16-9).

When you click this option, the right pane displays some information about the service. Click the Apply Now button to start the sign-up process.

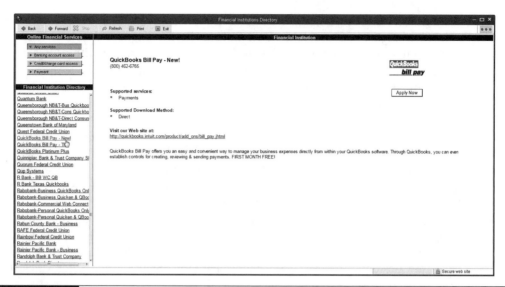

FIGURE 16-9 Sign up for the QuickBooks Bill Pay service to simplify your bill payment process.

Once you've completed the sign-up process, you can use either the Write Checks or Pay Bills feature in QuickBooks as you normally would. If you are writing a check instead of selecting To Be Printed, select Pay Online. Be sure to fill in the date that you want the payment to be delivered (you can schedule a payment up to one year in advance). If you are using the Pay Bills feature, pay your bills as you normally would and select Online Bank Payment as your payment method. Again, choose the date that you want the payment delivered.

After you've entered your checks or paid your bills, open the Bank Feeds Center and click the Send Items button.

If your vendor is set up to receive electronic payments (meaning that the company is part of the national electronic payment database), QuickBooks will electronically transfer your payments from your bank to your vendor/payee on the date you've specified. If your vendor is not able to receive electronic payments, a paper check (generated by the QuickBooks Bill Pay service) is sent via U.S. mail.

Transfer Money Between Accounts Online

If you have multiple accounts at your financial institution (for example, you may have a money market account for your business in addition to your checking account) and the financial institution uses Direct Connect, you can transfer money between those accounts within QuickBooks.

To transfer money online, you must have applied at your financial institution for online banking for both accounts. You'll probably have a unique PIN for each account. In addition, you must have enabled both accounts for online access within QuickBooks.

You can use one of two methods to transfer funds between online accounts: the online transfer funds function (as described next) or direct manual entry, which is covered in detail in Chapter 12.

Using the Transfer Funds Function

The simplest way to move money between your online accounts is to use the QuickBooks Transfer Funds Between Accounts window, which you reach by choosing Banking | Transfer Funds from the menu bar.

Specify the sending and receiving accounts (remember that both must be enabled for Direct Connect online access) and enter the amount you want to transfer. Be sure to select the option for Online Funds Transfer in the Transfer Funds Between Accounts window. Click Save & Close. Then choose Banking | Bank Feeds Center. Click the Send Items button to send the transfer to your bank.

ProAdvisor Tip: In the Account Information section of the Bank Feeds window, click the Transfers hyperlink to open the Fund Transfers To Be Sent window. Make sure the transfer transactions you want to send to your bank have check marks next to them. Close this window and click the Send Items button.

Entering Special Transactions Using General Journal Entries

Chapter 17

In this chapter:

- The QuickBooks Journal Entries window

- Make adjustments to the general ledger

- Depreciate fixed assets

- Use journal entries to post to outside payroll services

As you work in QuickBooks, the amounts involved in the financial transactions you complete—such as invoices and bills—are automatically posted to the appropriate accounts in your chart of accounts (the chart of accounts is covered in detail in Chapter 2). But, if necessary, you or your accountant can make an adjustment to an account directly. QuickBooks refers to this type of transaction as a general journal entry (aka journal entry).

Journal entries should be used to enter only financial data that cannot be added to an account via a standard transaction. For example, your accountant will often use a journal entry to adjust an account balance at year end to record annual depreciation of an asset and the associated depreciation expense.

The QuickBooks Journal Entries Window

The Make General Journal Entries window, shown in Figure 17-1, is accessed from the Company menu. The format of the transaction window is standardized and cannot be customized in the same way as, for example, an invoice template can be. There are columns for account names and debit and credit amounts. In addition, QuickBooks provides columns you can use to link the data you enter to customers and classes and also enter a memo.

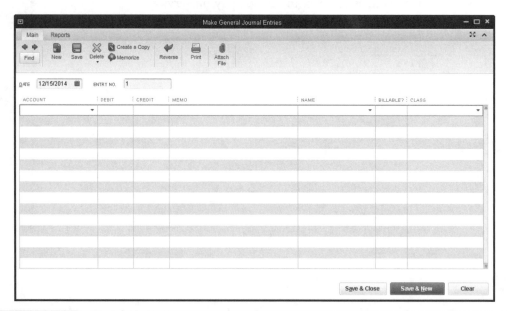

FIGURE 17-1 The QuickBooks Make General Journal Entries window has extra columns so you can track additional information about your entry.

To create a journal entry, follow these steps:

1. Choose Company | Make General Journal Entries. QuickBooks displays a message telling you that automatic numbers are now assigned to journal entries. (You can select the option Do Not Display This Message In The Future before you click OK.) You can enable or disable the automatic numbering feature in the Accounting category of the Preferences dialog.
2. In the Account column, select the account you need.
3. Move over to either the Debit or Credit column and enter an amount.
4. Optionally, make an entry in the Memo, Name, or Billable? columns.
5. Repeat Steps 2–4 for all the amounts in the journal entry.

As you enter each amount, QuickBooks presents the offsetting total in the next line. For example, if the line items you've entered so far have a higher total for the credit side than the debit side, the next entry presents the balancing offset (see Figure 17-2).

Here are some guidelines to using the columns available in the Make General Journal Entries window:

- Use the Memo column to write a comment about the reason for the journal entry. The memo text appears in the entry of the account's register and on reports, so you should enter the text on every line of the entry in order to see the explanation, no matter which account register you're viewing.

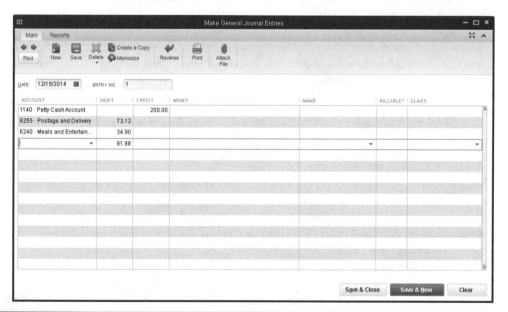

FIGURE 17-2 QuickBooks keeps the running offset figure available so you don't have to enter an amount for the last entry.

- Use the Name column to assign a customer, vendor, employee, or other name to the amount on this line of the entry, if you're linking the entry to a name. If the account you're posting to is an A/R (accounts receivable) or A/P (accounts payable) account, an entry in the Name column is required. Note, however, that you cannot use more than one A/R or A/P account in the same journal entry.
- The Billable? column indicates whether the amount is billable to the name in the Name column, if you are using an expense account and you enter a customer name in the Name column.
- If you are using the Class Tracking feature, a Class column is present and you can link the entry to a class. This can be useful if, for example, you'd like to allocate certain overhead costs or assets to different classes. (See Chapter 6 for information about setting up classes.)

➥ ProAdvisor Recommends

Creating Journal Entries for Changed Accounts

I've had many clients who, after they'd been using QuickBooks for a while, decided that they wanted to track their income or expenses differently. For example, instead of using only one income account to keep track of all the products and services they sold, they determined that having separate income accounts for service fees and for products sold made analyzing their business easier.

You can use a journal entry to split out these amounts to separate income accounts. First, create the new account and then take the appropriate amount of funds out of the original account and put it into the new account. Income, for example is a credit-side item, which means you'll want to do the following:

- Debit the original account to reduce the balance for the amount that belongs in the new account.
- Credit the new account to increase the balance for that amount.

Then, of course, you'll have to go to the Item List and change the impacted items by linking them to the new income accounts so you don't have to keep making journal entries.

The same decision is frequently made about expenses as well. Maybe you think your insurance accounts should be separated for car insurance, equipment insurance, building insurance, malpractice insurance, and so on.

Expense accounts are debit-side items, so the journal entry in this case is to do the following:

- Credit the original expense account to reduce the balance for the amount you're taking out of it and putting into the new account(s).
- Debit the new account(s) to increase the balance for the appropriate amount(s).

Create Journal Entries for Depreciation

Depreciation is a way to track the current value of a fixed asset that loses value as it ages. The basis of an asset's depreciation from an accounting point of view is determined by a complicated set of rules, including IRS rules, which can change frequently. Most small businesses enter the depreciation of their assets at the end of the year, but some companies perform depreciation tasks monthly or quarterly.

Depreciation is a special journal entry, because the accounts involved are very specific. The account that is being depreciated must be a fixed asset, and the offset entry is to a Depreciation Expense account found in the expense section of your chart of accounts.

Creating Accounts for Tracking Depreciation

It's not uncommon to have multiple fixed-asset accounts if you want to track different types of fixed assets separately. For instance, a chart of accounts could have three fixed-asset account categories: Equipment, Furniture & Fixtures, and Vehicles.

It's very useful to create a separate subaccount to capture the depreciation entries for each of your fixed assets as well as the purchase of an asset for that asset category. For example, the fixed-asset section of the chart of accounts for the three categories just described could look like this:

Parent Accounts	Subaccounts
Equipment Assets	
	Equipment Purchases
	AccumDepr-Equipment
Furniture & Fixtures Assets	
	Furn & Fixtures Purchases
	AccumDepr-Furn & Fixtures
Vehicle Assets	
	Vehicle Purchases
	AccumDepr-Vehicles

If you use numbers for your chart of accounts, create a numbering system that makes sense for this setup. For example, if Equipment is 16000, the subaccounts start with 16010; Furn & Fixtures starts with 16100, and the subaccounts start with 16110; Vehicle starts with 16200, and so on.

Post asset purchases to the subaccount created for purchases, and make the journal entry for depreciation in the AccumDepr subaccount. Avoid using the "parent" accounts when tracking fixed assets. There are several reasons for this:

- The transactions posted to both the asset subaccount and the AccumDepr subaccount should be consistent so that you (or your accountant) can look at either one to see a running total instead of a calculated net total.
- Tracing the year-to-year depreciation is easier. Just open the AccumDepr subaccount register—each line represents a year.
- The net value of the fixed assets is correct. A Balance Sheet report shows you the details in the subaccounts and automatically displays the total of the subaccounts in the parent account.

You can further refine this example by creating subaccounts and classes for specific fixed assets. For instance, you may want to create a subaccount for each vehicle asset (or one that covers all cars and another that manages all trucks) and its accompanying accumulated depreciation. If your equipment falls under a variety of depreciation rules (for example, manufacturing equipment versus computer equipment), you may want to have a set of subaccounts for each type. You can then use classes to categorize these assets by location or division.

Now, if you're really particular, you can create a different subaccount for each year of depreciation; for instance, under your AccumDepr-Vehicle subaccount, you could have Vehicle-Depr 2012, Vehicle-Depr 2013, Vehicle-Depr 2014, and so on. Then your balance sheet shows a complete year-by-year depreciation schedule instead of accumulated depreciation—and the math still works properly.

Creating a Depreciation Entry

To depreciate fixed assets, you'll need to have a Depreciation Expense account in the Expense section of your chart of accounts. Once that account exists, open the Make General Journal Entries window and choose the first asset depreciation subaccount. In the following example, it's the AccumDepr account under the fixed asset Equipment. Enter the depreciation amount in the Credit column. Notice the colon in the account names for the asset accounts—that's the QuickBooks indication of a subaccount.

ProAdvisor Tip: To help ensure that important transactions such as this depreciation journal entry are posted to the correct subaccount, you can turn on a company preference that tells QuickBooks to display only the lowest subaccounts—and not the parent accounts—when entering transactions. Select Edit | Preferences | Accounting | Company Preferences | Show Lowest Subaccount Only. Keep in mind that this option is available to you only if you use account numbers in your chart of accounts.

Choose the next asset depreciation subaccount and enter its depreciation amount in the Credit column as well. QuickBooks automatically puts the offsetting amount in the Debit column, but just keep moving to the Credit column as you work. Continue until all your depreciation figures are entered in the Credit column.

Now choose the Depreciation Expense account. The total amount of the credits you've entered is automatically placed in the Debit column. Click Save & Close.

Account	Debit	Credit
Equipment:AccumDepr-Equip		5,000.00
Furn & Fix:AccumDepr-Furn & Fix		700.00
LeaseholdImprov:AccumDepr-LeasImprov		1000.00
Depreciation Expense	6,700.00	

Use Journal Entries to Post to Outside Payroll Services

If you have an outside payroll service, you have to tell QuickBooks about the payroll transactions that took place. Your payroll service provider should be able to provide you with a report that gives the details of gross wages and any withholding or deductions, so you can enter this information into QuickBooks.

It's common for businesses to make this entry via a journal entry. Like all other journal entries, this one is just a matter of entering debits and credits. There are three parts to recording payroll:

- Transferring money to the payroll account (if you're using a separate bank account for your payroll)
- Entering the various payroll totals
- Entering the employer expense totals

Transferring Money to the Payroll Account

It's a good idea to have a separate bank account for payroll if you have an outside payroll service, because it makes it easier to record, keep track of, and reconcile payroll-related transactions. In fact, a separate payroll account is a good idea even if you do your own payroll using a QuickBooks Payroll service.

To transfer the money you need for a payroll, choose Banking | Transfer Funds. Select the account that you want to take the funds *from* and complete the transfer *to* your payroll account. Be sure to transfer enough money for the gross payroll, plus the employer payroll expenses, which include the following:

- Employer-matching contributions to FICA and Medicare
- Employer-matching contributions to pension plans
- Employer-matching contributions to benefits
- Employer state unemployment assessments
- Employer FUTA
- Any other government or benefit payments paid by the employer

Even though some of these aren't transmitted every payday, you should transfer the amounts at this time anyway. Then, when it's time to pay them, the correct amount of money will have accumulated in the payroll account.

Recording the Payroll

Running your payroll produces a fairly detailed set of debits and credits. If your payroll service takes care of remitting your payroll liabilities for you, you can record a single journal entry for the payment side of a payroll run and another, separate journal entry for the payment of the employer expenses when they're transmitted. An example of the journal entries you'll make to record this payroll processing scenario is shown in Table 17-1.

Account	Debit	Credit
Salaries and Wages (expense)	Gross Payroll	
FWT (liability)		Total Federal Withheld
FICA (liability)		Total FICA Withheld
Medicare (liability)		Total Medicare
Withheld State Income Tax (liability)		Total State Tax
Withheld Local Income Tax (liability)		Total Local Tax
Withheld State SDI (liability)		Total State SDI
Withheld State SUI (liability)		Total State SUI
Withheld Benefits Contrib. (liability)		Total Benefits
Withheld 401(k) Contrib. (liability)		Total 401(k)
Withheld Other Deductions (liability)		Total Other Deductions
Withheld Payroll Bank Account (asset)		Total of Net Payroll

TABLE 17-1   Typical Journal Entry to Record Payroll by an Outside Service

If your payroll service doesn't remit your liabilities, leaving you with that task, your check-writing activity will record the payments when you create those checks. So, in this instance, you don't need a second journal entry.

Table 17-1 shows a typical template for recording the payment side of a payroll run as a journal entry. It's possible that you don't have all the expenses shown in this table (for instance, not all states have employee unemployment assessments). And you may have additional withholding categories such as union dues, garnishments against wages, and so on. Be sure you've created a liability account in your chart of accounts for each withholding category you need and a vendor for each transmittal check.

Recording Liabilities

Next, you'll need to journalize the employer payment of the payroll liabilities recorded in the first journal entry, if your payroll service is taking care of them for you. As previously mentioned, if you do it yourself, just write the checks from the payroll account and each item will post to the general ledger. Table 17-2 is a sample journal entry for recording payroll remittances.

The entry involving the transmittal of withholdings is posted to the same account you used when you withheld the amounts. In effect, you "wash" the liability accounts; you're not really spending money—you're remitting money you've withheld from employees.

You can have as many individual employer expense accounts as you think you need, or you can post all the employer expenses to one account named "Payroll Expenses."

Account	Debit	Credit
Federal Payroll Expenses (expense)	Employer FICA and Medicare	
Federal Withholdings (liability)	All federal withholding	
State and Local Withholdings (liability)	All local withholding	
SUTA (expense)	Employer SUTA	
FUTA (expense)	Employer FUTA	
Employer Contributions (expense)	All employer benefit, pension, etc.	
Payroll Bank Account (asset)		Total of checks written

TABLE 17-2 Typical Journal Entry for Employer-side Transactions

Creating Your Own Payroll Entry Template

You can save a lot of time and effort by creating a template for the payroll journal entries. Open a Make General Journal Entries window and fill out the Account column only. Enter the first account, and then press the DOWN ARROW key and enter the next account; keep going until all accounts are listed (see Tables 17-1 and 17-2).

Press CTRL-M to open the Memorize Transaction dialog. Name the memorized transaction Payroll (or something similar), and select the Do Not Remind Me option (the reports from the payroll company are your reminder).

Close the Make General Journal Entries window. QuickBooks displays a message asking if you want to save the transaction you just created. Click No (you don't have to save a journal entry in order to memorize it). Do the same thing for the boilerplate journal entry you create to record employer remittances.

When you're ready to record a payroll, open the memorized transaction by pressing CTRL-T to open the Memorized Transaction List. Double-click your payroll boilerplate journal entry, enter the appropriate date, and then enter the data.

Click Save & New if you have to create another journal entry for the employer expenses; otherwise, click Save & Close.

Reconciling the Payroll Account

When you use journal entries to enter your payroll, the reconciliation process is a bit different. You don't have a record of the individual check numbers and payees. When you open the payroll account in the Reconcile window, you see the journal entry totals instead of the individual checks.

➡ ProAdvisor Recommends

Entering Payroll Check Details for Your Bank Reconciliation

If you want to perform a complete reconciliation in QuickBooks, you can use a workaround to enter individual "dummy" payroll checks for the sole purpose of making your bank reconciliation easier and more accurate. You have a little bit of setup to do, but the good news is you can reuse what you set up every payday.

1. Create a name in the Other Names List and name the new entity Payroll. You can use this name for every check and put the employee's name in the Memo field. If you prefer, you can create a name for each employee in the Other Names list using initials, last name only, or some other name that isn't the same as the original employee name as it exists in your Employee List.

(Continued)

➧ ProAdvisor Recommends

2. Open the Write Checks window. Using the bank account that you use for your payroll, enter the individual dummy payroll checks using these guidelines:

- The Date is the date of the payroll check.
- The No. field is the check number referenced in the report from the payroll service.
- You can use "Payroll" as the Pay To The Order Of name (unless you've entered all of your employee names as Other Names, in which case enter the appropriate name, which you can match to the right check number, too).
- The amount that you enter in the $ field is for the net paycheck (not the gross payroll) amount.
- The account is the *same* bank, meaning that the net effect on your bank account is zero and you're not double counting your payroll expenses, either.

QuickBooks flashes a message warning you that you're posting the payment to the source account. Click OK, because that's exactly what you want to do. You can check the Do Not Display This Message In The Future check box if you don't want to be reminded each time. You can also enter the checks the payroll service wrote to transmit your withholdings or pay your taxes.

You'll still have to enter your regular payroll journal entry (as described previously in the chapter), because the total of the checks written and posted to the bank account via the journal entry will need to be cleared as part to the reconciliation as well as the individual dummy checks you've entered that have cleared the bank.

Year-End Procedures

Chapter 18

The end of the year brings with it several inevitable tasks, and that's true for large corporations as well as for small businesses. There is so much to do: so many reports to run, corrections to make, entries to create, adjustments to apply—whew!

You can relax a bit. Everything doesn't have to be accomplished on January 1st. QuickBooks is date-sensitive, so you can continue to work in the new year without affecting the totals of the previous year. As long as the dates of new transactions are after the last day of your fiscal year, the transactions won't work their way into your year-end calculations.

The Year-End To Do List

Some of the tasks covered in this chapter, such as reconciling your bank account and running reports, may already be a part of your monthly routine. Others, however, can be done only at year end.

Consider creating a year-end To Do list based on the tasks covered in this chapter. You'll not only be ready for your accountant at tax time, but you can feel confident that your books will be in good shape for the new year.

Reconciling All Bank, Cash, and Credit Card Accounts

In January, when your December statements arrive from your bank and credit card company, be sure to either set those aside or print extra copies. Your cash position at year end is important when applying for credit and preparing your tax returns and for general business planning purposes. Performing a reconciliation for all your bank and credit card accounts will ensure that you can rely on the accuracy of these essential balances. It's also a good time to gather and enter all those petty cash receipts so you can reconcile that account, too. (Chapter 13 covers how to use the Reconcile feature in QuickBooks.)

Inventory Stock Status

Perform a physical inventory. While some businesses reserve the last day of the year to complete their physical inventory, others complete it in the days immediately following the end of the year. With the latter method, you'll need to adjust the physical count to account for changes (sales and receipt of goods) that occurred after the last day of the year, and then create an inventory adjustment dated the last day of the previous year. Refer to Chapter 15 to learn how to use inventory reports and the Adjust Quantity/Value On Hand window to ensure that QuickBooks accurately reflects your year-end inventory value.

Fixed Assets

Create a report on your fixed asset accounts to see purchases for the year. It's likely that your accountant will also need this report as the basis for calculating accumulated depreciation totals for fixed assets that were purchased in prior years.

The easy way to create this report is to select any fixed asset account in your chart of accounts and press CTRL-Q to open a QuickReport on that account. Click Customize Report, move to the Filters tab, and select Account in the Choose Filter list. Then select All Fixed Assets from the drop-down list in the Account field, and click OK. The resulting report displays detailed information about all your fixed assets, including purchases and accumulated depreciation.

Payroll

Payroll reports are always relevant as of the end of the calendar year, regardless of your company's fiscal year setup. See Chapter 21 to learn more about year-end payroll processes, including preparing W-2 forms.

If you use QuickBooks to run your payroll, QuickBooks primarily uses the paycheck date as the basis for calculating payroll totals. For example, if you pay employees on Friday for the pay period ending the previous Saturday, all payroll reports are based on the Friday paycheck date. That means for 2013, the last payroll figures are reported as of the last Friday in December. Paychecks issued in January 2014 for the period covering the end of December 2013 are not part of your payroll totals.

Some businesses prefer to track gross salaries and wages as a liability based on the work period and pay off that liability with the paycheck, so they create journal entries to track accrued salaries and wages. Using the same example, in 2013, that accrued entry covers December 23 through December 28 and will be paid with the paycheck issued January 3, 2014.

If you're accruing payroll entries and you file taxes on a cash basis, you need to make a journal entry for the accrued amounts that won't be paid by the end of the year. A reversing journal entry dated December 31, 2013, and reversed on January 1, 2014, takes care of maintaining the figures you need. Check with your accountant to see if a year-end accrual for payroll is applicable to your situation.

This is also the time to review any employee benefits that should be reported on W-2 forms and to make sure that you're up-to-date with changes in employee names and mailing addresses. This is important information to verify/gather, whether you'll be printing your own year-end payroll forms or passing on that information to an outside payroll processor.

Run Year-End Financial Reports

In addition to giving you and your accountant the information required to prepare your tax returns, the standard financial reports you run at year-end provide some additional benefits to you:

- They help you and your accountant assess the overall financial health of your business.
- They can provide you with the details behind each and every transaction you've made in QuickBooks for the year. This gives you one last opportunity to make sure everything is posted correctly *before* you finalize your financial information to determine what you owe in taxes.

Don't forget that these reports have date ranges such as "current year" and "last fiscal year." So if you're working in QuickBooks *after* the last date of your fiscal year, which is quite common, be sure you adjust the report dates to reflect the activities of your *last* fiscal year.

Profit & Loss Reports

Start with a Profit & Loss Standard report by choosing Reports | Company & Financial | Profit & Loss Standard. By default, when the report opens the date range is the current month to date. Be sure to change it to the fiscal year end that you're preparing for.

The report displays the totals for all the income and expense accounts in your general ledger that had any activity for the year. Examine the report, and if anything seems out of the ordinary to you, double-click the line to see a list of the postings to that account. If the data you see doesn't reassure you, double-click any of the individual posting lines to see the original transaction.

If a transaction seems to be in error, you can take corrective action. You should not delete or void a bill you paid or a customer invoice for which you received payment without consulting first with your accountant.

You may also find that you posted an expense or income transaction to the wrong general ledger account. If so, you can either change the posting account in the transaction or create a journal entry to correct it. (See Chapter 17 for information on creating journal entries.) Then run the year-end P&L report again and print it.

Year-End Balance Sheet

In many ways, your financial position is best represented on your balance sheet. In fact, it's a good idea to check out this report at regular intervals throughout the year and not just at the end of your fiscal year. To run a year-end balance sheet, choose

Reports | Company & Financial | Balance Sheet Standard. An analysis of your year-end balance sheet figures can lead to some important follow-up action items. Here are some examples:

- Perform a "reality check" with the balances that QuickBooks shows for your bank accounts with your bank's records: Are they in sync?
- If you track inventory, is the number that QuickBooks shows an accurate reflection of what's actually on your shelves?
- Try to pay your payroll withholding liabilities in the current year (the year in which they were accumulated) to clear them from the balance sheet. Do the same with any employer contributions you may owe.
- Check to see if your accounts payable and accounts receivable need some housekeeping: Is QuickBooks still showing some open customer invoices or vendor bills that you're quite sure have been paid?
- If you have an A/P balance, pay as many bills as you can afford in the current year, even if this means you pay vendor bills earlier than their due dates. If your taxes are reported on a cash basis, you can gain the expense deduction for this year.

Issue 1099 Forms

If any vendors are eligible for 1099 forms (QuickBooks supports only the 1099-MISC form), you need to print and mail the forms to them by January 31. Some of the work involved in issuing 1099 forms is done during company setup, where you set up the conditions for 1099 tracking. Then, during the year, you need to make sure the transactions you enter are posted to the accounts you identified when you configured these settings. It's also a very good idea to check the latest IRS rules about which vendors should receive a 1099 from you and about any other guidelines that you should be aware of.

Checking the 1099 Setup

First, make sure your file is set up to track and process 1099 forms: choose Edit | Preferences, click the Tax: 1099 icon, and move to the Company Preferences tab to see your settings (see Figure 18-1).

Be sure you've clicked Yes next to the Do You File 1099-MISC Forms? question. Optionally, you can click the first Click Here link (located near the top of the 1099 preference window), which opens to the Map Vendor Payment Accounts window (see Figure 18-2).

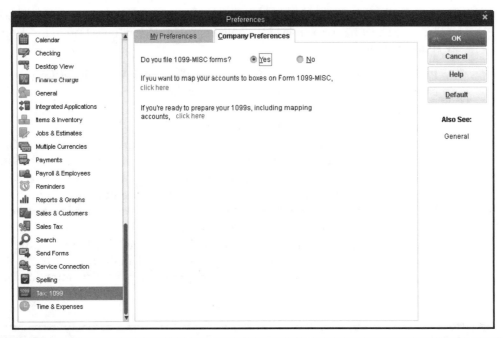

FIGURE 18-1 QuickBooks supports Form 1099-MISC. The links in the Tax: 1099 preferences window guide you through mapping your accounts to the categories (boxes) on the form.

QuickBooks lists for you the accounts that have payment transactions to 1099 vendors for the previous calendar year. From here, you tell QuickBooks which box (or category) on the 1099-MISC form you want the totals from each account to appear in, or you can simply have all amounts appear in Box 7 (Nonemployee Compensation). To assign an account to a 1099 category, select the category from the drop-down menu.

You also have the option of displaying your entire chart of accounts by selecting Show All Accounts in the drop-down menu at the top-right of the window. This will give you the opportunity to map additional accounts for 1099 reporting. Click Save & Close to assign all the accounts you've mapped.

You can assign multiple accounts to a 1099 category, but you cannot assign any account to more than one 1099 category. For example, if you have an expense account Sales Commissions and an expense account Outside Services, both of the accounts can be linked to the same 1099 category (Box 7–Nonemployee Compensation).

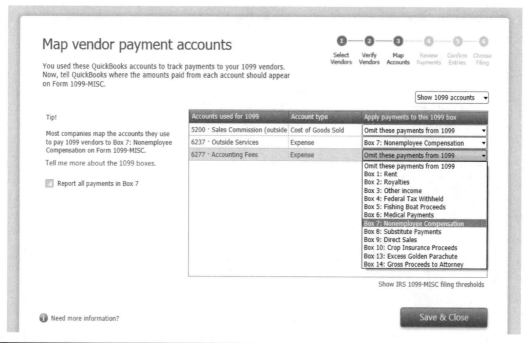

FIGURE 18-2 The Map Vendor Payment Accounts window lets you tell QuickBooks which boxes you want the totals from each account to appear in.

However, once you link those accounts to that category, you cannot use those same accounts in any other 1099 category. Note that you can also access this window via the 1099 Wizard, which is covered in the following section.

Using the 1099 Wizard

Before you print the forms, you need to run a checkup—it's essential to make sure everything is correct before you send forms to vendors and the government.

QuickBooks provides a wizard that walks you through the process to make sure every step is covered and every amount is correct. You can launch the QuickBooks 1099 wizard from 1099 Preferences (see the previous section) or by choosing Vendors | Print/E-File 1099s | 1099 Wizard (see Figure 18-3).

This wizard walks you through three important steps: verifying your 1099 vendor information, ensuring that the expense accounts that you associated with 1099 vendor payments are reported in the correct box on form 1099-MISC, and choosing a filing method.

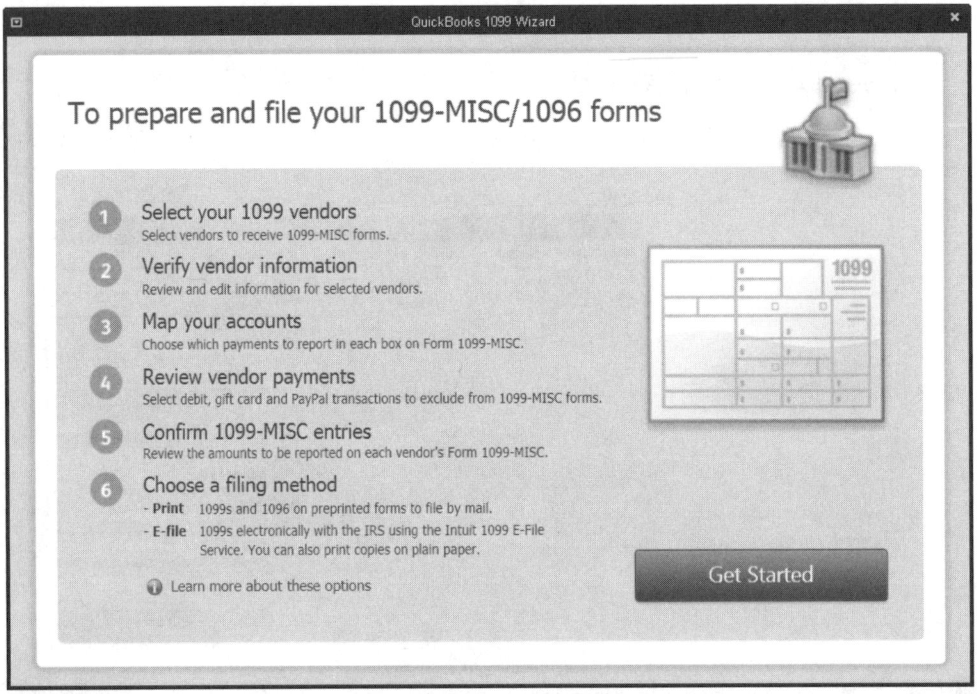

FIGURE 18-3 The QuickBooks 1099 Wizard makes it easy to issue 1099 forms.

Select Your 1099 Vendors

In this window, you'll see a list of all of the vendors you've entered into your QuickBooks company file. A check mark next to a name indicates that it's already been selected to receive a 1099. Add or remove a check mark in the Create Form 1099-MISC column to change the 1099 status of a vendor. Click Continue when you're ready to advance to the Verify Your 1099 Vendors' Information window.

Verify Your 1099 Vendors' Information

If any of the vendors you selected to receive a Form 1099-MISC are missing the required address and tax ID information (or have an invalid tax ID format), those missing fields will be outlined in red. Enter the missing information directly in the appropriate field(s). Click Continue when you're ready to advance to the Map Vendor Payment Accounts window.

Map Vendor Payment Accounts

This is the same window discussed in the previous section, "Checking the 1099 Setup," but the steps are worth repeating here.

QuickBooks lists for you the accounts that have payment transactions to 1099 vendors for the previous calendar year. From here, you tell QuickBooks which box(es) on the 1099-MISC form you want the totals from each account to appear in, or you can simply have all amounts appear in Box 7 (Nonemployee Compensation). To assign an account to a 1099 category, select the category from the drop-down menu.

You also have the option of displaying your entire chart of accounts by selecting Show All Accounts in the drop-down menu at the top-right of the window. This will give you the opportunity to map additional accounts for 1099 reporting. Click Continue to assign all the accounts you've mapped and to move onto the Review Payments For Exclusions window.

Review Payments for Exclusions

The IRS requires that you exclude from reporting on Form 1099-MISC any vendor payments you made by credit card, debit card, gift card, or third-party payment providers such as PayPal, because these payments are already being reported to the IRS by these networks directly.

QuickBooks will automatically exclude any payments you made to a vendor using a credit card account that's listed in your chart of accounts, but you'll need to "code" the other payment types so that you can exclude them from your 1099-MISC reporting. Use the View Included Payments report to identify and code these vendor payments that fall into this category, if you didn't do so when you originally entered the payment.

If you see a payment that needs to be coded for exclusion on this report, double-click that payment transaction, and in the check number field, enter one of the following codes that QuickBooks will recognize (be sure to save the updated transaction):

- Debit
- Debitcar
- DBT
- DBT card
- DCard
- Debit cd
- Visa
- Masterc
- MC
- MCard
- Chase
- Discover
- Diners
- PayPal

Once you've updated the information in the check number fields for all of the necessary payment transactions, click the View Excluded Payments button to confirm that the transactions you've modified will now be excluded from your 1099-MISC totals. Click Continue when all of your updates have been completed.

Confirm Your 1099 Entries

The Confirm Your 1099 Entries page of the 1099 Wizard shows all the vendors for which a form 1099-MISC will be created (see Figure 18-4). To the right of each vendor name, the following information appears:

- The tax ID number associated with that vendor
- The total of all payments included on the 1099
  - The total payments to be included in Box 7 (Nonemployee Compensation)
  - The total of all payments to that vendor posted to accounts not mapped to a 1099 category (box)
  - The total of all payments made to the vendor

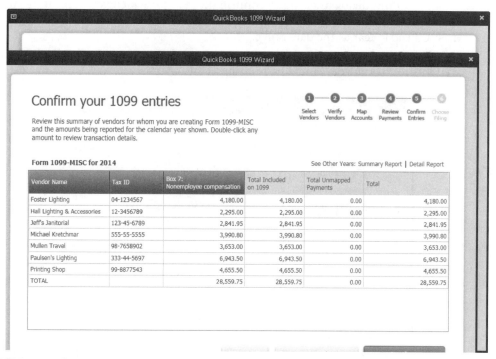

FIGURE 18-4 Make sure your vendor information is correct for 1099 forms.

To see the details behind the amounts being displayed for each vendor, double-click anywhere on the row that contains the vendor's information. The 1099 Detail report for that vendor opens, listing all payment transactions that make up the 1099 reporting balance. If you want to investigate—or modify—an individual payment, double-click the transaction in question on the report.

When you're satisfied that the amounts you'll be reporting are accurate, click Continue.

Choose a Filing Method

You have two options when choosing how to file your 1099-MISC information to your vendors, your state, and the IRS: E-file your federal and state forms with a printed copy to send to your vendor, or print all copies.

Click the Go To Intuit 1099 E-File Service button to e-file or to learn more about it (additional fees may apply). Click the Print 1099s button if you prefer to file using this method.

Printing 1099s

The 1099 Print dialog asks you to confirm the year for which you're printing. You'll likely be performing this task in January of the next year. In this case, you'll choose Last Calendar Year as the date range.

Click OK to move to the Select 1099s To Print dialog. QuickBooks displays the vendors for whom you should be printing 1099s.

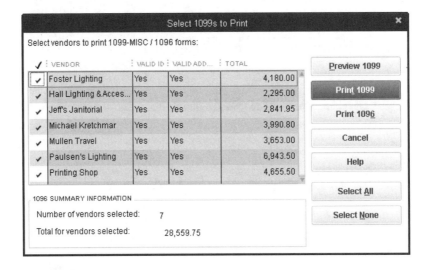

Click Preview 1099 to see what the form will look like when it prints. Zoom-in to make sure your company name, address, and employer ID number (EIN) are correct, and also check the vendor's information to make sure it's up-to-date.

Click Close on the Print Preview window to return to the Select 1099s To Print dialog. Then load the 1099 forms into your printer and click Print 1099. If you're using a laser or inkjet printer, set the number of copies at 3. Dot-matrix printers use three-part forms.

When the forms are printed, click Print 1096 in the Select 1099s To Print dialog. Enter the name of the contact person in your company who can answer questions about these forms (the name is printed on the 1096 form).

Print two copies of the 1096 so you have one for your files. Send each vendor a copy of the 1099 form by January 31. Send the government a copy of each 1099, along with a 1096 Transmittal Form.

Repeat these procedures for each box number of the 1099-MISC form you are required to print (most small businesses need only Box 7).

Make Year-End Journal Entries

Your accountant may want you to make some journal entries before you close your books for the year, such as the following:

- Enter depreciation.
- Move retained earnings to an account created to hold prior retained earnings, or move retained earnings to owner or partner equity retained earnings accounts.
- Create adjustments needed for cash versus accrual reporting (these are usually reversed on the first day of the next fiscal year).
- Adjust prepaid expenses from asset accounts to expense accounts.

You can send the P&L and Balance Sheet reports to your accountant by exporting the reports to Excel.

You can also send your accountant the Accountant's Copy of your company data and let him or her make the journal entries. You import the changes when the file is returned. (See Chapter 17 for detailed instructions on creating journal entries and Chapter 22 to learn how to use the Accountant's Copy feature.)

Getting Ready for Taxes

Most small businesses turn over the job of tax preparation to their accountants, but some business owners prepare their own taxes manually or use a tax software program such as TurboTax.

No matter which method you choose, you should run the reports that tell you whether your QuickBooks data files are ready for tax preparation. Is all the necessary data entered? Do the bottom-line numbers call for some special tax planning or special tax considerations? Even if your taxes are prepared by your accountant, the more organized your records are, the less time the accountant spends on your return, which, hopefully, makes your bill from the accountant smaller.

Checking Tax Line Information

If you're going to do your own taxes, every account in your chart of accounts that is tax related should have the correct tax form in the account's tax line assignment. To see if any tax line assignments are missing, choose Reports | Accountant & Taxes | Income Tax Preparation. When the report appears, all your accounts are listed, along with the tax form assigned to each account. If you created your own chart of accounts instead of accepting a chart of accounts during company setup, the number of accounts that lack a tax form assignment is likely to be quite large.

Before you can prepare your own taxes, you should edit each account to add the tax information. To do so, double-click each account listed as <Unassigned> on the Income Tax Preparation report to open the Edit Account dialog, or open the chart of accounts and select an account. Press CTRL-E to edit the account and select a tax form from the Tax-Line Mapping drop-down list.

Your selections vary depending upon the organizational type of your company (proprietorship, partnership, S-Corp, C-Corp, and so on).

ProAdvisor Tip: Be sure the Income Tax Form Used field is filled out properly on the Company Information dialog (on the Company menu). If it's blank, you won't see the tax information fields on any accounts.

Calculating Other Important Tax Information

Some taxable numbers aren't available through the normal QuickBooks reports. One of the most common is the report on company officer compensation if your business is incorporated.

If your business is a C-Corporation, you file tax Form 1120, while a Subchapter S-corporation files tax Form 1120S. Both of these forms require that you separate compensation for corporate officers from the other employee compensation. You will have to add those totals from payroll reports (either QuickBooks payroll or an outside payroll service).

You can avoid the need to calculate this by creating a separate Payroll item called Officer Compensation and assigning it to its own account (named something like Salaries & Wages—Officers), which you'll also have to create. Then open the Employee record for each officer and change the Earnings item to the new item. Do this for next year; it's probably too late for this year's end-of-year process.

Using TurboTax

If you use TurboTax to do your taxes, you don't have to do anything special in QuickBooks to transfer the information. Open TurboTax and tell it to import the data it needs from your QuickBooks company file.

Almost everything you need is transferred to TurboTax. You'll have to enter some details directly (for example, home-office expenses for a Schedule C form). You can learn more about TurboTax at www.turbotax.com.

Close Your Books

After all the year-end reports have been run, any necessary journal entries have been entered, and your taxes have been filed, it's customary to "close the books" so no user can add, remove, or change any transactions for that year. After taxes have been filed based on the information in your QuickBooks file, nothing should ever be changed. Typically, closing the books occurs some time after the end of the fiscal year, usually within the first couple of months of the current fiscal year, as soon as your business tax forms have been filed.

QuickBooks does not require you to close the books in order to keep working in the software. You can work forever, year after year, without performing a closing process. However, many QuickBooks users prefer to lock the transactions for the previous year as a way to prevent any changes to the data except by users with the appropriate permissions who know the password you created when you closed the books.

Closing the Year by Setting a Closing Date

In QuickBooks, you close the year by entering a closing date. This very important action essentially locks users out of that year's transactions. At the same time, you can configure user rights to enable or disable a user's ability to see, or even manipulate, closed transactions.

1. Choose Company | Set Closing Date.
2. In the Closing Date section of the dialog, click the Set Date/Password button.
3. In the Set Closing Date And Password dialog, enter the closing date (the last date of your fiscal year) and a password.

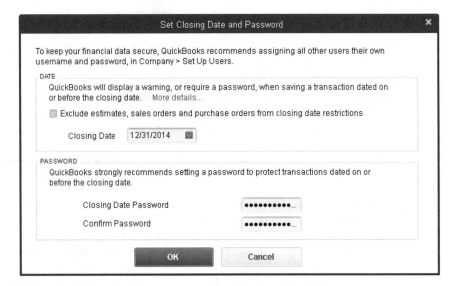

ProAdvisor Tip: If you've set up users and passwords for access to your QuickBooks data file, only the QuickBooks users named Admin or a user set up as an External Accountant can set the closing date and password.

Create a Year-End Backup

After all the numbers are checked, all the journal entries are made, and the books have been closed by entering a closing date, do a separate backup in addition to your normal daily backup. Don't put this backup on the same media you use for your normal backups—the best option is a CD, flash drive, or cloud-based backup service, which you can label "Year-End Backup 2013" and store off-site. See Chapter 23 to learn more about how to back up your QuickBooks files.

Part Four

Tracking Time and Paying Your Employees

If you have employees, the chapters in this section are required reading. In Chapter 19, you'll learn how to track the time your employees (and subcontractors) spend on customer jobs using the built-in QuickBooks time-tracking feature. You'll also learn how to use this information to bill your customers and in job costing reports.

Chapters 20 and 21 cover essentially everything you need to know about setting up and running your payroll in QuickBooks, including how to use the time tracked in a timesheet to prepare a paycheck as well as how to ensure that all payroll taxes due are remitted to the government on time.

Tracking Employee Hours with QuickBooks

n this chapter:

- Track time in QuickBooks

- Work with QuickBooks timesheets

- Track mileage

You can track time and mileage and use this information to recover reimbursable costs from customers, develop an accurate job costing system, analyze expenses, and pay employees. All the tools you need to perform these functions are available in QuickBooks, and they are covered in this chapter.

Your QuickBooks software includes built-in time-tracking that lets you record the amount of time you and your staff spend completing a project or doing work for a customer or for your company, such as administrative tasks. This chapter covers how to configure and use this feature.

Setting Up Time Tracking

If you used the Advanced Setup option to create your company file and responded "Yes" when asked if you want to track time, QuickBooks has already turned on the built-in time-tracking features for you.

If you're not sure whether you turned on time tracking when you created your company, choose Edit | Preferences from the QuickBooks menu bar. Select Time & Expenses by scrolling to the last category in the left pane, and click the Company Preferences tab. Make sure the Yes option is selected.

By default, QuickBooks assumes your work week starts on Monday. However, some businesses use a different work week, such as a Sunday-to-Saturday pattern for tracking time. If you're tracking time for employees and you plan to use the timesheets for payroll, it's a good idea to match the work week to the week your pay period covers.

Adding Timekeepers

You can track time for your employees, outside contractors (vendors), or yourself. Everyone who must keep track of his or her time must first exist in the system and, of course, must fill out a timesheet.

Setting Up Employees

If you're running the QuickBooks payroll feature, you already have employees in your QuickBooks system, and you can use timesheets to track their time. Optionally, you can also use their timesheet data to create a paycheck, using the number of hours reported on the timesheet. For this to work, however, you must modify the employee record as follows:

1. Choose Employees | Employee Center to open the Employee Center.
2. Click the Employees tab to display the list of employees.
3. Double-click the listing of the employee you want to link to time tracking.
4. Click the Payroll Info tab.
5. Select the Use Time Data To Create Paychecks check box on the bottom left (see Figure 19-1).
6. Click OK.

You don't have to link employees to time tracking for them to use timesheets to record their time—your employees can track time unconnected to the preparation of paychecks to make it possible to create job-costing reports or to invoice customers for their time.

Even if you're not doing your own payroll in QuickBooks, you can create employees (in the Employee Center) for the purpose of tracking time, and you can use the timesheet data for an outside payroll service.

Tracking Vendor Time

Any vendor in your system who is paid for his or her time can have that time tracked for the purpose of billing customers. Most of the time, these vendors are outside contractors or subcontractors. You don't have to do anything special to the vendor record to enable time tracking; you just need to record their time in a timesheet. If you want to bill the customer for those hours for which the service was performed, mark their time as "billable" on their timesheets (covered in the "Working with Timesheets" section later in this chapter).

FIGURE 19-1 Link employees to time tracking if you want to use timesheets to prepare paychecks automatically.

Tracking Other Worker's Time

You may need to track the time of people who are neither employees nor vendors. QuickBooks provides a system list called Other Names that you can use to collect names that don't fit in the other QuickBooks lists. Following are some situations in which you'll need to use the Other Names list:

- You have employees and use QuickBooks payroll, but you are not an employee because you take a draw instead of a paycheck. In this case, you should add your name to the Other Names list if you want to track your own time.
- You have no employees and your business is a proprietorship or a partnership. Owner or partner names should be entered into the Other Names list in order to track time.

Adding the Tasks

Most of the tasks you track in timesheets already exist in your Item List as service items. These are the items you use when you invoice customers for services. However, because you can use time tracking to analyze the way people in your organization spend their time, you may want to add service items that aren't connected to tasks performed for customers.

For example, if you want to track the time people spend performing administrative tasks for the business, you can add a service item called Administrative to your Item List. If you want to be more specific, you can name the particular administrative tasks you want to track; for example, bookkeeping, equipment repair, new sales calls, public relations, and so on.

To enter new items, choose Lists | Item List from the menu bar. When the Item List window opens, press CTRL-N to open the New Item dialog. Select Service as the item type (only service items are tracked in timesheets) and name the new item. Here are some guidelines for administrative items:

- If you're specifying administrative tasks, create a service named Administration and then make each specific administrative task a subitem of Administration.
- Don't put an amount in the Rate box unless every employee and outside contractor performing this service has the same hourly pay rate (highly unlikely). You can enter the amount when you make the payment (via payroll or vendor checks).
- Because QuickBooks requires that you assign an account to a service, choose or create a "dummy" (or placeholder) revenue account (such as Other Revenue or Time Tracking Revenue). Don't worry—no money is ever posted to the account, because you don't ever sell these services directly to customers.

Working with Timesheets

The built-in QuickBooks timesheet feature offers two methods for recording the time your timekeepers spend on tasks: Single Activity and Weekly Timesheet.

Single Activity is a form you use to enter what you did when you performed a single task at a specific time on a specific date. For example, a Single Activity form may record the fact that you made a telephone call on behalf of a customer, you repaired some piece of equipment for a customer, or you performed some administrative task for the company.

The Weekly Timesheet is a form in which you indicate how much time and on which date you performed work in a given week. Each Weekly Timesheet entry can also include the name of the customer for whom the work was performed. You can also print a blank timesheet that can be filled out manually and entered into QuickBooks all at once at the end of a week.

> **ProAdvisor Tip:** After you fill out and save a Single Activity form, you can open a Weekly Timesheet to view all the single activities that have been entered within that week—they are automatically inserted there for you.

Setting the Format for Displaying Time

When you enter time in the various timesheet forms, you can use either the minutes (*hh:mm*) format or a decimal format (6.5). To establish a default, choose Edit | Preferences and click the General category. Then select the Company Preferences tab and use the options in the Time Format section of the dialog to select the format you prefer.

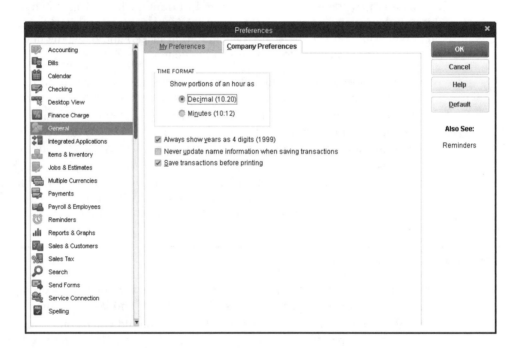

If you set the preference to decimal, and then enter time as 1:30, when you press TAB to move to the next field, QuickBooks changes the entry to 1.50 (or the other way around if you choose Minutes).

Tracking a Single Activity

To track one event or task with a Single Activity form (Figure 19-2), choose Employees | Enter Time | Time/Enter Single Activity.

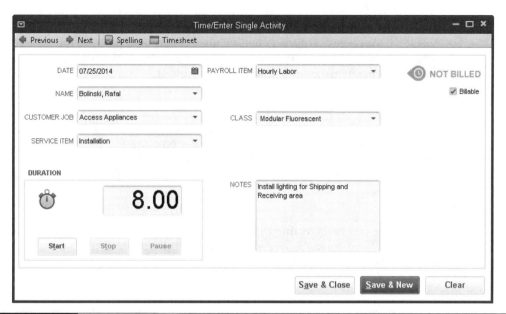

FIGURE 19-2 Fill out the details to indicate how you spent your time.

Follow these guidelines to use this form:

- The Date field is automatically filled in with the current date. If this activity took place previously, you can change the date (but you cannot change the date if you're using the stopwatch).
- Click the arrow to the right of the Name field and select the name of the person who performed the work from the drop-down list. This list contains vendors, employees, and names from the Other Names list. Most of the time, the person who performed the work is filling out the form.
- Select the customer or job in the Customer:Job field. Do this whether or not the customer is going to be billed for the time.
- In the Service Item field, select the task, and in the Duration box, enter the amount of time you're reporting.
- If this time is billable to the customer, the Billable check box should be marked (it is by default). If the time is not going to be billed to the customer, click the box to remove the check mark.
- If the Payroll Item field is available, select the payroll item that applies to this time (for example, salary or hourly wages). This field appears only if the selected name is an employee and the employee record has been linked to the time-tracking system (explained earlier in this chapter).

- If the Class field is available, you can optionally assign the time to a class.
- Use the Notes box to enter any comments or additional information you want to record about this activity. You can then transfer those notes onto the invoice that you generate using this timesheet data, and they can be included in job reports as well.

> **ProAdvisor Tip:** If you've linked the employee to the time-tracking system and you've also enabled class tracking, you won't see the Class field unless you turn on the Earnings Item option in Payroll & Employees Preferences (see Figure 19-3).

When you've finished creating the activity, click Save & New to fill out another Single Activity form (many workers perform multiple single activities each day), or click Save & Close to finish.

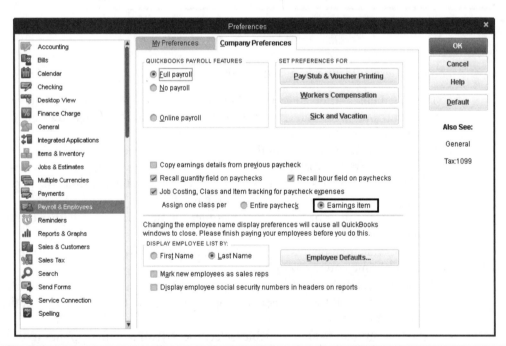

FIGURE 19-3 Enable the Earnings Item option in Payroll & Employees preferences if you want to assign an employee's payroll expense to a class.

Using the Stopwatch When Tracking a Single Activity

You can let QuickBooks track the time you're spending on a single task. Click the Start button in the Duration box of the Time/Enter Single Activity window when you begin the task. QuickBooks tracks hours and minutes as they elapse.

- To pause the counting when you're interrupted, click Pause. Then click Start to pick up where you left off.
- To stop timing, click Stop. The elapsed time is displayed.

The stopwatch always displays time in the *hh:mm:ss* format. If you set your format preference to decimal, QuickBooks converts the time when the stopwatch is stopped.

Using Weekly Timesheets

A Weekly Timesheet records the same information as the Single Activity form, except that the information is recorded in week-at-a-time blocks, and you have the option to "batch" enter the same timesheet information for multiple timekeepers (both employees and nonemployees).

To use the Weekly Timesheet form (shown in Figure 19-4), choose Employees | Enter Time | Use Weekly Timesheet. Use the instructions that follow to fill out the timesheet.

1. Select either an individual employee or a vendor name from the drop-down list in the Name field. Optionally, choose either Multiple Names (Payroll) or Multiple Names (Non-Payroll) (these options are located at the top of the Name drop-down list) to create multiple timesheets with the same information for the names you've selected in your list. This latter option is useful if you've got a team of employees or contractors working on the same project and performing the same work for the week.
2. The current week appears by default; click the calendar icon if you need to select a different week.
3. In the Customer:Job column, select the customer or job connected to the activity (or select the in-house listing to enter administrative work unconnected to a customer).
4. In the Service Item column, select the appropriate service item.
5. For an employee whose paycheck is linked to timesheets, use the Payroll Item column to select the payroll item that fits the activity. (If the name selected in the Name field is not an employee whose paycheck is linked to timesheets, the Payroll Item column disappears.)
6. In the Notes column, enter any necessary notes or comments.
7. Click the column that represents the day in which an activity occurred and enter the number of hours worked on this task. Repeat across the week for each day that the same activity was performed for the same customer or job.

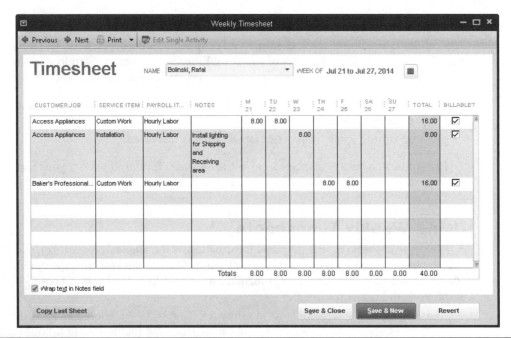

FIGURE 19-4 Some people find it easier to enter information on a weekly basis.

8. Move to the beginning of the next row to enter a different activity, or the same activity for a different customer, repeating this action until the timesheet is filled in for the week.

9. For each row, indicate whether the time is billable in the Billable column. Click the check box to remove the check mark in the Billable column if the time on this row is not billable.

10. Click Save & New to create a timesheet for a different week. Click Save & Close when you are finished entering time.

ProAdvisor Tip: By default, QuickBooks marks all time entries that are linked to a customer as billable. To change the default to Not Billable, choose Edit | Preferences, click the Time & Expenses category, and uncheck the option Mark All Time Entries As Billable.

Copying Previous Timesheets

You can copy the previous week's timesheet by clicking the Copy Last Sheet button after you enter the current date in the Timesheet window and select a name. This is useful for workers who have similar timesheet data every week. This description frequently applies to your office staff or to outside contractors who are performing large jobs that take multiple weeks.

For some employees whose work is usually for the office and not charged to a customer, the timesheet may be identical from week to week.

Reporting Timesheet Information

Before you use the information on the timesheets to invoice customers (covered later in this chapter in the section "Invoicing Customers for Time") or pay workers, you should go over the data on the timesheet reports. You can view and customize reports, edit information, and print the original timesheets.

Running Timesheet Reports

To run reports on timesheets, choose Reports | Jobs, Time & Mileage. You'll see a long list of available reports, but the following reports provide information on time tracking:

- **Time By Job Summary**   Reports the amount of time spent for each service on your customers and jobs.
- **Time By Job Detail**   Reports the details of the time spent for each customer and job, including dates and whether or not the time was marked as billable. A billing status of Unbilled indicates the time is billable but hasn't yet been used on a customer invoice.
- **Time By Name**   Reports the amount of time each user tracked.
- **Time By Item**   Shows an analysis of the amount of time spent on each service your company provides, including the customers for whom the services were performed.

Editing Entries in a Report

While you're browsing the report, you can double-click an activity listing to navigate to the original entry. You can make changes in the original entry, such as selecting or deselecting the billable option or change the Notes field by adding a note or editing the content of the existing note.

Editing the Original Timesheets

Before you use the timesheets for customer billing or payroll, make sure you examine them and make any needed corrections. In fact, you may want to take this step before you view any of the Jobs, Time & Mileage reports.

The most common revision is the billable status. If outside contractors or employees are filling out timesheets, it's not unusual to have some confusion about which customers receive direct time billings. In fact, you may have customers to whom you send direct time bills only for certain activities and provide the remaining activities as part of your basic services.

To check timesheets, open a new weekly timesheet and enter the name of the person connected to the timesheet you want to view. Use the Previous or Next arrows at the top of the Timesheet window or use the calendar icon to move to the timesheet you want to inspect. Then edit the information as necessary:

- If needed, change the number of hours for any activity item.
- Change the billable status.
- View (and edit if necessary) any notes.

Caution: If you've already used the timesheet data to create an invoice for the customer or to pay the employee, the changes you make to the timesheet do not automatically update these documents.

Printing Weekly Timesheets

It's a common practice to have employees print their weekly timesheets and deliver them to the person responsible for monitoring and managing employee hours. And it's not uncommon for this person to handle your payroll-related activities as well.

To print timesheets, choose File | Print Forms | Timesheets from the QuickBooks menu bar to open the Select Timesheets To Print window shown in Figure 19-5.

In this window, you can do the following:

- Change the date range to match the timesheets you want to print.
- By default, all timesheets are selected. To remove a timesheet, select its listing and click the column with the check mark to deselect that listing. You can click Select None to deselect all listings, and then select and add check marks to one or more specific users.
- To print any notes in their entirety, select the Print Full Activity Notes option. Otherwise, the default selection to print only the first line of any note is enabled.

The Select Timesheets To Print dialog has a Preview button, and clicking it displays a print preview of the selected timesheets. If you click the Print button in the Preview

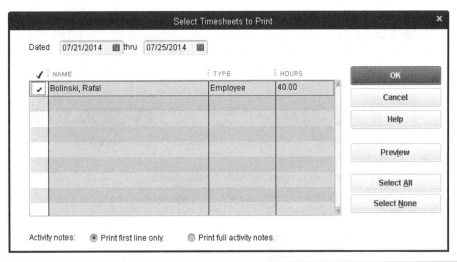

FIGURE 19-5   Print the timesheets for every person who tracks time.

window, the timesheets are sent to the printer immediately, giving you no opportunity to change the printer or any printing options. Clicking the Close button in the Preview window returns you to the Select Timesheets To Print dialog.

Click OK to open the Print Timesheets window, where you can change the printer or printing options. You should change the number of copies to print to match the number of people to whom you're distributing the timesheets.

One thing you should notice about printed (or previewed) timesheets is the last column, which indicates the billing status. The entries are codes, as follows:

- **B**   Billable but not yet invoiced to the customer
- **N**   Not billable
- **D**   Billable and already invoiced to the customer

Invoicing Customers for Time

Now that you've entered time, marked it as billable, and reviewed it for accuracy, it's easy to invoice your customer for the hours spent on their project or job—and you can do this right from the Create Invoice window.

From the Customers menu, select Create Invoices, and then select a customer name from the Customer:Job drop-down list. The first time you select a customer for which there is a timesheet entry, QuickBooks shows a message informing you that the customer or job you've selected has outstanding billable time. You'll be prompted to either select the outstanding billable time (as well as any costs) to add to the invoice or exclude time and costs now and leave them available for invoicing at a later date. You can also have QuickBooks save your choice by checking the box Save This As A Preference.

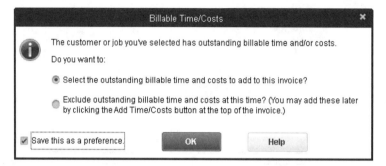

If you choose the option to add the outstanding billable time to your invoice, QuickBooks displays the Choose Billable Time And Costs window (Figure 19-6).

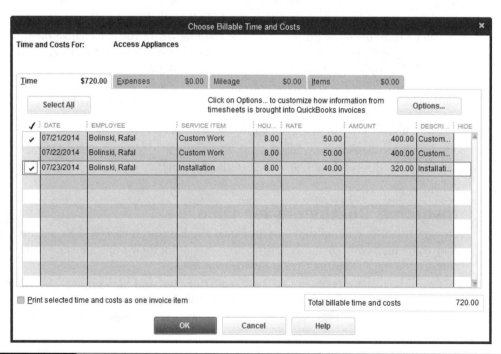

FIGURE 19-6 The Choose Billable Time And Costs window makes invoicing a customer for time an easy task.

Select the Time tab to view all the unbilled time assigned to that customer or job. Click the Select All button to invoice your customer for all the time that appears in this window, or place a check mark next to only those hours that you're ready to invoice the customer for.

By default, each time entry that has a different service item will appear as a separate line item on the invoice. To combine the hours for all items in this window as one line item on the printed copy of the invoice (the detailed view will still appear on your screen), place a check mark in the box next to Print Selected Time And Costs As One Invoice Item at the bottom of the window. Clicking the Options button gives you additional ways to customize how information from timesheets is included in invoices.

Tracking Mileage

QuickBooks provides a way to track the mileage of your vehicles. You can use the mileage information to track the expenses connected to vehicle use, to use mileage as part of your job-costing efforts, to bill customers for mileage expenses, or to maintain records for your vehicle-use tax deduction.

ProAdvisor Tip: Your accountant may be able to use the vehicle mileage data on your income tax return. You can deduct either the actual mileage expense or your other vehicle expenses; you can't deduct both. Your accountant, working with the figures you provide as a result of mileage tracking, will make the decision.

To track a vehicle, you first need to add that vehicle to your Vehicle list (covered in Chapter 6). Once the vehicle is in your QuickBooks system, you can begin tracking its mileage. Of course, you also need to make sure that everyone who uses the vehicle is tracking mileage properly, so you should create, print, and distribute a form for this purpose, with the following categories to fill in:

- Trip Start Date
- Trip End Date
- Starting Odometer
- Ending Odometer
- Customer:Job

Entering Mileage Rates

To track the cost of mileage, you must make sure you have accurate mileage rates in your system. These change frequently, so you'll have to keep up with the latest IRS figures. QuickBooks calculates the cost of mileage based on the information you enter. To get the current rate, check with the IRS (www.irs.gov) or ask your accountant. To enter mileage rates for your own use, use the following steps:

1. Choose Company | Enter Vehicle Mileage to open the Enter Vehicle Mileage dialog.
2. Click the Mileage Rates button on the toolbar to open the Mileage Rates dialog.
3. Select a date from the calendar as the Effective Date.
4. Enter the IRS rate for that date.
5. Click Close.
6. Close the Enter Vehicle Mileage dialog (unless you're using it to enter mileage).
7. The Mileage Rates dialog accepts multiple dates and rates. When you track mileage, QuickBooks uses the appropriate rate, based on the date of your mileage entry, to calculate costs.

Creating a Mileage Item

If you plan to invoice customers for mileage expenses, you must create an item (call it Mileage, Travel, or something similar). The item you create can be either a Service or Other Charge type.

- If you want to charge your customers for mileage as a reimbursable expense and post your reimbursements as income (as explained in Chapter 11), use an Other Charge item type and select the option This Item Is Used In Assemblies Or Is A Reimbursable Charge. Then enter the appropriate expense and income accounts.

- If you want to charge your customers for mileage and reduce your mileage expenses with reimbursed amounts, select the expense account to which you post your mileage expenses.

It's important to understand that the mileage rate you entered in the Mileage Rates dialog (described in the previous section) is *not* automatically transferred to the item you create for mileage. Therefore, you must manually fill in the rate for the item and update it when the IRS rate changes. You can use the same rate you used in the Mileage Rates dialog or enter a different rate to create a markup—or even a markdown, if you wish.

Entering Mileage

After you've configured your company file for mileage charges, you can track the mileage in the Enter Vehicle Mileage dialog as follows:

1. Choose Company | Enter Vehicle Mileage.

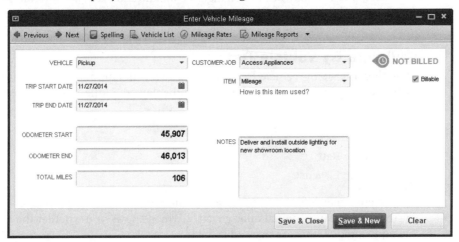

2. Select the appropriate vehicle from the drop-down list in the Vehicle field and enter the following data:
   - The dates of the trip.
   - The odometer readings (QuickBooks calculates the total miles for you). You can skip the odometer readings and enter the total mileage manually, but entering the odometer numbers creates a report entry that's closer to what an IRS auditor wants to see (the IRS likes "logs" that include odometer readings).
   - If you want to bill the customer for mileage, place a check mark in the Billable check box and select the Customer:Job, the item you created for mileage, and the Class (if you're tracking classes).
   - If you don't want to bill a customer but you want to track job costs, select the Customer:Job, but don't place a check mark in the Billable check box.

Mileage charges can be added to customer invoices in the same fashion as time (see the previous section, "Invoicing Customers for Time"). Reimbursable expenses are covered in Chapter 11.

Creating Mileage Reports

QuickBooks includes four vehicle mileage reports, which you can access by choosing Reports | Jobs, Time & Mileage and selecting the appropriate mileage report from the submenu. If you're working in the Enter Vehicle Mileage dialog, the reports are available in the drop-down list you see if you click the arrow next to the Mileage Reports button at the top of the dialog.

Mileage By Vehicle Summary

Use the Mileage By Vehicle Summary report to see the total miles and the mileage expense for each vehicle you're tracking. You can run this report for any date range that you want to check, which is a way to determine whether vehicles need servicing. For example, you may need to change the oil and filter every 6,000 miles or schedule a 50,000-mile checkup. If you deduct mileage expenses on your income tax form, use the entire year as the date range.

Mileage By Vehicle Detail

Use the Mileage By Vehicle Detail report to view details about each mileage entry you created. For each vehicle, the report displays the following information:

- Trip End Date
- Total Miles
- Mileage Rate
- Mileage Expense

No customer information appears in the report, but you can double-click any listing to open the original mileage entry, which shows you whether the trip is linked to a job and whether it's marked billable.

Mileage By Job Summary

Use the Mileage By Job Summary report to view the total number of miles linked to customers or jobs. The report displays total miles for all customers or jobs for which you entered an item and displays billable amounts for any mileage entries you marked billable.

Mileage By Job Detail

Use the Mileage By Job Detail report to see the following information about each trip for each customer or job:

- Trip End Date
- Billing Status
- Item
- Total Miles
- Sales Price
- Amount

To gain more insight, you can modify the report by clicking the Customize Report button on the report window to open the Modify Report dialog. In the Display tab, select additional columns to reflect what you want to see in this report. For example, you may want to add the Mileage Rate or Mileage Expense (or both). Memorize the report so you don't have to repeat the modifications next time. Memorizing reports in QuickBooks is covered in Chapter 26.

Paying Your Employees with QuickBooks Payroll

Chapter 20

*I*n *this chapter:*

- Choose a payroll service

- Run a manual payroll

- Set up payroll items

- Set up employee information

- Enter historical data

- Issue payroll checks

- Use the Employee Center

If you plan on processing your payroll through QuickBooks, the information you need to set it up is in this chapter. Now may also be a good time to consult with your accountant for advice on choosing the payroll option that best fits your business needs and to ensure that your setup is fully compliant with your local and state taxing authorities.

QuickBooks Payroll Services

QuickBooks offers a variety of payroll services designed to work with your company data. Here's a brief recap of what's currently available:

- **Basic Payroll** provides tax tables and automatic calculations of paycheck deductions and employer expenses for up to three employees. No tax forms are included, so you either need to work with your accountant on tax filings or prepare your tax forms manually. QuickBooks makes it easy to prepare tax forms manually by providing detailed reports in Excel (covered in Chapter 21).
- **Enhanced Payroll** adds tax forms and e-filing for both federal and state reporting.
- **Full Payroll** turns the job of running your payroll, depositing withholdings, paying employer contributions, and printing and filing government forms over to QuickBooks. All you have to do is enter your employees' hours.

Additional plans are available, such as Intuit's Online Payroll service, which does not require that you use QuickBooks for your accounting, and Enhanced Payroll for Accountants, which lets you prepare payroll for up to 50 companies (including preparing federal and state forms) and includes After The Fact payroll data entry capability. If you're looking for a complete solution, consider the Intuit Full Service option—you enter your employees' time, and Intuit handles the rest.

Enabling a QuickBooks Payroll Service

If you haven't already done so, be sure the Full Payroll feature preference is enabled in your QuickBooks company file by choosing Edit | Preferences | Payroll & Employees | Company Preferences | Full Payroll. Selecting this option enables payroll-related information fields for employees and also adds a Turn On Payroll button in the Employee section of the QuickBooks Home Page. Click the Turn On Payroll button to learn about and sign up for one of the QuickBooks payroll offerings.

When the sign-up process is completed, download the files you need to run payroll. The new files are automatically added to your QuickBooks system; you don't have to do anything to install them. In addition to the payroll software, the current tax table is added to your system. After payroll is installed, your Employees menu has all the commands you need to run payroll.

➨ ProAdvisor Recommends

Processing Your Payroll Manually in QuickBooks

Some small businesses with one or two employees may choose to run a manual payroll through QuickBooks. Keep in mind that if you choose to process your payroll manually, no withholding or tax will automatically be calculated for any paycheck you create—you have to sign up for the QuickBooks payroll service for that. But you can use your own printed tax table (Employer's Circular E from the IRS), calculate the deductions, and enter them manually when you create paychecks.

However, you'll need to set up your file to allow you to enter these amounts manually, and the only way to tell QuickBooks you want to exercise this option is via the Help menu:

1. Select QuickBooks Help from the main Help menu to open the Have A Question? window.

2. In the Search field, type **manual payroll**, and then click the magnifying glass (search) icon. QuickBooks will display several Help articles—click the article titled "Process Payroll Manually (Without A Subscription To QuickBooks Payroll)." Within this article is a topic titled "If You Prefer to Process Your Payroll Manually." Locate and click the link Manual Payroll Calculations that's embedded within this topic.

3. From here, you'll be brought to a new Help article called "Are You Sure You Want to Set Your Company File to Use Manual Calculations?" Click the link at the end of this article—Set My Company File To Use Manual Calculations.

If you do elect to process your payroll manually, you'll still need to set up Employees and Payroll Items and track Payroll Liabilities—all of which are covered in the following sections.

It may seem like quite a lot to go through, so the decision to run a manual payroll should be made only after careful consideration and consultation with your accountant and if you're running a very simple payroll for only one or two employees. It will be up to you to ensure that the calculations are correct and you have a system in place to remit your withholdings to the appropriate agency in a timely manner.

Setting Up Your Payroll

To produce accurate paychecks, you need to add accounts to your chart of accounts; create payroll items (salary, wages, and so on); and identify the payroll taxes you have to withhold, the payroll taxes you have to pay as an employer, and company contributions or deductions. And you also need to set up tax information for each employee, such as dependents and deductions.

You can set up these payroll elements in either of two ways:

- Manually
- Using the Payroll Setup wizard

The following sections cover all the steps involved in setting up payroll manually, and later in this chapter you'll learn to use the Payroll Setup wizard. You can review both to decide which way you want to approach the setup.

Adding Payroll Accounts to the Chart of Accounts

You may need to create new accounts in your chart of accounts for payroll. For example, some businesses use a bank account specifically for payroll instead of using their main bank account. QuickBooks automatically adds the Payroll Liabilities and Payroll Expenses accounts when you enable payroll.

You should use subaccounts for payroll liabilities and payroll expenses, because it makes it easier to keep track of individual liabilities and expenses (see Figure 20-1). Be sure to link your payroll items to these subaccounts and not to the parent account. Then, when you create reports, any balances in the subaccounts are totaled in the parent account.

Adding Vendors

Running payroll creates liabilities for payroll taxes and employee benefits that are withheld or deducted. In QuickBooks, the government agency or employee benefit provider to which you remit these withheld amounts needs to be set up as a vendor. Then when you set up the payroll item that tracks the withholding or deduction (discussed in the next section), you can assign that item to the appropriate vendor.

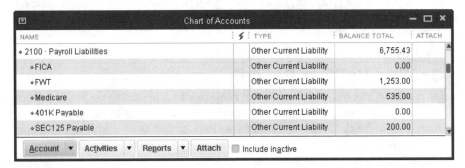

FIGURE 20-1 Use subaccounts to make it easier to track payroll liabilities and expenses.

For withholding of federal income taxes, Medicare, FICA, and the matching employer Medicare and FICA payments, you can assign the United States Treasury Department as the vendor.

For local and state income tax, unemployment, disability, workers comp, and deductions for benefits such as health insurance, set up a vendor for each agency you need to pay. Most states now offer electronic payments for payroll remittances on their websites, but if you use checks you probably have forms or coupons that should accompany your payments.

ProAdvisor Tip: Beginning January 1, 2011, the IRS requires that all payroll tax deposits be made electronically using the Employer Federal Tax Payment System (EFTPS). EFTPS deposits can be made online or by telephone, from the convenience of your home or office. If you haven't already done so, you'll need to go to the EFTPS website (www.eftps.gov) to learn more and enroll.

Adding Payroll Items

QuickBooks uses *payroll items* to list compensation or deduction amounts on a payroll check. The number of individual payroll items that make up a paycheck may be more than you thought. Consider this list, which is typical of many businesses:

- Salaries
- Wages (hourly)
- Overtime (time and a half)
- Double-time
- Federal tax withholdings (including FIT, FICA, and Medicare)
- State tax withholdings
- State unemployment and disability withholdings
- Local tax withholdings
- Pension plan deductions
- Medical insurance deductions
- Life insurance deductions
- Garnishes (such as child support)
- Union dues
- Reimbursement for auto expenses
- Bonuses
- Commissions
- Holiday pay
- Sick pay
- Advanced Earned Income Credit

Whew! And don't forget that you also have to track company-paid payroll items, such as matching FICA and Medicare, employer contributions to unemployment (both state and federal), state disability funds, pension and medical benefit plans, and more.

You can view your payroll items and create new payroll items by choosing Lists | Payroll Item List to open the Payroll Item List seen in Figure 20-2. QuickBooks adds some items to the list automatically when you enable payroll services. Usually, local taxes, medical benefits deductions, and other payroll items are missing and the items that *do* exist may be missing information about the vendor, so you'll have to edit them to add that information.

To add a new payroll item, from the Payroll Item List window, press CTRL-N (or right click) to open the Add New Payroll Item wizard shown in Figure 20-3. In this window, you're asked to select one of two payroll item setup methods: EZ Setup or Custom Setup.

Following is an explanation of what to expect with each option.

EZ Setup of Payroll Items

If you select the EZ Setup option, when you click Next you see a list of payroll item types. The descriptions are brief, but basically you can create any type of pay, deduction, or company benefit, paid by the company, the employee, or both. The only types of payroll items you cannot create in EZ Setup are state and local payroll taxes, including state unemployment and/or disability taxes.

ITEM NAME	TYPE	AMOUNT	LIMIT	TAX TRACKING	PAYABLE TO	ACCOUNT ID
Sick - Hourly	Hourly Wage			Compensation		
Vacation - Hourly	Hourly Wage			Compensation		
Bonus (one-time cash award)	Addition			Compensation		
Employee Advance	Addition			None		
Mileage Reimbursement	Addition	0.55		Compensation		
125 -Health Insurance (pre-tax)	Deduction		-1,200.00	None	Sec125 Administrator	Acct# 870547
401(k) Emp.	Deduction			401(k)	401K Administrator	45632010
Owner's Labor Deduction	Deduction	0.00		None		
Advance Earned Income Credit	Federal Tax			Advance EIC Paym...	State Tax Agency	55-5555555
Federal Unemployment	Federal Tax	0.6%	7,000.00	FUTA	State Tax Agency	55-5555555
Federal Withholding	Federal Tax			Federal	State Tax Agency	55-5555555
Medicare Company	Federal Tax	1.45%		Comp. Medicare	State Tax Agency	55-5555555
Medicare Employee	Federal Tax	1.45%		Medicare	State Tax Agency	55-5555555
Social Security Company	Federal Tax	6.2%	113,700.00	Comp. SS Tax	State Tax Agency	55-5555555
Social Security Employee	Federal Tax	6.2%	-113,700.00	SS Tax	State Tax Agency	55-5555555

FIGURE 20-2 Some payroll items are created automatically by QuickBooks, while others may need to be added by you.

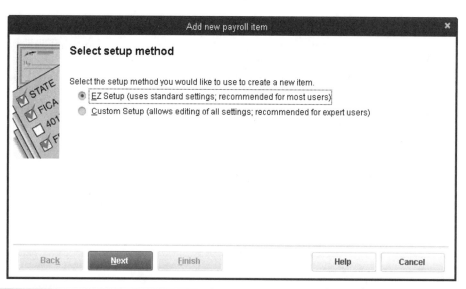

FIGURE 20-3   The Add New Payroll Item wizard helps you create a payroll item.

When you use the EZ Setup option, after you select the type of item, QuickBooks loads the Payroll Setup wizard and then displays the Add New dialog from that feature. The questions and explanations you see in the Payroll Setup wizard are more basic than the questions you're asked if you select the Custom Setup option for setting up a payroll item. You need less knowledge of payroll processing to complete the setup, but you'll spend more time moving through more wizard windows, because most of the data you provide is entered one wizard window at a time. This does not mean you can set up a payroll item accurately if you know nothing about deductions, benefits, or the accounting and legal issues involved with payroll benefits and deductions (which is why it's always a good idea to consult with an accounting professional when payroll is involved). What it does mean, however, is that the explanations you see when you're asked to provide information are easy to understand.

For example, if you're setting up a benefit such as health insurance, pension benefit, or any form of a benefit in a cafeteria plan, the wizard asks you if the benefit cost is borne entirely by the company, entirely by the employee, or shared between both. Depending on your answer, the wizard moves through the subsequent windows to set up the necessary payroll item(s). In addition, if the employee contributes some or all of the cost, you have to know whether it's a pre-tax or after-tax deduction, and you have to know how the deduction affects the employee's W-2 form. Perhaps yet another reason to discuss your payroll setup with your accountant first!

Custom Setup of Payroll Items

If you select the Custom Setup option, the list you see when you click Next is all inclusive. You can set up all the payroll item types offered in the EZ Setup list of payroll types, plus you can also set up state and local payroll items. You'll find that, unlike the EZ Setup wizard, each window in the Custom Setup wizard contains most all the fields for the required information, resulting in fewer steps needed to complete the setup of a payroll item.

Keep in mind, however, that if you have a health benefit with costs shared between the company and the employee, the Custom Setup wizard isn't going to remind you that you have to set up two items: first one for the employee deduction and another for the company payment. In this instance, you have to start the wizard again to select Company Contribution in the second wizard window to set up the company side of the health benefits item.

Set Up Employees

The information about your employees *must* be accurate; otherwise, you may find yourself having to adjust payroll information inside QuickBooks and then having to report these changes to the IRS—which means more work for you and potential confusion with the IRS about your payroll withholding data.

There is a great deal of information to fill out for each employee, and some of it is probably the same for all or most of your employees. For example, many of your employees may share the same type of pay (salary or hourly wage) or the same deductions for medical insurance.

To save yourself a lot of time, you can create a new employee default (or New Employee Default (template). The information you put into the template is then automatically added to the Payroll Info tab for each new employee you create.

Creating an Employee Template

To access the template, you open the Employee Center by choosing Employees | Employee Center from the menu bar.

In the Employee Center window, click the Manage Employee Information button at the top of the window and choose Change New Employee Default Settings from the submenu that appears. This opens the Employee Defaults window, where you can enter the data that applies to most or all of your employees.

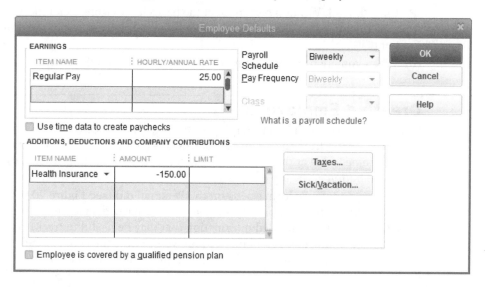

1. Click in the Item Name column of the Earnings box, and then click the arrow to see a list of earnings types that you've defined as payroll items. Select the one that is common enough to be suitable for a template.

2. In the Hourly/Annual Rate column, enter a wage or salary figure if one applies to most of your employees. If not, just skip it; you can enter each employee's rate in the individual employee record later.

3. Click the arrow in the field to the right of the Payroll Schedule field and select a schedule. If you don't have any established payroll schedules, you can add a new one here if you wish. See the section "Payroll Schedules" later in this chapter for more information.

4. Select a Pay Frequency (if you created schedules and selected one, QuickBooks automatically uses that schedule to fill in the Pay Frequency field).

5. Use the Class field if you've enabled classes to track data.

6. If you're using QuickBooks time-tracking features to pay employees, you'll also see a Use Time Data To Create Paychecks check box. Put a check mark in the check box to enable that feature.

7. If all or most of your employees have the same additional adjustments (such as insurance deductions, 401(k) deductions, or reimbursement for car expenses), click in the Item Name column in the Additions, Deductions, And Company Contributions box, and then click the arrow to select the appropriate adjustments.

8. Click the Taxes button to open the Taxes Defaults dialog and select those taxes that are common and therefore suited for the template. The State tab and the

Other tab (usually local payroll taxes) contain tax data that probably applies to all or most of your employees.

9. Click the Sick/Vacation button to set the terms for accruing sick time and vacation time if your policy is similar enough among employees to include it in the template.

10. When you are finished filling out the template, click OK to save it.

Creating Employees

You're now ready to add your employees to QuickBooks. Choose Employees | Employee Center from the menu bar. The details about how to work in the Employee Center can be found at the end of this chapter, but for now, start by clicking the New Employee button at the top of the window to add your first employee.

The New Employee form opens on the Personal tab (see Figure 20-4). This tab has several fields that not only allow you to enter basic data about your new hire, but also capture more detailed information that may be useful to track. For example, your state unemployment form may require you to note the gender of all employees; your medical or life insurance carrier may require the date of birth.

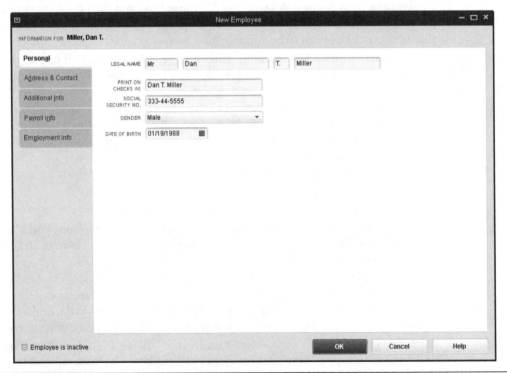

FIGURE 20-4 Start by entering personal information about the employee.

You'll also see additional tabs for the following categories:

- **Address & Contact** Here you can enter a primary address as well as multiple phone numbers, e-mail, and emergency contacts. Remember that an employee's address is required to file W-2 forms.

- **Additional Info** Use this tab to enter an employee number (optional). This tab also contains a Define Fields button, so you can create custom fields to track such things as the date of an employee's last raise or the name of a spouse or partner.

- **Payroll Info** This is where you enter information about earnings, taxes, and deductions (see Figure 20-5). If you've previously completed the default template, this tab will contain the employee's payroll items and amounts already filled in from the default template. If you did not complete the template and the amount of the earnings or the deduction is the same every week, enter an amount. If it differs from week to week, don't enter an amount here. Enter that information when you create the employee's payroll check instead.

- **Employment Info** Enter information about the employee's hiring date and other job details and assign an employment type. See "ProAdvisor Recommends: Understanding Employment Types" a bit later to learn more about using employment types in QuickBooks.

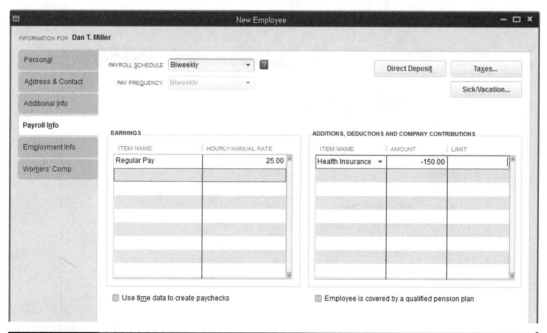

FIGURE 20-5 Enter information about this employee's compensation and deductions.

- **Workers' Comp** This tracking feature is available only if you've signed up for either the Enhanced or Assisted Payroll service. When you use either one of these payroll services, the workers comp tracking feature is automatically enabled, but you can disable it in the Payroll & Employees Preferences (refer to Chapter 24 to learn more about setting Preferences in QuickBooks). Assign the workers comp code that applies to the employee, or select Exempt if this employee is exempt from workers comp.

Click the Taxes button to open the Taxes dialog, which starts with Federal tax information, as shown in Figure 20-6. Fill in any data that wasn't automatically filled in from the employee template, and then modify data that is different for this employee.

Move to the State tab and configure the employee's status for the state. QuickBooks has built in a great deal of state information and, depending on the state, you should see the appropriate withholdings and company-paid items. For example, states that don't deduct SUI from employees have a check box for SUI (Company Paid), while states that collect disability funds from employees will display the appropriate check box.

On the Other tab, apply any local payroll tax that applies to this employee. If you haven't already configured that tax in the Payroll Item List, you can click <Add New> in the Item Name column to enter it now. Click OK to save the tax status information and return to the Payroll Info tab.

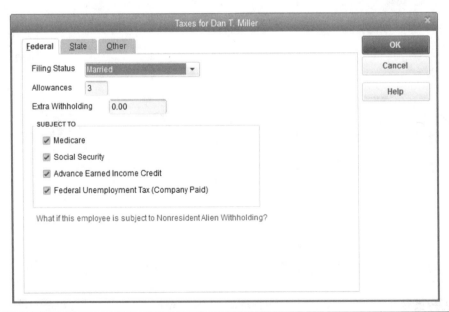

FIGURE 20-6 Configure the employee's tax information.

Click the Sick/Vacation button and enter the hours and dates for this employee. When you are finished, click OK to return to the Payroll Info tab.

Click the Direct Deposit button to establish direct deposit of the employee's paycheck to his or her bank account. If you haven't signed up for direct deposit, the window that opens offers the chance to enroll. Click OK to save your selections and return to the New Employee form.

▶▶ ProAdvisor Recommends

Understanding Employment Types

The Type field on the Employment Info tab of the New Employee form offers four choices. Because the selection you make can have an impact on the way your tax returns are prepared, you should check with your accountant if you have any questions about the type you should assign to any employee.

Regular Employee   A regular employee is exactly what it seems to be: a person you hired for whom you deduct withholdings, issue a W-2, and so on. It's a good idea to have every employee fill out a W-4 form every year even if nothing has changed from the last year. (If you need extra W-4 forms, you can download them from the IRS at www.irs.gov. Go to the forms section, select W-4, and print the form or download it and print as many copies as you need.)

Officer Employee   An *officer* is someone who is an officer of a corporation. If your business isn't incorporated, you have no officers. On federal corporate tax returns, you are required to report payroll for officers of the corporation separately from the regular payroll amounts. Selecting Officer as the type has no impact on running your payroll (calculations, check printing, and so on); it only affects reports.

Statutory Employee   A *statutory employee* is someone who works for you that the IRS has decided qualifies as an employee instead of as an independent contractor. The list of the job types that the rules cover and the definition of *independent contractor* is the subject of much debate (especially in IRS audit hearings). The IRS has a list of criteria that must be met in order to qualify as an independent contractor (which means you don't have to put that person on your payroll, you don't have to withhold taxes, and you don't have to pay employer taxes). The rules that govern this change frequently, so it's important to check the rules in Circular E or with your accountant.

Owner Employee   QuickBooks payroll won't perform payroll tasks for any employee of this type. This employee type is appropriate if you own a company that is a proprietorship, because the money you pay yourself should be posted to an equity account called Owner's Draw, or if the business is a partnership, which has multiple owners. In this case, the amounts paid to the owners are considered distributions.

Handling Year-To-Date Payroll Data

If you start using QuickBooks mid-year, you must enter the historical information about paychecks that have been issued thus far. This is the only way for QuickBooks to perform all of the required year-end tasks when the time comes—you cannot give your employees two W-2 forms: one from your "pre-QuickBooks" system and another from QuickBooks.

No matter what your fiscal year is, your payroll year is the calendar year. Even though you can start using QuickBooks payroll for the current period before you enter the historical data, remember that the absence of historical data may affect some tax calculations. Also, year-to-date payroll information on pay stubs for the employees will be incorrect until you enter historical payroll data. If there are withholding amounts that cease after a certain maximum (perhaps your state only requires SUTA/SUI for the first $7,500.00 in gross payroll), you'll have to adjust the deductions on the current paychecks manually so that QuickBooks can calculate the maximum deduction properly and stop deducting these amounts.

> **P r o A d v i s o r   T i p :** To make historical data entry easier, consider going live with payroll at the beginning of a calendar quarter.

Entering Year-To-Date Totals

The year-to-date payroll totals from before the QuickBooks payroll start date need to be entered into your QuickBooks company file. Here are some guidelines to help you understand how your QuickBooks payroll start date can affect this task:

- Historical payroll amounts need to be totaled and entered by quarter, because your 941 reports are due quarterly.
- You can't enter summarized data for the quarter that's current (the quarter your start date falls in). Instead, for the current quarter, you must enter data for each individual pay period (weekly, biweekly, semimonthly, or monthly). For previous quarters, you can enter quarterly totals.
- If your start date is any date in the first quarter, you have to enter historical data for each pay period, because you don't have a full quarter to summarize.
- If your start date is in the second quarter, enter a quarterly total for the first quarter and then enter the individual pay period numbers for the second quarter, up to the go-live date.
- If your start date is in the third quarter, enter quarterly totals for the first two quarters and then enter each pay period up to the go-live date.
- If your start date is in the fourth quarter, you can follow the same pattern, but it might be just as easy to wait until next year to begin using QuickBooks payroll.

Manually Entering Payroll History in Batches

If you have already entered all your employees in QuickBooks, you can use a shortcut that launches a wizard for entering year-to-date payroll information. The wizard replicates the historical balance entry windows that the QuickBooks Payroll Setup wizard (covered in the next section) offers, but some people find this method easier to use, especially if they've chosen to set up their payroll manually.

1. Choose Help | About QuickBooks Pro 2014 to display the product information window. Then press CTRL-SHIFT-Y. The Set Up YTD Amounts wizard opens to walk you through the steps of entering year-to-date summary information for each employee (see Figure 20-7). Click Next to begin.

2. In the next two windows, the wizard asks you to specify three dates, as described next. It's important to note that the dates you enter might not be the same for all three categories. See "ProAdvisor Recommends: Choosing the Correct Dates when Entering Year-To-Date Payroll."

   • The date your payroll liability and expense accounts are affected. In other words, When should the data you're entering be posted to liability and expense accounts that are associated with payroll items?

   • The date your payroll bank accounts are affected. In other words, When should the net paycheck amounts be posted to your payroll bank account?

   • The check date of the first paycheck you'll create using QuickBooks payroll. This paycheck posts to all relevant accounts; there are no historical balances. Click Next when you've entered this third date.

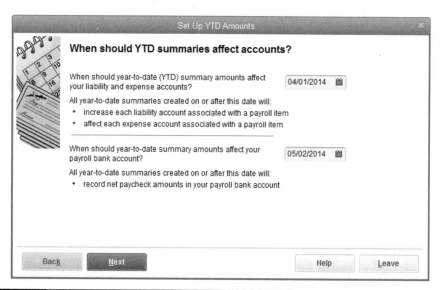

FIGURE 20-7 It's important to know the correct dates needed to enter year-to-date payroll information.

▶▶ ProAdvisor Recommends

Choosing the Correct Dates when Entering Year-To-Date Payroll

Here's an example of a scenario that should help you understand how to enter the dates in these categories. For the purpose of these examples, let's assume you're entering historical information as of the end of April 2014, and your first QuickBooks-produced paychecks will be Friday, May 2, 2014.

- Your first posting of liabilities and expenses should be April 1, 2014, because you would have already remitted the withholdings and employer contributions for the quarter ending March 31, 2014 (see Figure 20-7).
- Your first posting of bank account amounts should be May 2, 2014, the date of the first QuickBooks-produced paycheck (see Figure 20-7).
- Your "first paycheck using QuickBooks" date is your first payday in May. In this example, that day is May 2, 2014.

Nov 30, 2018
Dec 15, 2018
Dec 15, 2018

3. On the Employee summary information page, you'll see your list of employees. Highlight a name and then click the Enter Summary button to open the YTD Adjustment window for that employee.

4. Enter the YTD amounts for wages and withholdings for each payroll period. Click OK after you've completed the entries for each employee. You'll be brought back to the Employee summary information page in the Set Up YTD Amounts wizard.

5. Click the Leave button to close the Set Up YTD Amounts wizard.

Use the QuickBooks Payroll Setup Wizard

When you use the QuickBooks Payroll Setup wizard to set up your payroll, the setup process can take more time than it takes to perform those tasks manually, as described earlier in this chapter. But the wizard does have some advantages: It's user-friendly with explanations throughout, and you can use it to set up all the components required for payroll including entering your historical data. It also has a Finish Later button that you can click if you have to do other work or you get tired or bored. When you open the wizard again, you pick up where you left off.

Regardless of whether you use the Payroll Setup wizard to set up all your components or to enter historical data only, be sure to set up all the vendors and accounts you need to remit payroll withholding and employer payroll expenses first.

To get started, choose Employees | Payroll Setup from the QuickBooks menu bar. The wizard window opens with all the tasks listed in the left pane (see Figure 20-8).

The first few screens are informational, indicating the data you need to complete the wizard (the same information about employees, payroll items, deductions, and so on, that were discussed earlier in this chapter). The real work starts with the Company Setup pages, where the wizard begins to guide you through the necessary details of your payroll setup.

Company Setup Section

In the Company Setup section, the wizard starts with compensation, which means payroll items for salary, hourly wages, bonuses, and so on. When you've finished with that section, the wizard moves on to other payroll item types.

If you've already created your payroll items manually, they appear in the wizard window, and you can click Edit to view or change the settings. If you haven't yet set up payroll items, click Add New to open a mini-wizard that walks you through the process.

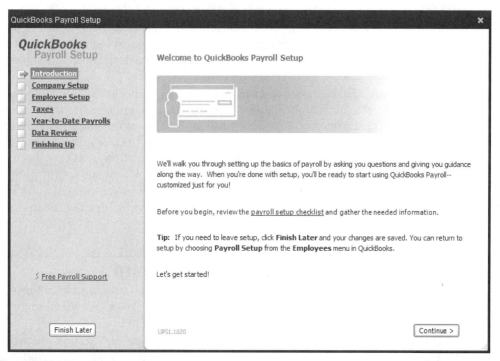

FIGURE 20-8   The QuickBooks Payroll Setup wizard is divided into logical sets of tasks.

The types of payroll items the Company Setup section of the wizard helps to set up include the following:

- Types of compensation, such as salary, hourly wages, overtime, bonuses, commissions, tips, and so on.
- Benefits, such as insurance, pension, and so on. For each benefit you select, you configure the employee/employer contribution rates.
- Paid time off, such as sick leave and vacations. You can configure how QuickBooks calculates vacation time and sick time (if you let employees accrue time according to time worked).
- Other additions and deductions, such as workers comp, auto expense reimbursement, garnishments, union dues, and so on.

Setting Up Employees in the Wizard

After the Company Setup section, the wizard moves on to the Employee Setup section. If you didn't set up your employees manually, you can add each employee in the wizard, moving through a series of windows in which you enter information about the employee's personal information, pay structure, and tax status. For each employee, you designate the taxes and benefits that affect the employee.

When you finish entering employee information, the wizard displays the list of employees. If any employee is missing information, the wizard indicates the problem (if you entered your employees manually, the wizard automatically finds the employee records and displays the same list if problems exist).

Some missing information isn't critical to issuing paychecks, but QuickBooks requires the information in the employee record. If any employee in the list has the notation Fix This Error Now, it means critical information is missing and the system either won't be able to issue a paycheck or won't be able to issue a W-2 form at the end of the year. Regardless of whether the missing information is critical or not, select the employee and click Edit to move through the wizard and fix the problem.

Incidentally, if you use the wizard to set up employees, when you fail to fill in required information, the wizard displays a reminder—something that doesn't happen when you set up employees manually.

Setting Up Payroll Taxes in the Wizard

In the Taxes section, you tell the wizard about the federal, state, and local taxes you're responsible for. These are payroll items, so if you haven't set up all these items beforehand, you can use the wizard.

If you're setting up your taxes in the wizard, as you finish each section, the wizard displays a list of all the taxes for that section. If you set up your taxes as payroll items manually, the wizard finds those entries and uses them to populate the list.

If the wizard finds anything amiss in your setup of any tax, the problem is displayed in the Description column. Choose Edit to make the needed changes.

Entering Payroll History in the Wizard

In the Year-to-Date Payroll section, you enter your historical payroll data. The wizard presents a set of windows, starting with a window that asks if you've issued paychecks this year (meaning outside of QuickBooks, of course). If you answer Yes, the next window displayed is the Payroll Summary window, where you have access to three preformatted tables into which you'll enter the following year-to-date information:

- Paychecks (monthly totals for each employee)
- Payroll tax payments
- Nonpayroll tax payments (company contributions to benefits, and so on)

Click the Edit button next to each of these payroll categories to open the associated worksheet.

Running Data Review

Next is the Data Review section, which you can run if you choose. If you do, QuickBooks asks if you'd like to go over your payroll settings; if you select Yes, the wizard runs a payroll checkup routine.

▶▶ ProAdvisor Recommends

Running a Payroll Checkup

You can run a Payroll Checkup whenever you make changes to your payroll components (employees, taxes, and so on) by choosing Employees | My Payroll Service | Run Payroll Checkup. The QuickBooks Payroll Setup wizard walks through all the elements required for running payroll (a task list). Each section of the wizard's task list is checked for errors. The errors the checkup may find include missing information, invalid information (the format of an EIN number or state reporting number may be incorrect), or any other data that doesn't match the standards built into the QuickBooks payroll feature.

The program reports on the integrity of the data for prior quarters (unless you're working in the first quarter, of course), and then, separately, the integrity of the data for the current quarter.

Then the program asks you about the federal and state forms you've filed to remit withholdings and pay employer taxes. After you've filled in the information, the program reconciles the totals against the payroll totals you entered previously. If it finds errors, the specifics are displayed, and you can correct the problem and rerun the checkup.

Finishing Up

At this point, your setup is complete, and from here you can click Finish or go straight to the Payroll Center, where you'll have access to essentially everything that relates to managing your payroll.

Payroll Schedules

A payroll schedule is a way to create different payroll intervals. For example, if your company pays salaried employees and officers on a weekly basis and pays hourly workers on a biweekly basis, you can run payroll by selecting the appropriate schedule to make sure you pay the right employees on the right dates.

When you create a payroll schedule, you define how often you pay your employees: weekly, biweekly, or semimonthly, for example. You also define the pay period (the workdays covered by the paycheck), the date on the paycheck, and the date you prepare the payroll.

> **C a u t i o n :** The date you prepare the payroll differs from the paycheck date if you're using direct deposit, which requires you to transfer payroll information two days before the paycheck date.

Creating a Payroll Schedule

To create a payroll schedule, choose Employees | Add Or Edit Payroll Schedules. When the Payroll Schedule List window opens, press CTRL-N to create a new payroll schedule. In the New Payroll Schedule dialog, fill out the required information, as follows:

- A name for this schedule. Use descriptive text if you're setting up multiple payroll schedules, such as "weekly-checks," "weekly-DirDep," "CommissionsOnly," and so on.
- The pay period frequency for this schedule.
- The next pay period end date. This is the time period covered by the paycheck, which often is not the same as the paycheck date. For example, you may issue paychecks on Thursday for the period ending the previous Friday.
- The next paycheck date.

If your payroll is monthly or semimonthly, the dialog includes additional fields. For example, if you issue paychecks semimonthly, you can select specific dates, such as the 10th and the 25th, or you can select one midmonth date and then select Last Day Of Month for the second check in that month.

After you create the schedule, QuickBooks offers to assign the schedule automatically to any employees who are configured for the same pay frequency as the new schedule.

Assigning Payroll Schedules to Employees

Each employee record has a field for the applicable payroll schedule in the Payroll Info tab. When you link the payroll schedule to the appropriate employees, those employees appear when you select the schedule on the day you're preparing paychecks.

Special Payroll Runs

QuickBooks offers a way to issue a paycheck, or multiple paychecks, outside of the schedules you create. When you choose Employees | Pay Employees, in addition to the subcommand Scheduled Payroll, you see two commands you can use for special payroll runs:

- **Unscheduled Payroll**   Select this special payroll category if you need to create bonus checks, commission checks, or any other type of paycheck that differs from a regularly scheduled payroll run. You also have the option of adding the additional compensation to a "regular" paycheck instead of running an unscheduled payroll.
- **Termination Check**   To use this option, you must first enter a Release Date in the Employment Info tab of the employee's record. Be sure this release date is after the check date, because QuickBooks removes the name from the Enter Payroll Information window (which means that you can't create a final paycheck for them) as of that date.
  When you're ready to create the check, select the terminated employee by placing a check mark in the column to the left of the employee name. Next, fill in the pay period ending date, the check date, the termination date, and the hours (or amount the employee is salaried). Click Continue, approve or change the paycheck details; then print the check, assign a check number for a manual check, or issue a direct deposit check.

Run Payroll

It's payday. All the historical data is entered. It's time to run the payroll. Begin creating payroll checks as follows:

- If you don't use payroll schedules, choose Employees | Pay Employees | Unscheduled Payroll to open the Enter Payroll Information dialog seen in Figure 20-9.

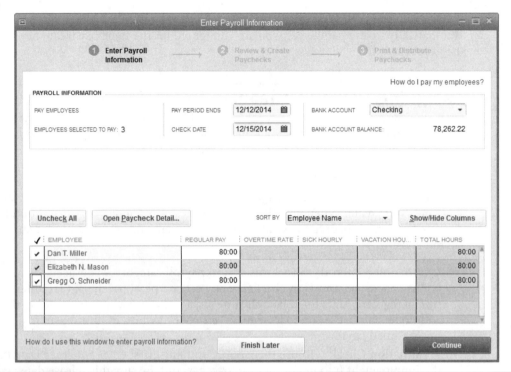

FIGURE 20-9 Begin configuring paychecks in the Enter Payroll Information dialog.

- If you have payroll schedules, choose Employees | Pay Employees | Scheduled Payroll to open the Employee Center with the Payroll tab selected (the Pay Employees function appears in the right pane). Select the appropriate schedule and click Start Scheduled Payroll to open the Enter Payroll Information dialog, which looks the same as Figure 20-9 but lists only the employees linked to this payroll schedule.

Select the employees to pay. If all the employees are receiving paychecks (the usual scenario), click Check All.

- For hourly employees who are configured for automatic payroll amounts using timesheets, the number of hours is prefilled.
- For hourly employees who are not paid from timesheets, you must fill in the number of hours for this paycheck.

Changing Paycheck Data

If you want to make changes to a paycheck, click the employee's name to open the Preview Paycheck dialog. You can add a payroll item such as a bonus, assign the paycheck to a customer or job, or add a deduction such as a repayment of a loan or garnishment. Click Save & Next to move to the next employee or click Save & Close to return to the Enter Payroll Information dialog. (There's also a Save & Previous button in case you think you should go back to a previous check.)

Reviewing the Payroll Run

Click Continue in the Enter Payroll Information dialog to display the Review And Create Paychecks window (see Figure 20-10), which displays all the financial information for this payroll run. If anything looks incorrect, click Back to reconfigure the paychecks or make other needed corrections.

Fill out the options for producing the paychecks (print the checks or automatically assign check numbers in the bank account register for manual checks), and then click Create Paychecks. QuickBooks creates the checks and displays the Confirmation And Next Steps dialog.

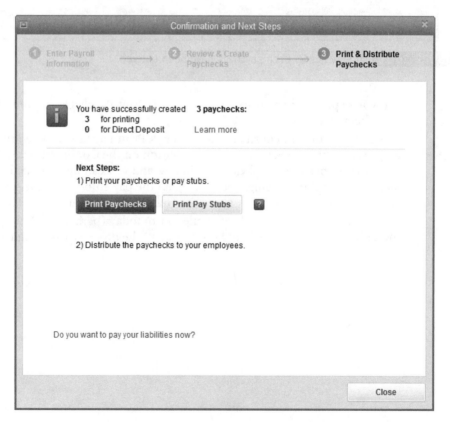

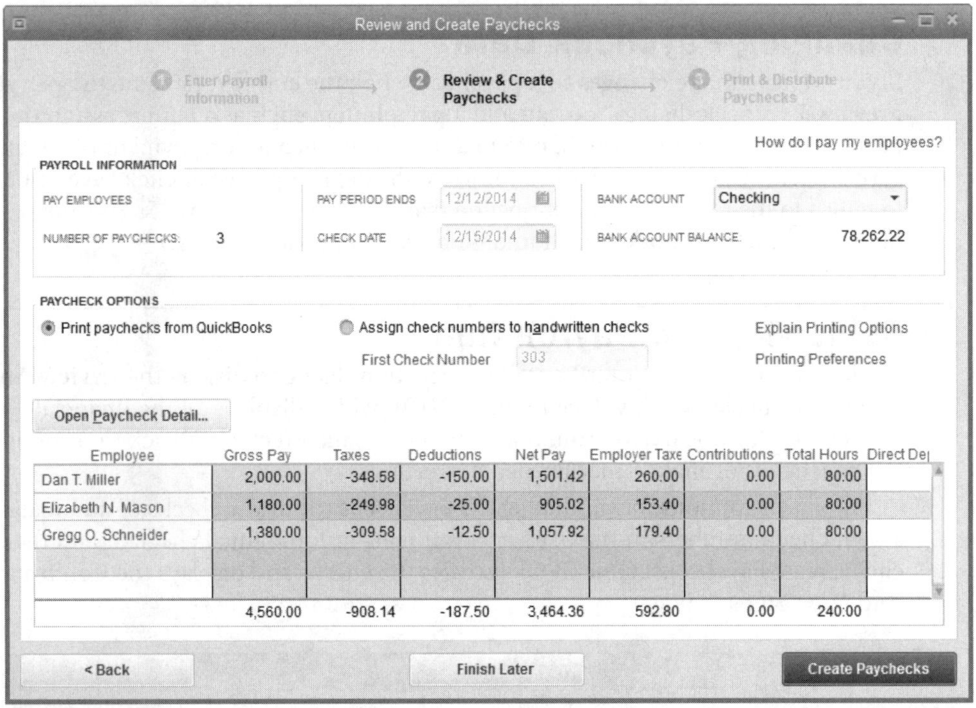

FIGURE 20-10 The details for each paycheck have been entered.

If you're printing paychecks, you can click Print Paychecks, or you can wait and print them by choosing File | Print Forms.

If you have direct deposit employees, click Print Pay Stubs. When the pay stubs are printed, click the Send Payroll Data button on the Confirmation And Next Steps dialog. This opens the Send Center window, and you can upload the direct deposit data to Intuit for processing. You can e-mail the pay stubs using the security standards built into the process (see the Help files for details).

If you have another payroll schedule to run today (perhaps both weekly and biweekly employees are paid today), repeat all the processes as outlined here.

➼ **ProAdvisor Recommends**

Net to Gross Calculations for Enhanced Payroll Subscribers

If you subscribe to the Enhanced Payroll service, you can enter the net amount of a check and let QuickBooks calculate the gross amount. This is useful for bonus checks or another special payroll check for which you need to make sure the employee receives a net check of a certain amount.

During the payroll run (either a regular payroll or a special payroll for this individual paycheck), select the employee for this payroll run. In the Preview Paycheck window, select the option Enter Net/Calculate Gross, located in the lower-right corner, and then enter the net amount for this paycheck. QuickBooks automatically calculates the gross amount and the deductions to arrive at the net amount you entered.

The Employee Center

All the employee information you've entered and the payroll schedules and paychecks you've created are easily accessed via the Employee Center (shown in Figure 20-11). The Employee Center not only contains reporting information about your payroll, but it also provides links to all the functions in the payroll system. It's a central location for everything you need to do or need to know.

To open this window, choose Employees | Employee Center from the menu bar.

ProAdvisor Tip: Users who do not have QuickBooks permissions to see payroll or other sensitive information do not see payroll financial information when they open the Employee Center.

If you subscribe to a QuickBooks payroll service, the left pane of the Employee Center contains three tabs: Employees, Transactions, and Payroll. If you don't have a payroll plan subscription, the pane lacks a Payroll tab.

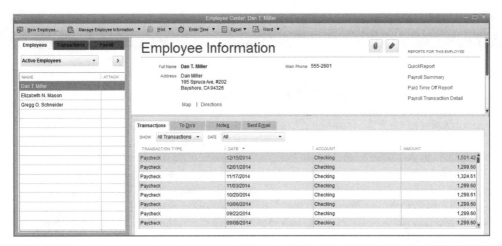

FIGURE 20-11 The Employee Center is the repository of all payroll information and functions.

Employees Tab

When you select an employee on the Employees tab, QuickBooks displays information from the employee's record on the top part of the right pane and displays transaction information for that employee on the bottom part of the right pane. You can change the choices in the Show and Date fields to filter the transactions information. Notice the three additional tabs located just above the employee transaction information. They allow you to add and manage To Do's, Notes, and e-mails sent to an employee.

You can open any listed transaction by double-clicking its listing. For example, if you open a paycheck, you can see the original check along with a summary of the financial information. If you need to check any of the details, click Paycheck Detail to see all the calculated amounts.

Transactions Tab

The Transactions tab (see Figure 20-12) lists all payroll-related transaction types. Select a type to display the transactions you've created. You can use the Date field to narrow the range of the information displayed.

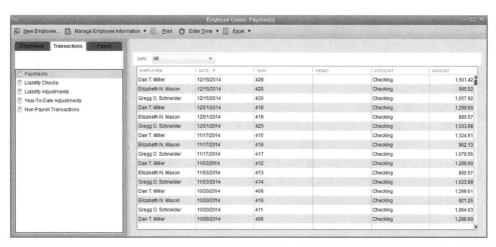

FIGURE 20-12   The Transactions tab lets you view transactions of the selected type.

Payroll Tab

The Payroll tab provides a one-stop center for all your payroll tasks. At a glance, you can view upcoming liability payments (and those that may be overdue), create transactions, and generate the payroll forms you need. Visit this tab periodically to make sure you don't miss any deadlines. The details behind how to pay, report, and remit payroll liabilities is covered in the next chapter.

Customizing the Employee Center

You can tailor the way the Employee Center displays information. Resize the panes by moving your mouse pointer over the edge of any pane; when the pointer changes to a vertical bar with right and left arrows, drag the pane in either direction. In addition, you can expand the pane to show the full list view by clicking the arrow button located at the top of the Employees tab. Use the same button to collapse the pane to show both the list and the detail panes.

You can customize the columns that QuickBooks displays in the left pane of the Employees tab by right-clicking anywhere on the list and choosing Customize Columns.

You can also customize the information displayed in the right pane when you select an employee's name in the Employees tab or when you select a transaction type on the Transactions tab. Right-click anywhere in the right (Transaction) pane and select Customize Columns.

Tracking and Remitting Payroll Liabilities

In *this chapter:*

- Confirm payroll liability payment schedules

- Pay liabilities

- Prepare quarterly and annual returns

- Print W-2 forms

- Work with payroll data in Excel

There's a logical order to all the tasks involved in reporting on and paying your payroll liabilities using QuickBooks, although the steps may differ depending on the state and municipality you're in. These tasks, and the order in which most businesses have to perform them, are covered in this chapter.

Confirm Payroll Payment Schedules

When you run payroll, QuickBooks maintains a payment schedule behind the scenes that keeps track of the amounts and due dates for all the payroll liabilities and employer expenses that are accumulating. You'll use this payment schedule to make sure you remit your payroll obligations on time. Most of the information required for scheduling payments is probably already in your system as a result of the information you provided when you set up payroll items. To view the schedule and correct any problems, choose Employees | Payroll Taxes And Liabilities | Edit Payment Due Dates/Methods.

This opens the Payroll Setup wizard's Tax Payments window. As you move through each page, if any data is missing or does not match the content or format the payroll system expects, the wizard highlights the listing with a problem icon (see Figure 21-1).

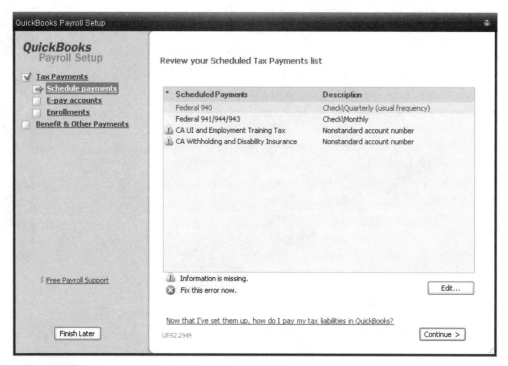

FIGURE 21-1 If an item listed has a problem icon, an error needs to be fixed.

Double-click the problem listing so you can edit it and fix the problem. QuickBooks usually provides a hint about the problem in the window that opens. In Figure 21-1, for example, the problem with the two listings is the format of the account numbers for state unemployment and withholding in California. QuickBooks knows that the account number has to follow a specific format, and this data was originally entered in the wrong format.

Report and Remit Payroll Liabilities

When you create payroll checks, QuickBooks tracks the taxes that are due as liabilities. To see your scheduled liabilities, choose Employees | Payroll Taxes And Liabilities | Pay Scheduled Liabilities. The Pay Liabilities tab in the Employee Center shows the list of taxes and other liabilities currently owed (see Figure 21-2).

Select the liability you want to pay and click the View/Pay button. The first time you pay liabilities, QuickBooks asks you to select the appropriate bank account (if you have more than one bank account).

The Liability Payment transaction window opens, as seen in Figure 21-3. Continue to view and pay until all the current liabilities are remitted.

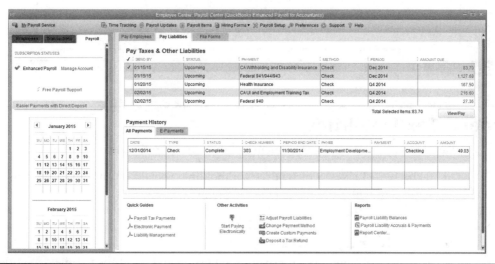

FIGURE 21-2 QuickBooks tracks your payroll liabilities automatically.

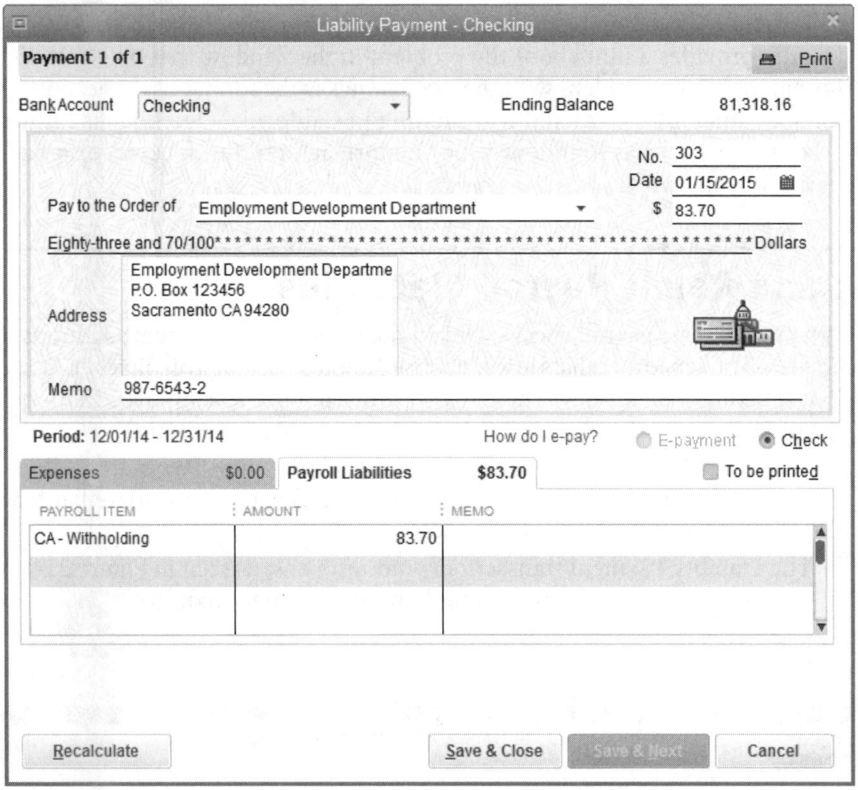

FIGURE 21-3 This liability check is posted to the appropriate account and is ready to print.

Federal Tax Liabilities

Payments to the federal government involve two payroll taxes:

- 941/944/943 taxes, which cover withholding, Social Security, and Medicare
- 940 taxes, which are the federal unemployment taxes

941/943 Payments

The federal government requires you to report on and remit the withheld amounts, along with the matching employer contributions, at a specified time. That time period is dependent upon the size of the total withholding amount you've accumulated. You may be required to remit monthly, semimonthly, weekly, or within three days of the payroll. Check the current limits with the IRS or your accountant.

There's a formula for determining the size of the 941/943 payment—it's the sum of the following amounts for the period:

- Federal withholding
- FICA withholding
- Medicare withholding
- FICA matching contribution from employer
- Medicare matching contribution from employer

You don't have to do the math—QuickBooks does it for you. But it's a good idea to know what the formula is so you can check the numbers yourself and make sure you have sufficient funds in your bank account to cover the next payment.

In addition, the IRS requires that you remit your payments electronically, either through QuickBooks Enhanced Payroll or by using the Electronic Federal Tax Payment System (EFTPS) operated by the IRS; the payee is the US Treasury. If you haven't already done so, you'll need to go to the EFTPS website (www.eftps.gov) to learn more and enroll. If, however, your employment taxes for a quarterly period are less than $2,500, you can remit the taxes with your quarterly (Form 941) return in lieu of depositing them.

Creating a 941/943 Form

Unless you've been notified that you're a Form 944 filer (where your annual payroll withholding liability is less than $1,000/year), you must file a 941 or 943 form every quarter to report the total amount you owe the federal government for withheld taxes, FICA, and Medicare. If you have been making your deposits regularly and on time, no amount is due with the 941/943.

- If you underpaid, you can use the EFTPS system to remit your payment for the underpaid amount or remit the underpayment with your form. The vendor for the check entry you make in QuickBooks is the United States Treasury.
- If you overpaid, you can select the option to take a credit toward the next 941/ 943, or you can select the option for a refund.

QuickBooks will prepare your 941/943 report using the information in your QuickBooks payroll registers. If QuickBooks isn't preparing your federal forms (either because you're doing payroll manually or you subscribed to the QuickBooks Basic Payroll service), you can prepare your forms manually with the use of Excel worksheets that QuickBooks provides. See the section "Tax Form Worksheets in Excel" at the end of this chapter. Creating the form is quite easy.

Follow these steps to create a 941/943 form:

1. Choose Employees | Payroll Tax Forms & W-2s | Process Payroll Forms. The Payroll tab in the Employee Center opens to show the list of tax forms available for filing.
2. Select Federal Quarterly Form 941/Sch B – Employer's Quarterly Federal Tax Return (or Federal Quarterly Form 943A – Employer's Annual Federal Tax Return for Agricultural Employees) and click the File Form button. The File Form window opens.
3. Select the Filing period. You can also click the Auto-Fill Contact Info button to have QuickBooks automatically copy the contact information you provide in this window to future tax forms you need to complete. Click OK.
4. The Payroll Tax Form window opens to the form selected (see Figure 21-4). The first window is an interview; enter the appropriate data, and click Next to continue.
5. Use the guidelines presented in the following sections to move through the wizard.

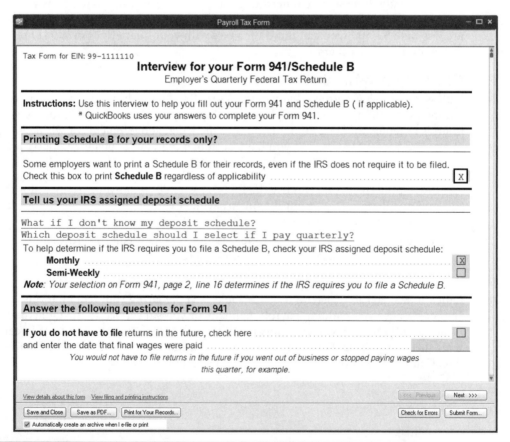

FIGURE 21-4 Start by answering questions; the answers are transferred to the form in the appropriate places.

Filling In Blank Fields

To enter information in a blank field, click your cursor in the field to activate it, and then type the data. The typed text appears in blue, but that's just a signal to you that the data was entered manually; QuickBooks doesn't print the form in color.

Editing Prefilled Data

Follow these steps to edit data:

1. Right-click the field and choose Override from the menu that appears.
2. Enter the replacement data in the override box and press the TAB key.
3. The new data replaces the original data in the field, and the text is green (to remind you that you manually replaced the data that was exported from QuickBooks).

If you change your mind and decide that the data automatically supplied by QuickBooks should remain in the form, right-click in the field and choose Cancel Override.

Data You Cannot Change

Do *not* edit the following types of data on the Form 941 (or on any payroll tax form for that matter):

- Federal Employer Identification Number (EIN)
- Filing period (if you're trying to change the filing period, start the process again and select the appropriate date range)
- Totals (these are calculated by QuickBooks; if a total is wrong, edit the erroneous number and QuickBooks will recalculate the total)

Checking for Errors

Before you finalize the contents of Form 941/943, click the Check For Errors button. QuickBooks examines the content and displays any errors in the Errors box that opens at the top of the form. If there aren't any problems, the Errors box reports this, too.

Click any error to move automatically to the field that's causing the problem, and then correct the information.

- If the problem is in a field you filled out, correct the data and press the TAB key.
- If the problem is in a field that was prefilled but you changed the content by overriding the data, right-click the field and select Cancel Override.

When you press TAB to replace the data in the field, the error listing should disappear from the Errors box. If it doesn't, you have to do some homework to figure out what's wrong with the data in the affected field and then correct it.

When the error is fixed, you can close the Errors box by clicking the Close Errors button.

Saving and Reopening an Unfinished Form

If you get interrupted or confused while you're preparing your 941, 943, or 940 form, you can save the form with the data you already filled in, so you don't have to start from scratch when you resume your work. Click Save And Close to save the form with its current contents. To return to work on the saved form, you'll need to open the form again following the steps from the previous section, again selecting the form and a date range. QuickBooks asks if you want to use the saved draft.

Keep in mind that when you open a saved draft, QuickBooks does not refresh the form with your QuickBooks payroll data. So if you made changes, you'll have to start a new form instead of opening a saved draft. Changes could include an additional paycheck being issued within the date range for some reason or a payment you made the IRS as a remittance for this report period.

Printing or Submitting Form 941/943

You can print the form from QuickBooks, save it as a PDF, or submit the form electronically. If you choose to print, be sure to use these printing criteria:

- The form must be printed with black ink on white or cream-colored paper.
- The paper size must be 8.5-by-11 inches.
- The paper must be 20-pound weight or heavier.

➡ ProAdvisor Recommends

Using the 944 Form for Payroll Liability Reporting

If your annual payroll withholding liability is less than $1,000 per year, you may be eligible to file Form 944—a simplified version of the 941 form. If you were notified by the IRS that you should file Form 944 instead of Form 941, follow the instructions in the previous sections to open the federal form list and select Form 944. You can remit your liabilities when you send the form, or, if you wish, you can make deposits against your 944 liability by using the deposit coupon (8109), filling in the circle for Form 944, and taking the check to the bank.

You cannot use Form 944, even if you qualify financially, unless you've been notified by the IRS that you are a Form 944 filer. This form is shorter than Form 941, has no additional schedules, and has an annual filing frequency, all of which combine to make this a desirable filing method. If you think you qualify financially but you didn't receive a notification to use Form 944, you can contact the IRS to request a notification at www.irs.gov.

The printed report doesn't look exactly like the blank form you received, but it's close. More importantly, it's perfectly acceptable to the government. Print two copies: one to mail and one for your files.

If you've set up for e-filing with your QuickBooks Payroll subscription, click the Submit Form button to file your 941/943 electronically. If you have not set up this form for e-filing, open the Employee Center and click the Payroll Tab to open the Payroll Center. Then click the File Forms tab and click Start Filing Electronically in the Other Activities area. (If you've already chosen e-file for any form filing, click Manage Filing Methods instead.)

940 Payments

The Federal Unemployment Tax Act (FUTA) provides unemployment compensation to workers who have lost their jobs, usually after the workers' state benefits have been exhausted. The FUTA tax is paid by employers; no deductions are taken from employee wages. Companies must make FUTA payments if either of the following scenarios exists:

- During this year or last year, you paid wages of at least $1,500 in any calendar quarter.
- During this year or last year, you had one or more employees for at least part of a day for a period of 20 weeks (the weeks do not have to be contiguous).

You don't have to make the deposit until you owe the entire amount, but you can make deposits until you reach that amount if you wish.

Currently, the FUTA tax is 6 percent of gross wages up to $7,000 per employee, but the federal government gives employers up to a 5.4 percent credit for paying their state unemployment taxes. So if you're entitled to the maximum 5.4 percent credit, the FUTA tax rate after the credit is 0.6 percent. QuickBooks assumes you're paying your state unemployment taxes and calculates your FUTA liability accordingly.

Preparing the 940 Form

The 940 form (FUTA) is filed annually; there are no quarterly forms to file. To create your Form 940, follow these steps:

1. Choose Employees | Payroll Tax Forms & W-2s | Process Payroll Forms. The Payroll tab in the Employee Center opens to show the list of tax forms available for filing.
2. Select Annual Form 940/Sch A – Employer's Annual Federal Unemployment (FUTA) Tax Return. Click the File Form button. The File Form window opens.

3. Select the Filing period. You can also click the Auto-Fill Contact Info button to have QuickBooks automatically copy the contact information you provide in this window to future tax forms you need to complete. Click OK.

4. The Payroll Tax Form window (it's the first window of a wizard) opens with the Form 940 Interview displayed. The top section of the interview window asks about your state and federal unemployment payments. Below that section is a series of questions aimed at determining whether any of your payroll expenses covered exempt payment types. Exempt payments are wages you paid that are exempt from FUTA taxes. QuickBooks checks your payroll items to track several categories of exempt payments, and if you've used these payroll items, QuickBooks fills in the amounts. If you had any exempt payments that are not in the payroll items that QuickBooks automatically checks, fill in the amount directly on the appropriate field. Check the IRS rules for preparing Form 940, or check with your accountant. You can also get more information about this form by clicking the link "View details about this form" located at the bottom of the Payroll Tax Form window.

5. Click Next to see the form itself. Fill out any fields that aren't automatically prefilled by QuickBooks from your payroll records. Continue to click Next and follow the instructions that appear on the screen.

State and Local Income Taxes

Your state and local payroll liabilities vary depending upon where your business is located and where your employees live (and pay taxes). Besides income taxes, you may be liable for unemployment insurance and disability insurance.

Most states have some form of an income tax, which might be calculated in any one of a variety of ways:

- A flat percentage of gross income
- A sliding percentage of gross income
- A percentage based on the federal tax for the employee

Local (municipal or county) taxes are also widely varied in their approach:

- Some cities have different rates for employees of companies that operate in the city. There may be one rate for employees who live in the same city and a different rate for nonresidents.
- Your business might operate in a city or town that has a *payroll head tax* (a once-a-year payment that is a flat amount per employee).

QuickBooks Enhanced Payroll supports most state forms. State and local taxing authorities also provide coupons or forms or an online service for remitting income tax withholding. The frequency with which you must pay might depend on the size of your payroll, or it might be quarterly, semiannual, or annual, regardless of the amount. Some municipal authorities have e-pay available.

Other State Liabilities

If your state has SUI (state unemployment insurance) or SDI (state disability insurance) or both, you have to pay those liabilities when they're due. Commonly, these are quarterly payments.

P r o A d v i s o r   T i p : It's a good idea to create different vendor names for SUI, SDI, and state income tax withholding to make sure you don't accidentally send checks for the wrong component and to prevent QuickBooks from issuing a single check for the grand total. The vendor record for each vendor name may have the same payee (State Department of Revenue), but the vendor names are different.

Not all states have SUI or SDI, and some have one but not the other. Some states collect SUI and SDI from the employee and the company; some collect only from the company. Check the rules for your state.

Other Non-Tax Payroll Liabilities

The rules for remitting the paycheck deductions and employer contributions for other reasons—such as health benefits, pension, and workers compensation—are specific to your arrangements with those vendors.

There are many ways to handle how these payments are posted, and you have to decide what makes sense to you (or to your accountant). For example, if you pay a monthly amount to a medical insurer, you may want to post the employee deductions back to the same expense account you use to pay the bill. That way, only the net amount is reported as an expense on your taxes.

To remit liabilities that are not a Scheduled Liability in QuickBooks, you can use the Unscheduled Liabilities window. Choose Employees | Payroll Taxes And Liabilities | Create Custom Liability Payments. Select the paycheck date range you need, and then select the liability you want to remit.

Workers Comp

QuickBooks Enhanced and Assisted Payroll offerings include workers comp, and the setup options are available in the Payroll & Employees category of the Preferences dialog. Click the Workers Compensation button on the Company Preferences tab to open the Workers Comp Preferences dialog. Select Track Workers Comp to enable the feature.

When workers comp is enabled, you can also opt to see reminder messages to assign workers comp codes when you create paychecks or timesheets. In addition, you can select the option to exclude an overtime premium from your workers comp calculations (check your workers comp insurance policy to see if you can calculate overtime amounts as regular pay).

Prepare W-2 Forms

On or before January 31, you must print and send W-2 forms to your employees for the previous calendar year. And by February 28, you'll need to send or e-file copies to the appropriate government agencies as well.

When you run your payroll in QuickBooks, this process is very straightforward. You start by selecting the form and the employees, and then move to the process of creating and printing or electronically sending the forms.

Here are the step-by-step instructions:

1. Choose Employees | Payroll Tax Forms & W-2s | Process Payroll Forms. The Payroll tab in the Employee Center opens to show the list of tax forms available for filing.
2. Select Annual Form W-2/W-3 –Wage And Tax Statement/Transmittal. Click the File Form button. The File Form dialog opens.

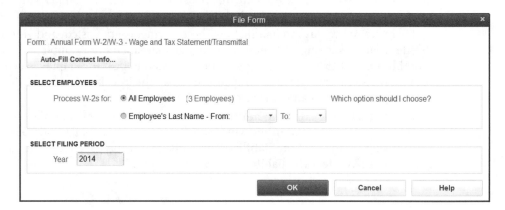

3. Select the filing period and the employees for which you want to process W-2 forms. You can also click the Auto-Fill Contact Info button to have QuickBooks automatically copy the contact information you provide in this window to future tax forms you need to complete. Click OK.

4. The Select Employees For Form W-2/W-3 window opens, listing all your employees that have received a paycheck during the year (see Figure 21-5). By default, all employees are selected and the current status of the W-2 printing process is noted.

5. Click Review/Edit to display the first page of the Payroll Tax Form window (shown in Figure 21-6), which explains the steps you'll go through as you step through the wizard. Click Next to move through the wizard.

6. In the screens that follow, each employee's W-2 form is presented. If any nonfinancial data is missing (such as an address or ZIP code), you must fill it in. If prefilled information is incorrect, right-click the appropriate field and select Override. Enter the correct information, and press TAB to add that information into the field.

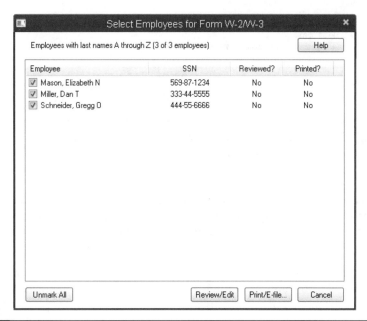

FIGURE 21-5   Confirm or change the employees that should receive a W-2.

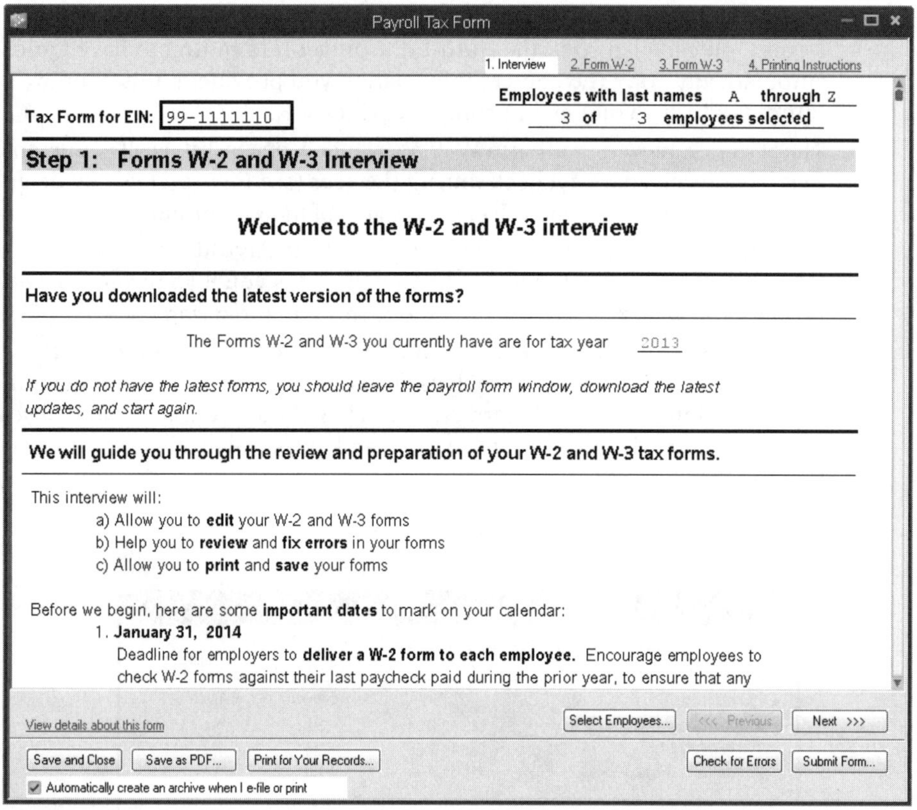

FIGURE 21-6 The first page of the Payroll Tax Form window will guide you through the preparation of your W-2 and W-3 forms.

> **C a u t i o n :** Changes you make to nonfinancial information are not written back to the employee record. You must make the same changes there.

7. Click the Check For Errors button to see if anything is amiss on any employee's form. If errors appear in the Errors box at the top of the form, click the error's listing. QuickBooks automatically takes you to the appropriate field to correct the information.

8. When everything is correct, load your W-2 forms in the printer (even if you're e-filing, you'll likely be printing the copy that goes to the employee) and click Submit Form to open the Print/E-file Form dialog.

9. If you enrolled in an agency's e-filing program, have an active Enhanced Payroll subscription, and there are no errors on the form, the option to e-file these forms will be available to you. Otherwise, only the Print button will be active. Select the option to open the Print W-2 And W-3 Forms window.

10. Click Print when all of these settings are just the way you want them. You must also print or e-file the W-3 form, which is a summary of your W-2 forms.

ProAdvisor Tip: You can make your employees' W-2 forms available online at no extra charge if you have a QuickBooks payroll subscription. Using this service eliminates the need for you to print and mail W-2 forms to your employees since they can view and print their own W-2 information directly from an Intuit website called ViewMyPaycheck.com. Also, if your employees use TurboTax to prepare their own personal tax returns, they can view and download their W-2 forms directly into TurboTax. To learn more about this service, click the "Tell me more" link at the bottom of the Print W-2 And W-3 Forms window.

Tax Form Worksheets in Excel

If QuickBooks isn't preparing your payroll forms (either because you're doing payroll manually or you subscribed to the QuickBooks Basic Payroll service), you can prepare your forms manually with the use of Excel worksheets that are available from QuickBooks.

To access the worksheets, choose Reports | Employees & Payroll | More Payroll Reports In Excel | Tax Form Worksheets. Because this Excel file has macros, depending on how you've configured Excel's security options, you might have to tell Excel to let the macros run.

When the QuickBooks Tax Worksheets dialog appears, select the form and filing period you need. Next, click the Options/Settings button to open the QuickBooks

Tax Forms Workbook – Options/Settings dialog, where you'll configure the report using the guidelines discussed in the following sections.

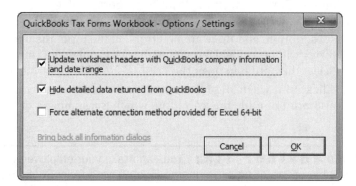

Configuring Worksheet Headers

By default, the option to update worksheet headers is checked. This means that the header of a printout of the worksheet contains the company name and address information, as well as the date range of the report (the date range you selected in the previous dialog). If you are planning to print the report, it's important to know the date range, so make sure this option is selected.

Configuring the Level of Detail

By default, the Hide Detailed Data Returned From QuickBooks option is selected, which means that the workbook displays only the information connected to the report you selected.

If you deselect the option to hide detailed data, QuickBooks adds a second worksheet named Data to the workbook, as shown in Figure 21-7. This worksheet contains detailed information about the employees, the payroll items, and the job-costing links (if you use timesheets to do job costing for payroll) on separate rows.

Forcing an Alternate Connection Method

Microsoft Office 2010 products are available in both 32-bit and 64-bit versions. If you are using a 64-bit version of Excel (which is included in Office 2010), the Force Alternate Connection Method Provided For Excel 84-Bit option (located on the QuickBooks Tax Forms Workbook – Options/Settings dialog) should be checked to complete the export.

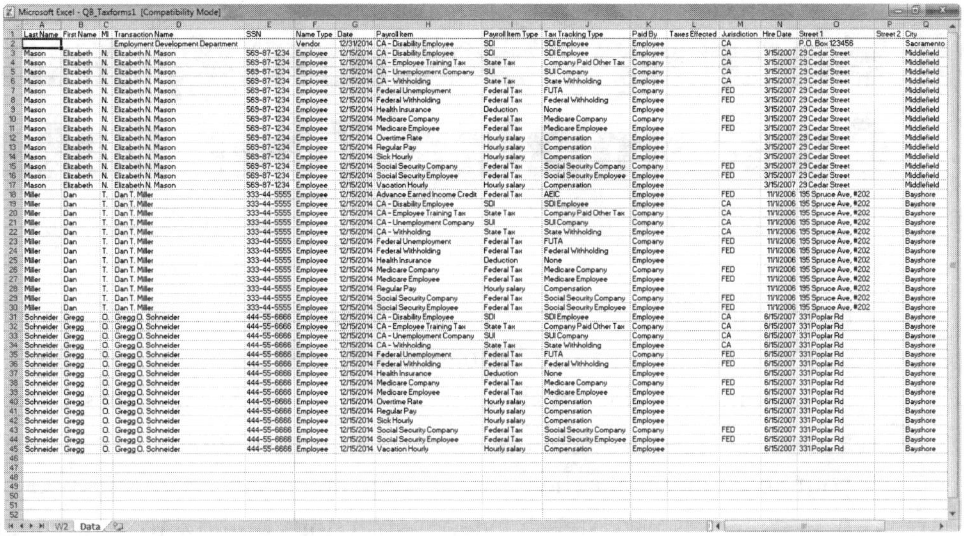

Microsoft Excel - QB_Taxforms1 [Compatibility Mode]

	A	B	C	D	E	F	G	H	I	J	K	L	M	N	O	P	Q
1	Last Name	First Name	MI	Transaction Name	SSN	Name Type	Date	Payroll Item	Payroll Item Type	Tax Tracking Type	Paid By	Taxes Effected	Jurisdiction	Hire Date	Street 1	Street 2	City
2				Employment Development Department		Vendor	12/31/2014	CA - Disability Employee	SDI	SDI Employee	Employee		CA		P.O. Box 123456		Sacramento
3	Mason	Elizabeth	N.	Elizabeth N. Mason	569-87-1234	Employee	12/15/2014	CA - Disability Employee	SDI	SDI Employee	Employee		CA	3/15/2007	29 Cedar Street		Middlefield
4	Mason	Elizabeth	N.	Elizabeth N. Mason	569-87-1234	Employee	12/15/2014	CA - Employee Training Tax	State Tax	Company Paid Other Tax	Company		CA	3/15/2007	29 Cedar Street		Middlefield
5	Mason	Elizabeth	N.	Elizabeth N. Mason	569-87-1234	Employee	12/15/2014	CA - Unemployment Company	SUI	SUI Company	Company		CA	3/15/2007	29 Cedar Street		Middlefield
6	Mason	Elizabeth	N.	Elizabeth N. Mason	569-87-1234	Employee	12/15/2014	CA - Withholding	State Tax	State Withholding	Employee		CA	3/15/2007	29 Cedar Street		Middlefield
7	Mason	Elizabeth	N.	Elizabeth N. Mason	569-87-1234	Employee	12/15/2014	Federal Unemployment	Federal Tax	FUTA	Company		FED	3/15/2007	29 Cedar Street		Middlefield
8	Mason	Elizabeth	N.	Elizabeth N. Mason	569-87-1234	Employee	12/15/2014	Federal Withholding	Federal Tax	Federal Withholding	Employee		FED	3/15/2007	29 Cedar Street		Middlefield
9	Mason	Elizabeth	N.	Elizabeth N. Mason	569-87-1234	Employee	12/15/2014	Health Insurance	Deduction	None	Employee			3/15/2007	29 Cedar Street		Middlefield
10	Mason	Elizabeth	N.	Elizabeth N. Mason	569-87-1234	Employee	12/15/2014	Medicare Company	Federal Tax	Medicare Company	Company		FED	3/15/2007	29 Cedar Street		Middlefield
11	Mason	Elizabeth	N.	Elizabeth N. Mason	569-87-1234	Employee	12/15/2014	Medicare Employee	Federal Tax	Medicare Employee	Employee		FED	3/15/2007	29 Cedar Street		Middlefield
12	Mason	Elizabeth	N.	Elizabeth N. Mason	569-87-1234	Employee	12/15/2014	Overtime Rate	Hourly salary	Compensation	Employee			3/15/2007	29 Cedar Street		Middlefield
13	Mason	Elizabeth	N.	Elizabeth N. Mason	569-87-1234	Employee	12/15/2014	Regular Pay	Hourly salary	Compensation	Employee			3/15/2007	29 Cedar Street		Middlefield
14	Mason	Elizabeth	N.	Elizabeth N. Mason	569-87-1234	Employee	12/15/2014	Sick Hourly	Hourly salary	Compensation	Employee			3/15/2007	29 Cedar Street		Middlefield
15	Mason	Elizabeth	N.	Elizabeth N. Mason	569-87-1234	Employee	12/15/2014	Social Security Company	Federal Tax	Social Security Company	Company		FED	3/15/2007	29 Cedar Street		Middlefield
16	Mason	Elizabeth	N.	Elizabeth N. Mason	569-87-1234	Employee	12/15/2014	Social Security Employee	Federal Tax	Social Security Employee	Employee		FED	3/15/2007	29 Cedar Street		Middlefield
17	Mason	Elizabeth	N.	Elizabeth N. Mason	569-87-1234	Employee	12/15/2014	Vacation Hourly	Hourly salary	Compensation	Employee			3/15/2007	29 Cedar Street		Middlefield
18	Miller	Dan	T.	Dan T. Miller	333-44-5555	Employee	12/15/2014	Advance Earned Income Credit	Federal Tax	AEIC	Employee		FED	11/1/2006	195 Spruce Ave, #202		Bayshore
19	Miller	Dan	T.	Dan T. Miller	333-44-5555	Employee	12/15/2014	CA - Disability Employee	SDI	SDI Employee	Employee		CA	11/1/2006	195 Spruce Ave, #202		Bayshore
20	Miller	Dan	T.	Dan T. Miller	333-44-5555	Employee	12/15/2014	CA - Employee Training Tax	State Tax	Company Paid Other Tax	Company		CA	11/1/2006	195 Spruce Ave, #202		Bayshore
21	Miller	Dan	T.	Dan T. Miller	333-44-5555	Employee	12/15/2014	CA - Unemployment Company	SUI	SUI Company	Company		CA	11/1/2006	195 Spruce Ave, #202		Bayshore
22	Miller	Dan	T.	Dan T. Miller	333-44-5555	Employee	12/15/2014	CA - Withholding	State Tax	State Withholding	Employee		CA	11/1/2006	195 Spruce Ave, #202		Bayshore
23	Miller	Dan	T.	Dan T. Miller	333-44-5555	Employee	12/15/2014	Federal Unemployment	Federal Tax	FUTA	Company		FED	11/1/2006	195 Spruce Ave, #202		Bayshore
24	Miller	Dan	T.	Dan T. Miller	333-44-5555	Employee	12/15/2014	Federal Withholding	Federal Tax	Federal Withholding	Employee		FED	11/1/2006	195 Spruce Ave, #202		Bayshore
25	Miller	Dan	T.	Dan T. Miller	333-44-5555	Employee	12/15/2014	Health Insurance	Deduction	None	Employee			11/1/2006	195 Spruce Ave, #202		Bayshore
26	Miller	Dan	T.	Dan T. Miller	333-44-5555	Employee	12/15/2014	Medicare Company	Federal Tax	Medicare Company	Company		FED	11/1/2006	195 Spruce Ave, #202		Bayshore
27	Miller	Dan	T.	Dan T. Miller	333-44-5555	Employee	12/15/2014	Medicare Employee	Federal Tax	Medicare Employee	Employee		FED	11/1/2006	195 Spruce Ave, #202		Bayshore
28	Miller	Dan	T.	Dan T. Miller	333-44-5555	Employee	12/15/2014	Regular Pay	Hourly salary	Compensation	Employee			11/1/2006	195 Spruce Ave, #202		Bayshore
29	Miller	Dan	T.	Dan T. Miller	333-44-5555	Employee	12/15/2014	Social Security Company	Federal Tax	Social Security Company	Company		FED	11/1/2006	195 Spruce Ave, #202		Bayshore
30	Miller	Dan	T.	Dan T. Miller	333-44-5555	Employee	12/15/2014	Social Security Employee	Federal Tax	Social Security Employee	Employee		FED	11/1/2006	195 Spruce Ave, #202		Bayshore
31	Schneider	Gregg	O.	Gregg O. Schneider	444-55-6666	Employee	12/15/2014	CA - Disability Employee	SDI	SDI Employee	Employee		CA	6/15/2007	331 Poplar Rd		Bayshore
32	Schneider	Gregg	O.	Gregg O. Schneider	444-55-6666	Employee	12/15/2014	CA - Employee Training Tax	State Tax	Company Paid Other Tax	Company		CA	6/15/2007	331 Poplar Rd		Bayshore
33	Schneider	Gregg	O.	Gregg O. Schneider	444-55-6666	Employee	12/15/2014	CA - Unemployment Company	SUI	SUI Company	Company		CA	6/15/2007	331 Poplar Rd		Bayshore
34	Schneider	Gregg	O.	Gregg O. Schneider	444-55-6666	Employee	12/15/2014	CA - Withholding	State Tax	State Withholding	Employee		CA	6/15/2007	331 Poplar Rd		Bayshore
35	Schneider	Gregg	O.	Gregg O. Schneider	444-55-6666	Employee	12/15/2014	Federal Unemployment	Federal Tax	FUTA	Company		FED	6/15/2007	331 Poplar Rd		Bayshore
36	Schneider	Gregg	O.	Gregg O. Schneider	444-55-6666	Employee	12/15/2014	Federal Withholding	Federal Tax	Federal Withholding	Employee		FED	6/15/2007	331 Poplar Rd		Bayshore
37	Schneider	Gregg	O.	Gregg O. Schneider	444-55-6666	Employee	12/15/2014	Health Insurance	Deduction	None	Employee			6/15/2007	331 Poplar Rd		Bayshore
38	Schneider	Gregg	O.	Gregg O. Schneider	444-55-6666	Employee	12/15/2014	Medicare Company	Federal Tax	Medicare Company	Company		FED	6/15/2007	331 Poplar Rd		Bayshore
39	Schneider	Gregg	O.	Gregg O. Schneider	444-55-6666	Employee	12/15/2014	Medicare Employee	Federal Tax	Medicare Employee	Employee		FED	6/15/2007	331 Poplar Rd		Bayshore
40	Schneider	Gregg	O.	Gregg O. Schneider	444-55-6666	Employee	12/15/2014	Overtime Rate	Hourly salary	Compensation	Employee			6/15/2007	331 Poplar Rd		Bayshore
41	Schneider	Gregg	O.	Gregg O. Schneider	444-55-6666	Employee	12/15/2014	Regular Pay	Hourly salary	Compensation	Employee			6/15/2007	331 Poplar Rd		Bayshore
42	Schneider	Gregg	O.	Gregg O. Schneider	444-55-6666	Employee	12/15/2014	Sick Hourly	Hourly salary	Compensation	Employee			6/15/2007	331 Poplar Rd		Bayshore
43	Schneider	Gregg	O.	Gregg O. Schneider	444-55-6666	Employee	12/15/2014	Social Security Company	Federal Tax	Social Security Company	Company		FED	6/15/2007	331 Poplar Rd		Bayshore
44	Schneider	Gregg	O.	Gregg O. Schneider	444-55-6666	Employee	12/15/2014	Social Security Employee	Federal Tax	Social Security Employee	Employee		FED	6/15/2007	331 Poplar Rd		Bayshore
45	Schneider	Gregg	O.	Gregg O. Schneider	444-55-6666	Employee	12/15/2014	Vacation Hourly	Hourly salary	Compensation	Employee			6/15/2007	331 Poplar Rd		Bayshore

W2 Data

FIGURE 21-7 See the details behind your report totals.

Sharing, Securing, and Customizing Your Data

Part Five of this book covers features in QuickBooks that allow you to share your company information with others, including your accountant. You'll learn about how to make an Accountant's Copy, a special copy of your file that allows your accountant to examine your books and make the necessary adjustments to your QuickBooks data. You'll also see step-by-step instructions on how to secure and maintain the integrity of the important financial information you track in QuickBooks.

This section also covers ways that you use Preferences to customize the QuickBooks experience—for all users or just one.

Using the Accountant's Copy

n this chapter:

- Understand the Accountant's Copy

- Create an Accountant's Copy

- Merge the accountant's changes into your file

Many accountants specialize in supporting QuickBooks, which means they understand the software and know how to use it. Many have a specialized version of QuickBooks for accounting professionals on their own computers.

At various times during the year, your accountant might want to look at your books. There might be quarterly reports to analyze or prepare. Or maybe a physical inventory uncovered serious discrepancies in your on-hand quantities, requiring an adjustment to the inventory account on your balance sheet. Almost definitely your accountant will want to examine your QuickBooks file at the end of the year to help you close your books and prepare your tax returns.

Some accountants may ask for a copy of the company file, a backup of your company file (which they restore onto their computer), or a portable company file in order to review and make changes to your QuickBooks file.

If they use any of these methods, you shouldn't work in your QuickBooks file at the same time. If you do continue to work on your local copy on your computer, the transactions you enter will be lost once you restore the copy your accountant returns to you. Why? Because restoring a regular backup overwrites the company file you continued to use. Not a good solution.

Understanding the Accountant's Copy

QuickBooks has a better solution. Give your accountant a specially designed copy of your company file called the *Accountant's Copy*. Let your accountant do the work back at her office while you continue to work in your copy. When the file comes back to you with the accountant's changes, QuickBooks can merge the changes from the Accountant's Copy into your copy of the company file, which means the work you do while the accountant is working isn't replaced by the work your accountant does.

When you create an Accountant's Copy, QuickBooks imposes restrictions on the type and extent of transactions you and your accountant can do to make sure you don't work at cross purposes.

Creating an Accountant's Copy

QuickBooks provides two methods for delivering the accountant's copy you create to your accountant:

- **Save a file** You can save an Accountant's Copy on removable media (CD, DVD, or flash drive) and send or deliver it that way. You can also send it via e-mail, although sometimes people can't e-mail the file because of the size limits set by their ISP (Internet service provider) and/or their accountant's ISP.

- **Send a file to your accountant using a QuickBooks secure server** If your accountant has subscribed to this service, you can upload for free an Accountant's Copy to a secure server provided by QuickBooks and have your accountant download the file. QuickBooks notifies the accountant of the existence of the file by e-mail and provides a link to the file in the e-mail message.

> **ProAdvisor Tip:** Only the Admin or External Accountant user can create an Accountant's Copy, and the company file must be operating in Single-User mode to accomplish this task.

Saving the Accountant's Copy

To create an Accountant's Copy and save it to a location on your computer or on removable media, choose File | Accountant's Copy | Save File. In the Save Accountant's Copy dialog, be sure the Accountant's Copy option is selected.

Click Next to move to the window to set the dividing date for this Accountant's Copy. Your accountant will be able to work on transactions dated on or before that date in his copy while you can continue to work and create transactions that are dated after the dividing date in your company file. To learn more about this important date, be sure to read the section "Choosing the Dividing Date." Click Next to save the file.

QuickBooks opens the Save Accountant's Copy dialog and creates a filename that incorporates your company filename as well as the date and time of the file's creation. That's an excellent filename, and there's no reason to change it. By default, QuickBooks saves the Accountant's Copy to your desktop, but you can change the location if you wish.

If you're sending the file on a flash drive, change the location by choosing the flash drive in the Save In field at the top of the dialog. If you're planning to send the file on a CD or DVD, save the file to your hard drive and then transfer the file to the CD/DVD. After you save the file, QuickBooks displays a message reminding you of the dividing date and also reminding you to send the file to your accountant.

If you've password-protected your QuickBooks data file, you must give your accountant the Admin password so he can open it.

Sending an Accountant's Copy to the QuickBooks Server

To create an Accountant's Copy that is uploaded to a secure server maintained by QuickBooks from which your accountant can download the file, choose File | Accountant's Copy | Send To Accountant, which opens the Send Accountant's Copy dialog that explains the process.

Click Next to establish a dividing date. Your accountant will be able to work on transactions dated on or before that date in his copy while you can continue to work and create transactions that are dated after the dividing date in your company file. To learn more about this important date, be sure to read the next section, "Choosing the Dividing Date."

In the next window, enter your accountant's e-mail address twice to confirm the data, your name, and your e-mail address. If an e-mail address exists in the e-mail field of the Company Info dialog (in the Company menu) window, that address is automatically entered as your e-mail address, but you can change it.

In the next window, enter a password your accountant needs to open the company file in the Accountant's version of QuickBooks. It must be a *strong password,* which means it contains at least seven characters, a mixture of letters and numbers, and at least one letter is in a different case from the other letters (usually, this means one letter is uppercase).

If your Admin password is a strong password because you enabled credit card security, as explained in Chapter 3, you can use the Admin password for the upload/download server access.

You can also enter a message for your accountant that will appear in the body of the e-mail message, notifying your accountant that you've uploaded the file. E-mail text is not encrypted as it travels around the Internet, so don't use this message to give your accountant the password.

Click Send to upload the file to the server. QuickBooks displays a message telling you it must close all windows to create an Accountant's Copy; click OK to continue. When the Accountant's Copy has been created and uploaded, QuickBooks displays a success message.

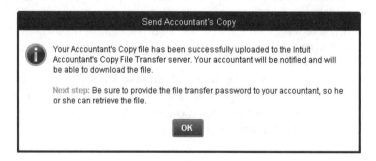

QuickBooks then sends an e-mail to your accountant (see Figure 22-1) and to you (see Figure 22-2).

intuit.

Accountant's Copy File Available

An Accountant's Copy Transfer File is now available for download on the Intuit Accountant's Copy File Transfer secure server. Click the link and then click **Save** in the File Download dialog. Save the file in any convenient location.

About this Accountant's Copy Transfer File:

File Name:	wholesale-distribution business (QuickBooks2014 Acct Transfer Aug 04,2014 02 19 PM).QBX
Sent by:	Leslie, info@samplecompany.com
Note:	Here's our file for your quarterly review.
Uploaded:	08-04-2014 11:21 AM
Expires:	**08-18-2014**

What Next?

No automatic notification is sent to your client when you download the file. Please contact your client to confirm receipt of this file.

To use the transfer file, start QuickBooks Accountant Edition. On the **File** menu, choose **Accountant's Copy** and then choose **Open and Convert Accountant's Copy Transfer File**. The system will prompt you for a password to decrypt the file. Your client must give you that password.

NEED HELP?

Click here for help, or contact QuickBooks Technical Support.

FIGURE 22-1   QuickBooks notifies your accountant that the file is available and explains what to do next.

intuit.

Upload Successful

Your Accountant's Copy file has been successfully uploaded to the Intuit Accountant's Copy File secure server. Your accountant has been notified by email to download the file. The file is available on the server for 14 days, through **08-18-2014**.

File Transfer Password

Please be sure to let your accountant know the file transfer password that is required to open the file.

Just in Case....

Please save this message, in case you need it in the future. If your accountant does not receive the notification message, you can forward this message to your accountant. Your accountant can download your Accountant's Copy Transfer File from the Intuit Accountant's Copy File Transfer secure server by clicking the link and then clicking **Save** in the File Download dialog.

About your file:

File Name:	wholesale-distribution business (QuickBooks2014 Acct Transfer Aug 04,2014 02 19 PM).QBX
Sent to:	info@samplecompany.com
Note:	Here's our file for your quarterly review.
Uploaded:	08-04-2014 11:21 AM
Expires:	**08-18-2014**

NEED HELP?

Click here for help, or contact QuickBooks Technical Support.

FIGURE 22-2   QuickBooks also sends you information about the file transfer.

FIGURE 22-3   The dividing date establishes boundaries and limits for the type of work you and your accountant can perform.

Choosing the Dividing Date

The text in the Set The Dividing Date window (see Figure 22-3) explains that your accountant works on transactions dated on or before the dividing date, and you work on transactions dated after the dividing date. You and your accountant should discuss the dividing date you select.

While your accountant is working with the Accountant's Copy, you can continue to work in your QuickBooks file, adding transactions dated *after* the dividing date. There are some limitations, however, in what you can change in your file while an Accountant's Copy is outstanding:

- You can add a new account but not subaccounts. You can also make new accounts inactive. But you cannot add a subaccount to an account that existed prior to creating the Accountant's Copy.
- If you perform a reconciliation of your bank account (or other account) and clear transactions dated on or before the Accountant's Copy dividing date, be sure to advise your accountant that you're performing a reconciliation. Otherwise, if the accountant performs a reconciliation for the same month and/or clears the same transactions, the reconciliation will be undone in your QuickBooks file when you import the accountant's changes.

ie period for which you need your te needed changes, which may not be a

with a dividing date matching the date such as an income statement and/or of an existing or potential line of credit. oved" detailed report of transactions for ciation's board (usually a month, quarter,

ich to insert changes, such as adjusting , set the dividing date about two weeks the report you need is as of the end of the three weeks after the last quarter end date.

hanges into Your File

ot a complete QuickBooks company file; accountant. In addition, the file is encrypted so it can be imported only into the company file you used to create it.

Use the following steps to open the file and import it into the original company file:

1. Be sure the company file from which you created the Accountant's Copy is open.
2. Choose File | Accountant's Copy | Import Accountant's Changes From File (if the file is on removable media) or From Web (if your accountant is using Intuit's file transfer service).
3. Navigate to the location where you saved the file your accountant sent, and double-click the file listing; the file has the naming format <CompanyName> (Acct Changes).qby.
4. The Incorporate Accountant's Changes window opens so you can preview the changes that will be merged into your company data file and read any notes your accountant wrote. (Before you import the changes, you can save the report as a PDF file or print it.)
5. Click Incorporate Accountant's Changes. QuickBooks walks you through the process of backing up your current file before importing the changes and then merges the changes into your company data file.

If any transactions failed to merge with your company file, a message appears informing you of the failure. The window includes buttons you can click to save (as PDF) or print the information. QuickBooks, however, will automatically create a PDF and save it in the same location as your QuickBooks data file.

Click Close. QuickBooks displays a message asking if you'd like to set a closing date and password-protect the closed period as of the dividing date you set. If the dividing date on this Accountant's Copy was the last day of the previous fiscal year, this is a good idea, so click Yes; if not, use your own judgment. (You can learn about setting a closing date to protect data in the previous fiscal year in Chapter 18.)

QuickBooks opens your company file, the text on the title bar changes back to its normal contents (instead of displaying a notice that an Accountant's Copy is outstanding), and you can work in the file with no restrictions.

> **ProAdvisor Tip:** After you're up and running again normally, you can delete the file your accountant sent you, and you can also delete the Accountant's Copy file you created if you saved it instead of uploading it.

Cancel the Accountant's Copy

Sometimes, accountants report that they have no changes to make; sometimes, accountants send you an e-mail to notify you of a small change and ask you to enter the transaction manually; and sometimes, you decide you made the Accountant's Copy in error and don't want to wait for a file to come back (don't forget to tell the accountant about your decision). Whatever the reason, if you're not going to get a file back from your accountant, you can cancel the Accountant's Copy in order to work normally in your company file.

Another reason to cancel the Accountant's Copy is because you simply don't want to import the changes you saw in the Incorporate Accountant's Changes window. Call your accountant and discuss the problem. If the end result is that you prefer not to import the changes, close the Incorporate Accountant's Changes window without importing the changes and cancel the Accountant's Copy.

To return everything to normal, choose File | Accountant's Copy | Remove Restrictions. QuickBooks asks you to confirm your decision. Select the Yes, I Want To Remove The Accountant's Copy Restrictions option, and click OK.

> **Caution:** If you cancel the Accountant's Copy and then later decide you want to import and accept the changes, you cannot import the copy you've just canceled. You'll have to create a new Accountant's Copy, send it to your accountant again, and she, in turn, will need to redo whatever changes were made in the Accountant's Copy.

Keeping Your QuickBooks Data Secure and Healthy

Chapter 23

The bookkeeping chores you complete in QuickBooks ensure that you're tracking important information about your business and how it's performing. Just as important as these tasks is the need to take care of the "health" of your QuickBooks company data file. In particular, it's important to keep your software up to date and make sure your data is not cluttered with very old or irrelevant transactions and list items. Finally, it's critical that you decide on and adopt a backup routine that you can rely on.

Delete Company Files

Sometimes, you have a valid reason to get rid of a company file. Perhaps you created a company to experiment with and you no longer use it, or someone is taking over your job and you no longer need to keep a QuickBooks company file on your local computer.

QuickBooks doesn't have a Delete File command from within the program itself, but you can delete the file from your hard drive through Windows Explorer or My Computer. Before you delete the file, however, read the following sections carefully so you don't encounter a problem the next time you open QuickBooks.

How QuickBooks Loads Company Files

QuickBooks automatically opens the company file that was loaded when you last exited the software. It's best to make sure that you don't have the about-to-be-deleted company file loaded when you close QuickBooks. Otherwise, the next time you open the program, it will try to "find" the deleted file, which can be confusing to both you and the software. To prevent this, take one of the following actions:

- Choose File | Open Or Restore Company to select another company file other than the one you're about to delete, and then exit the program.
- Choose File | Close Company/Logoff to close the current file and have no company file loaded if you shut down QuickBooks and reopen it.

Deleting the File

To delete a company file, open My Computer or Windows Explorer and navigate to the folder that holds your company files. Then delete the file *companyname*.qbw and the associated *companyname*.dsn and *companyname*.nd files. To complete the task, you'll also need to delete the *companyname*.tlg file separately (you may also see an LGB file that can be removed as well).

ProAdvisor Tip: It's a good idea to create a separate folder on your hard drive for your QuickBooks company files. Store all the import and export files you create that are associated with your QuickBooks files in that folder, too. Having a separate folder makes it easy to find files, and you can back up everything simply by backing up the folder.

Eliminating Deleted Files from the Company File List in QuickBooks

QuickBooks tracks the company files you've opened and lists the most recently opened files on the Open Previous Company submenu (under the File menu) to make it easier to move among files. You don't have to open a new dialog to select one of those files; you just click the appropriate listing. The submenu lists the company files you've opened, starting with the most recent.

After you delete a company file, its "ghost" listing may still appear on the Open Previous Company submenu or in the No Company Open window. You or another user could inadvertently select it, which produces a delay followed by an error message, and then possibly followed by a user panic attack.

You can clear the list of company files that you see in the Open Previous Company menu or in the No Company Open window by clicking the Edit List link on the No Company Open window.

In the QuickBooks Edit Company List window, select a company file that you want to hide from the list and click OK.

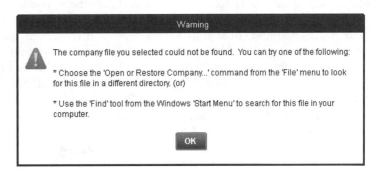

This changes the company files that are listed in the Open Previous Company menu as well as the No Company Open Window to the current company file only. QuickBooks again begins to track the files that you're working on, so as you open different company files, it rebuilds the list.

Back Up and Restore Files

Backing up your QuickBooks data is an incredibly important task and should be done on a daily basis. In addition, once a week, it's a good idea to use removable media to make an extra backup, and then take that backup off-site.

If you need to use a backup file, you don't open it the way you open a regular company file; instead, it has to be restored, using the QuickBooks Restore command as discussed in the following section.

Backing Up

Do this every day! You don't have to create a manual backup every day, as described here, or you can set up a scheduled backup; you'll still be making a daily backup—you just won't have to remember to initiate it. More about scheduling backups later in this chapter.

To create a local backup of the company currently open in QuickBooks, choose File | Back Up Company | Create Local Backup. This opens the Create Backup wizard window seen in Figure 23-1 with the Local Backup option pre-selected. If you select File | Backup Company | Setup/Activate Online Backup, QuickBooks opens a browser and takes you to a website with information about the QuickBooks online backup service (a fee-based service). From there, you can learn more about the service (which allows you to back up not only your QuickBooks data, but also your entire computer) or sign up for the service. If you do payroll in-house, any payroll forms you saved (940, 941, W-2, etc.) are not backed up. Luckily, you can back up those forms separately by copying them to your backup media. Look for a folder named *<YourCompanyFile> Tax Forms* in the folder that holds your company files; all the forms you saved are in that folder.

With the Local Backup option selected, click the Options button to set the location of the backup in the Backup Options dialog seen in Figure 23-2. Use the guidelines in the following sections to select options in this dialog.

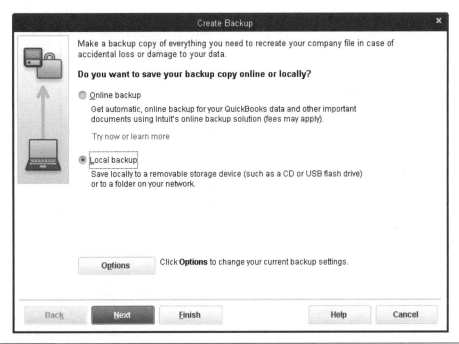

FIGURE 23-1 Select the type of copy you want to create—in this case, it's a local backup.

▶▶ ProAdvisor Recommends

Backing Up a File on a Network

If you're using QuickBooks on a network, you should run the QuickBooks backup routine on the same computer that the QuickBooks data file is stored on to ensure a complete backup is made. This may require you to install the full QuickBooks program on your QuickBooks "server" computer if only the QuickBooks Database Server Manager is installed there now. Refer to Appendix A to learn more about the QuickBooks Database Server Manager.

If you create a backup over a network from a client computer that's running QuickBooks, you may be creating a backup that is incomplete and that may require additional configuration if you ever need to restore your QuickBooks data file from it.

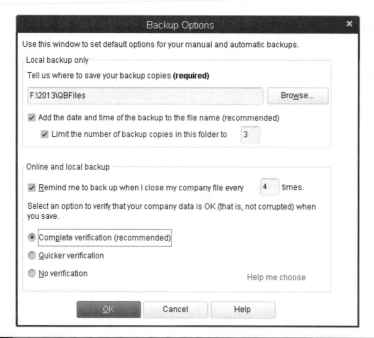

FIGURE 23-2 Configure the options for this backup.

Selecting a Location for the Backup

Click the Browse button to select the location for this backup. The optimum location is a universal serial bus (USB) drive, a CD/DVD, or a drive on another computer on your network (if you have a network). If you select a local drive that also holds your QuickBooks company file, QuickBooks issues a warning message when you click OK.

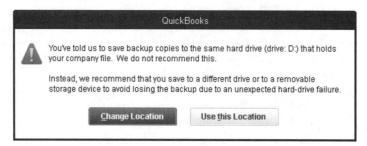

Unless you're saving the file to a folder on the drive that is going to be backed up later in the day or at night, heed the warning. Putting a backup on your hard drive could make your backup irretrievable if your hard drive experiences a catastrophic failure.

Adding Time Stamps to Backup Filenames

You can select the option to append a date/time stamp to the filename, which lets you tell at a glance when the backup file was created. The backup filename has the following format:

```
CompanyFilename(Backup Jun 01,2014 04 36 PM).QBB
```

When you select the time-stamp option, you're creating multiple backups in the same location, and you can limit the number of backups you save in a specific location. Multiple backups over continuous days provide an option to restore a backup from two days ago (or longer) if you think the backup you made yesterday may have some corrupted data. During backup, QuickBooks notes the number of backups you opted to keep and, when a backup is made that exceeds that number, QuickBooks asks if you want to delete the extra backup, always choosing the oldest backup as the one to delete.

Setting Backup Reminders

You can ask QuickBooks to remind you about backing up when you close a company file by selecting that option and then indicating the frequency. Hopefully, this prompt won't be necessary because you are already backing up every day. However, if you think you'll still need to be reminded to back up your file, use this option.

Choosing File Verification Options

If you wish, you can ask QuickBooks to verify the data in your company file before backing up by selecting either verification option. This can increase the amount of time it takes to complete the backup, so if you're performing a quick backup because you want to make changes in your file, or you're about to perform some other action that makes you think you want a quick safety backup, you can select the option No Verification.

If you choose this option, however, you'll want to be sure that when time permits, you run the verify utility by selecting File | Utilities | Verify Data. See the section "Verify and Rebuild a Company File," later in this chapter, for more information on completing this very important task.

Choosing When to Save the Backup

After closing the Backup Options dialog, click Next to choose when to create this backup. You have three choices:

- Save It Now
- Save It Now And Schedule Future Backups
- Only Schedule Future Backups

The second and third choices are concerned with scheduling automatic and unattended backups, a subject that's covered later in this chapter in the section "Scheduling Backups."

Assuming you're creating a backup now (the option chosen by default), click Next. QuickBooks opens the Save Backup Copy dialog with your location selected and the backup filename in the File Name field. Click Save.

Backing Up to a CD

If you're using QuickBooks on a computer running Windows XP, Windows 2003 Server, Windows Vista, Windows 7, or Windows 8, you can select your CD drive as the backup target.

QuickBooks saves the backup to the default folder on the hard drive that holds files waiting to be written to a CD, and the software displays a message telling you your data has been backed up successfully to that location. When you click OK, QuickBooks may display a dialog offering online backup (you can choose to learn more about this service or close the dialog to proceed). From here, you can choose to burn the CD using the Windows CD Wizard (Burn Now) or using your own CD-burning software (Burn Later).

You may see a balloon over the notification area of your taskbar, telling you that files are waiting to be written to the CD (the standard notification when you burn CDs in Windows). You don't have to click the balloon to open the folder that holds the file, because the QuickBooks backup feature automatically opens the Windows CD Writing Wizard and copies the file to the CD.

If you choose Burn Later, when you're ready to burn your CD, Windows looks in the folders under your name in C:\Users\\<username>\My Documents (in Windows 7, it saves the file to C:\Users\<username>\AppData\Local\Microsoft\Windows\Burn) and uses the backup files that QuickBooks created to burn to the CD. You can open your CD-burning software and direct it to that location, or you can use the Windows CD Writing Wizard by following these steps:

1. Select the CD drive in My Computer, where Windows displays the file(s) waiting to be written to the CD.
2. Choose File | Write These Files To CD (in Windows 7, you see a Burn To Disc command).
3. When the Windows CD Writing Wizard appears, follow the prompts to move your backup file to the CD.

Scheduling Backups

QuickBooks offers both automatic backups and unattended backups (which are also automatic). You can schedule either or both of these types of backups from the same wizard that walks you through the backup process described in the previous sections. Click through the wizard windows until you get to the second window titled Create Backup. You'll see two options that allow you to schedule future backups:

- Select Save It Now And Schedule Future Backups if you want to create a manual backup and also set up automatic and/or unattended backups.
- Select Only Schedule Future Backups if you just want to set up automatic and/ or unattended scheduled backups.

Clicking Next after either selection brings you to the wizard window shown in Figure 23-3.

Configuring Automatic Backups

An automatic backup is one that takes place whenever you close the company file. Closing a file is an action that can take place under any of the following circumstances:

- You open another company file.
- You choose File | Close Company (or File | Close Company/Logoff if you've set up users for the company).
- You close QuickBooks with this company file loaded.

FIGURE 23-3   Set up automatic backup procedures to make sure your data is always safe.

Set the frequency of automatic backups to match the way you use QuickBooks and the way you work in this company file. For example, if you open QuickBooks with this company file loaded in the morning and keep QuickBooks open all day without changing companies, set a frequency of 1 to make sure you have at least one backup each day (you can also set up another scheduled backup for that evening). The automatic backup is created using the settings, including the location, you configured in the Options dialog.

Configuring Scheduled Backups

You can configure QuickBooks to perform a backup of your company files at any time, even if you're not working at your computer. This is a cool feature, but it doesn't work unless you remember to leave your computer running when you leave the office. Before you leave, make sure QuickBooks is closed so all the files are available for backing up (open files are skipped during a scheduled backup). Also, keep in mind that scheduled backups cannot be made to a CD/DVD.

To create the configuration for an unattended backup, click New to open the Schedule Backup dialog seen in Figure 23-4.

FIGURE 23-4 Configure the specifications for an unattended backup.

You can give the backup a descriptive name (it's optional), but if you're going to create multiple unattended backup configurations, it's a good idea to identify each by name. For example, if you're backing up to a USB stick drive that's had its drive letter assigned as F:, a good description of a backup scheduled for 10 P.M. is "10PM to F."

C a u t i o n : Be sure the target drive is available—insert the Zip, USB, or other removable drive before leaving the computer, or be sure the remote network computer you're using for backup storage isn't shut down at night.

If you don't want to overwrite the last backup file every time a new backup file is created, select the option Number Of Backup Copies To Keep, and specify the number. QuickBooks saves as many backup files as you specify (up to 99), each time replacing the first file with the most recent backup and copying older files to the next highest number in the filename. These backup files are saved with the file extension .qbb and include a date and time stamp.

Create a schedule for this unattended backup by selecting a time and a frequency. In the example shown in Figure 23-4, the backup occurs every night.

If you're on a network, QuickBooks displays the Enter Windows Password dialog. The password in question is not to your QuickBooks user and password configuration; it's your Windows logon name and password. You can create multiple unattended backups and configure them for special circumstances. For instance, in addition to a nightly backup, you may want to configure a backup every four weeks on a Saturday or Sunday (or during your lunch hour on a weekday) to create a backup on a removable drive that is earmarked for off-site storage. Be sure to bring your backup media to the office on that day and take it back to the off-site location when the backup is finished.

Mapped drives are unique to your Windows login name. If you log off of Windows before you leave the office (not the same as shutting down the computer, which would prevent the backup from running), you cannot use a mapped drive to create your backup. While it's not common to take the trouble to log off of Windows, if you do normally log off, use the full path to the remote folder you're using as the target backup location instead of the mapped drive letter. The format of the full path (called *Universal Naming Convention* or UNC) is

```
\\ComputerName\ShareName
```

Restoring a Backup

You just turned on your computer and it sounds different—noisier. In fact, there's a grinding noise. You wait and wait, but the usual startup of the operating system fails to appear. Eventually, an error message about a missing boot sector appears (or some other equally troubling message). Nonetheless, you have invoices to send out, checks to write, and tons of things to do, and if you can't accomplish those tasks, your business suffers. It may be time to replace your hard drive or get a new computer.

Maybe your computer is fine, and it's your QuickBooks program that won't open, or it opens but reports a data error when it tries to open your file. In either case, follow these steps to restore your latest backup file:

1. Start QuickBooks. If the opening window tells you there's no company file open and suggests you create one (if this is a fresh installation of the software), ignore that message.

2. If you backed up to removable media, put the disc or USB flash drive that contains your last backup into its slot. If you backed up to a network share, be sure the remote computer is running. If you purchased the QuickBooks online backup service, be sure you've configured your Internet connection in QuickBooks.

3. Choose File | Open Or Restore Company. Choose Restore A Backup Copy and click Next.

4. Select Local Backup if your backup files are on removable media or on a remote computer on the network. Select Online Backup if you subscribe to that QuickBooks service. Then click Next. (If you use the QuickBooks online backup service, at this point, follow the prompts to restore your backup.)

5. If you selected Local Backup, the Open Backup Copy dialog appears. Navigate to the folder or drive where your backup is stored.

6. Select the backup file—if you store multiple backups with time stamps embedded in the filename, select the most recent backup.

7. Click Open, and then click Next to continue with the Restore Wizard.

8. In the Save Company File As dialog, select the folder to which you're restoring the file and click Save.

9. If you're restoring to an existing company because the problem was a corrupt data file, QuickBooks asks if you want to replace the existing file. Click Yes. Then, just to make sure, QuickBooks displays a warning that you're about to overwrite/delete the existing file. That's fine; it's what you want to do, so type **Yes** in the dialog and click OK.

QuickBooks displays a message that your data files have been restored successfully and opens the file (if you have to log in, the login dialog displays first, and the success dialog appears after you log in).

The Portable Company File

A portable company file is a copy of your QuickBooks company file that has been condensed to save disk space to make it "portable," that is, smaller than a backup (QBB) copy. Portable files are designed to move data between computers, such as your home computer and your office, so you can work at home and then bring the updated file back to the office.

Creating a Portable Company File

To create a portable company file, choose File | Create Copy, select Portable Company File, and click Next. In the Save Portable Company File dialog, select a location for the file (by default, QuickBooks selects Desktop as the location).

If you're taking the file to another computer (perhaps you're taking it home), choose removable media such as a Zip or USB drive, and take the media with you. Or, save the file on your hard drive and then send it to the person who will be working with the file (such as your accountant), either by e-mail or by burning it to a CD and sending the CD to the recipient.

ProAdvisor Tip: Do not substitute making a full backup as part of your regular backup routine with creating a portable company file. Why? Because a portable company file does not contain an important transaction log file that a full backup (QBB) file has. This file is located in the same folder as your company file (the QBW file), and its filename is <YourCompanyFilename>.tlg. In many cases, Intuit Technical Support can use the log file and your most recent backup to recover data up to the point of the transactions saved at the time of the backup file you supply.

Click Save. QuickBooks displays a message telling you it has to close the company file to create the portable file. Click OK.

It takes a while to create the file, and when it's done, QuickBooks issues a success message.

➡️ **ProAdvisor Recommends**

Overwriting Your Data File by Restoring a Backup or Portable File

Restoring a portable or backup file to a computer that has an existing QuickBooks company file may cause you to lose any work you've performed in the existing file. The process of overwriting the existing file with the portable or backup copy deletes the existing file and replaces it with the data in the portable or backup copy.

If you're the only person who works in the company file and you take a portable or backup file to another computer (such as your home computer), then work on the file and bring it back to the office, it's safe to overwrite the office copy with the changes that are made when you restore. Nobody has created any transactions since you created the portable or backup file, so deleting the original file doesn't delete any new transactions.

However, if you send a portable or backup file to someone else and then continue to work in the original file, you can't restore the file when it's returned unless you're prepared to lose all the work you did in the meantime. You have four ways to avoid this situation:

- Stop working on the file until the portable or backup file is returned. Then, when you restore to the company file, you don't lose any data.
- Have the person who's performing work in the portable or backup file send you a list of the transactions that were entered, instead of returning the file, and enter those transactions in the existing company file.
- Restore the file to a different location, or use a different filename (or both). You can open the restored company file and see what's new and then add that data to your real company file.
- Send an Accountant's Copy to the person doing the off-site work (this person needs to be using QuickBooks Accountant's edition). Creating and working with an Accountant's Copy is covered in Chapter 22.

To restore a portable company file, either on your home computer or on the office computer after you've worked on the file at home and saved it as a portable file, follow these steps to use the wizard that guides you through the process:

1. Choose File | Open Or Restore Company.
2. In the Open Or Restore Company window, select Restore A Portable File and click Next.

3. In the Open Portable Company File dialog, navigate to the folder or removable media drive that holds the file, select the file, and click Open.

4. The next window that appears is the informational window about where to restore the file. Click Next.

5. The Save Company File As window opens, which allows you to choose where you want to save the restored file. Use one of the guidelines described next to select a location and filename:

   • **Replacing the Existing Company File with the Portable File** If you're deliberately replacing a company file, select the folder that holds the original company file and use the same filename as your company file. QuickBooks displays a warning that you're about to overwrite the existing file and asks if you want to replace it; click Yes. To make sure you really understand what you're about to do, QuickBooks displays the Delete Entire File dialog and asks you to confirm your action. Type **Yes** and click OK to continue.

   • **Creating a Different Company File from the Portable File** If you want to create a separate company file to avoid overwriting the work you did in your real company file, change the location or the filename (or both) before you click Save.

After the portable company file is uncompressed, it's loaded in the QuickBooks window so you can work in it.

Verify and Rebuild a Company File

QuickBooks includes utilities to verify and rebuild the data in your company file. They're both found on the File | Utilities submenu.

Verifying a company file checks the integrity of your QuickBooks data. If QuickBooks finds any issues with your data, you're prompted to rebuild the file. Before you start the rebuild, QuickBooks asks you to make a backup and reminds you *not* to use your existing backup disk (or location)—heed this advice!

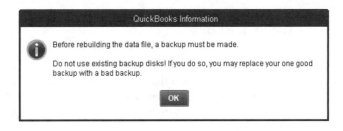

In many cases, the Rebuild routine will resolve the issue with the data (the best way to determine this is to run the Verify routine again). If it does not, the problems that are encountered are written to a log file named qbwin.log. If you wish, you can view the contents of the log within QuickBooks by pressing F2 to open the Product Information window and then pressing F3 to open the Tech Help window. Click the tab named Open File, select qbwin.log, and click Open File.

Sometimes, the log file has clear, helpful information about the problem and you can remove the problem transaction or list element from the data file. However, if you can't easily decipher the log contents or the Rebuild routine continues to indicate a problem with the data, you should call Intuit Technical Support for help. The support technician may ask you to send the log file, along with other files available in the QuickBooks Tech Help window, using the Send Log Files To Intuit Support button on the Open File tab.

Condense Your Data

To help reduce the size of your data file, QuickBooks provides a feature that enables you to remove certain transaction and list data in your company file that you no longer use or need. This is a handy feature, but keep in mind that it can result in the loss of details about transactions.

Understanding the Condense Data Process

The Condense Data utility is a process that allows you to delete closed transactions and replace them with a journal entry that shows totals posted to accounts. (If you subscribe to any QuickBooks payroll services, no current-year transactions are condensed.) Open transactions, such as unpaid invoices and bills and estimates that are not marked "Closed," are not removed. Before removing the data, QuickBooks creates an archive copy of your company file, which you can open to see the original transactions that were removed.

Choosing a Date

QuickBooks asks you for the date you want to use as the cutoff date. Everything you no longer need before that date is removed, if it can be safely removed without interfering with the transactions that remain. No open transactions are removed; only those that are completed and safe to remove are affected. Also, any transactions before the cutoff date that affect current transactions are kept so the details are maintained in the file.

Understanding Summary Transactions

The transactions that fall within the parameters of the condensing date are deleted and replaced with summary transactions. Summary transactions are nothing but journal entry transactions that show the totals for the removed transactions, one for each month. The account balances are not changed by removing data because the summary transactions maintain those totals.

What to Expect After the Condense Process Is Complete

After you clean up the file, you won't be able to run detail reports for those periods before the cutoff date. However, summary reports will be perfectly accurate in their financial totals. You will be able to recognize the summary transactions in the account registers because they will be marked with a transaction type GENJRNL. You can open the archived file if you need to see the original transaction details.

Run the Condense Data Utility

To run the Condense Data utility, choose File | Utilities | Condense Data. The Condense Data wizard opens, offering two cleanup methods (see Figure 23-5). You may see a warning about losing your budget data when your file is condensed, because some budgets are based on detailed postings. Click Yes. (Chapter 27 explains how to export your budgets to Excel and import them back into QuickBooks.)

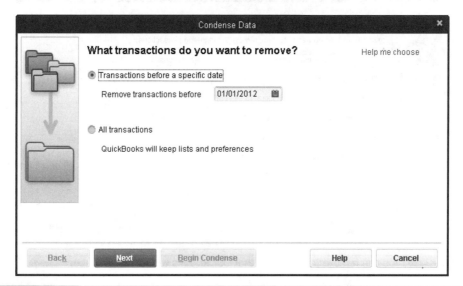

FIGURE 23-5   You can choose to clean up your file or remove all transactions, leaving your lists behind.

For this discussion, select the Transactions Before A Specific Date option. (Read "Removing All Transactions" later in this section to learn about the other option.) By default, QuickBooks inserts the first day of the previous fiscal year as the date. Usually, it's a good idea to go back a bit more if you've been using QuickBooks for several years without performing a cleanup. Click Next when you've entered the cutoff date.

Condensing Inventory Transactions

If you're tracking inventory in your QuickBooks file, the next window will ask you how you want QuickBooks to handle the removal of transactions that involve inventory. If your file is not set up to track inventory, you'll be asked to tell QuickBooks about the transactions you want to remove from your file.

Selecting Additional Transactions to Remove

In the next wizard window, you can select one or more types of existing transactions to remove, even though they wouldn't be removed automatically during a file cleanup process (see Figure 23-6). For example, if you have a transaction marked "To Be Printed" that's more than a year old, you probably aren't planning to print it (and you probably forgot you ever created it). When you've made your selections, click Next.

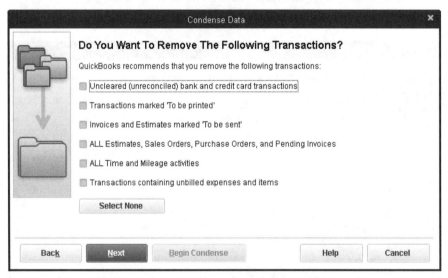

FIGURE 23-6 You can remove transactions that QuickBooks would normally keep.

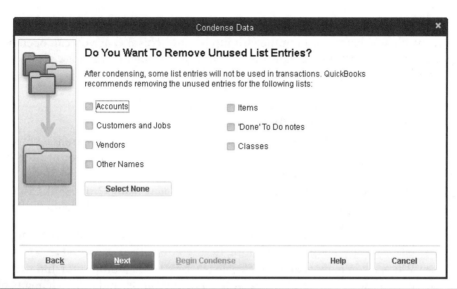

Removing Unused List Entries

In the next window, you can select the lists that may have entries that won't be used after old transactions are removed (see Figure 23-7). Click the list(s) you want QuickBooks to examine to determine whether there are unused listings and, if so, remove them.

Click Next to see an informational window in which the condense process is explained. Click Begin Condense to start the process. QuickBooks automatically makes a full copy of your file for you and at the end of the condense process displays a message giving you the location on your computer that this copy was saved to.

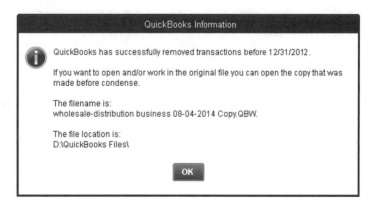

This is not an everyday backup; it's a full copy of your data file—just the way your file was before you ran the cleanup feature. This means you can open it if you need to see transaction details the next time a customer or vendor calls to discuss an old, old transaction.

Removing All Transactions

The Condense Data feature offers an option to strip the file of all transactions, leaving behind only the lists and the configuration settings you created for printers and Edit | Preferences categories.

Often, this function is used shortly after you start using QuickBooks as a way to "start all over." The other reasons you may use this option include the following:

- To start a new file at the beginning of a new year when the current company file has become so large that working in it is slower than you'd like.
- When a company changes its legal structure (from a proprietorship to a corporation or to an LLC), payroll, equity accounts, and other elements of the file must be changed to reflect the new organization type.

QuickBooks creates a backup of the file before beginning the process and creates an archive of the file before clearing the transactions, so you don't really wipe out the company's history permanently.

C a u t i o n : The Remove All Transactions choice won't run if you have payroll transactions for the current year or if your file contains bank or credit card accounts that are still enabled for online access.

Update QuickBooks

QuickBooks provides an automatic update service you can use to make sure your software is up to date and trouble free. This service provides you with any maintenance releases of QuickBooks that have been created since you purchased and installed your copy of the software. A maintenance release is distributed when a problem is discovered and fixed, or when a new feature is added to the software. Note that this service does not provide upgrades to a new version; it just provides updates to your current version.

You can enable automatic updates, which means QuickBooks periodically checks the Intuit update site on the Internet for updates to your version of QuickBooks. If new files exist, they're downloaded to your hard drive. If you turn off automatic updates, you should periodically check for new software files manually. Use the Update Now tab to select and download updated files.

Configuring QuickBooks Update Service

Choose Help | Update QuickBooks and move to the Options tab to configure the Update feature. You can enable or disable the automatic check for updates.

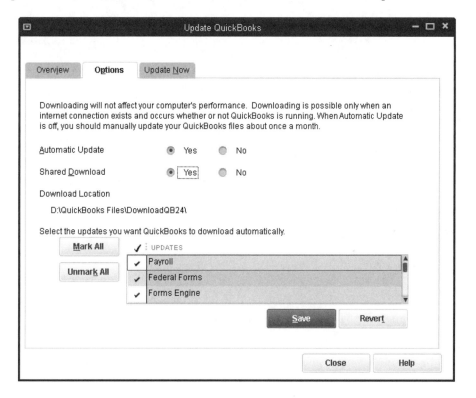

If you're using QuickBooks on a network, you can configure the update service to share downloaded files with other users. When this option is enabled, QuickBooks creates a subfolder on the computer that holds the shared QuickBooks data files, and the other computers on the network use that subfolder as the source of updated files instead of going online and downloading files.

For this to work, every user on the network must open her copy of QuickBooks and configure the Update options for Shared Download to reflect the folder location on the host computer. The folder location is displayed on the Options tab when you select the Shared Download option.

Customizing QuickBooks for Your Business

n this chapter:

- Configure preferences

- Customize transaction templates

The Preferences settings you establish in QuickBooks allow you to control the way you complete tasks, how data is entered, and how it is reported. It's not uncommon for QuickBooks users to change or tweak these preferences periodically. In fact, the more you use QuickBooks and understand the way it works, the more comfortable you'll be with changing preferences.

Many of the templates that QuickBooks uses allow customization so that you can capture additional information about your transactions. Once captured, this information is available in reports. The ability to customize templates also means that you can modify the way information is displayed in a transaction window, which makes it easier to fill in a form with just the information that you need.

Customize Settings and Options

Your settings and options for the available QuickBooks features are maintained in the Preferences dialog, which you open by choosing Edit | Preferences from the QuickBooks menu bar.

Each category in the Preferences dialog is accessed by clicking the appropriate icon in the left pane. While every category has the two tabs My Preferences and Company Preferences, not every category will have options available on each tab.

- The My Preferences tab is where you configure your preferences as a QuickBooks user. Each user you create in QuickBooks can set her own My Preferences. QuickBooks will apply the correct preferences as each user logs into the company file.
- The Company Preferences tab is the place to configure the way the QuickBooks features work for the current company, regardless of which user logs in. Only the Admin or an External Accountant user can change settings in the Company Preferences tab.

As you configure options and move from one category of the Preferences window to another, you're asked whether you want to save the changes in the section you just left.

For convenience, all of the Preferences categories are covered in this chapter. However, you may also find some additional details about a specific preference category in a relevant chapter.

Accounting Preferences

Click the Accounting icon on the left pane of the Preferences dialog to open the Accounting preferences (see Figure 24-1). There are only Company Preferences available for this section; the My Preferences tab has no options available.

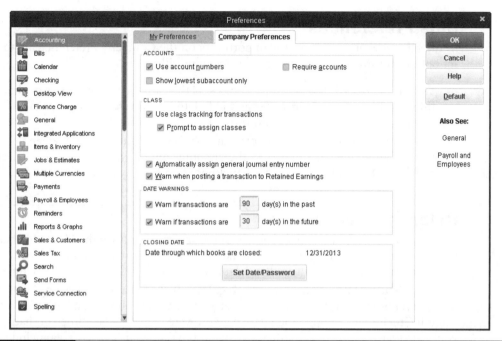

FIGURE 24-1 Configure the way basic accounting functions work.

You can select the option to use account numbers, and if so, you should also select the option Show Lowest Subaccount Only. The latter option is useful because it means that when you see an account number in a drop-down list (in a transaction window), you see only the subaccount. If the option is not selected, you see the parent account followed by the subaccount, and since the field display doesn't show the entire text unless you scroll through it, it's hard to determine which account has been selected.

The option to require accounts means that every item and transaction you create in QuickBooks has to be assigned to an account. If you disable this option, transaction amounts that aren't manually assigned to an account are posted to Uncategorized Income or Uncategorized Expense. These amounts will show as such on reports—not really useful when you want to analyze your business.

You can also enable the Class feature, which lets you create Profit & Loss reports for divisions, departments, or other categories by which you've decided to analyze your business.

The other options on this dialog are self-explanatory, except for the Closing Date section, which is discussed in detail in Chapter 18.

Bills Preferences

In the Bills category, you have the opportunity on the Company Preference tab to set options for the way you enter and pay vendor bills:

- You can set default terms (QuickBooks sets this at ten days, but you can change this default). When you create terms and link those terms to vendors, QuickBooks ignores this default for any vendor that has terms configured.
- You can tell QuickBooks to take discounts and credits automatically when you're paying vendor bills. If you choose the discounts option, you'll be asked to select a Default Discount Account that QuickBooks will post your discounts to.

Calendar Preferences

All the settings available in this preference area are found only on the My Preferences tab. This means that the choices you make here will apply when you log into QuickBooks. Other users will see the default settings unless they also make changes.

The Calendar Settings area on this tab gives you several alternatives on the view (daily, weekly, monthly) that should be set as your default. If you can't decide, you can tell QuickBooks to open the view that you were using the last time you had your calendar window open. Other options in the Calendar Settings area include the number of days you want to appear for each week and the type of transactions your calendar should display for you.

The Upcoming & Past Due Settings area gives you control over which future and past-due transactions will make their way onto your calendar.

Checking Preferences

This category has options in both the My Preferences and Company Preferences tabs. On the My Preferences tab, you can select default bank accounts for different types of transactions. Skip these options if you only have one bank account.

The Company Preferences tab (see Figure 24-2) offers several options concerned with check printing, which are described in the following paragraphs.

Print Account Names On Voucher

This option is useful only if you print your checks and the check forms you purchase have vouchers (stubs). If so, selecting this option means that the text on the stub will display posting accounts. That information is of no interest to your vendors, so only use this option if you keep and file check vouchers instead of leaving them attached to the check.

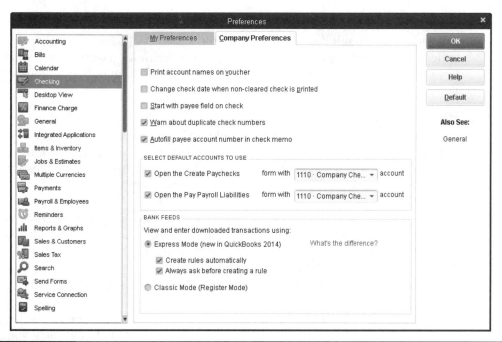

FIGURE 24-2 Select the options you need to make check writing more efficient.

Change Check Date When Non-cleared Check Is Printed

Selecting this option means that at the time you print checks, the current date becomes the check date. If you don't select this option, the check date you specified when you filled out the check window is used, even if that date has already passed.

Start With Payee Field On Check

Enabling this option forces your cursor to the Payee field when you first bring up the Write Checks window. If the option is not enabled, the Bank Account field is the first active field. If you always write checks from the same bank account, enable this option to save yourself the inconvenience of pressing TAB.

Warn About Duplicate Check Numbers

This option means that QuickBooks will warn you if you attempt to save a check with a number that already exists.

Autofill Payee Account Number In Check Memo

Most vendors maintain an account number for their customers, and your own account number with that vendor can be included on the checks you print. In order for this to occur, you must fill in your account number in the Account No field on the Payment Settings tab in the vendor record. The printout appears in the Memo section on the lower-left section of the check.

Select Default Accounts To Use

You can set the default bank accounts for different types of payroll transactions, which is important if you have a separate bank account for payroll. Then, when you create these checks, you don't have to select the bank account from a drop-down list in the transaction window.

Bank Feeds

If you use the Bank Feeds (aka Online Banking) to download your banking transactions, you can choose how you want to view and enter transactions. Express mode (which was a new addition in QuickBooks 2014) uses a Transaction List window, which you'll use to add or match transactions to your QuickBooks company file.

Express mode also gives you more robust options on how your transactions are matched to existing QuickBooks names (called renaming rules). Specifically, you can control whether QuickBooks automatically creates an "alias" name for you or whether you want to be asked to create an alias name.

If you select Classic (Register) mode, the work of processing and categorizing your transactions happens while in a register view.

As you make your decision on the Bank Feeds mode that you want to use, keep in mind that the renaming rules you set in Express mode are not available if you switch to Register mode—and vice versa.

Desktop View Preferences

This is where you can modify the way the QuickBooks window looks and acts. The My Preferences tab (see Figure 24-3) contains basic configuration options. In the View section, you can specify whether you always want to see one QuickBooks window at a time or view multiple windows.

- Choose One Window to limit the QuickBooks screen to show one window at a time, even if you have multiple windows open. The windows are maximized and stacked atop each other, with only the top window visible. A convenient way to switch between multiple windows is by using the Open Window List. To add this list to the left side of your QuickBooks window, select View | Open Window List.
- Choose Multiple Windows to make it possible to view multiple windows on your screen. Selecting this option activates the arrangement commands on the Window menu item, which allows you to stack or arrange windows so that more than one window is visible at a time.

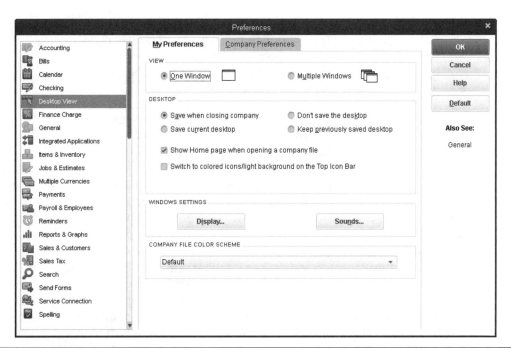

FIGURE 24-3 Configure the look and behavior of the QuickBooks window.

In the Desktop section, you can also specify what QuickBooks should do when you open and exit the software, choosing among the following options:

- **Save When Closing Company** This means that the state of the desktop is remembered when you close the company or exit QuickBooks. Whichever QuickBooks windows were open when you left will reappear when you return. You can pick up where you left off. If you select the option Show Home Page When Opening A Company File, that option overrides this option, so if you close the company file after closing the Home page, the Home page appears on top of any open windows when you open the company file.
- **Save Current Desktop** When you choose this option, the next time you open QuickBooks, it displays the desktop as it was the last time you worked in your company file.
- **Don't Save The Desktop** This tells QuickBooks to display an empty QuickBooks desktop (unless you enable the Show Home Page When Opening A Company File option) when you open this company file or when you start QuickBooks again after using this company file. The desktop isn't really empty—the menu bar, Icon Bar, and any other navigation bars are on the desktop, but no transaction or list windows are open.

- **Keep Previously Saved Desktop**   This is available only when you select Save Current Desktop. This option tells QuickBooks to display the desktop as it was the last time you used the Save Current Desktop option.
- **Show Home Page When Opening A Company File**   This tells QuickBooks to display the Home page when you open the company file.

Buttons are available to configure Windows settings for display and sounds. Clicking either button opens the associated window in your Windows Control Panel. The display and sounds configuration options you change affect your computer and all your software, not just QuickBooks.

Use the drop-down menu under Company File Color Scheme to change the color associated with the QuickBooks file that you're working in. Changing colors can be an effective way to quickly differentiate one QuickBooks company file from another—especially helpful if you find you're often doing work in multiple company files.

In the Company Preferences tab, you can customize some of the contents of the Home page. If you want to add an icon on the Home page for a particular feature (such as Estimates), this tab also tells you whether that feature has been enabled in your company file. If the feature hasn't been enabled, click the feature's name to open its category in the Preferences dialog. Turn the feature on to add its icon to the Home page, and then click the Desktop View icon to return to this window.

Finance Charge Preferences

In the Company Preferences tab, you can turn on, turn off, and configure finance charges. Finance charges can get complicated, so read the complete discussion about this topic in Chapter 10.

General Preferences

This dialog contains options for the way you work in QuickBooks. There are settings on both the My Preferences and Company Preferences tabs.

The My Preferences tab (shown in Figure 24-4) offers a number of options that are designed to let you control the way QuickBooks behaves while you're working in transaction windows.

Pressing Enter Moves Between Fields

Use this option to tell QuickBooks that you want to use the ENTER key to move between fields rather than the default method, which is the TAB key.

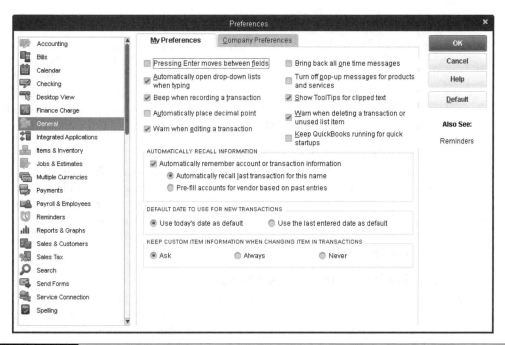

FIGURE 24-4 The My Preferences tab in General Preferences helps you control the way QuickBooks behaves when you're the logged-in user.

Automatically Open Drop-Down Lists When Typing

This is a handy option that's used when you're making selections from drop-down lists. When you begin typing the first few letters of the listing you need, the drop-down list appears and you move to the first listing that matches the character(s) you typed.

Beep When Recording A Transaction

If you don't want to hear sound effects as you work in QuickBooks, you can deselect the option. But if you select this option (which is the default QuickBooks setting), you can control what sounds you want to hear and when you want to hear them on the My Preferences tab of the Desktop View Preferences.

Click the Sounds button to open the Sounds window. Click the tab labeled Sounds. Use the slider in the Program Events area to find the list of QuickBooks actions that trigger a sound. Highlight an action to specify which sound you want to hear for that action.

Automatically Place Decimal Point

This is a useful feature once you get used to it. When you enter numbers in a currency field, a decimal point is placed automatically to the left of the last two digits when you enable this feature. Therefore, if you type 5421, when you move to the next field, the number changes to 54.21. If you want to type in even dollar amounts, type a period after you enter 54, and QuickBooks will automatically add two zeros to the right of the period.

Warn When Editing A Transaction

This option, which is selected by default, tells QuickBooks to flash a warning message when you change any transaction and try to close the transaction window without explicitly saving the changed transaction. This means you have a chance to change your mind. If you deselect the option, the edited transaction is saved as changed, unless it is linked to other transactions, in which case, the warning message explaining that problem appears.

Bring Back All One Time Messages

One-time messages are those informational dialogs that include a Don't Show This Message Again option. If you clicked that Don't Show option on any message dialogs, select this check box to see those messages again (and you can once again select the Don't Show option).

Turn Off Pop-Up Messages For Products And Services

Selecting this option stops pop-up messages from QuickBooks that are connected to products and services available from Intuit.

Show ToolTips For Clipped Text

Enabling this option means that if text in any field is truncated, hovering your mouse over the text displays the entire text. This saves you the trouble of selecting the field and using the arrow keys to read the entire text.

Warn When Deleting A Transaction Or Unused List Item

When selected, this option produces a warning when you delete a transaction or a list item that has not been used in a transaction—it's a standard message asking you to confirm your action. If you try to delete an item or a name that has been used in a transaction, QuickBooks won't permit you to complete the deletion.

Keep QuickBooks Running For Quick Startups

When enabled, QuickBooks will start automatically and run in the background whenever you start your computer. When you close QuickBooks, it remains running in the background so it starts quickly the next time you open it.

Automatically Remember Account Or Transaction Information

Enabling this option tells QuickBooks to prefill information in a bill, check, or credit card transaction window, based on previous transactions for the same vendor. If this option is enabled, you can choose either of the suboptions:

- Automatically Recall Last Transaction For This Name, which duplicates the information in the last transaction. This is handy for transactions that don't change (or don't change often), such as the check to your landlord, which is always for the same amount and posted to the same account.
- Pre-fill Accounts For Vendor Based On Past Entries, which examines the history of transactions for the current vendor. If the same information appears in all or most of the historical transactions, QuickBooks autofills the transaction window (same as the previous option). If historical transactions differ, QuickBooks does not prefill the transaction window, saving you the trouble of removing the data if it doesn't match this transaction.

ProAdvisor Tip: In addition to these "auto recall" options that QuickBooks provides for vendor transactions, you can prefill accounts for vendors right in the vendor record. Learn more about that feature in Chapter 4.

Default Date To Use For New Transactions

Use this option to tell QuickBooks whether you want the Date field to show the current date or the date of the last transaction you entered when you open a transaction window. If you frequently enter transactions for the same date over a period of several days (for example, you start preparing invoices on the 27th of the month, but the invoice date is the last day of the month), select the option to use the last entered date so you can just keep going.

Keep Custom Item Information When Changing Item In Transactions

The selection you make for this option determines what QuickBooks does when you change the description text or the price for an item you insert in a sales transaction form and then change the item:

- If you select Always, QuickBooks will keep the descriptive text you wrote, even though you changed the item. This descriptive text is linked to this different item only for this invoice; no changes are made to any item record.

- If you select Never, QuickBooks just fills in the description that goes with the new item you selected.
- If you select Ask, as soon as you change the item, QuickBooks asks if you want to change only the item and keep your customized description on the invoice. You can answer Yes (or No), and you can also tell QuickBooks to change this Preferences option permanently to match your answer.

The same thing happens if you entered a different price (instead of, or in addition to, the description) and then changed the item.

The Company Preferences Tab in General Preferences

The Company Preferences tab in the General section has the following options:

- **Time Format**   Select a format for entering time, choosing between decimal (for example, 11.5 hours) or minutes (11:30).
- **Always Show Years As 4 Digits**   If you prefer to display the year with four digits (01/01/2014 instead of 01/01/14), select this option.
- **Never Update Name Information When Saving Transactions**   By default, QuickBooks asks if you want to update the original information for a name when you change it during a transaction entry. For example, if you're entering a sales receipt and you change the customer's address, QuickBooks offers to make that change on the customer's record (you can choose Yes or No when QuickBooks asks). If you don't want to be offered this opportunity and always want the record to remain as is, select this option.
- **Save Transactions Before Printing**   The rule that a transaction must be saved before it's printed is a security precaution. Keeping this option enabled will help to prevent an employee (or others who have access to your QuickBooks file) from printing an invoice or check without the transaction being recorded. It's recommended that you keep this default setting.

Integrated Applications Preferences

You can let third-party software access and share the data in your QuickBooks files. Click the Integrated Applications icon and move to the Company Preferences tab to specify the way QuickBooks works with other software programs.

When you use a third-party program that links to QuickBooks, you're asked to approve that link the first time that other application attempts to make a connection to the QuickBooks file you're working in. If you click Yes, basic information for that program is recorded and appears in this dialog so that you do not have to reapprove future connections.

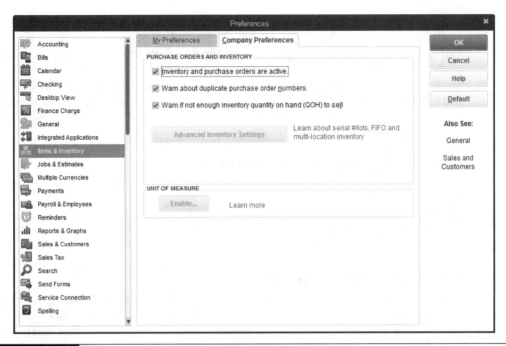

FIGURE 24-5   Set up your QuickBooks file to track inventory.

Items & Inventory Preferences

Use this dialog to enable the inventory function and set options for processing inventory transactions. Only the Company Preferences tab has options (see Figure 24-5).

Inventory And Purchase Orders Are Active

Select this option to tell QuickBooks that you want to enable the inventory feature; the ability to create and track purchase orders is automatically enabled with that option.

Warn About Duplicate Purchase Order Numbers

When this option is enabled, any attempt to issue a purchase order with a PO number that already exists will generate a warning.

Warn If Not Enough Inventory
Quantity On Hand (QOH) To Sell

This option turns on the warning feature that is useful during customer invoicing. If you sell ten widgets but your stock of widgets is fewer than ten, QuickBooks displays a message telling you there's insufficient stock to fill the order. You can still complete the invoice; it's just a message, not a functional limitation, but you should order more widgets immediately.

The Company Preferences tab of the Items & Inventory Preferences dialog also contains an Advanced Inventory Settings and a Unit Of Measure button. If you find that both of these buttons are not "live," it's because these features are only available in the QuickBooks Premier and Enterprise editions (Advanced Inventory is only available at the Enterprise level). Click the Learn More links to see if either of these features is a fit for your business and learn how to upgrade to either one of these versions of QuickBooks.

Jobs & Estimates Preferences

Use the Company Preferences tab to configure the way your estimates work. While the options are self-explanatory, if you plan on using estimates you should read Chapter 9 to learn everything about creating estimates and how to save time and increase accuracy by creating invoices from estimates.

Multiple Currencies Preferences

The Company Preferences tab is where you enable the ability to do business in multiple currencies. The available options are Yes and No, but if you select Yes, QuickBooks prompts you to make a backup of your company file before finalizing your decision since this feature cannot be turned off once it's been turned on. From this window, you'll also tell QuickBooks what your home currency is.

Even if you're sure you want to work in multiple currencies in QuickBooks, make a backup, and use a name for the backup file that indicates what you're doing (such as *<Company Name>*PreMulticurrency.qbb). Then, if you decide you don't want to use this feature, you can restore your backup file and proceed as before. Using the multiple currencies feature in QuickBooks is covered in Appendix B.

Payments Preferences

Use the Payments preferences (Company Preferences tab only) to learn more about or to sign up for the Intuit Payment Network. With this service, you can choose from credit card processing, paper check processing, or electronic check processing (additional fees may apply).

In the Receive Payments section, you'll find three options.

Automatically Apply Payments

This option tells QuickBooks to apply payments automatically to open invoices. If the payment amount is an exact match for an open invoice, it is applied to that invoice. If the payment amount is smaller than any open invoice, QuickBooks applies the payment to the oldest invoice. If the payment amount is larger than any open invoice, QuickBooks applies payments, starting with the oldest invoice, until the payment amount is used up.

Without this option, you must manually apply each payment to an invoice. That's not as difficult as it may sound, and in fact, is quite common because the customer's check almost always indicates the invoice the customer wants to pay, even if the check doesn't cover the entire amount of that invoice. Sometimes, customers don't mark the invoice number on the check and instead enclose a copy of the invoice in the envelope. Read Chapter 10 to learn about receiving and applying customer payments.

Automatically Calculate Payments

When this option is enabled, you can begin selecting invoices to pay in the Receive Payments window before entering the amount of the customer's payment check. When you've finished selecting invoices, either paying them entirely or applying a partial payment, the amounts you've applied should equal the amount of the check you received.

This is efficient if a customer has many invoices (some of which may have credits or may have an amount in dispute) and has attached instructions about the way to apply the checks.

Use Undeposited Funds As A Default Deposit To Account

Selecting this option automates the process of depositing all cash received into the Undeposited Funds account. If the option isn't selected, each cash receipt transaction window (customer payment and sales receipt) offers the choice of depositing the cash into a bank account or into the Undeposited Funds account.

Invoice Payments

In this section, you can learn more about or sign up for the Intuit Payment Network. And if you're already signed up for this service, this is where you can go to turn it off. When you sign up for the Intuit Payment Network, a link with a web address set up just for your business is included on your invoices. Your customer can use this link to pay you online. Click the Learn More or Explain link to activate this service or to get more information about how it works. Additional fees may apply.

Payroll & Employees Preferences

Use the Company Preferences tab of this category to set all the configuration options for payroll. Refer to Chapter 20 for an explanation of the selections in this window.

Reminders Preferences

The Reminders category of the Preferences dialog has options on both tabs. The My Preferences tab has one option, which enables the display of the Reminders List when you open the company file.

The Company Preferences tab lists all the available reminders, and you can select the ones you want to use (see Figure 24-6). Keep in mind that these selections won't take effect unless you select the Show Reminders List When Opening A Company File check box on the My Preferences tab.

For each item, decide whether you want to see a summary (just a listing and the total amount of money involved), a complete detailed list, or nothing at all. You can also determine the amount of lead time you want for your reminders. If you notice that some of the options are grayed out, it's because they're only available in QuickBooks Premier or Enterprise edition.

Reports & Graphs Preferences

This is another section of the Preferences window that has choices on both tabs, so you can set your own user preferences and then set those options that affect the current company.

Using the My Preferences tab, you can customize your experience when working with reports and graphs.

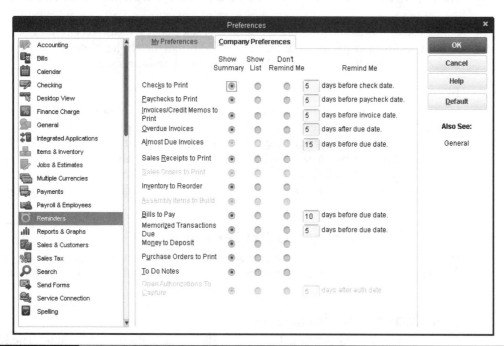

FIGURE 24-6 Decide which tasks you want to be reminded about.

Prompt Me To Modify Report Options Before Opening A Report

If you find that almost every time you select a report you have to customize it, you can tell QuickBooks to open the Modify Report window whenever a report is brought to the screen by selecting this option.

Reports And Graphs Settings

While you're viewing a report or a graph, you can make changes to the format, the filters, or the data behind it. Most of the time, QuickBooks automatically changes the report or graph to match the changes. Sometimes, however, if there is anything else going on (perhaps you're also online, or you're in a network environment and other users are manipulating data that's in your report or graph), QuickBooks may not make changes automatically. The reason for the shutdown of automatic refreshing is to keep your computer running as quickly and efficiently as possible. At that point, QuickBooks has to make a decision about when and how to refresh the report or graph. You must give QuickBooks the parameters for making the decision to refresh:

- Choose Prompt Me To Refresh to see a message asking you whether you want to refresh the report or the graph after you've made changes to the data behind it. When the reminder appears, you can click Yes to refresh the data in the report.
- Choose Refresh Automatically if you want up-to-the-second data and don't want to bother to click the Refresh button. If you work with QuickBooks across a network, this could slow down your work a bit because whenever any user makes a change to data that's used in the report/graph, it will refresh itself.
- Choose Don't Refresh if you want to decide for yourself, without any reminder from QuickBooks, when to click the Refresh button on the report window.

Graphs Only

Give QuickBooks instructions about creating your graphs, as follows:

- Choose Draw Graphs In 2D (Faster) to have graphs displayed in two dimensions instead of three. This doesn't limit your ability to see trends at a glance; it's just not as high-tech. The main reason to consider this option is that the 2-D graph takes less time to draw on your screen.
- Choose Use Patterns to draw the various elements in your graphs with black-and-white patterns instead of colors. For example, one pie wedge may be striped, another speckled. This is handy if you print your graphs to a black-and-white printer.

Move to the Company Preferences tab of the Reports & Graphs category to set company preferences for reports (see Figure 24-7).

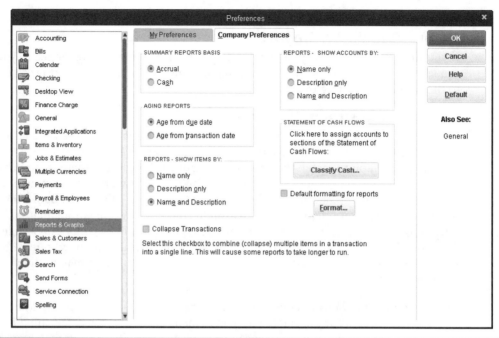

FIGURE 24-7   Set the default Company Preferences options for reports.

Summary Reports Basis

Specify whether you want to see summary reports as accrual-based or cash-based. You're only setting the default specification here, and you can always change the basis in the Modify Report dialog when you actually display the report.

Aging Reports

Specify whether you want to generate A/R and A/P aging reports using the due date or the transaction date.

Reports—Show Accounts By

Specify whether you want reports to display account names, account descriptions, or both. If you enabled account numbers, those numbers are part of the account names.

Reports—Show Items By

Specify whether you want reports that include items to display just the item name, the item description, or both.

Setting Report Format Defaults

You can set the default formatting for reports by clicking the Format button and making changes to the default configuration options for parts of reports that aren't data related but instead control the look of the reports. Use this feature if you find yourself making the same modifications to the formats over and over.

Configuring the Statement Cash Flows Report

A cash flow report is really a complicated document, and before the days of accounting software, accountants spent many hours creating such a report (and charged a lot of money for doing so). QuickBooks has configured a cash flow report format that is used to produce the Statement Of Cash Flows, which is available in the list of Company & Financial reports.

You can view the format by clicking the Classify Cash button, but if you plan on using this report on a regular basis, it's a good idea to check with your accountant before you reassign accounts. You can learn about cash flow reports in Chapter 27.

Collapse Transactions

Selecting this option will collapse (combine) a transaction that includes multiple items into one line on a report. When you run a report with this option, you can then use the Expand button at the top of the report window to display the details.

Sales & Customers Preferences

You can set options in the Sales & Customers category on both the My Preferences and Company Preferences tabs. On the My Preferences tab, set the options for invoicing customers for reimbursable expenses and billable time.

Prompt For Time/Costs To Add

Choosing this option tells QuickBooks to open a dialog that displays the current outstanding reimbursable expenses and time associated with a customer whenever you create an invoice or sales receipt for a customer. This is the option to select if you typically need to rebill your customers for out-of-pocket expenses or for time spent on a project.

Don't Add Any

Selecting this option prevents the automatic display of any dialogs about reimbursable expenses when you create a sales transaction. Choose this option if you rarely (or never) seek reimbursement from your customers. If you decide that you *do* want to collect reimbursable expenses during invoice creation, you can click the Add Time/Costs button on the sales transaction form.

Ask What To Do

Select this option to tell QuickBooks to ask you what you want to do whenever you create a sales transaction for a customer with outstanding reimbursable costs. Depending on your selection in that dialog, you can either add the costs to the sales transaction or omit them. You can learn how to bill customers for expenses and time in Chapter 9.

On the Company Preferences tab, set the default options for sales transactions.

Usual Shipping Method

Use this to set the default shipping method if you use the same shipping method most of the time. This saves you the trouble of making a selection from the drop-down list unless you're changing the shipper for a particular invoice.

Usual FOB

Set the FOB language for invoices. FOB (Free On Board) is the location from which shipping is determined to be the customer's responsibility. This means more than just paying for freight; it's a statement that says, "At this point, you have become the owner of this product." The side effects include assigning responsibility if goods are lost, damaged, or stolen. FOB settings have no impact on your financial records.

Warn About Duplicate Invoice Numbers

This option tells QuickBooks to warn you if you're creating an invoice with an invoice number that's already in use.

Choose Template For Invoice Packing Slip

Select a default packing slip to use when you print packing slips. If you've created customized packing slips, you can make one of them the default.

Enable Collections Center

Selecting the Enable Collections Center check box makes the Collections Center feature available. Once enabled, an icon with the same name is added to the Customer Center for easy access. Its purpose is to help you keep track of past due and almost past due customer balances while also giving you an easy way to send e-mail reminders to the customers that are listed there.

Custom Pricing

Choose one of two options: No Custom Pricing and Enable Price Levels. Price levels are a way for you to customize your prices by customer. Learn more about how to use price levels in Chapter 6.

Sales Tax Preferences

If you collect sales tax, you must set your sales tax options. Most of the selections are predefined by state tax laws and state tax reporting rules. Check with your accountant and read the information that came with your state sales tax license. For more information about managing sales taxes in QuickBooks, see Chapter 5.

Search Preferences

The Search feature allows you to quickly search in all areas of your company file for things like transactions, names, amount, dates, QuickBooks features, and so on. By default, the Search field is included on the QuickBooks Icon Bar—whether you use the Top or Left Icon bar. If you use the Top Icon bar, you can remove the Search field on it by unchecking that option at the top of the My Preferences tab (learn how to customize the QuickBooks Icon Bar in Chapter 1). You can also tell QuickBooks whether to search the Help files or your QuickBooks file when a search term is entered in this field.

The preferences listed on the Company Preferences tab give you the option of updating your search information either automatically (as often as every five minutes) or manually.

Send Forms Preferences

If you send transactions to customers via e-mail, the My Preferences tab offers the opportunity to automatically select the Email Later option on a sales transaction if the current customer is configured for e-mail as the preferred send method.

You can choose whether to send this information via Outlook or a compatible web e-mail service like Yahoo! or Gmail. You can also use QuickBooks E-mail, which is a subscription-based offering. Click the Check For Valid Subscriptions button to learn more or to confirm your own subscription.

On the Company Preferences tab, you can use Email Templates to design multiple versions of the message that accompanies an e-mailed transaction (like invoices, estimates, sales receipts, reports, and employee pay stubs, to name a few).

Service Connection Preferences

If you use QuickBooks services on the Internet, use this category to specify the way you want to connect to the Internet for those services.

The My Preferences tab contains options related to online banking if your bank uses the Web Connect method of online access. (Chapter 16 has detailed information about online banking services.)

- **Give Me The Option Of Saving A File Whenever I Download Web Connect Data**   Select this option if you want QuickBooks to provide a choice to save Web Connect data for later processing instead of automatically processing the transactions. QuickBooks provides the choice by opening a dialog that lets you choose whether to import the data immediately or save it to a file so you can import it later (you have to supply a filename). The QuickBooks dialog also includes an option to reset this option. This option only works when you select Open on the File Download dialog. If you disable this option, the file is automatically opened and the data is imported into QuickBooks.
- **If QuickBooks Is Run By My Browser, Don't Close It After Web Connect Is Done**   Selecting this option means that when QuickBooks is launched automatically when you download Web Connect data from your financial institution (after selecting Open on the Download dialog), QuickBooks remains open after you process the data. If you deselect this option, QuickBooks closes automatically as soon as your data is processed.

The following connection options are available on the Company Preferences tab (these options don't apply to payroll services or online banking):

- Automatically Connect Without Asking For A Password lets all users log into the QuickBooks Business Services network automatically.
- Always Ask For A Password Before Connecting forces users to enter a login name and password in order to access QuickBooks Business Services.
- Allow Background Downloading Of Service Messages lets QuickBooks check the Intuit website for updates and information periodically when you're connected to the Internet.

Spelling Preferences

The Spelling section presents options only on the My Preferences tab. This is where you control the way the QuickBooks spell checker works. You can instruct QuickBooks to check spelling automatically before saving, sending, or printing any form.

In addition, you can specify those words you want the spell checker to skip, such as Internet addresses, numbers, and all capital letters that probably indicate an abbreviation.

Tax:1099 Preferences

If you need to file 1099-Misc forms, select the Company Preferences tab of this window to access a wizard that will help you establish the 1099 form options you need. For each type of 1099 payment, you must assign an account from your chart of accounts. To make these assignments, use the Click Here link under If You Want To Map Your Accounts To Boxes On Form 1099-MISC. If you're ready to prepare your 1099s, including mapping accounts, use the Click Here link to launch the 1099 wizard (see Figure 24-8). See Chapter 18 for detailed information about configuring and issuing 1099 forms.

Time & Expenses Preferences

Use this section in the Company Preferences tab to turn on time tracking and to tell QuickBooks the first day of your work week (which becomes the first day listed on your timesheets). Read all about tracking time in Chapter 19. In addition, you can configure invoicing options, as explained in the following sections.

Mark All Time Entries As Billable

Selecting this option will automatically make hours entered in a timesheet that are associated with a customer or job billable to that customer.

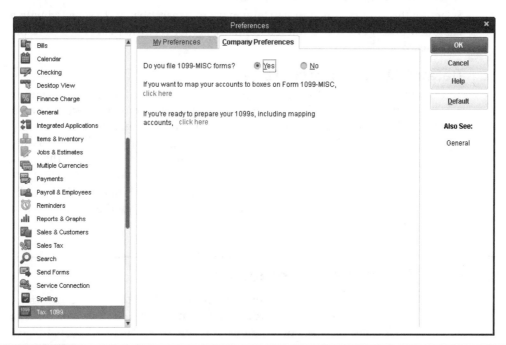

FIGURE 24-8 Use the 1099 Preferences window to launch the wizard that will guide you through the process of configuring your QuickBooks file for 1099 reporting.

Track Reimbursed Expenses As Income

Selecting this option changes the way your general ledger handles customer payments for reimbursements. When the option is enabled, the reimbursement is assigned to an income account instead of posting back to the original expense account. As a result of enabling this option, QuickBooks adds a new field to the dialog you use when you create or edit an expense account so you can enter the associated income account.

Whenever you post a vendor expense to this account and also indicate that the expense is reimbursable, the amount you charge to the customer when you create an invoice for that customer is automatically posted to the income account that's linked to this expense account.

QuickBooks requires a separate income account for each reimbursable expense. If you have multiple expense accounts for which you may receive reimbursement (a highly likely scenario), you must also create multiple income accounts for accepting reimbursed expenses. See Chapter 11 to learn how to enter expenses as reimbursable.

Mark All Expenses as Billable

Selecting this option will automatically make expenses that are associated with a customer or job billable to that customer, whether recorded via check, bill, or credit card.

Default Markup Percentage

You can preset a markup for reimbursed expenses and also for items that have both a cost and price. QuickBooks uses the percentage you enter here to automate the pricing of inventory items. When you're creating an inventory item, as soon as you enter the cost, QuickBooks automatically adds this percentage and displays the result as the price. If your pricing strategy isn't consistent, don't enable this option because you may find yourself having to frequently re-enter an item's selling price.

If you enter a default markup percentage, use the Default Markup Account field to select an account from your chart of accounts that you want the resulting markup amounts to be posted to.

Customize Transaction Templates

QuickBooks makes it easy to customize the forms you use to create transactions. Forms such as invoices, purchase orders, statements, and so on, are called *templates* in QuickBooks, and there are two options available when customizing templates.

The first allows you to create brand-new template designs from an online template gallery. You can then save these templates to your template list. The second option gives you the ability to work with and modify the appearance of an *existing* template or to create a new template based on an existing one from within the program. The focus of this section is on the second option.

You can use an existing template as the basis of a new template, copying what you like, changing what you don't like, and eliminating what you don't need. Existing templates can be customized in two ways:

- **Basic customization** Change the appearance by customizing the fonts, colors, and other output settings only—these are minor changes (a form of "window dressing") that can be made to your templates, including the built-in Intuit templates.
- **Additional customization** Customize the fields and columns that appear on the template—these are major changes and require you to create a new template with a new template name.

Basic Customization of Templates

To make minor changes to an existing template, locate and open the desired template in the Templates list by choosing Lists | Templates. Double-click the desired template to open the Basic Customization window.

You can also open a template to the Basic Customization window when you're working to create a new transaction (like an invoice, for example). In this case, on the Formatting tab located on the ribbon bar at the top of the form window, select Manage Templates. Choose the template you want to modify and click OK to open the Basic Customization window (see Figure 24-9).

P r o A d v i s o r   T i p : Templates that have the word "Intuit" in the template name are designed to work with preprinted forms you purchase from Intuit (although you can use them with blank paper or letterhead). Except for the Intuit Packing Slip, you can only perform basic customization on these templates. To use Intuit templates as the basis of additional customization, you must make a copy of the template and create a new template, as shown next.

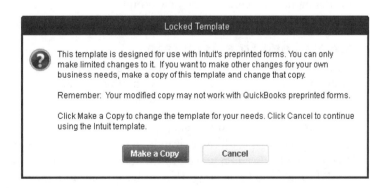

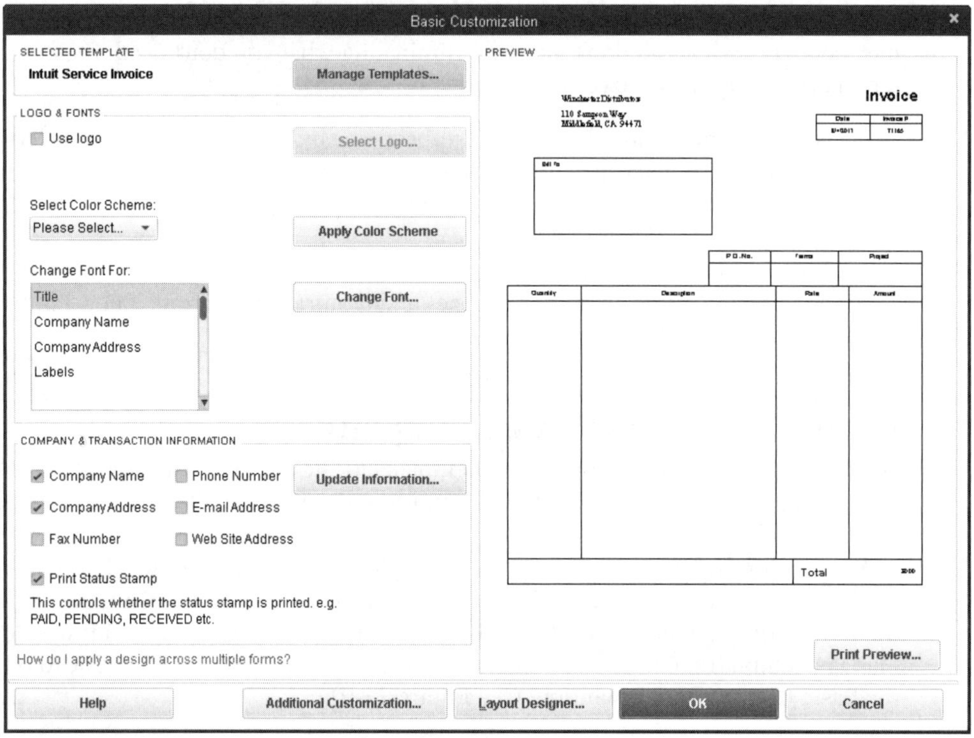

FIGURE 24-9 Change the appearance of a template in the Basic Customization dialog.

Managing Templates

Click Manage Templates to view, copy, or rename a template. The Preview pane (on the right) displays a layout of the template as it currently looks and displays the template name at the top. In the Template Name field at the top of the Preview pane, you can delete the current name (unless it's an original Intuit template) and replace it with the name you want for the new template. Clicking OK returns you to the Basic Customization dialog.

Adding a Logo to a Template

You can add your company logo to a template by selecting the Use Logo check box. Navigate to the folder that has your logo graphic file, and select the file. Use the following guidelines to add a logo to a template:

- The logo should be a square shape to fit properly on the template.
- QuickBooks accepts all the common graphic formats for your logo. However, the graphic loads when you print the template, and graphic files saved with a BMP format tend to be larger than other formats and may take quite some time

to load each time you print. The most efficient format, in terms of size and resolution, is JPG.

- Your logo appears in the upper-left corner of the form, unless you open the Layout Designer (covered later in this chapter) to reposition it.
- You won't see the logo on the screen version of the template.
- If you can't place the logo in the size and position you prefer, consider having stationery printed and using it as the paper source for the template.

Customizing Colors on a Template

You can change the color of the lines that appear on the template by selecting a color scheme from the drop-down list in the Select Color Scheme field. Click Apply Color Scheme to save the change and see its effect in the Preview pane on the right side of the dialog.

You can also change the color of any text that's printed on the form by using the features for changing fonts (covered next) and selecting a color for the font.

Customizing Fonts on a Template

To change the fonts for any elements on the template, select the element in the Change Font For list and click Change Font. Select a font, size, style (such as bold or italic), effects, or color.

Customizing the Company Information on a Template

You can select and deselect the text that appears in the name and address block of your templates. The data is taken from the Company Information dialog, which you can open by clicking Update Information to make sure that the data exists.

Printing Status Stamps on Templates

You can select or deselect the option to print the status stamp on a transaction template (PAID, RECEIVED, and so on). The status stamp prints at an angle across the center of the header section of the template. If you deselect the status stamp, you are only removing it from the printed copy of the form; the screen copy always shows the status.

Additional Customization of Templates

You can make major changes in templates to suit your needs as well as your taste. QuickBooks calls this the Additional Customization feature. Start your customization by selecting an existing template on which to base your new template. Select the Customize Data Layout button located on the Formatting tab, which is located on the ribbon bar at the top of the form's window. If you are attempting to modify an Intuit template, the Locked Template dialog appears instructing you to make a copy of the template; otherwise, the Additional Customization window opens (see Figure 24-10).

➡ ProAdvisor Recommends

The List of Templates

If you've just started using QuickBooks, you may be confused by the template names you see in the Templates list (Lists | Templates). The templates that appear in the list depend on the preferences you set and the transactions you've created.

By default, QuickBooks installs Invoice templates, a Statement template, and a Packing Slip template. You won't see a Purchase Order template unless you enable Inventory & Purchase Orders (covered earlier in this chapter) and also open the built-in Purchase Order template by choosing Vendors | Create Purchase Orders. As soon as the Create Purchase Orders transaction window opens, the Purchase Order template appears on the list (you can close the transaction window without creating a PO if your only purpose was to add the template to the list). The same convention applies to Sales Receipts, Estimates, and other QuickBooks templates.

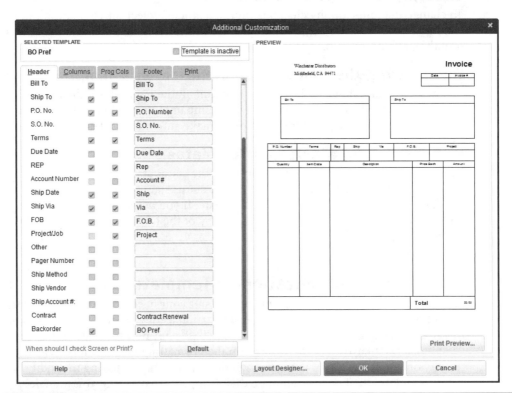

FIGURE 24-10 The Additional Customization dialog lets you point and click to redesign a template.

Notice that in Figure 24-10, the name of this template includes the text "BOPref," which refers to a custom field that was created for tracking customer preferences for back orders. This field will only display on the screen version of the template (the field serves as a guideline when filling an order), but not on the printed version that is sent to the customer.

Custom fields you create in a Names list appear in the Header section of transaction windows—custom fields you create in the Item List appear in the Columns section of transaction windows.

Customizing the Template Header

The header section of the Additional Customization dialog includes all the fields that appear above the line items in a transaction form. You can add or remove fields on the screen form, the printed form, or both. The Preview pane on the right is a preview of the printed form, and as you add or remove fields from the printed form, you see the changes reflected there.

There are some changes to the header section that you may want to make based on the way you've set up your QuickBooks company file. For example:

- If you assign account numbers to your customers, you may want to display the Account Number field (only available on the printed version).
- If you use reps, either as commissioned salespersons or as customer support contacts, you can add the Rep field to both the screen and printed versions.
- If you're tracking jobs for the majority of your customers, add the job name to the form (only available in the printed version). QuickBooks uses the term "project" because that's the commonly used term in most businesses (the exception is the construction trade, where "job" is a common term). If you refer to jobs as "jobs" with your customers, you can change the text.

Customizing the Template Columns

On the Columns tab of the Additional Customization dialog (see Figure 24-11), you can add or remove columns that appear in the line item section of the transaction form. If you created custom fields for items, they're available for any template you design.

If progress invoicing is turned on, another columns tab, called Prog Cols, is available for customizing the transaction form you use when you create a progress invoice against an estimate (to learn how to create estimates and progress invoices, read Chapter 9).

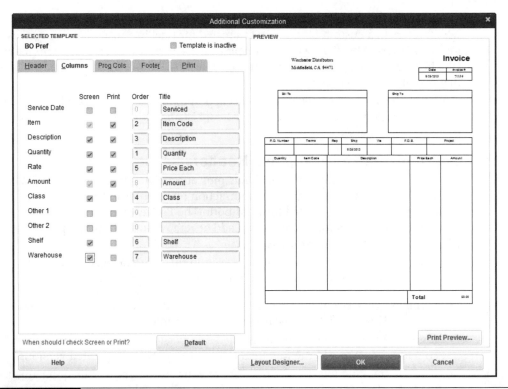

FIGURE 24-11 Add columns to specify details of the items you're including in the transaction.

Customizing the Template Footer

The Footer tab (see Figure 24-12) contains the elements that appear at the bottom of the transaction form. If you want to add fields to this section of the printed transaction form, you'll have to use the Layout Designer to maneuver the positioning because you don't have a lot of space to work with.

Setting the Print Option

On the Print tab, you can configure the printer settings for just this template by selecting the option Use Specified Printer Settings Below For This Invoice. If you want to use the same invoice printer settings that you used in your printer setup (File | Printer Setup | Invoices), you can select that option as your default.

FIGURE 24-12 Add fields from the Footer tab to add more information to the transaction form.

Using the Layout Designer

As you customize the printed forms, you can see the effects in the Preview pane. If you notice some overlapping fields, or you think the layout looks too crowded, you can use the Layout Designer to reposition the elements on the form. Click Layout Designer to open your template in the Layout Designer window, as seen in Figure 24-13.

The Layout Designer is a powerful and complicated feature, and it's beyond the scope of this book to go into deep detail about it. The more you work with it, however, the better you'll get at making it work for you. It's a good idea to make a copy of an existing invoice template and experiment on that copy before you make changes to your "live" template.

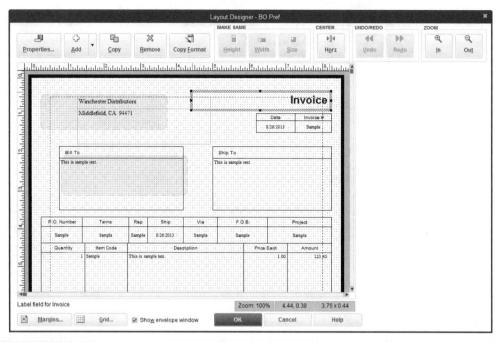

FIGURE 24-13 You can reposition the elements in the form to create your own design.

If you use window envelopes to mail your invoices, be sure the Show Envelope Window option at the bottom of the Layout Designer is selected before you start. The areas of the form that appear in envelope windows are highlighted in green. This helps you avoid moving any fields into that area.

Select any element to put a frame around it. Now you can perform an action on the frame, as follows:

- To change the size of the element, position your pointer on one of the sizing handles on the frame and then drag the handle to resize the element.
- To move an element, position your pointer inside the frame and, when your pointer turns into a four-headed arrow, drag the frame to a different location on the form.

- Double-click an element's frame to see a Properties dialog that permits a variety of changes for the selected element.

- To change the margin measurements, click the Margins button at the bottom of the Layout Designer.
- Click the Grid button to open the Grid And Snap Settings dialog, where you can eliminate the dotted line grid, change the spacing between grid lines, or turn off the Snap To Grid option (which automatically aligns objects to the nearest point on the grid).
- Use the toolbar buttons to align, resize, and zoom into the selected elements.

There are also Undo and Redo buttons, just in case.

When you finish with the Layout Designer, click OK to move back to the Additional Customization window. If everything is just the way you want it, save your new template by clicking OK. This new template name appears on the drop-down list when you create transaction forms.

Part Six

Using QuickBooks Reports, Budgets, and Planning Tools

Part Six of this book covers how to gain insight into your company's finances by using the information that you've entered into your QuickBooks file.

In Chapter 25, you'll learn how to run the reports you need to analyze your business and pay your taxes. The External Accountant, which is a special user login identity that lets your accountant examine, troubleshoot, and fix data entry problems, is also covered in this chapter. In Chapter 26, you'll find step-by-step instructions for customizing reports so they display exactly the data you and your accountant want to see. And in Chapter 27, you'll learn how to create a budget and also become familiar with the other planning and forecasting tools that come with your QuickBooks software.

Useful QuickBooks Reports and Analysis Tools

Chapter 25

In this chapter:

- The QuickBooks Report Center
- Standard financial reports
- Financial activity reports
- Company Snapshot
- The External Accountant
- Client Data Review tool

By now, you've probably already discovered how QuickBooks makes it easy for you to enter and keep track of your businesses transactions. Now it's time to run and analyze the reports that will not only help you better manage your day-to-day operations, but also give you insight into how your business is doing.

This chapter is designed to introduce you to the most common reports that QuickBooks users rely on and to explain the information contained in them. Chapter 26 builds upon what you learn in this chapter by explaining how you can customize and memorize *any* QuickBooks report with your preferred settings.

Start with the Report Center

In the Report Center, you can get a dynamic preview of the built-in reports that are available in QuickBooks. It's also where you can access reports that have been contributed by other QuickBooks users and keep track of reports that you especially like by adding them to your list of favorites. Choose Reports | Report Center or click the Reports icon on the Top Icon Bar to get there (see Figure 25-1).

There are many ways you can view samples of the reports that belong to a particular category. Start by selecting a report category from the Standard tab on the left. QuickBooks displays a sample and a short description of the reports available for that category in the main window, depending on the view you've chosen. Next, select the view in which you want to display the category. The Report Center has three view types: Carousel, List, and Grid (the default view). All views provide the same

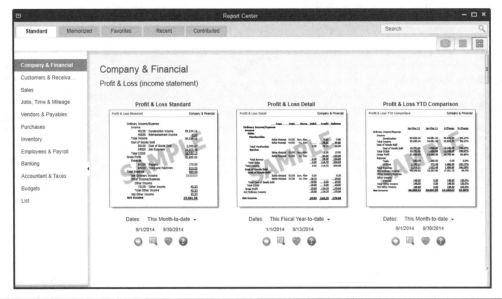

FIGURE 25-1   The Profit & Loss Standard report as seen in the Grid view in the Report Center

options and quick access to multiple reports, but they're arranged in different ways. Experiment with the different views to find the one that works best for you.

If you double-click the report display or description itself, the report opens; it's not a sample report—it's an actual report on your company.

In addition to the Standard tab that is displayed by default when the Report Center opens, four other tabs give you quick access to reports that you've memorized, chosen as favorites, and viewed most recently. You can also see reports that have either been shared by you or contributed by others.

Drill Down for Details

When you create and view a report, you can investigate the information that's shown by drilling down to the details behind the displayed totals. Position your mouse over a total, and your mouse pointer turns into a magnifying glass with the letter "Z" (for zoom). Double-click to see the details behind the number.

- If the report is a summary report, the detail report that opens is a list of transactions that made up the total on the original report. You can drill down into each listing to see the original transaction.
- If the report is a detail report, the list of individual transactions is displayed. You can drill down into each listing to see the original transaction.

Standard Financial Reports

Accountants, bookkeepers, and business owners can keep an eye on the company's health and financial status with a group of reports that are generally referred to as the *standard financial reports*.

These are also likely the reports your banker will ask to see for loans and lines of credit, and if you're selling your business, these are the initial reports the potential buyer wants to see.

Profit & Loss Report

Your Profit & Loss report is probably the one you'll run most often. It's natural to want to know if you're making any money. A Profit & Loss report is sometimes called an *income statement*. It shows the total of all your income accounts and all your expense accounts, and then puts the difference between the two totals on the last line. If you have more income than expenses, the last line is a profit; if not, that last line is a loss.

There are several variations of the Profit & Loss report available in QuickBooks. The ones most widely used are covered in the following section and can be accessed by choosing Reports | Company & Financial.

Profit & Loss Standard Report

The Profit & Loss Standard report (shown in Figure 25-2) is a basic report that follows a conventional format:

- The income is listed and totaled by both account and subaccount.
- The Cost Of Goods Sold accounts are listed, and the total is deducted from the income total to show the gross profit.
- The expenses are listed and totaled by both account and subaccount.
- The difference between the gross profit and the total expenses is displayed as your net ordinary income (or loss).

ProAdvisor Tip: Click the Collapse button on the report menu bar to show income and expense totals by parent account only. To return the report to its default format, click the Expand button to view report totals by account and subaccount.

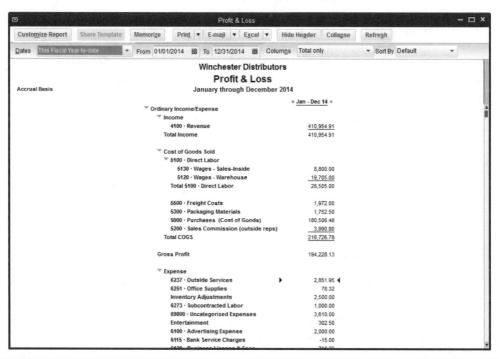

FIGURE 25-2   The Profit & Loss report is probably the report you'll run most often.

When you run a Profit & Loss report, the default date range that QuickBooks sets is the current month to date. This means that you'll need to change the date range to year to date—otherwise, you'll be looking at information from only the current month.

Click the arrow to the right of the Dates field and change the date range to This Fiscal Year-To-Date. The resulting display is what you want to see—an income statement for your business so far this year.

Profit & Loss Detail Report

The Profit & Loss Detail report lists every transaction for every account in the Profit & Loss format. This report is a good one to run if you notice some numbers that seem "not quite right" in the standard P&L, or if you just want to ensure that each and every transaction you've entered for a period of time has made its way to the account that you expected.

Profit & Loss YTD Comparison Report

The YTD (year-to-date) Comparison report compares the current month's income and expense totals with the year-to-date totals. Each income and expense account is listed.

Profit & Loss Prev Year Comparison Report

This is a Profit & Loss report for the current year to date, with an additional column that shows last year's figures for the same period. This gives you an easy way to see how your business is doing relative to the previous year. What are really useful are the two additional columns that show you the difference between the years in either dollars or percentage.

Balance Sheet

A Balance Sheet report is specifically designed to show only the totals of the Balance Sheet accounts (assets, liabilities, and equity) from your chart of accounts—information that's critical to understanding your business's financial health.

The Balance Sheet balances because it's based on the age-old accounting formula:

Total Assets = Total Liabilities + Total Equity

QuickBooks offers several Balance Sheet reports, and each of them is explained in this section. Select the one you want to see from the Report Center, or choose Reports | Company & Financial and then click one of these reports.

Balance Sheet Standard Report

The Balance Sheet Standard report lists the balance in every Balance Sheet account (unless the account has a zero balance) and subtotals each type of asset, liability, and equity in addition to reporting the totals of those three categories. By default, the report displays totals as of the fiscal year-to-date figures, but you can change the As Of date.

Balance Sheet Detail Report

This report displays every transaction in every Balance Sheet account. By default, the report covers a date range of the current month to date. Even if it's early in the month, this report is lengthy. If you change the date range to encompass a longer period (the quarter or year), the report goes on forever.

If you want to see a Balance Sheet report just to get an idea of your company's financial health, this is probably more than you wanted to know.

Balance Sheet Summary Report

This report is a quick way to see totals, and it's also the easiest way to answer the question, "How am I doing?" All the Balance Sheet accounts are subtotaled by type, as shown in Figure 25-3.

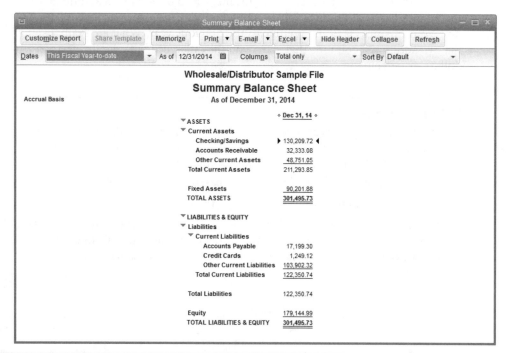

FIGURE 25-3 Check your financial health with the Balance Sheet Summary report.

Balance Sheet Prev Year Comparison Report

This report is designed to show you what your financial situation is compared to a year ago, and it displays the following four columns:

- The year-to-date balance for each Balance Sheet account
- The year-to-date balance for each Balance Sheet account for last year
- The amount of change in dollars between last year and this year
- The percentage of change between last year and this year

If you've just started using QuickBooks this year, there's little reason to run this report. Next year, however, it'll be interesting to see how you're doing compared to this year.

Trial Balance

A *trial balance* is a list of all the accounts in your chart of accounts and their current balances. It's a quick way to see what's what on an account-by-account basis. Most accountants ask to see a trial balance when they're preparing your taxes or analyzing the health of your business.

To see a trial balance, choose Reports | Accountant & Taxes | Trial Balance. Your company's trial balance is displayed on your screen, and you can scroll through it to see all the account balances. The bottom of the report shows a total for debits and a total for credits, and they're equal.

By default, the trial balance displays every account (including inactive accounts), even if an account has a zero balance. That's because most accountants want to see the entire list of accounts, and sometimes the fact that an account has a zero balance is meaningful.

Cash Flow Reports

The list of reports in the Company & Financial submenu includes two cash flow reports: Statement Of Cash Flows and Cash Flow Forecast. The difference between them is that the Statement Of Cash Flows displays historical information based on the data in your company file, and the Cash Flow Forecast looks ahead and forecasts cash flow based on the history in your company file.

Statement Of Cash Flows

The Statement Of Cash Flows report displays the history of your cash position over a given period (by default, the Dates field is set to This Fiscal Year-To-Date, but you can change the interval). This is one of the reports you'll probably be asked for by a banker or a potential buyer; it's not a report that provides quick analysis about whether you're making a profit.

This is an accrual report that self-modifies to report on a cash basis, and the lines on the report show you the adjustments that were made behind the scenes to provide cash-based totals. If you have no asset accounts that involve money owed to you—such as accounts receivable (A/R), or loans you made to others—and no liability accounts that involve money you owe—such as accounts payable, or loans—then no adjustments have to be made because you're essentially operating your business on a cash basis.

A cash flow report has several categories and, depending on the general ledger postings, QuickBooks provides category totals as follows:

- **Operating Activities** The postings involved with general business activities
- **Investing Activities** The postings involved with the acquisition and sale of fixed assets
- **Financing Activities** The postings involved with long-term liabilities and, if the business is not a C-Corp, postings of owner/partner investments in the business and draws from the business

QuickBooks uses specific accounts for this report, and you can view and modify those accounts as follows:

1. Open the Statement Of Cash Flows report.
2. Click the Classify Cash button at the top of the report window to open the Reports & Graphs Preferences window.
3. On the Company Preferences tab, click the Classify Cash button.
4. In the Classify Cash dialog, add or remove accounts or move an account to a different category.

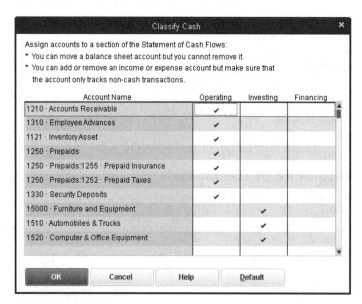

Cash Flow Forecast

The Cash Flow Forecast report predicts your cash flow as of a specific date range (by default, the next four weeks, but you can change this). The forecast predicts cash in and cash out and then displays the cash balances that result from those cash flows.

This report is based on income predicted from current receivables and outgo predicted by current payables. If your business operates mostly on a cash basis (you usually collect payment from customers at the time of the sale and you usually write direct disbursement checks instead of entering vendor bills), there's not much future cash flow for QuickBooks to predict.

This report assumes that both you and your customers pay bills based on their terms. If your customers pay late, you can tell QuickBooks to "re-predict" the flow of cash and the dates you can expect that cash by using the Delay Receipts field at the top of the report window. Enter the number of days after the due date you expect to receive money from your customers. For example, if your terms to customers are 30 Days Net, and you know from experience that most of your customers pay you in 60 days, enter **30** in the Delay Receipts field. QuickBooks has no field on the report window for you to enter the number of days you take beyond the terms your vendors offer; this report assumes you always pay on time.

Other Useful Reports

QuickBooks offers many other financial reports on your transactions that are categorized by the type of activity for those transactions. Here's a brief overview of those reports.

Sales Reports

If you choose Reports | Sales, you'll see a list of built-in reports you can open to see your sales reported in a summarized or detailed fashion. Table 25-1 explains the contents of each report. Refer to Chapter 26 to learn how these reports can be customized to include additional data or "filtered" to only display information of particular importance to you.

Vendor Reports

Choose Reports | Vendors & Payables to track financial data related to vendor payments. The list of reports in the submenu includes A/P aging, Form 1099 data, and other useful information. Many businesses find the Unpaid Bills Detail report most useful since it lists every outstanding bill and vendor credit as of the report date.

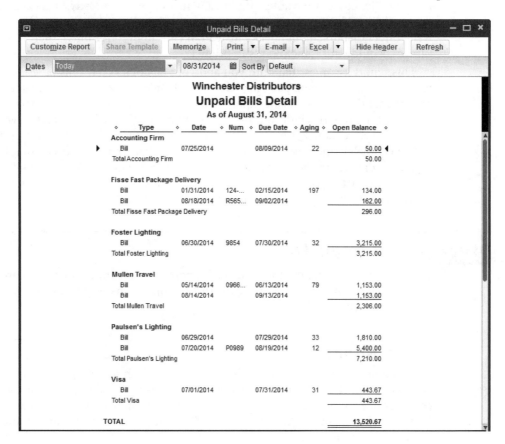

Report	Contents
Sales By Customer Summary	Total sales for each customer and job; does not include reimbursed expenses or sales tax
Sales By Customer Detail	Each transaction that's included in the Sales By Customer Summary report
Sales By Item Summary	Summary of sales, subtotaled by item type
Sales By Item Detail	Each transaction that's included in the Sales By Item Summary report
Sales By Rep Summary	Summary of sales totaled by sales rep; does not include reimbursed expenses or sales tax
Sales By Rep Detail	Each transaction that's included in the Sales By Rep summary report
Sales By Ship To Address	Totals for each unique address you ship to
Sales Graph	Bar and pie graphs of sales totals (you can display data by customers, items, and reps)
Pending Sales	All sales transactions currently marked "Pending"

TABLE 25-1 Sales Reports Built into QuickBooks

Inventory and Purchasing Reports

If you've enabled inventory tracking, choose Reports | Purchases *or* Inventory. QuickBooks provides the following useful reports:

- **Purchases Reports** These give detail on purchases you've made and can be sorted and totaled by vendor or item. Open Purchase Order reports can also be found on the Purchases submenu, and can be listed by item or customer.
- **Inventory Reports** There are several reports available here that you can use to get your inventory value and stock status as of the report date. The Inventory Valuation Detail report is one report you can use to quickly determine how

QuickBooks has calculated your current on-hand quantities and inventory asset value.

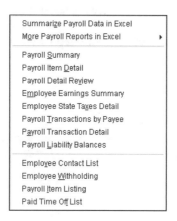

			Inventory Valuation Detail					— □ ×

Customize Report | Share Template | Memorize | Print ▼ | E-mail ▼ | Excel ▼ | Hide Header | Refresh

Dates Custom ▼ | From 01/01/2014 📅 To 12/31/2014 📅 Sort By Default ▼

Winchester Distributors
Inventory Valuation Detail
January through December 2014

Type	Date	Name	Num	Qty	Cost	On Hand	Avg Cost	Asset Value
Inventory								
Bath/Vanity Fixtures								
5029-03-55 (Brushed Nickel with Opal Glass)								
Bill	06/30/2014	Foster Lig...	9854	30	555.00	111	18.50	2,053.50
Invoice	08/15/2014	Baker's Pr...	71135	-4		107	18.50	1,979.50
Invoice	09/23/2014	Cole Home...	71090	-2		105	18.50	1,942.50
Total 5029-03-55 (Brushed Nickel with Opal Glass)						105		1,942.50
5030-03-02 (Solid Brass with Etched Glass, 2 Light)								
Invoice	10/15/2014	Thompson...	71140	-11		9	32.60	293.36
Invoice	11/05/2014	Valesha J...	71103	-4		5	32.60	162.98
Invoice	12/15/2014	Kern Light...	71136	-5		0	32.60	0.00
Total 5030-03-02 (Solid Brass with Etched Glass, 2 Light)						0		0.00
5030-04-02 (Solid Brass with Etched Glass, 4 light)								
Bill	06/30/2014	Foster Lig...	9854	50	950.00	123	19.00	2,337.00
Invoice	08/17/2014	Cole Home...	71075	-1		122	19.00	2,318.00
Invoice	08/24/2014	Cole Home...	71074	-1		121	19.00	2,299.00
Invoice	08/31/2014	Cole Home...	71073	-1		120	19.00	2,280.00
Total 5030-04-02 (Solid Brass with Etched Glass, 4 light)						120		2,280.00
6520-01-03 (White with Satin White Glass)								
Bill	06/30/2014	Foster Lig...	9854	20	300.00	54	15.00	810.00
Invoice	08/17/2014	Cole Home...	71075	-2		52	15.00	780.00
Invoice	08/24/2014	Cole Home...	71074	-2		50	15.00	750.00
Invoice	08/31/2014	Cole Home...	71073	-2		48	15.00	720.00
Invoice	10/15/2014	Thompson...	71140	-7		41	15.00	615.00
Invoice	12/03/2014	Lavery Lig...	71139	-15		26	15.00	390.00

Employees & Payroll Reports

The Employees & Payroll submenu provides a number of reports that range from important to useful, depending on how you and your accountant want to analyze your financials.

Summarize Payroll Data in Excel
More Payroll Reports in Excel ▸

Payroll Summary
Payroll Item Detail
Payroll Detail Review
Employee Earnings Summary
Employee State Taxes Detail
Payroll Transactions by Payee
Payroll Transaction Detail
Payroll Liability Balances

Employee Contact List
Employee Withholding
Payroll Item Listing
Paid Time Off List

Banking Reports

To track your bank balance activities, you can display reports on them, including check and deposit detail data, missing check numbers, and reconciliations. See Chapter 13 to learn about reconciliation processes and troubleshooting reconciliation problems with the reconciliation reports in this Reports submenu.

Reporting by Class

If you've enabled class tracking and have assigned classes to all of your income and expense transactions, you can run two types of reports:

- Individual class reports
- Reports on all classes

Reporting on a Single Class

To report on a single class, open the Class List and select the class on which you want to report. Then press CTRL-Q to open a QuickReport on the class. This report will give you a list of all the transactions that have been assigned to that class. When the Class QuickReport appears, you can change the date range or customize the report as needed. Using the Sort By drop-down list, you can also sort the report by type to group together transactions of the same type (such as invoice, bill, and so on).

Reporting on All Classes

If you want to see one report on all the classes, open the Class List and click the Reports button at the bottom of the list window. Choose Reports On All Classes, and then select Profit & Loss By Class, Profit & Loss Unclassified, or Graphs. The Graphs menu item offers a choice of an Income & Expenses graph or a Budget Vs. Actual graph.

- **Profit & Loss By Class Report**   The Profit & Loss By Class report is the same as a standard Profit & Loss report, except that each class uses a separate column. The Totals column provides the usual P&L information for your company for each class that you've created. This report is also available on the submenu by choosing Reports | Company & Financial.
- **Profit & Loss Unclassified Report**   This report displays P&L totals for transactions in which items were not assigned to a class. You can drill down to the transactions and add the appropriate class to each transaction. (This will likely be a rather lengthy report if you enable class tracking after you've already begun using QuickBooks.)
- **Graphs That Use Class Data**   You can also display graphs for income and expenses sorted by class or a graph that compares budget versus actual figures sorted by class.

Accountant & Taxes Reports

The reports that you or your accountant will need for year end or to identify entries that may need adjusting can be found on this submenu under the Reports menu. Choose Reports | Accountant & Taxes.

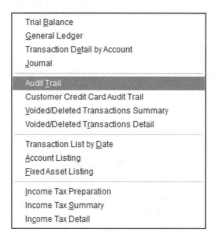

Trial Balance
General Ledger
Transaction Detail by Account
Journal

Audit Trail
Customer Credit Card Audit Trail
Voided/Deleted Transactions Summary
Voided/Deleted Transactions Detail

Transaction List by Date
Account Listing
Fixed Asset Listing

Income Tax Preparation
Income Tax Summary
Income Tax Detail

Audit Trail Report

QuickBooks has a feature called the Audit Trail that is automatically—and behind the scenes—keeping track of all the accounting transactions that you (and all your QuickBooks users) add, modify, or delete in your company file. The Audit Trail report lists these transactions along with the date; the time; and the user who entered, modified, or deleted the transaction. The Audit Trail report should be your go-to report if you notice any suspicious activity in your QuickBooks file (like missing or changed transactions). Choose Reports | Accountant & Taxes | Audit Trail.

Voided and Deleted Transactions Reports

QuickBooks offers two reports you can use to track voided and deleted transactions. Both reports are available by choosing Reports | Accountant & Taxes and then selecting either of these reports: Voided/Deleted Transactions Summary or Voided/Deleted Transactions Detail.

Voided/Deleted Transactions Summary Report

This report displays a summary of all voided and deleted transactions in the selected period. The report shows the current state (void or deleted) and the original state (including the amount) of each affected transaction.

Voided/Deleted Transactions Detail History Report

This report provides more information about both the original transaction and the change. In addition to the information provided by the Voided/Deleted Transactions Summary report, this report displays the credit and debit postings and the posting accounts. If items (including payroll items) were involved in the transaction, they're also displayed.

Company Snapshot

You can get a quick answer to the question "How's business?" in the Company Snapshot window (see Figure 25-4). Click Snapshots from the Icon Bar to open this window.

In addition to displaying an easy-to-understand summary of the money that's moved in and out, this customizable window provides information on tasks you should perform, account balances, and A/R and A/P data by customer/vendor. Clicking the Add Content link at the top of the window allows you to add graphs and tables to your "dashboard." Double-clicking an area of interest in a graph or table will display a more detailed report or bring you to an account's register. You can also modify the report content (such as date ranges), rearrange the positions, or completely remove a graph or table from the Snapshot window.

FIGURE 25-4 View a summary of your financial status using the Company Snapshot.

For example, to see details about a specific customer's A/R balance, double-click the customer name in the Customers Who Owe Money listing to display an Open Balance report for that customer, sorted and totaled by job.

In addition, selecting the Payments or Customer tab opens new snapshot windows that give you quick access to the details on money due your business and the particulars on the customers that you do business with (like how long they've been customers and how long, on average, they take to pay you). To view more detail on any of the information presented in the snapshot view, just double-click an element.

The data displayed in the Company Snapshot window is always appropriate for the permissions granted to the current user. If the user does not have permission to see sensitive financial data, no bank balances appear in the Account Balances section of the window. In addition, the Income And Expense Trend graph section has no data; instead, the user sees a message explaining that he or she needs permission to view the area. Various elements of the window are displayed or hidden, depending on the current user's permissions. (Learn about configuring users and permissions in Chapter 8.)

External Accountant

An External Accountant is a specific type of user who has the same rights as the QuickBooks Admin but with the following exceptions:

- The External Accountant cannot create, edit, or remove users.
- The External Accountant cannot view customer credit card numbers if the QuickBooks Credit Card Protection feature is enabled (covered in Chapter 3).

You should create an External Accountant user so that when your accountant (or a bookkeeper from your accountant's office) comes to your office, the Client Data Review tools (discussed in the next section) are available.

Creating an External Accountant

To create a user who is an External Accountant, you must be logged into QuickBooks as the Admin (only the QuickBooks Admin can create users).

1. Choose Company | Set Up Users And Passwords | Set Up Users.
2. In the User List dialog, select Add User.
3. Enter the user name and password, and click Next.
4. Select External Accountant and click Next.
5. QuickBooks asks you to confirm this action—click Yes.
6. Click Finish to create the External Accountant.

Converting an Existing User to an External Accountant

Many companies have already set up a user name for the accountant. Even if the accountant's login provides full permissions, the Client Data Review tool isn't available on the Company menu unless an External Accountant is logged in (except in Premier Accountant Edition). You can edit the accountant's user account to convert it to an External Accountant.

Select the accountant's user account and click Edit User. Don't change the user name and password data. Click Next, and in the next window, select External Accountant and follow the prompts to save this user name as an External Accountant.

Client Data Review

The Client Data Review tool is only available via the Company menu when a user logs into your QuickBooks file as an External Accountant.

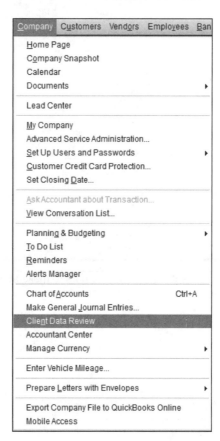

Your accountant can use this tool to examine your QuickBooks data and troubleshoot any data entry mistakes or other potential problems in your company file (see Figure 25-5). In addition, any changes made by the External Accountant during a review are separated from the changes made by regular QuickBooks user, including the Admin user, in the Audit Trail report.

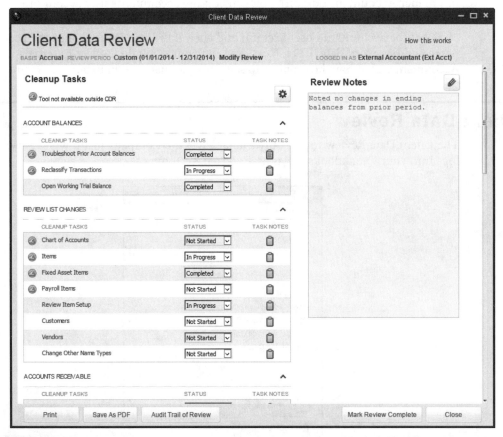

FIGURE 25-5 Your accountant can review your data to make sure your financial information is correct.

Modifying and Creating Reports

n this chapter:

- Use the report customization tools
- Memorize customized reports
- Share report templates

QuickBooks offers report customization tools that allow you to work with and view your financial information in the way that makes the most sense for you. Using these tools, you can select and sort almost any piece of information stored in your QuickBooks company file, from the smallest detail to the broadest overview. This chapter covers where to find and how to use these report customization tools.

Customization Starts with a Standard Report

All report customization efforts start with opening one of the standard QuickBooks reports. For this discussion, the Sales By Customer Detail report is opened with the date range set for a full year. Figure 26-1 shows you what it looks like before any customization.

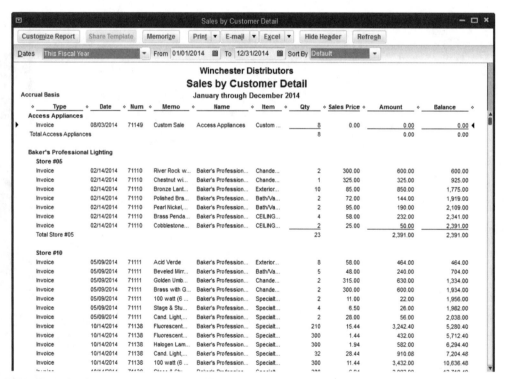

FIGURE 26-1 This report has a lot of detail, but sometimes you won't need all this information; other times, you may need slightly different data.

Click the Customize Report button to open the Modify Report dialog. This is where you begin the process of customizing the format and content of the report. Each part of the Modify Report dialog is discussed in the following sections.

The Display Tab

The Display tab (see Figure 26-2) is in the foreground when you open the Modify Report dialog, and it's filled with customization options. Some of these options are also right on the report window itself, such as the Dates and Sort By fields.

FIGURE 26-2 Use the Display tab to determine what type of data appears on the report and how it's sorted.

▶▶ ProAdvisor Recommends

QuickBooks Report Types

Built-in QuickBooks reports come in two flavors: summary and detail. A summary report displays summarized transactions that are grouped together and show a single total for a reporting group. The Display tab in this type of report will show customization options that allow you to compare current and previous periods, calculate percentages of an account total in relation to others listed in a row or a column, and change how the information is totaled and displayed in the report.

Detail reports display the individual transactions that make up the totals for a reporting group. In addition to allowing you to change how the information is totaled and displayed in a report, the Display tab allows you to add or remove columns from the report that make up the report totals.

Selecting the Report Basis

You can select accrual or cash basis for most QuickBooks reports:

- When you run a cash basis report, the report only shows actual cash transactions. This means that, for example, an invoice (revenue) won't show on a report if a customer has not yet paid you, and a bill (expense) won't appear on the report if you have not yet paid the vendor for that bill.
- When you run an accrual basis report, the report shows all the transactions you've entered. This means that, for example, revenue is reflected in the report when you create an invoice, and expenses are reflected when you enter a bill.

By default, QuickBooks displays financial reports as accrual-based reports because accrual-based reports are more useful for getting an overview of the state of your business. However, if you file taxes on a cash basis, a cash-based report is easier to use for tax preparation.

Selecting Columns

The real power in the Display tab is in the Columns list (which exists only in detail reports, not in summary reports). You can select and deselect columns so the report displays only the information you need.

For example, in this report, you may not care about the contents of the Memo field but you'd like to know whether the invoice is paid. In the Columns list, deselect Memo and select Paid, and then click OK to return to the report where the Memo column is gone and the appropriate data ("Paid" or "Unpaid") appears in the Paid column.

ProAdvisor Tip: Any custom fields you created appear in the Columns list, which adds even more power to your ability to customize reports in a meaningful way.

Advanced Options

Some reports have an Advanced button on the Display tab of the Modify Report dialog to open the Advanced Options dialog, which lets you specify the way QuickBooks selects data for the report.

The options you see on the Advanced Options dialog may vary, depending on the report. The following sections describe what you might see.

Include Option

The following options determine which accounts appear in transaction detail reports:

- **All**   All accounts, whether or not the account had postings in the date range selected for the report
- **In Use**   Only those accounts that had postings in the date range selected for the report

Open Balance/Aging Options

The following options specify the way QuickBooks calculates an open balance in an aging report:

- **Current (Faster)**   Displays the open balance as of today, including all payments received through today's date
- **Report Date**   Displays the open balance as of the ending date of the report, and payments received after the ending date of the report are not included in the calculation

Display Rows Options

These options (typically found in summary reports) specify the rows to include or exclude, as follows:

- **Active**   Only rows in which some financial activity occurred, which includes amounts of $0.00 if that total resulted from financial transactions
- **All**   All rows, regardless of activity or balance
- **Non-Zero**   Only rows in which activity occurred and where the amounts are other than zero

Display Columns Options

These options (also typically found in summary reports) specify whether to include or exclude columns based on whether financial activity occurred in the time frame specified for the report, as follows:

- **Active Only**   Columns in which some financial activity occurred, which includes amounts of $0.00 if that total resulted from financial transactions
- **All**   All columns, regardless of activity or balance
- **Non-Zero**   Only columns in which activity occurred and where the amounts are other than zero

Reporting Calendar Options

These options specify the calendar basis of the report, as follows:

- **Fiscal Year**   Uses the fiscal year as specified in the Company Info window, starting with the first month of the fiscal year. For example, if your fiscal year begins in October, configuring the report's date range to First Fiscal Quarter displays transactions from October through December.
- **Calendar Year**   Uses the calendar year (starts in January).
- **Tax Year**   Uses a year that starts in the first month of your company's tax year, as specified in the Company Info window.

ProAdvisor Tip: Some Budget reports (like the Budget Overview) have a Show Only Rows And Columns With Budgets option, which you can use to customize a report so it displays only accounts that are used in your budgets.

The Filters Tab

The Filters tab (see Figure 26-3) gives you a robust set of tools that you can use to customize a report to display the exact information that you want it to. Some examples are covered here, but I encourage you to explore all the options in this tab to get a feel for its capabilities and power.

For the sales report used in our previous example, suppose you want to see only those transactions that are higher than a certain amount. Refer to Figure 26-4 for this example.

1. Select Amount in the Filter list. The filter changes to reflect the options available for the Amount item.
2. Select the greater than or equal to (> =) option.
3. Enter the amount on which to filter the transaction—in this example, $1000.00.
4. Press TAB to add the filter to the Current Filter Choices list.
5. Click OK to return to the report, where the contents have changed to match your filter.

FIGURE 26-3 Change what's reported by filtering the data to meet your own criteria.

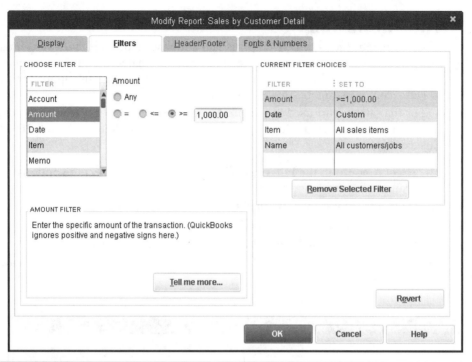

FIGURE 26-4 You can create filters to show precisely the information you want to see.

If you want to see only certain types of transactions on the report, use the Transaction Type filter to select the type you want to see; for example, in this report on sales and customers, you might want to see only credit memos. At that point, you've effectively created a "Credit Memos By Customer Detail" report. This is an example of the kind of report you memorize so you can use it frequently (memorizing customized reports is covered later in this chapter).

If you select multiple filters, make sure they don't interfere with each other. In this discussion, I mentioned filtering for amounts and also for transaction type. If you were following along and creating the same filters I created, at this point, you're seeing only credit memos that exceed the amount you entered in the amount filter.

If you want to see all credit memos, select the Amount filter in the Current Filter Choices list and click Remove Selected Filter.

Keep in mind that each filter has its own options. As you add and configure filters and notice the effect on your reports, you'll learn to use filters effectively.

Customize Report Headers and Footers

You can customize what appears on the header and footer of your report by changing the options on the Header/Footer tab, shown in Figure 26-5. The options you set here have no bearing on the figures in the report; they are simply a descriptive label on the report that appears in either the header or footer. While most of the fields are self-explanatory, the most frequently used settings are described next.

In the Show Header Information section:

- To display the date and/or time the report was prepared, select the Date or Time Prepared check box.
- To display the report basis, select the Report Basis check box. Your options are either Cash or Accrual.
- To remove an informational line from the header, clear the check box for that line.
- If you want the header information to appear only on the first page of the report, clear the Print Header On Pages After First Page check box.

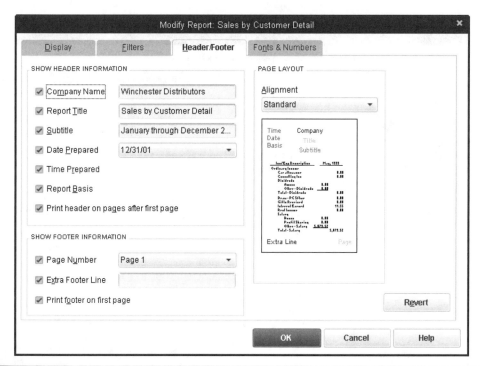

FIGURE 26-5 Customize the information that appears on the top and bottom of the report page using the Header/Footer tab.

In the Show Footer Information section:

- Click the drop-down menu next to Page Number to choose a different numbering style.
- Clear the Page Number check box to remove page numbering altogether.
- Fill in the Extra Footer Line field to add an extra line of information below the page number.
- Clear the Print Footer On First Page check box if you don't want the footer to appear on the first page.

Customize Report Fonts and Numbers

The Fonts & Numbers tab, shown in Figure 26-6, lets you further customize your report by changing fonts and also giving you control over the way numbers display on the report. Use The Change Font For list to select an element (like a column label or report totals) of the report that you want to change the font size or style for.

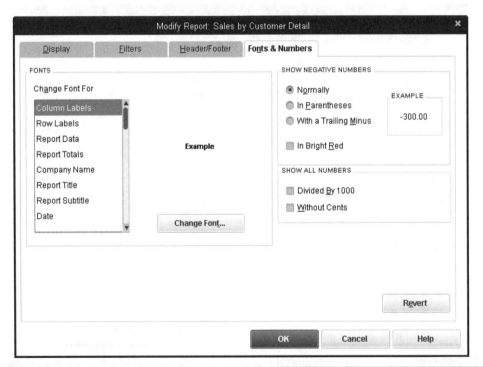

FIGURE 26-6 Change the fonts and format of the data in the report.

On the right side of the Fonts & Numbers tab, you can control the way numbers display and print on your report. Select a method for showing negative numbers. If you wish, you can also select a method for displaying all the numbers on the report.

- **Divided By 1000** Reduces the size of the numbers by showing them as multiples of 1,000. This is useful for companies that report seven- and eight-digit numbers.
- **Without Cents** Eliminates the decimal point and the two digits to the right of the decimal point from every amount. Only the dollars show, not the cents. QuickBooks rounds the cents to the nearest dollar. (Accountants frequently enter numbers in this manner for tax preparation purposes.)

Memorize Customized Reports

After you've customized a report to display the information you want in the manner in which you want it, you can avoid the need to go through all this work again by memorizing the report.

> **ProAdvisor Tip:** Before you memorize a report, change its name in the Header/Footer tab so when you use it in the future you know exactly what you're looking at.

Click the Memorize button on the report's button bar to open the Memorize Report window, where you can give this customized report a name. QuickBooks gives you the option to save the report in a report group and to share the report you've just customized with others (both of these options are discussed in this chapter).

By default, QuickBooks uses the report name in the Header/Footer tab. If you didn't change that title, be sure to use a reference to the report type in the memorized name. If you use a name such as My Report, you'll have no idea what the report displays.

Memorize Report	✕
Name: Sales by Customer Detail - Over $1000.00	
☑ Save in Memorized Report Group: Customers ▼	
☑ Share this report template with others	
OK Cancel	

Using a Memorized Report

Open a memorized report by choosing Reports | Memorized Reports from the QuickBooks menu bar and selecting the report from the submenu.

When you open the report, all your customized settings are the way you configured them, but the data changes to reflect up-to-date information. Incidentally, it's not uncommon for experienced QuickBooks users to open a memorized report, look at the data, and think, "Hmm, this makes me think that I'd like to know more about X than Y when I do my quarterly analysis." When that happens, use your memorized report as the basis of another customized report, and memorize that one, too.

Using Memorized Report Groups

After you discover the power available in creating and memorizing customized reports, you may find yourself creating special-data reports like crazy. After a while, it can become difficult to select the report you need in the list of memorized reports. To save time and confusion, QuickBooks has a handy feature called Memorized Reports Groups to help. These report groups let you store reports by category, which makes it easier to locate exactly the report you need.

Creating a Memorized Report Group

Memorized report groups are displayed in the Memorized Report List window, as well as on the submenu you see when you select Memorized Reports on the Reports menu. However, to create or manipulate groups, you have to work in the Memorized Report List window.

1. Choose Reports | Memorized Reports | Memorized Report List to open the Memorized Report List window.

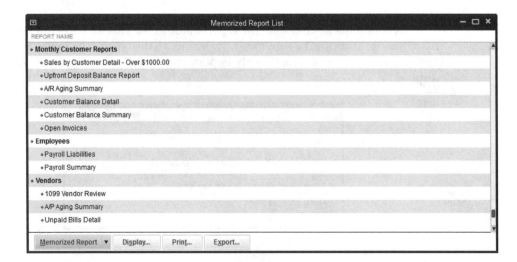

2. Click the Memorized Report button at the bottom of the window to display the window's menu, and choose New Group. Enter a name for this group in the New Memorized Report Group dialog and click OK. The group you created appears in the window list, and its listing is boldfaced. Continue to add groups to reflect the types of memorized reports you've already created or expect to create in the future.

ProAdvisor Tip: Choose a name that fits the category for the group you're creating. Common names for these groups are Year-End, Monthly, and so on. The more straightforward the name, the easier it is to place reports in the group and find those reports when you need them.

Moving Existing Memorized Reports into Groups

Start by moving your existing memorized reports into the appropriate groups, and then you can save reports you memorize directly in the right group (covered next). You can use either of the following methods to move a report into a group:

- **Edit each report to add the name of the group.** Select the report's listing and press CTRL-E. Select the Save In Memorized Report Group option, and then select the appropriate group from the drop-down list.
- **Drag each report to a group by indenting the report name under the group name.** First, drag each report listing (using the diamond icon to the left of the report name) so it's under the group listing, and then drag to the right, indenting the report name under the group name.

Note that any report listing indented under a group listing is automatically a member of that group.

ProAdvisor Tip: You can drag listings to groups only if the Report Name column heading bar at the top of the window is the only column heading. If you see a column to the left that has a diamond as the heading, click the diamond to hide that column. (To reverse the process, click the Report Name heading to reveal the diamond.)

Saving a Memorized Report in a Group

After you've created groups, you can save memorized reports directly to a group. When you've perfected the customizations you need, click Memorize on the report window. In the Memorize Report dialog, enter the report name, select the Save In Memorized Report Group option, and then select the appropriate group from the drop-down list.

Processing Report Groups

One of the cool things about creating groups for your memorized reports is that QuickBooks makes it easy to process all the reports in a group at once. You can print all the reports in one fell swoop or display all the reports (and then export them to Excel for your accountant).

For example, if you've created reports that are important at the end of each month or each quarter and placed them in a group named End of Month or End of Quarter, you can display or print all the reports with a single mouse click.

To process a group of reports, double-click the group's listing in the Memorized Report List window to open the Process Multiple Reports dialog shown in Figure 26-7. You can deselect any report you don't need at the moment.

Adding Standard Reports to Memorized Reports Groups

Often, the report you want to include in a group is a standard, built-in report, available on the Reports menu. To add the report to a group, open the standard report and click the Memorize button. In the Memorize Report dialog, put the report into the appropriate group.

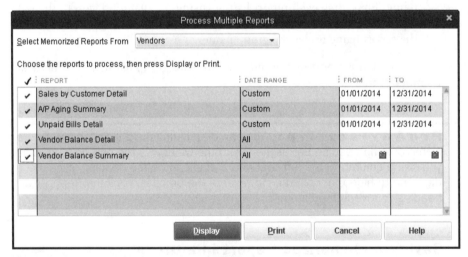

FIGURE 26-7 When it's time to review your businesses performance at month's end, print everything you need.

Sharing Reports You've Customized

It's nice to share—and when you modify a report, you can share its template (meaning only the customized report structure you've created and not your company's actual financial data) with other QuickBooks users. Simply click the Share Template button at the top of the report window and give your report a title and description. You can decide if you want to share the report with the rest of the QuickBooks world.

Your shared report will then be listed on the Memorized tab in the Report Center (covered in Chapter 25). What's more, you can access reports that others have decided to share. In the Report Center, select the Contributed tab. Be sure to check in from time to time to see what reports may have been added by other QuickBooks users in your industry.

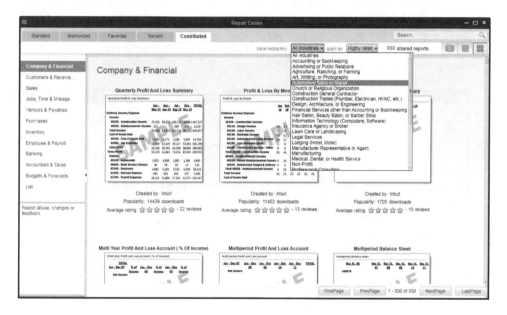

➡ **ProAdvisor Recommends**

Exporting Your Report Data to Excel

This chapter points out the many ways you can work with and customize standard reports inside QuickBooks. But there may be times when you'll need to perform some additional analysis of your QuickBooks data or even change the appearance of a report in ways that QuickBooks itself doesn't allow. The ability to easily send the contents of a QuickBooks report to Excel enhances the power of QuickBooks reports and the value of all the important information that you enter into QuickBooks every day.

At the top of every report window is an Excel drop-down menu that has two options: Create New Worksheet or Update Existing Worksheet (as shown next). If you choose the first option, QuickBooks can either create a new file (workbook) that contains a new worksheet, or it can create a new worksheet in an existing workbook. If you choose the second option, QuickBooks opens a window that allows you to browse to an existing Excel workbook. QuickBooks can send the report information and update the existing Excel report data accordingly, using much of the existing formats and formulas in the workbook.

Using the QuickBooks Budget and Planning Tools

In this chapter:

- Create a budget
- Report on budget versus actual figures
- Export budgets
- Project cash flow

A budget is a tool for tracking your business's progress against your plans. A well-prepared budget can also help you decide when it's best to make a major purchase, hire additional staff, or draw money out of your business account.

The ability to project profitability and cash flow by using actual data and then applying "what if" scenarios helps you decide whether you can increase or decrease expenses and prices. How to make the budgeting and planning tools built into QuickBooks work for you is what this chapter is all about.

How QuickBooks Handles Budgets

Before you begin creating a budget, you need to know how QuickBooks manages budgets and the processes connected to them. This section presents an overview of the QuickBooks budget features so you can understand them and keep them in mind when you create your budgets.

Types of Budgets

QuickBooks offers several types of budgets:

- Budgets based on your Balance Sheet accounts
- Profit & Loss budgets based on your income and expense accounts
- Profit & Loss budgets based on income and expense accounts and a customer or job
- Profit & Loss budgets based on income and expense accounts and a class

Profit & Loss budgets can be created from scratch or by using the actual figures from the previous year. The latter option, of course, works only if you've upgraded to QuickBooks 2014 from an earlier version.

Budget Data Is Saved Automatically

In QuickBooks, once you begin creating a budget, the data you record is stored in the budget window and reappears whenever you open that window. You create a budget by choosing Company | Planning & Budgeting | Set Up Budgets.

You can create only one of each type of budget for the same year. For example, if you create a Profit & Loss budget, enter and record some figures, and then decide to start all over by launching the Create New Budget wizard, you can't create a new Profit & Loss budget for the same year. Instead of creating a new budget, the wizard displays the data you already configured. You have no way of telling QuickBooks, "Okay, save that one; I'm going to do another one with different figures." You can change the figures, but the changes replace the original figures. You're editing a budget; you're not creating a new budget document.

Creating Multiple Budgets

Once you've created your first budget, regardless of type, the next time you select Company | Planning & Budgeting | Set Up Budgets, the budget window opens with the last budget you created.

If the budget is a Profit & Loss or Balance Sheet budget, you cannot create a second budget of the same type for the same year. However, you can create a budget of a different type, such as Profit & Loss with Customer:Job or Profit & Loss with Class. To do so, click the Create New Budget button in the budget window and go through the wizard to select different criteria (Customer:Job or Class).

After you've created a Customer:Job budget or a Class budget, you can create another budget using a different customer or job or a different class (or using different accounts for the same customer, job, or class). See the sections "Customer:Job Budgets" and "Class Budgets" for instructions on creating multiple budgets of those types.

Deleting a Budget

QuickBooks lets you delete a budget. This means if you want to create multiple budgets of the same type (perhaps you feel better if you have a "Plan B" budget), you have a workaround to the "no two budgets of the same type" rule. Export the original budget to Microsoft Excel, and then delete the original budget and start the process again. See the section "Work with Budget Data Outside of QuickBooks" later in this chapter.

To delete a budget, choose Edit | Delete Budget from the QuickBooks menu bar while the budget window is open.

Understanding the Budget Window

Before you start entering figures, you need to learn how to manage your work using the buttons on the budget window:

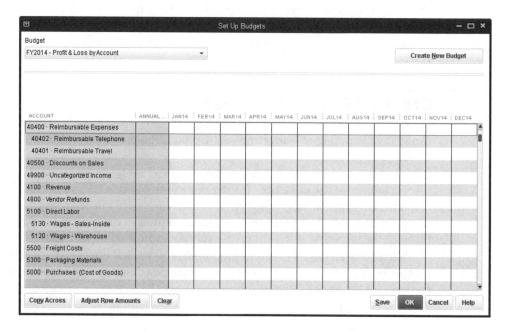

- **Clear** Deletes all figures in the budget window—you cannot use this button to clear a row or column.
- **Save** Records the current figures and leaves the window open so you can continue to work.
- **OK** Records the current figures and closes the window.
- **Cancel** Closes the window without offering to record the figures.
- **Create New Budget** Starts the budget process anew, opening the Create New Budget wizard. If you've entered any data, QuickBooks asks if you want to record your budget before closing the window. If you record your data (or have previously recorded your data with the Save button), when you start anew, the budget window opens with the same recorded data, and you can change the figures.

The other buttons in the budget window are used when you're entering data, and they're covered later in this chapter in the section "Enter Budget Amounts."

Tasks to Perform Before You Start Your Budget

Before you create a budget, you need to check the following details:

- Make sure the accounts you need exist; adding accounts while you're working in a budget doesn't work properly because you won't see the accounts unless you close and reopen the budget.
- The first month of the budget must be the same as the first month of your fiscal year.
- All the accounts you want to include in the budget must be active; inactive accounts aren't available in the budget window.

Profit & Loss Budgets

The most common and useful budget you can create is a Profit & Loss budget, which helps you plan for future income and expenses. If you've set up a well-thought-out chart of accounts, creating this type of budget is quite easy.

1. Choose Company | Planning & Budgeting | Set Up Budgets. If this is the first budget you're creating, the Create New Budget wizard opens to walk you through the process. (If you've already created a budget, the Set Up Budgets window appears with your existing budget loaded. Click Create New Budget to launch the Create New Budget wizard.)

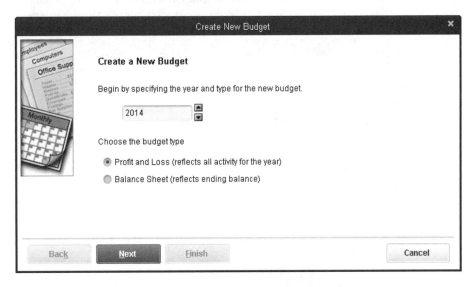

➡ ProAdvisor Recommends

A Word About Balance Sheet Budgets

A Balance Sheet budget can be challenging to build because it's difficult to predict the amounts for most Balance Sheet accounts—with the exception of fixed assets and loans. In fact, the transactions that affect fixed assets and loans are usually planned and therefore don't need budget-to-reality comparisons to allow you to keep an eye on them.

If you still feel you need to create a Balance Sheet budget, choose Company | Planning & Budgeting | Set Up Budgets. If this is your first budget, the Create New Budget wizard opens. Otherwise, when an existing budget appears, click the Create New Budget button. When the Create New Budget wizard opens, select the year for which you want to create the budget and select the Balance Sheet option. Then click Next, and because the next window has no options, there's nothing for you to do except click Finish. The budget window opens, listing all your Balance Sheet accounts, and you can enter the budget figures.

See the following sections on creating Profit & Loss budgets to learn the detailed procedures for entering budget figures.

2. Enter the year for which you're creating the budget and select the Profit And Loss option.

3. Click Next and select No Additional Criteria for this budget. Creating budgets that include customers or classes is covered later in this chapter.

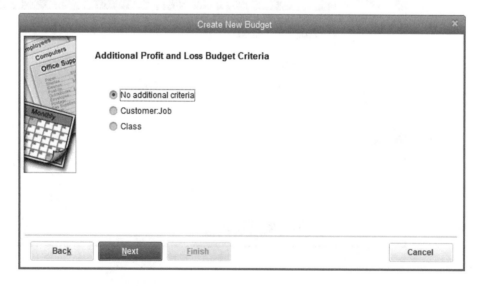

4. Click Next to choose between creating a budget from scratch or from the figures from last year's activities, and then select the option to create a budget from scratch.

5. Click Finish to open the budget window, where all your income and expense accounts are displayed (see Figure 27-1).

Enter Budget Amounts

To create budget figures for an account, select the account and then click in the column of the first month for which you want to budget. Enter the budget figure, press TAB to move to the next month, and enter the appropriate amount. Repeat until all the months for this account have your budget figures. As you enter each monthly amount and press TAB, QuickBooks automatically calculates and displays the annual total for the account (see Figure 27-2).

Using Budget Entry Shortcuts

To save you from having to manually complete some of the more repetitive tasks when entering budget figures, QuickBooks provides the following shortcuts (refer to Figure 27-2).

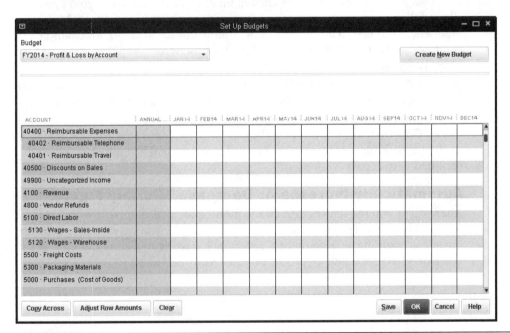

FIGURE 27-1   All active income and expense accounts are available for your Profit & Loss budget.

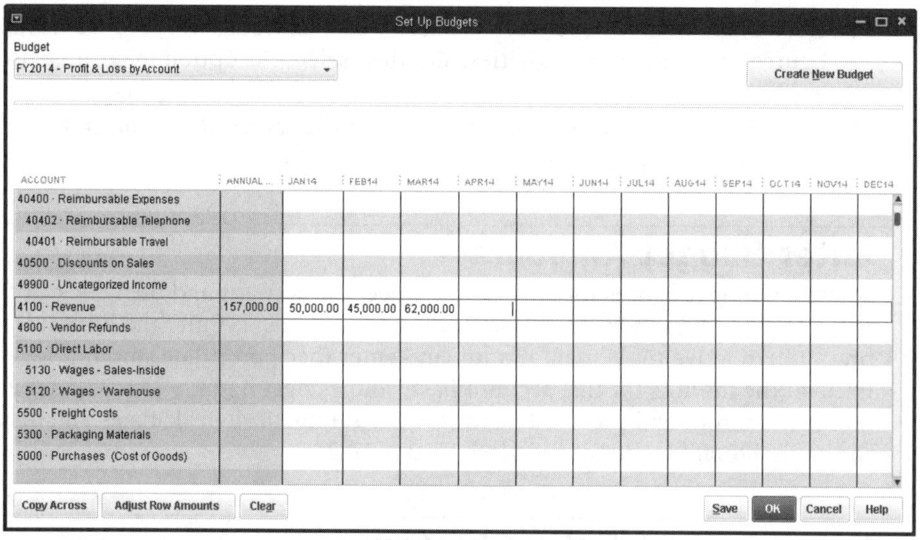

FIGURE 27-2 QuickBooks takes care of tracking the running totals.

Copy Numbers Across the Months

To copy a monthly figure from the current month (the month where your cursor is) to all the following months, enter the figure and then click Copy Across button. The numbers are copied to all the rest of the months of the year. So, for example, if you enter your rent in the first month and click Copy Across, you'll save yourself a lot of manual entry time!

However, suppose your landlord sends you a notice that your rent is increasing beginning in July. To adjust the July–December budget figures, just move your cursor to July, enter the new rate, and click Copy Across.

The Copy Across button is also the only way to clear a row. Delete the figure in the first month (or enter a zero) and click Copy Across. The entire row is now blank (or filled with zeros).

Automatically Increase or Decrease Monthly Figures

After you've entered figures into all the months on an account's row, you can raise or lower monthly figures automatically. For example, you may want to raise an income account by an amount or a percentage starting in a certain month because you expect to sign a new customer or a new contract.

Select the first month that needs the adjustment, and click the Adjust Row Amounts button to open the Adjust Row Amounts dialog.

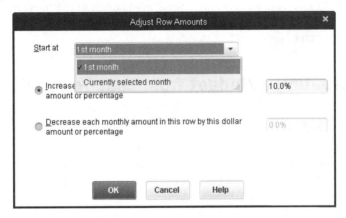

Choose 1st Month or Currently Selected Month as the starting point for the calculations:

- You can choose 1st Month no matter where your cursor is on the account's row.
- You must click in the column for the appropriate month if you want to choose Currently Selected Month (you can click the first month to make that the currently selected month).
- To increase or decrease the amount in the selected month and all the months following by a specific amount, enter the amount.
- To increase or decrease the amount in the selected month and all columns to the right by a percentage, enter the percentage rate and the percentage sign.

Compound the Changes

If you select Currently Selected Month, the Adjust Row Amounts dialog adds an option named Enable Compounding.

When you enable compounding, the calculations for each month are increased or decreased based on a formula starting with the currently selected month and taking into consideration the resulting change in the previous month. QuickBooks can calculate a compounded increase (or decrease) using a dollar amount or percentage.

Creating a Budget from Last Year's Data

If you used QuickBooks last year, you can create a budget based on last year's figures. To use last year's real data as the basis of your budget:

1. Open the Create New Budget wizard by choosing Company | Planning & Budgeting | Set Up Budgets. When the Create New Budget wizard opens, enter the year for which you're creating the budget, and select the Profit And Loss budget option. Click Next.
2. Select any additional criteria, such as a customer, job, or class. Click Next.
3. Select the option to create the budget from the previous year's actual data, and click Finish.

The budget window opens with last year's actual data used for the budget figures. For each account that had activity, the ending monthly balances are entered in the appropriate month. You can change any figures you wish using the procedures and shortcuts described earlier in this chapter.

Customer:Job Budgets

If you have a customer or a job that warrants it, you can create a Profit & Loss budget to track the financials for that customer or job against a budget.

To create your first budget for a customer or a job:

1. Choose Company | Planning & Budgeting | Set Up Budgets. If you already created another budget of a different type (Profit & Loss or Class), the budget window opens with the last budget you created. Click the Create New Budget button in the budget window to launch the Create New Budget wizard. If this is your first-ever budget, the Create New Budget wizard appears automatically.
2. Select the year for your budget, and choose Profit And Loss as the type. Click Next.

3. Select the option Customer:Job. Click Next

4. In the next window, specify whether you want to create the budget from scratch or from last year's data. Click Finish.

In the Set Up Budgets window, select the Customer:Job for this budget from the drop-down list. Enter budget figures using the following guidelines:

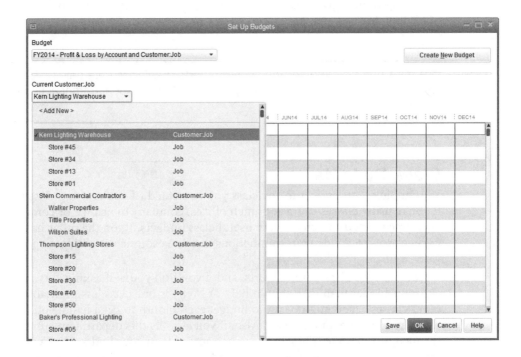

- The expenses you track depend on the scope of the job. For example, you may only want to budget the cost of outside contractors or supplies, so if prices rise, you can have a conversation with the customer about overruns.

- Enter a monthly budget figure for each account or for each month the project exists, or enter a total budget figure in the first month. The last option lets you compare accumulated data for expenses against the total budgeted figure by creating modified reports, where you change the report date to reflect the elapsed time for the project and filter the report for this job only.

- If the project is lengthy, you may budget some accounts for some months and other accounts for other months. For example, if you have a project that involves purchases of goods followed by installation of those goods, or training for the customer's employees, you might choose to budget the purchases for the first few months and then the cost of the installation or training (either by tracking payroll or outside contractors) for the months in which those activities occur.
- If you want to track payroll costs against a job, use the QuickBooks Time and Billing features that are discussed in Chapter 19.

C a u t i o n : Customer:Job budget reports aren't accurate unless you're faithful about assigning every appropriate revenue or expense transaction to the customer or job.

Class Budgets

You can link your budget to any class you've created (if you're using class tracking). If you're using classes to track branch offices, company divisions, or company departments, you can create very useful class budgets. If, on the other hand, you're using classes to divide your transactions in some esoteric way, budgeting may not work well.

Look at your class-based reports, and if you find yourself asking, "Aren't those expenses higher than they should be?" or "Why is one class less profitable than the other classes?" you might want to budget each month to get a handle on where and when expenses got out of hand. Also, if you ask, "Is this department contributing the income I expected?" include income accounts in your budget. You can use income accounts in class budgets to provide incentives to your employees—perhaps a bonus to a manager if the reality is better than the budget.

To create a class-based budget, use the steps described earlier to create a budget and choose Class in the Additional Profit And Loss Budget Criteria window. When the budget window opens, a Current Class field appears. Select the class for which you're creating a budget from the drop-down list. Then begin entering data.

To create additional class budgets (for other classes, of course), use the same approach discussed in the previous section on creating additional customer or job budgets.

Budget Reports

QuickBooks provides a number of budget reports you can use to see how you're doing. I'll discuss each of them in this section. To get to the reports, choose Reports | Budgets from the menu bar, and then select one of the following reports:

- Budget Overview
- Budget vs. Actual
- Profit & Loss Budget Performance
- Budget vs. Actual Graph

Budget Overview

This report shows the accounts you budgeted and the amounts you budgeted for each month. Accounts that you didn't include in the budget aren't displayed.

Profit & Loss Budget Overview

If you created multiple budgets, select the budget you want to view from the drop-down list and click Next. In the next window, select a report layout (the options differ, depending on the type of budget). Click Next, and then click Finish. Essentially, the Overview report type produces the display you'd see if the window you use to create a budget had a button labeled Print The Budget.

This report includes inactive accounts if an account was used when preparing the budget and then subsequently made inactive. This may be confusing if you print this report as the "official" budget for your company.

If you use subaccounts in your budget but only want to see parent account budget totals, you can click the Collapse button at the top of the report window. The button name changes to Expand, and clicking it puts the subaccount lines back into the display.

To condense the numbers, use the Columns drop-down list to select a different interval. The default is Month, but you can choose another interval and QuickBooks will calculate the figures to fit. For example, you might want to select Quarter to see four columns of three-month subtotals (and a Total column).

If you want to tweak the budget or play "what if" games by experimenting with different numbers, click the Excel button to send the report to Microsoft Excel.

Balance Sheet Budget Overview

If you created a Balance Sheet budget, select <FYxxxx> Balance Sheet By Account for the budget in the first window, and then click Next. QuickBooks displays a graphical representation of the report's layout (it's a monthly layout similar to the layout for the Profit & Loss budget). Click Finish to see the report.

Customer:Job Budget Overview

If you created budgets for customers or jobs, select <FYxxxx> Profit & Loss By Account And Customer:Job in the first window and click Next. Select a report layout from the drop-down list (as you select each option from the list, QuickBooks displays a diagram of the layout). The following choices are available:

- **Account By Month**   Lists each account you used in the budget and displays the total budget amounts for all customer budgets you created, for each month that has data. No budget information for individual customers appears.
- **Account By Customer:Job**   Lists each account you used in the budget and displays the fiscal year total for that account for each customer (each customer has its own column).
- **Customer:Job By Month**   Displays a row for each customer that has a budget and a column for each month. The budget totals for all accounts—individual accounts are not displayed—appear under each month. Under each customer's row is a row for each job that has a budget.

ProAdvisor Tip: The name of each layout is a hint about the way it displays in the report. The first word represents the rows, and the word after "by" represents the columns. So, for Customer:Job By Month, Customers:Jobs are shown in rows and months are displayed as columns.

Class Budget Overview

If you created a Class budget, select Profit & Loss By Account And Class in the first window and click Next. Select a report layout from the drop-down list. You have the following choices:

- **Account By Month**   Lists each account you used in the budget and displays the total budget amounts for all Class budgets you created, for each month that has data. No budget information for individual classes appears.
- **Account By Class**   Lists each account you used in the budget and displays the yearly total for that account for each class (each class has its own column).

- **Class By Month** Displays a row for each class that has a budget and a column for each month. The total budget (not broken down by account) appears for each month.

Budget vs. Actual

This report's name says it all—it shows you how your real numbers compare to your budget figures. For a standard Profit & Loss budget, the report displays the following data for each month of your budget, for each account:

- Amount posted
- Amount budgeted
- Difference in dollars
- Difference in percentage

The choices for the budget type are the same as the Budget Overview report, so you can see account totals, customer totals, or class totals to match the budgets you've created.

When the report opens, only the accounts you used in your budget show budget figures.

You can also use the options in the Modify Report window to make the following changes:

- Change the report dates.
- Change the calculations from accrual to cash to remove any unpaid invoices and bills so that only actual income and expenses are reported.

You should memorize the report so you don't have to make these modifications the next time you want to view a comparison report. Click the Memorize button at the top of the report window and then give the report a meaningful name. Only the formatting changes you make are memorized, not the data. Every time you open the report, it displays current data. To view the report after you memorize it, choose Reports | Memorized Reports from the QuickBooks menu bar.

Profit & Loss Budget Performance

This report is similar to the Budget vs. Actual report, but it's based on the current month and the year to date. For that time period, the report displays your actual income and expenses compared to what you budgeted.

By default, the date range is the current month, but you can change that to see last month's figures or the figures for any previous month. This report is also available for all types, as described in "Budget Overview," earlier in this section, and can also be modified to customize the display.

Budget vs. Actual Graph

This report just opens; you have no choices to select first. All the choices are in the graph that displays in the form of buttons across the top of the report window. Merely click the type of report you want to see.

Work with Budget Data Outside of QuickBooks

If you need to manipulate your budget data or have report formatting needs beyond what QuickBooks offers, you can export this data to Excel or to a delimited text file. Exporting to Excel can be useful for creating customized budget reports using your QuickBooks data, while exporting to a text file gives you the option to make changes to your budget data that can be imported back into QuickBooks.

Exporting a Budget Report to Excel

Although you can export any budget report to Excel, it's common to use the Profit & Loss Budget Overview report for this purpose. Choose Reports | Budgets | Budget Overview. Select the desired Profit & Loss report and click Next. Select a report layout, click Next, and then click Finish.

With the report open, click the Excel button at the top of the report window. From here, you can choose to create a new worksheet or update an existing worksheet (Chapter 26 covers how to use the Excel export feature on all reports.) Select Create New Worksheet if this is the first budget you're exporting. If you're exporting multiple budgets in this manner, you can select an existing workbook and create separate worksheets for each budget.

Exporting Budgets to Delimited Text Files

When you export budgets to a delimited text file (QuickBooks adds the file extension .iif to the exported file), you can't select specific budgets to export—it's all or nothing. To export your budget data:

1. Choose File | Utilities | Export | Lists To IIF Files from the QuickBooks menu bar.
2. When the Export dialog opens, it displays all the QuickBooks lists. Select the item named Budgets, and click OK.

3. Another Export dialog opens. Select a folder in which to save this exported file, or leave it in your QuickBooks folder (the default location).

4. Give the exported list a filename (for example, QBBudgets). QuickBooks will automatically add the extension .iif to the filename.

5. Click Save. QuickBooks displays a message telling you that your data has been exported successfully.

6. Click OK.

Open the file using Excel (or any spreadsheet program). Note that the file shows a row of budget data for every year that you've created one in QuickBooks.

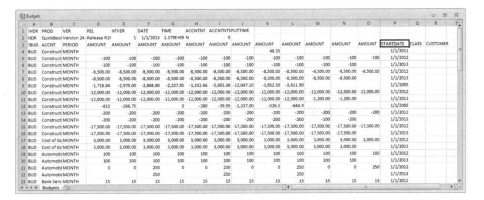

If you only want to work on the figures for one year, you'll have to delete the unwanted rows. The budget year is indicated by the date found in the STARTDATE column. Updating the date in the STARTDATE column will create a budget for the year you've entered when the file is imported back into QuickBooks.

Be sure that any changes you make to the file while it is open in Excel are saved in the original text (.iif) format if you plan on importing your changes back into your QuickBooks file.

Importing Budgets Back into QuickBooks

The only practical reason you'd import budgets back into QuickBooks is to copy a budget to another year to use as the basis for another year's budget. While you can also edit the actual budget figures you've exported to an .iif file, it's easier to work directly in the QuickBooks budget window. To play "what if" games or to sort the budget differently, it's easier to work in Excel or some other spreadsheet program.

Before you can import the file, you must save it as a delimited text file, choosing Tab as the delimiter. You must also change the filename extension to .iif. Then follow these steps to bring the budget into QuickBooks:

1. Choose File | Utilities | Import | IIF Files from the menu bar to open the Import dialog.
2. Locate and double-click the file you saved.
3. When QuickBooks displays a message telling you the import was successful, click OK.

You can view the imported budgets in any budget report or in the budget window. QuickBooks checks the dates and changes the budget's name to reflect the dates.

When you select a budget report or choose a budget to edit in the budget window, the available budgets include both the budgets you created in QuickBooks (FY2013, for example) and the budgets you imported after changing the date (FY2014).

Project Cash Flow

The Cash Flow Projector is a tool you can use to build a report that projects your cash flows using your own criteria. This tool uses data in your company file and then lets you remove and add accounts and even adjust figures. These features make it easier to achieve the projection parameters and results you need.

The Cash Flow Projector is rather powerful if you understand the accounting terminology and principles of determining cash flows. You can design specific cash flow scenarios, which might be useful in planning for an expansion or other major business event.

It's beyond the scope of this book to provide a detailed explanation of the best ways to use this tool, but this section gives you an overview.

To ensure accuracy, make sure you've entered all transactions, including memorized transactions, into your QuickBooks company file. Then launch the Cash Flow Projector by choosing Company | Planning & Budgeting | Cash Flow Projector. The program operates like a wizard, and the opening window (see Figure 27-3) welcomes you and offers links to information you should read before you begin.

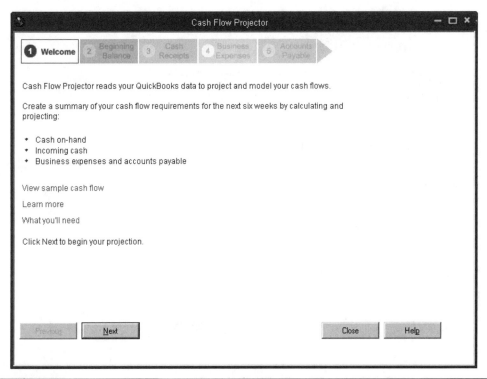

FIGURE 27-3   Use the links to familiarize yourself with the information the wizard needs.

ProAdvisor Tip: Each ensuing wizard window has a button labeled Preview Projection. Click it to see your results so far.

Click Next to display the Beginning Balance window (see Figure 27-4), and select the cash accounts you want to include in your projection.

The software calculates a beginning balance by adding together the balances of all the accounts you select. You can make an adjustment to that calculated balance to change the beginning balance of the cash flow projection. This is useful if you know that the current balance of any account contains an amount that you don't want included in the projection, such as an income item that is earmarked for spending today or tomorrow and therefore shouldn't be counted.

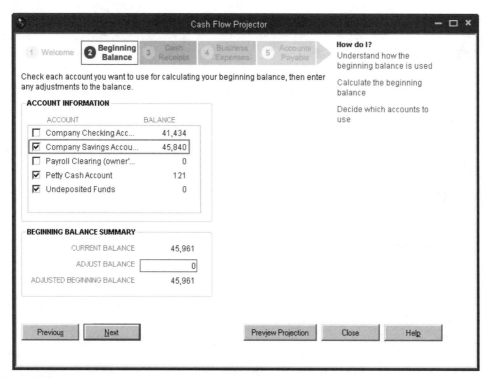

FIGURE 27-4 Select the accounts to use to project your cash flow.

Click Next to move to the Cash Receipts window (see Figure 27-5). You must select a projection method from the drop-down list. If you don't understand the terminology in the list, discuss it with your accountant. One of the choices is I Want To Project Cash Receipts Manually, which is useful if your accountant has some particular method in mind or if you don't have A/R totals to guide you because you run a retail business.

The next two wizard windows look similar to Figure 27-5, but they deal with expenses, starting with expenses that are not accounts-payable expenses (expenses for which you write direct checks instead of entering bills, and any unique expenses that qualify as "one-time-only"), and moving on to accounts-payable expenses, including recurring bills you've entered into your system. In both windows, you can enter specific expenses or adjusted total expenses.

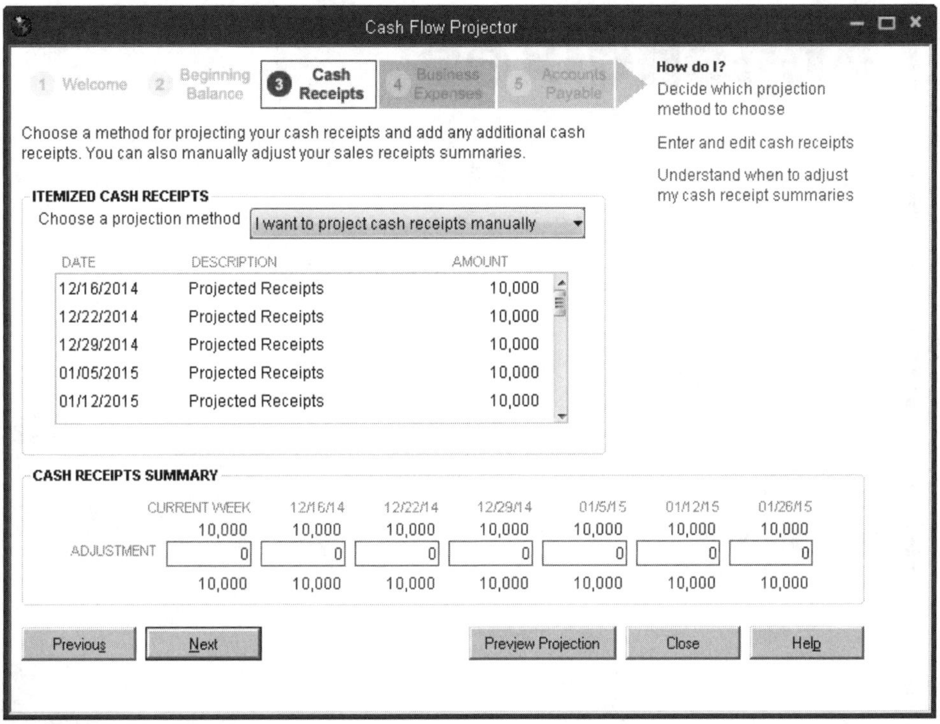

FIGURE 27-5 Summarize your projected cash receipts on a weekly basis.

This brief discussion should give you a basic understanding of the ways you can use this tool to better run your business. If you think you'd benefit by generating a variety of cash flow scenarios, you should introduce this tool to your accountant— together, you can see all the ways it can be applied to suit your business needs.

Part Seven

Appendixes

Installing QuickBooks on a Network

n *this appendix:*

- License requirements

- Understand the different installation options

- Set up and configure QuickBooks in a multi-user environment

Soon after you launch the QuickBooks installer, you're asked to make some choices about how the program should be installed on your computer and other computers on your network. Although the choices are presented in a straightforward manner during the installation, it may not be obvious which choice is right for you when more than one user needs simultaneous access to your QuickBooks file.

This appendix will provide you with the background information you need to know, along with some tips to help ensure your multi-user installation goes as smoothly as possible.

License Requirements for a Multi-user Installation

You'll need to purchase a separate QuickBooks license for each computer that will have simultaneous access to your QuickBooks data file. In addition, all computers must use the same version—in this case, QuickBooks Pro 2014. QuickBooks Pro comes in one-, two-, or three-user license packs, allowing for up to three simultaneous users (with three unique user login names) to access a company file on a network. You can also purchase a two-user and a three-user pack that allows you to have up to five simultaneous users accessing the company file (again, each user is required to have a unique user login name). Setting up users and permissions is covered in Chapter 8.

Multi-user Installation Options

Multi-user installation options are dependent on the type of network configuration you plan to use. Specifically, the options you choose depend on whether you plan on using a dedicated server to host your QuickBooks company file or a peer-to-peer network, where one of the computers on the network runs QuickBooks and also stores the file.

It's beyond the scope of this appendix to provide instruction on which configuration is best in your situation and the steps required for setup. You'll want to contact your system administrator for that; if you don't have one, find a local IT expert.

Installing QuickBooks on a Peer-to-Peer Network

First, ensure that all the computers that need access to the QuickBooks file are on a network running Windows 7, 8 (all editions except Starter and Basic), Vista, or XP. It's also a good idea to make sure your operating system is up to date with the latest release. Other important tasks to add to your preinstall checklist include these:

- Deciding which computer on your network will hold the QuickBooks company file. It should be the fastest computer on your network, and it will be the first computer that you install QuickBooks on.

- Ensuring that the other QuickBooks computers on the network have full read/write access to the folder in which you plan on storing your QuickBooks data file.

Insert the QuickBooks CD in your CD drive, or, if you downloaded the program, run the Download Manager to launch the Intuit QuickBooks Installer. A Welcome screen confirms the launch. Click Next and follow these steps:

1. Review and accept the terms of the Intuit Software End User License Agreement. Click Next.
2. In the Choose Your Installation Type window, select Custom And Network Options (see Figure A-1). Click Next.
3. The Custom And Network Options window opens, giving you three choices. Select the middle option, I'll Be Using QuickBooks On This Computer, AND I'll Be Storing Our Company File Here So It Can Be Shared Over Our Network (see Figure A-2). Click Next.
4. Enter your license and product information (found either on your CD or in the e-mail received from Intuit that included your product download link). Click Next.
5. Enter your Intuit ID (which is likely the e-mail address you used when you purchased the software) and click the Validate button. If you don't know your Intuit user name or password—or you don't want to enter it at this time—click the "Skip this" link to advance to the next window.

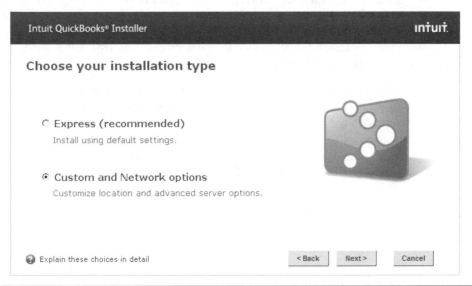

FIGURE A-1 Choose the installation type Custom And Network Options.

FIGURE A-2 This installation option lets you store the file on your computer, run QuickBooks, and give others access to your QuickBooks company file.

6. If this is your first version of QuickBooks, you can accept the suggested folder that the installer recommends. If you're upgrading from a previous version of QuickBooks, you'll have the option of replacing your previous version with QuickBooks 2014 or changing the install location (which keeps the existing version of QuickBooks on your computer). I recommend you select the option Change The Install Location (see the next ProAdvisor Tip). Click Next, and then click the Install button.

For the next several minutes, you'll see a series of informational windows about various QuickBooks features and additional services. Each of these windows contains a status bar to keep you apprised of the progress of your installation.

When the installation is complete, you'll receive a congratulations message and the option to open QuickBooks directly, get help getting started, or both. For the discussion that follows, select Open QuickBooks and click Finish.

ProAdvisor Tip: Most installations are trouble-free. But there are times when a setting on your computer that you are not aware of—or perhaps even an emergency situation in your office—interrupts your installation. Whatever the reason, choosing not to overwrite and replace your existing QuickBooks installation lets you continue working in your QuickBooks file until any issues with the installation have been resolved. Later, after you're up and running with the new version, you can confidently uninstall the previous version using the appropriate utility in Windows Control Panel.

File Hosting and the Database Server Manager

With your QuickBooks company file open, select File | Switch To Multi-User Mode. Click OK. When you turn on multi-user mode on the first computer on which you've installed QuickBooks, you automatically designate this computer as the *host* of your QuickBooks data file.

In addition, behind the scenes, QuickBooks installs a Database Server Manager program. Running this program along with QuickBooks ensures that other QuickBooks users will be able to access the company file even if the QuickBooks program is not open on this computer (the computer itself, however, has to be turned on).

Here's how to open and run the Database Server Manager:

1. On the Windows Start menu, select All Programs | QuickBooks | QuickBooks Database Server Manager.
2. On the Scan Folders tab, click the Add Folder button to browse to the QuickBooks file you want to make available to other users. The default location that QuickBooks uses to save company files (which will have a .qbw extension) is C:\Users\Public\Documents\Intuit\QuickBooks\Company Files.
3. When the folder where your QuickBooks file resides is listed in the Folders That Contain QuickBooks Company Files box, click the Scan button. Your file will be configured to ensure that others on the network can open your QuickBooks file (see Figure A-3).

Installing QuickBooks on the Client Computers

With your QuickBooks host computer up and running, you're ready to install the program on the other networked computers. Follow these steps:

1. Complete Steps 1 and 2 from the previous section.
2. In the Custom And Network Options window, select the first option, I'll Be Using QuickBooks On This Computer (see Figure A-4). Click Next.

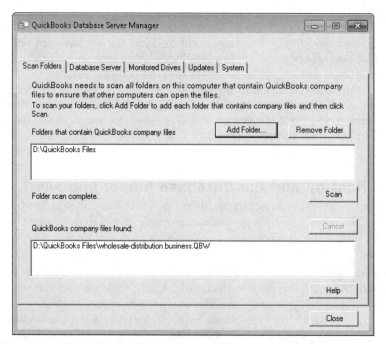

FIGURE A-3 Running the Database Server Manager makes your QuickBooks company file available to other users on your network.

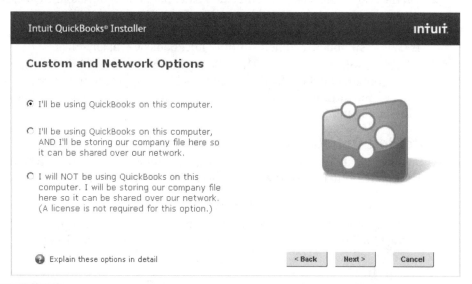

FIGURE A-4 When you install QuickBooks on client computers, choose the option I'll Be Using QuickBooks On This Computer.

3. Enter your license and product information (found either on your CD or in the e-mail received from Intuit that included your product download link).

4. Enter your Intuit ID (which is likely the e-mail address you used when you purchased the software) and click the Validate button. If you don't know your Intuit user name or password—or you don't want to enter it at this time—click the "Skip this" link to advance to the next window.

5. If this is your first version of QuickBooks, you can accept the suggested folder that the installer recommends. If you're upgrading from a previous version of QuickBooks, you'll have the option of replacing your previous version with QuickBooks 2014 or changing the install location (which keeps the existing version of QuickBooks on your computer). I recommend you select the option Change The Install Location. (See the earlier ProAdvisor Tip.) Click Next, and then click the Install button.

   For the next several minutes, you'll see a series of informational windows about various QuickBooks features and additional services. Each of these windows contains a status bar to keep you apprised of the progress of your installation.

6. When the installation is complete, you'll receive a congratulations message and the option to open QuickBooks directly, get help getting started, or both. For the discussion that follows, select Open QuickBooks and click Finish.

7. In the No Company Open window, click the Open Or Restore An Existing Company button.

8. In the Open Or Restore Company window, select the option to Open A Company File. Click Next.

9. Browse to and open your QuickBooks company file located on the QuickBooks host computer.

ProAdvisor Tip: After you click Finish, and before proceeding to the No Company Open window, QuickBooks may ask if you want to use this computer to host multi-user access. Answer No to ensure that the first computer that you installed QuickBooks on remains the host computer. If you answer Yes to this question, this computer will become the host, which means that not only will QuickBooks need to be open on this computer, but a user will need to be logged into the company file before any of the other users on the network can work in the file.

Installing QuickBooks on a Client-Server Network

To use QuickBooks on a network with a dedicated server, you must be running one of the following: Microsoft Windows XP (SP2 or later), Vista (w/ UAC on), 7 or 8 (w/ UAC on), Windows Server 2003, Windows Server 2008, or Small Business Server 2008. Once you've confirmed that your server operating system meets one of these requirements, follow these installation instructions:

1. On the server computer, insert the QuickBooks CD into the CD drive; if you downloaded the program, run the Download Manager to launch the Intuit QuickBooks Installer. A Welcome screen confirms the launch. Click Next.
2. Review and accept the terms of the Intuit Software End User License Agreement. Click Next.
3. In the Choose Installation Type window, select the Custom And Network Options. Click Next.
4. The Custom And Network Options window opens giving you three choices. Select the last option, I Will NOT Be Using QuickBooks On This Computer. I Will Be Storing Our Company File Here So It Can Be Shared Over Our Network (see Figure A-5). Click Next.

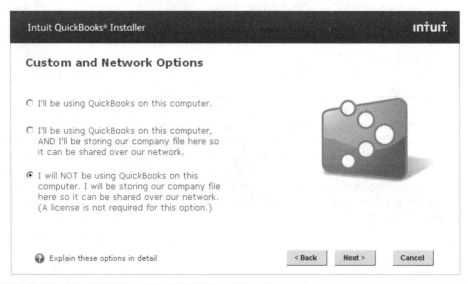

FIGURE A-5 Choosing the option I Will NOT Be Using QuickBooks On This Computer installs the Database Server Manager only.

5. QuickBooks suggests an installation location for the Database Server Manager Program. You can change the location if you wish by clicking Change The Install Location. Click Next, and then click the Install button.

6. For the next several minutes, you'll see a series of informational windows about various QuickBooks features and additional services. Each of these windows contains a status bar to keep you apprised of the progress of your installation. When the installation of the Database Server Manager is complete, you'll receive a congratulations message and the option to get help getting started. For the discussion that follows, click Finish.

Configure the Database Server Manager

Here's how to open and configure the Database Server Manager:

1. From the Windows Start menu, select All Programs | QuickBooks | QuickBooks Database Server Manager.

2. On the Scan Folders tab, click the Add Folder button to browse to the QuickBooks file you want to make available to other users.

▶▶ ProAdvisor Recommends

Installing Both QuickBooks and the Database Server Manager on Your Server

Selecting the I Will Not Be Using QuickBooks On This Computer option (as shown in Figure A-5) installs the QuickBooks Database Server Manager program and not the full version of QuickBooks. Although this is a perfectly acceptable installation option when installing in a client-server environment, it's also acceptable to install both QuickBooks and the Database Server Manager on the server computer (which is the middle option shown in Figure A-5). This can be a good idea because two very important utilities are built into the full QuickBooks program: the verify and rebuild utilities (they are covered in Chapter 23). These utilities should only be run locally, meaning that the QuickBooks file being verified and rebuilt should reside on the same computer as the full QuickBooks program.

When both QuickBooks and the Database Server Manager are installed, the QuickBooks program will be "silent" and used only occasionally for maintenance purposes. As a result, it will not affect your licensing requirements, but it will give you peace of mind knowing that you can easily perform routine maintenance on your QuickBooks file when you need to.

3. When your folder is listed in the Folders That Contain QuickBooks Company
   Files box, click the Scan button. Your file will be configured to ensure that others
   on the network can open your QuickBooks file (refer to Figure A-3).

You're now ready to install the QuickBooks program on the other client
workstations by following the instructions in the earlier section, "Installing
QuickBooks on the Client Computers."

Multiple Currencies

n this appendix:

- Set up and configure multiple currencies

- Set up and configure customers and vendors for multiple currencies

- Create transactions in other currencies

- Run reports

This appendix provides an overview of the multiple currencies feature in QuickBooks. If you do business with customers or vendors in other countries, this feature allows you to create transactions in their currencies and track the exchange rates so you always know what the transactions mean to you in US Dollars.

Set Up and Configure Multiple Currencies

Before you can begin creating transactions in different currencies, you have to complete some configuration and setup tasks.

It's important to be aware that, unlike most of the configuration preferences available in QuickBooks, once you enable multiple currencies, you can't disable it. If you're already using QuickBooks (either because you updated your company files from a previous version or because you began creating transactions before deciding to use multiple currencies), be sure to back up your company file before enabling this feature.

Creating a Special Backup

When you create your backup before turning on multiple currencies, don't use your normal backup routine. Instead, name the backup file differently so you can identify it easily and avoid having the multicurrency backup file overwritten with "regular" backups. For example, when you save your backup file, you might change the name of the file from the usual *<CompanyFileName>*.QBB to *<CompanyFileName>*-BeforeMulticurrency.QBB.

If you change your mind later and decide not to use multiple currencies and you don't want to restore the backup (because you'd have to re-enter all the transactions you'd created while multiple currencies was enabled), it's okay to keep using the company file with multiple currencies enabled as long as you use customers, vendors, and accounts that are not linked to another currency. Some windows and dialogs will continue to have an extra field for currency, but no financial information will be compromised.

Enabling Multiple Currencies

To enable the multiple currencies feature, choose Edit | Preferences and click the Multiple Currencies category icon in the left pane. In the Company Preferences tab (see Figure B-1), select Yes, I Use More Than One Currency.

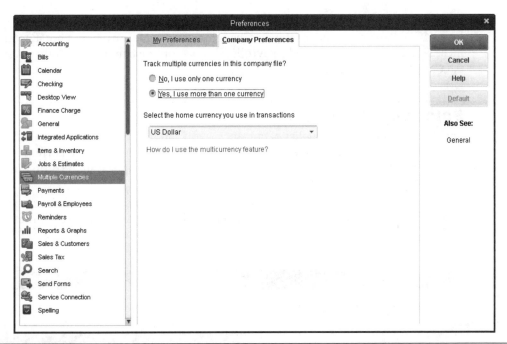

Enable multiple currencies and select your home currency.

When you select Yes, QuickBooks displays a warning message:

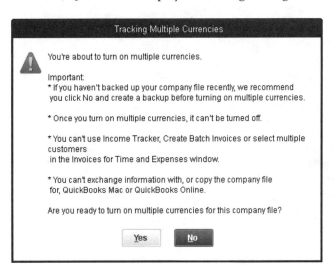

If you've already made a backup, as discussed in the previous section, you can continue. If not, stop the process and create your backup. Then enable multiple currencies.

The Preferences window offers the opportunity to change your home currency from US Dollars to another currency. Changing your home currency is not a good idea, because QuickBooks tracks payroll, sales tax, online banking, and other basic data in US Dollars only.

Selecting Currencies

QuickBooks provides a long list of currencies you can use, but by default only the commonly used currencies are active. You can change the list of active currencies to suit your own needs. Remember that only active currencies appear in the drop-down list when you're assigning a currency to a customer or vendor.

Choose Company | Manage Currency | Currency List to open the Currency List window seen in Figure B-2. If the list includes only active currencies, select the Include Inactive check box to see the entire list.

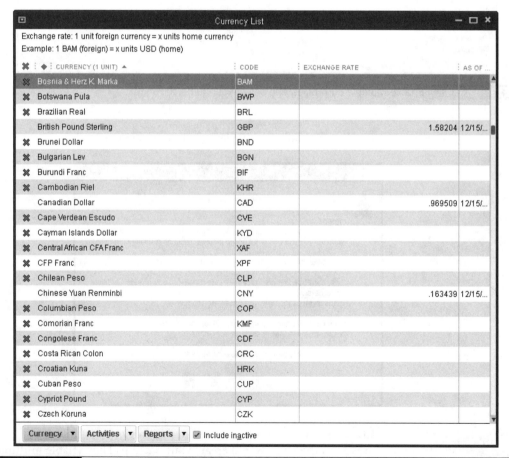

| FIGURE B-2 | Activate the currencies you need. |

To activate an inactive currency, click the X in the leftmost column to remove the X; to make an active currency inactive, click the leftmost column to place an X in the column.

Notice that each currency has a three-letter abbreviation; for example, US Dollar is USD. You can, if necessary, create a currency if the one you need doesn't appear on the list, but keep in mind that QuickBooks can't download exchange rates for currencies you add manually. With the Currency List window open, press CTRL-N to open the New Currency dialog and configure the currency.

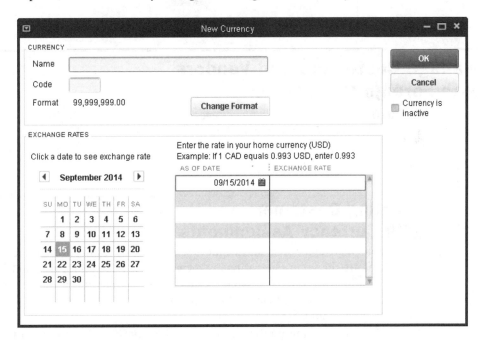

Tracking Exchange Rates

Because QuickBooks tracks both the customer/vendor currency and its worth in your home currency, you need to make sure the exchange rate is accurate. If the exchange rate isn't accurate, your financial reports, which use US Dollars, won't be accurate.

To update the exchange rate for all your active currencies, choose Company | Manage Currency | Download Latest Exchange Rates. QuickBooks goes online to get the current rates (you don't see an Internet page; all of this is done in the background).

When your active currencies have been updated, QuickBooks displays a success message, and you can now see the updated exchange rates in the Currency List.

Manage Customers and Vendors with Foreign Currencies

You need to identify the currency of every customer and vendor in your company file. QuickBooks automatically assigns your home currency (USD) to all customers and vendors, so you need to change only those that do business in a different currency.

Creating Customers and Vendors with Currency Assignments

When you create customers and vendors who do business in another currency, the basic steps are the same as creating any new customer or vendor in QuickBooks. The only differences are the existence of a Currency Field in the New Customer or New Vendor dialog and the lack of an Opening Balance field when you select a currency other than USD.

As you can see in Figure B-3, QuickBooks inserts US Dollar in the Currency field, but you can choose another currency from the drop-down list (which displays only those currencies you've marked Active).

ProAdvisor Tip: As you create a new customer or vendor and assign them a new currency, QuickBooks automatically adds the following accounts to your chart of accounts: an Accounts Receivable account for each currency and an Accounts Payable account for each currency.

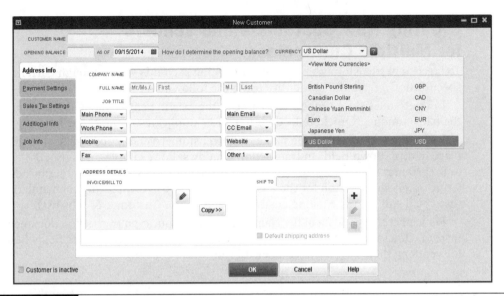

FIGURE B-3 If new customers or vendors you're creating use a foreign currency, select their currency from the drop-down list.

Changing Currency for Existing Customers and Vendors

You can change the currency assignment for existing customers and vendors only if they have *no transactions* associated with their names. It doesn't matter whether the current open balance is $0.00; the existence of any transaction prevents you from changing the currency. For those customers and vendors, you must create a new entity with the new currency.

In addition, you cannot merge customers or vendors that use different currencies. To edit the currency of an existing customer or vendor that has no existing transactions, open either the Customer or Vendor Center, select the name that you want to edit, and click the Edit icon in the upper-right of the Information pane. Select the currency from the drop-down list in the Currency field, and click OK.

If you need to change the currency assignment for customers or vendors who have transactions associated with their name, or you need to do business with them in more than one currency, see the next section.

Creating New Customers and Vendors for Multiple Currencies

To create a new customer or vendor for existing accounts with a foreign currency specification, create the new entity using the following guidelines.

In the Name field, use the same name as the existing entity, but add text to make the name unique. (QuickBooks does not allow duplicates in the Name field.)

It's best to add text after the name, so the customer/vendor appears in the right place in drop-down fields in transaction windows. For example, in Figure B-4, a new customer is created to assign a new currency to an existing customer by adding a three-digit abbreviation for the customer's currency to create a unique name (note that you'll still see the existing customer name in the Customer & Jobs list).

Remember that the data in the Name field doesn't appear on transaction documents; instead, QuickBooks uses the data in the Company Name and Address fields (and for vendors, there's even a field labeled Print Name On Check As).

FIGURE B-4   The currency is added to the new customer's name; everything else is the same as the existing customer.

Managing Existing Open Transactions

When you create new customers and vendors, you have to manage existing open transactions using the original customer or vendor since you cannot accept or make a payment linked to the original entity using the new entity. When the open balance for the original entity becomes zero, you can make the original customer or vendor inactive so the listing doesn't appear in drop-down lists in transaction windows. Be sure to use the new entity you created for all new transactions.

Viewing Currency Data in Customer and Vendor Centers

After you've enabled multiple currencies, the Customer Center and Vendor Center display currency information in both panes.

In addition, QuickBooks makes the following changes automatically:

- In the List pane, the currency is noted for each customer/vendor and the current balance total displays using the customer/vendor currency.
- In the Transactions tab of the Details pane, the Amount and Open Balance columns display amounts in the currency of the customer or vendor.

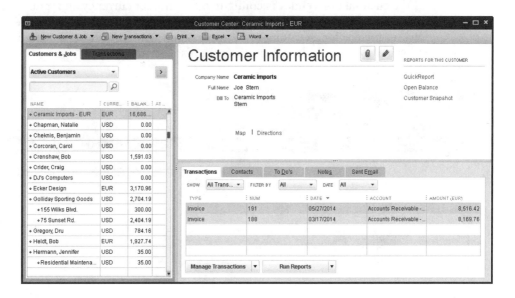

You can change these default settings to make it easier to understand the data you see in the centers.

Configuring the List Pane

In the List pane, you can add the current balance total in USD to save yourself the need to calculate the "real money."

You can either remove the Balance Total column for the foreign currency or display both Balance Total columns. If you frequently talk to vendors or customers about current balances, it's handy to have the foreign currency balance in front of you, so having both amounts display makes sense. However, to save room in the List pane, remove the Currency column.

You can add (or remove) columns to the list by right-clicking anywhere in the list and choosing Customize Columns.

Create Transactions in Other Currencies

When you open a sales or payment transaction window, QuickBooks automatically takes care of the currency issues by adding fields to the transaction window.

If the customer or vendor currency is USD, you won't see much difference between the transaction window for multiple currencies and the same transaction window before you enabled multiple currencies. The only real difference is that the text "USD" appears for "Total" amounts.

If the customer or vendor is configured for another currency, the transaction window changes to provide the information you need. For example, Figure B-5 shows an invoice for a customer in Europe, and Figure B-6 shows a vendor bill for a vendor in the UK who does business in Euros.

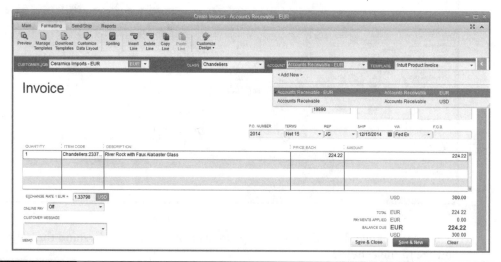

FIGURE B-5 This invoice displays all the data needed to see the sales total for this invoice in both US Dollars and Euros.

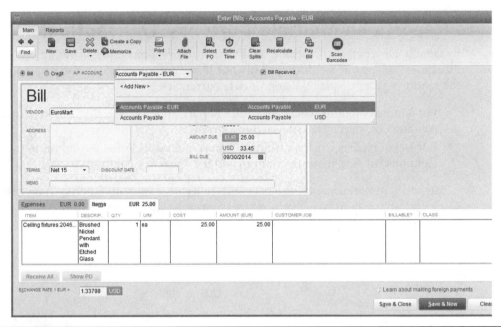

FIGURE B-6 When the amount of the bill is entered in Euros (which is what the bill that arrived showed), QuickBooks also displays the amount in USD.

Notice the following about these transaction windows:

- The A/R or A/P account is specific to the currency.
- The amounts in the line items are displayed in the customer/vendor currency.
- There are two totals: one for the transaction currency and one for USD.
- The Exchange Rate field displays the exchange rate used when this transaction was created.

The printed versions of transactions that are sent to customers (invoices, credits, and so on) and vendors (checks) do not display any fields or data related to USD; those fields appear on the screen only for your convenience.

Decide on an exchange rate update schedule that makes sense to you. Keep in mind that if the exchange rate changes between the day you enter an invoice or bill and the day you receive a payment or make a payment, QuickBooks automatically adds an Other Expense account named Exchange Gain or Loss to track the net amounts that accrue from adjustments in exchange rates for current open balances.

Create Reports on Multiple Currency Transactions

By default, all reports on customer and vendor transactions (such as Aging, Sales, Purchases, and so on) are displayed in your home currency (USD). You can modify the reports so they display the appropriate currencies.

- For Summary reports, click Customize Report, and in the section labeled Display Amounts In, select The Transaction Currency.
- For Detail reports, click Customize Report and select Foreign Amount in the Columns list. You may also want to add the Currency column.

Memorize these reports, using a name that reflects the contents (such as Transaction Currency), so you don't have to customize them each time you create them.

Index

• J

• R

• W